The C# Programmer's Study Guide (MCSD)

Exam: 70-483

Ali Asad
Hamza Ali

Apress®

The C# Programmer's Study Guide (MCSD)

Ali Asad
Sialkot, Pakistan

Hamza Ali
Sialkot, Pakistan

ISBN-13 (pbk): 978-1-4842-2859-3
DOI 10.1007/978-1-4842-2860-9

ISBN-13 (electronic): 978-1-4842-2860-9

Library of Congress Control Number: 2017944951

Cover image designed by FreePik

Managing Director: Welmoed Spahr
Editorial Director: Todd Green
Acquisitions Editor: Celestin Suresh John
Development Editor: Anila Vincent and Laura Berendson
Technical Reviewer: Syed Lakhtey Hussnain
Coordinating Editor: Sanchita Mandal
Copy Editor: Larissa shmailo
Compositor: SPi Global
Indexer: SPi Global
Artist: SPi Global

Distributed to the book trade worldwide by Springer Science+Business Media New York, 233 Spring Street, 6th Floor, New York, NY 10013. Phone 1-800-SPRINGER, fax (201) 348-4505, e-mail orders-ny@springer-sbm.com, or visit www.springeronline.com. Apress Media, LLC is a California LLC and the sole member (owner) is Springer Science + Business Media Finance Inc (SSBM Finance Inc). SSBM Finance Inc is a **Delaware** corporation.

For information on translations, please e-mail rights@apress.com, or visit http://www.apress.com/rights-permissions.

Apress titles may be purchased in bulk for academic, corporate, or promotional use. eBook versions and licenses are also available for most titles. For more information, reference our Print and eBook Bulk Sales web page at http://www.apress.com/bulk-sales.

Any source code or other supplementary material referenced by the author in this book is available to readers on GitHub via the book's product page, located at www.apress.com/978-1-4842-2859-3. For more detailed information, please visit http://www.apress.com/source-code.

Printed on acid-free paper

*Dedicated to my family (Mama[**Samina**], Papa[**Asad**], brother[**Hamza**],
sisters [**Rimsha, Aima, Azma**]); and to my dearest friend, **Sundus Naveed**.
Thank you for supporting me and believing in me. Most importantly, you guys never tried
to change me; instead, you gave me the confidence and the freedom to work on my dreams.
For that, I'm eternally grateful. Thank you!!!*

—Ali Asad

*Dedicated to my father [**Muhammad Arif**], who always encourages and supports
me to learn and deliver knowledge, and my whole family (Mother [**Yasmeen Tahira**],
my brothers [**Adil Ali** and **Awais Ali**], my sister-in-law [**Noureen Azmat**],
my cute niece [**Zoha Adil**], my sisters [**Iram Suhaib** and **Aqsa Hamid**],
and my beloved fiancée [**Zunaira Shafqat Ali**].)*

—Hamza Ali

Contents at a Glance

Contents

About the Authors

Ali Asad is one of the top C# programmers of Pakistan. He is a Microsoft Specialist (MS) in C# since 2015. In Pakistan, he is well known for his popular Microsoft C# Certification training, which helped so many students to pass their Microsoft Certification Exams.

Ali is an active community member; he speaks about *Game Development* and *C# Programming* at different conferences and workshops.

You can reach out to Ali Asad through:

- twitter.com/imaliasad
- facebook.com/imaliasad
- linkedin.com/in/imaliasad
- imaliasad@outlook.com

Hamza Ali is a Microsoft Specialist (MS in C#) since 2015 and an independent trainer teaching .NET technologies and the Cloud platform in general, and Microsoft C# certification training and ASP.NET MVC, in particular. Hamza is also exercising his expertise in JaSol Technologies (emerging Software House in Market own by him) as CTO.

He speaks at different tech talks and gives sessions on different tools and technologies, and frameworks including ASP.NET Core, Angularjs, Reactjs, Visual Studio Team Services, WCF Services, and Web APIs, using his expertise and experience.

You can reach out to Hamza Ali through:

- linkedin.com/in/hamzaali2
- facebook.com/hamZaali.003
- hamzaaliarif@hotmail.com
- twitter.com/arreez11

About the Technical Reviewer

Syed Lakhtey Hussnain is a Software Engineer in a wide range of applications with solid experience in developing web applications (including ERPs,CRMs) with ASP.NET MVC. Lakhtey is working as a Technology Strategist with Senior Development team from Barracuda Inc. to reconstruct entire web application that serves the business purposes. Lakhtey has also been working as a trainer in a Startup called '7Colors' where he gave trainings to his community members on .NET certifications. He is also a Microsoft Certified Solution Developer in Web Applications and AppBuilder.

Lakhtey has his deep interest in Music and Art and enjoys it a lot. Lakhtey lives in Kharian, Pakistan with his Parents.

Lakhtey can be reached at:

- lakhtey_hussnain@hotmail.com
- https://twitter.com/lakhtey22
- https://www.facebook.com/hassan.lakhtey
- https://www.linkedin.com/in/lakhtey/

Acknowledgments

Ali Asad: It is my honor and privilege to have worked with Apress. I'd like to thank each person who contributed a lot to the book:

- To **Celestin Suresh John** for providing me the opportunity to write this book.

- To **Sanchita Mandal** for your tremendous support and coordination that helped me a lot in the writing process.

- To my co-author **Hamza Ali** for your great partnership. Without your support, this book wouldn't get the quality that it has now.

- To **Syed Lakhtey Hussnain** for your technical reviewing skills. It helped me to correct the mistakes I made.

- To **David V Cobin** for taking the time to read this book and providing your valuable foreword.

- To the entire team at **Apress**, who made this book possible.

There are people in life who are special, who inspire you, support you and make you the person you are today. I have been so blessed for having such people in my life, because without them I wouldn't be able to write this book.

- To **Ali Raza** (AlizDesk) for guiding me to take the Microsoft Certification Exam.

- To **Mubashar Raffique** for supporting me in the academy, where we trained students and professionals for their Microsoft Certification Exams.

- To **Usman Ur Rehman** for all your valuable advice and support that helped me a lot during my time working at the Microsoft Innovation Center, Lahore.

- To **Faqeeha Riaz** for doing my semester assignments and helping me to prepare for final exams because, without your support, I wouldn't be able to give my complete focus to this book.

- To my parents (Mama[**Samina**], Papa[**Asad**]) for giving me the freedom to do good work in life.

- Last but not least, to **Sundus Naveed** for all your patience, support, and love.

Hamza Ali: I am honored to work with **Apress,** one of the quality-oriented book publishers. I'd like to acknowledge the contributions done by:

- **Celestin Suresh John:** for providing the opportunity to write this book.

- **Sanchita Mandal:** for your committed and continuous support to maintain and complete the book on time.

- **Ali Asad:** my co-author, for your big contribution along with your support to write, complete, and maintain the quality of the book and, obviously, the opportunity for the book.

- **Syed Lakhtey Hussnain:** for technical review and pointing out some deep mistakes, which improved the quality.

- **David V Cobin:** for writing the foreword for this book.

- **Zunaira Shafqat Ali:** for your support and understanding throughout the process of book writing.

I'd also like to thank:

- **my family:** for encouragement and support.

- **Ali Imran:** for support and guidance.

- **Mubashar Rafique:** for availability and useful thoughts.

Introduction

This book covers basic to advanced-level knowledge required to pass the Exam 70-483. It covers the usage and techniques used for professional development.

This book covers all the objectives listed in the official syllabus for Exam 70-483.

This book is suitable for students or readers who have a basic knowledge of C#, to lead them to an advanced level fit for experienced developers.

Target Audience

Students or readers with a basic understanding of C# and the learner beyond this stage are the target audience. Microsoft recommends one year of experience in C# before appearing for Exam 70-483, but this book (with its synced and basic to advanced explanation structure) leads basic, intermediate, or advanced-level students or developers to that level where they can easily appear for the Exam 70-483 with satisfactory preparation that also helps for concepts' clarity.

This book prepares readers for Exam 70-483 and, by passing this exam, "Microsoft Certified Professional" and "Microsoft Specialist: Programming in C#" certificates are awarded by Microsoft.

Content Covered

This book covers the content listed in the official syllabus for Exam 70-483 along with the building block topics related to official contents, so that synchronicity can be maintained and readers can understand the content step-by-step.

This book uses C# 5.0 and .NET Framework 4.5 in its content and examples. Exam-type questions for each chapter are also covered by this book to give readers better understandability, as well as Exam Challenges to improve the coding skills of readers.

Book Requirements

To read and implement code examples, you will need:

- A system (PC) with Windows 10
- Microsoft Visual Studio 2015 Community (this edition is freely available) Or above.
  You can download this version from the following link:

  https://www.visualstudio.com/downloads/

Structure of Book

The book is structured so that the knowledge base builds gradually. The chapter's structure is as follows:

- Each chapter contains the objective to cover.
- Real world examples to clear the concepts of readers.
- Mapping of real world examples into code.
- Notes and tips from authors for best practices.
- Useful resources links added where required.
- At the end, exam structured MCQs are given to test the capability of the reader based on his/her understanding of the chapter.

Each chapter is mapped to 4 main objectives of Exam 70-483 with respect to its contents. The objectives are:

1. Manage Program Flow 25-30%
2. Create & Use Types 25-30%
3. Debug Application & Implement Security 25-30%
4. Implement Data Access 25-30%

The objectives (with their sub-objectives) explained in this book with respect to chapters are:

Manage Program Flow 25-30%

This objective explains how you can use simple C# programs that execute all its logic from top to bottom, and also use complex C# programs that do not have a fixed program flow. In this objective, we'll cover following sub-objectives:

1. Implement Multithreading and Asynchronous Processing. (Chapter 8)
2. Manage Multithreading. (Chapter 8)
3. Implement Program Flow. (Chapter 1)
4. Create and Implement Events and Callbacks. (Chapter 5)
5. Implement Exception Handling. (Chapter 9)

Create & Use Types 25-30%

This objective explains the default type system in .NET and explains how you can use it in a simple C# program. This objective also explains how you can create your custom types by using struct, enums, and classes, and use them effectively to create complex C# programs by using object-oriented principles. In this objective, we'll cover the following sub-objectives:

1. Create Types. (Chapter 2)
2. Consume Types. (Chapter 2)
3. Enforce Encapsulation. (Chapter 3)

4. Create & Implement Class Hierarchy. (Chapter 3)

5. Find, Execute, and Create Types at Runtime. (Chapter 14)

6. Manage Object Lifecycle. (Chapter 6)

7. Manipulate Strings. (Chapter 4)

Debug Application & Implement Security 25-30%

This objective explains how you can debug an application by validating user inputs, managing assemblies, etc. Also, you'll learn how to secure your application by implementing different encryption techniques (i.e., symmetric and asymmetric) and much more. In this objective, we'll cover the following sub-objectives:

1. Validate Application Input. (Chapter 9)

2. Perform Symmetric & Asymmetric Encryption. (Chapter 13)

3. Manage Assemblies. (Chapter 14)

4. Debug an Application. (Chapter 15)

5. Implement Diagnostics in an Application. (Chapter 15)

Implement Data Access 25-30%

This objective explains how you can use .NET libraries to manipulate data in a file system. It explains how you can use LINQ to query data, use ADO.NET to access a database, and much more. In this objective, we'll cover the following sub-objectives:

1. Perform I/O Operations. (Chapter 10)

2. Consume Data. (Chapter 12)

3. Query and Manipulate Data and Objects by Using LINQ. (Chapter 6)

4. Serialize and Deserialize Data. (Chapter 11)

5. Store Data in and Retrieve Data from Collections. (Chapter 4)

Keep in Touch

We have created a small and effective community on a Facebook group for readers of this book. We highly encourage you to join our Facebook group so, if you face any problem, feel free to post questions or start a discussion related to Microsoft Certification Exam 70-483 at: https://www.facebook.com/groups/Exam70483/.

Foreword

As a professional developer for multiple decades, I have seen and been involved in many different certification programs. Microsoft has invested heavily in a set of exams and certifications that are indicative of a candidate's ability to apply the relevant knowledge to real world situations.

When I was first approached about writing a foreword for this book on the 70-483 Exam, I was cautious. Over the years, I have seen far too many publications that do not provide any real understanding of the underlying material. However, upon receipt of the draft for this book, those concerns were eliminated.

The chapters contain topics ranging from the very basic to advanced C# language capabilities, using a combination of narrative text and code samples. Even if you are a seasoned C# developer, starting preparation for the exam from the beginning is highly recommended.

The Exam policies and FAQ page on the Microsoft site specifically states: "The best way to prepare for an exam is to practice the skills." I encourage all readers of this book to also spend hands-on time with the material; fire up Visual Studio, enter the sample code, write some little programs of your own related to the capability, and use the debugger to step through the code.

With the material in this book, the diligent reader should be well on their way to the level of understanding needed to do well on the 70-483 Exam. Even if your immediate focus is not on certification, there are always learning, review, and reference needs that can be addressed by keeping a copy of this book handy.

David V. Corbin
President/Chief Architect
Dynamic Concepts Development Corp.

CHAPTER 1

■ ■ ■

Fundamentals of C

To prepare for **Microsoft Certification Exam 70-483**, it is essential to learn the **fundamentals** of C# programming. This chapter teaches you **how to:**

1. Write your first program in C#.

2. Work with variables, primitive data types & operators.

3. Use implicit & explicit type casting.

4. Use var keyword.

5. Work with arrays.

6. Define decision structure.

7. Define decision operators.

8. Work with loops.

9. Use jump statements.

10. Use & define methods.

To get more out of this chapter, grab a pencil and paper, note down each point, and writing code snippets in Microsoft Visual Studio 2012 or above. At the end of this chapter, you can practice all concepts by: reviewing the summary, completing code challenges, and solving multiple choice questions. Good luck!

Program Structure & Language Fundamentals

This section helps us to get started with program structure by learning **basic building blocks** of C# programming. These building blocks include:

- Write first program in C#

- Work with variables, primitive data types & operators

- Understand expressions in C#

- Understand type casting in C#

- Use var keyword

- Array in C#

© Ali Asad and Hamza Ali 2017
A. Asad and H. Ali, *The C# Programmer's Study Guide (MCSD)*, DOI 10.1007/978-1-4842-2860-9_1

First Program in C#

Writing your first C# program is as simple as writing a program in C++/Java or in any high-level programming language. We prefer to write code in the **console application** to practice all topics for **Exam 70-483**. It is necessary that we know how to create an empty C# console project in Visual Studio to write the program.

To create an empty C# console project in Visual Studio 2012 or above, follow these steps, beginning with (Figure 1-1):

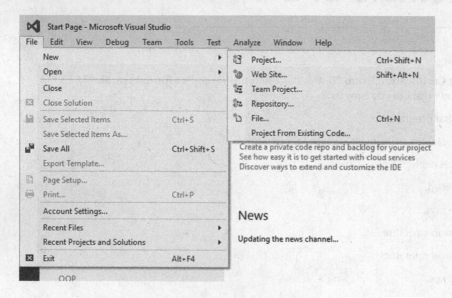

Figure 1-1. *Open a new project in Microsoft Visual Studio*

Open Visual Studio, Click on **File ➤ New Project**.

A window (Figure 1-2) will pop up to create a .NET project. Follow the below steps to create an empty C# console project in Visual Studio.

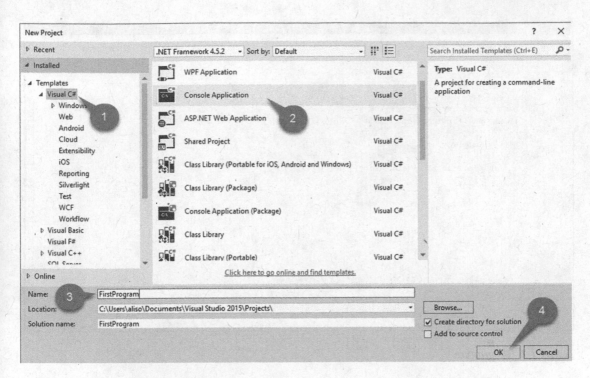

Figure 1-2. *Choose project template*

1. Select template "Visual C#" from left pane.

2. Select "Console Application" as a project type.

3. Write a unique name for your project.

4. Select "OK" to create the project.

Program.cs class will appear, which contains some default code. These codes are divided into different segments (using, namespace, class, main).

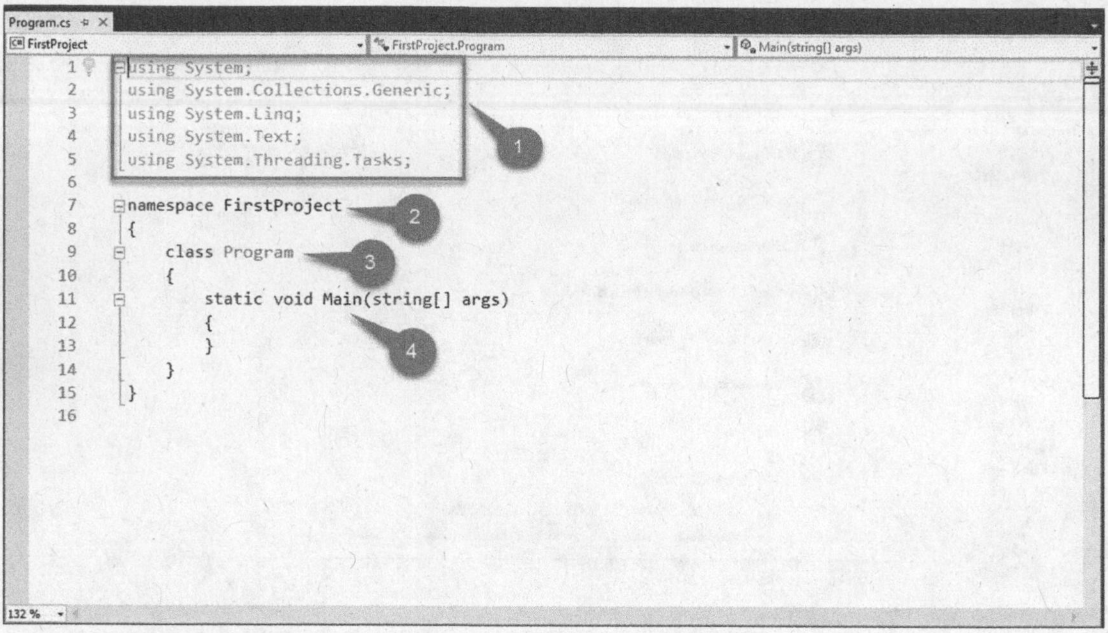

Figure 1-3. Program.cs

1. ***using***: statement helps to import namespace in the program. These namespaces have types that we can use to develop applications.

2. ***namespace FirstProject***: C# strictly follows object-oriented design. Therefore, when we created an empty console project, it creates a namespace with a project name. Inside namespace we write types for our project.

3. ***class Program***: C# creates a default class inside namespace called "Program". Inside classes we write methods, fields, properties, and events that we can reuse in the project.

4. ***Main***: C# program must contain a main method. It is where execution of the program begins.

Inside main method, write the following line of code to print a nice message on the output screen as shown in Listing 1-1.

Listing 1-1. First C# Program

```
static void Main (string [] args)
{
    Console.WriteLine("Welcome devs!");
}
```

To run the above code press *"f5"* or click on the **start** button from the toolbar in Visual Studio. It will print "Welcome devs!" on the output screen.

■ **Note** *Console.WriteLine* is a method that takes the message and prints it on the output screen.

Congratulations, you've successfully written your first application in Visual Studio using C#. Now you are ready to begin your journey to become a Microsoft Certified Professional & Specialist: Programming in C#.

Variables & Data Types

Data is **everywhere**. Our job as a developer is to manipulate data and produce required results. Data have numerous types (for example, text, audio, and video, etc.). Each type of data can hold a different size in memory. The same concept applies while writing an application in C#. We have *variables* to store data and *data types* to describe what type/size of data can be stored in a variable.

Syntax

```
Date_Type  Variable_Name  =  Value;
```

Code Snippet

Listing 1-2. Initialize an integer variable "age"

```
int age = 10;
```

Data Types in C#

There are some Data Types in C# which are common, used frequently, and have different sizes in memory. In Table 1-1 we have listed some of them.

Table 1-1. *Common data types in C#*

Data Type	Example	Default Value	Memory Size	Classification
int	456	0	4 bytes	Value Type
float	10.05f	0.0f	4 bytes	Value Type
Double	19.5D	0.0D	8 bytes	Value Type
Char	'A'	'\0'	2 bytes	Value Type
byte	5	0	8 bit	Value Type
string	"Dev"	Null	(2 bytes) * (length of string)	Reference Type
bool	true	False	1 byte	Value Type

Variables in C#

Variables are **placeholders**, to store data in memory for a temporary period of time. In programming, a variable is used frequently to retrieve and edit data in memory to produce required results. When defining a variable, there are some rules which we must follow.

- Name of a variable must start with an alphabet or underscore (_). Variables can also be *alphanumeric*.

- Name must be unique and it cannot be a keyword (e.g., "using").

- Do not insert space while defining a name, use camel case (studentName) or pascal case (StudentName).

Operator in C#

Operators are **special symbols**, used with variables (operands), to manipulate data with the aim of producing required results. Operators lie in different categories. Some of them are listed below:

- Arithmetic Operator

- Relational Operator

- Boolean Logical Operator

Arithmetic Operator

We use arithmetic operators on **numeric** values to perform mathematical operations. For example, in the following (Table 1-2), each arithmetic operator is used to perform a different mathematical operation.

Table 1-2. *Arithmetic Operators in C#*

Operator	Description	Example	
+	**Add Operator** used to add two numeric values	`int add = 10 + 5;`	`//add = 15`
-	**Subtract Operator** used to subtract two numeric values	`int min = 10 - 5;`	`//min = 5`
*	**Multiply Operator** used to multiply two numeric values	`int mul = 10 * 5;`	`//mul = 50`
/	**Division Operator** used to divide two numeric values	`int div = 10 / 5;`	`//div = 2`
%	**Modulus Operator** used to return remainder of two numeric values	`int mod = 10 % 5;`	`//mod = 0`

Relational Operator

Relational operator is used to **compare** two values (operands) and return **Boolean** as a result.

Table 1-3. *Relational Operators in C#*

Operator	Description	Example
>	**Greater than operator** returns "True", if first value is greater than the second value. Otherwise it will return "False".	`bool check = 4 > 3;` //True `bool check = 3 > 4;` // False
<	**Less than operator** returns "True", if first value is less than the second value. Otherwise it will return "False".	`bool check = 2 < 4;` //True `bool check = 4 < 2;` //False
==	**Equal to operator** returns "True", if first value matches with second value. Otherwise it will return "False".	`bool check = 2 == 2;` //True `bool check = 2 == 3;` //False
!=	**Not equal to operator** returns "True", if first value does not match with second value. It returns "False" when both values are equal.	`bool check = 2 != 3;` //True `Bool check = 2 != 2;` //False
>=	**Greater than Equals to operator** returns "True", if first value is greater or equal to second value. Otherwise it will return "False".	`bool check = 2 >= 1;` //True `bool check = 2 >= 2;` //True `bool check = 1 >= 2;` //False
<=	**Less than Equals to operator** returns "True", if first value is less than or equal to second value. Otherwise it will return "False".	`bool check = 2 <= 3;` //True `bool check = 2 <= 2;` //True `bool check = 2 <= 1;` //False

Boolean Logical Operators

Logical operators are used between **two** bool values. Some logical operators are described in the table below.

Table 1-4. *Boolean Logical Operators in C#*

Operator	Description	Example
&&	**And operator**, returns "True" if both Boolean values are true. Otherwise it will return "False".	`Bool check = True && True;` //True `Bool check = True && False;` //False
||	**OR operator**, returns "True" if any of two values have "True" value. If all values are "False" then it returns "False".	`Bool check = True || False;` //True `Bool check = False || False;` //False
!	**Not operator**, if value is "False" it returns "True" and if value is "True" it returns "False".	`Bool check = ! (false);` //True `Bool check = ! (true);` //False

Expression in C#

Expression helps us to evaluate the result from simple or complicated statements. It's actually a **series** of one or more operands, literal values and method invocations with zero or more operators that helps to **evaluate a result**.

Code Snippet

Listing 1-3. Write a simple expression in C#

```
int i = 4;
int j = (i * 4) + 3;
//Output j = 19
```

Type Casting

C# is **strongly** typed language, which means the type of variable **must match** with its value in both **compile and runtime**. In most cases, we need to convert the type of a data to store it in some other type. For example, we are getting string data ("10") and we want to convert it into int32 to perform an arithmetic operation.

There are two ways C# helps you to convert the type of an object or variable, by using:

- Implicit Conversion
- Explicit Conversion

Implicit Conversion

Implicit conversion happens **automatically** by the compiler itself. No special casting syntax is required and no data is lost during implicit conversion.

Example

Listing 1-4. Implicit conversion of small to larger integral data

```
int i = 10;
double d = i;
```

Listing 1-5. Implicit conversion of derived to base type

```
object o = new Program();
```

Explicit Conversion

Special casting/syntax is required when data cannot convert into other types automatically. Data might be lost in explicit conversion.

Example

Listing 1-6. Explicit conversion of larger data to smaller data type

```
double d = 3.1417;
int i = (int)d;
// use (type) to convert a type explicitly
```

Listing 1-7. Explicit conversion of string in primitive data type with "Parse" method

```
string s = "22";
int age = int.Parse(s);
```

■ **Note** Each permitive type has a Parse method. It helps to convert string data into that associated permitive type.

---

var keyword

Var is an **implicit** type, used to **store any value** of an expression. The type of var variable **depends on the value** that is assigned on **compile time**. If the value of an expression, object, or variable is string, then the type of var variable is string. If the value is int32, the type of var variable will become int32.

var keyword is highly recommended when:

- you prefer good variable names over type;
- The type name is long;
- the expression is complex and you don't know the type of value it returns.

Syntax

```
var variable_name = data;
```

Code Snippet

Listing 1-8. Assign any value in var variables

```
var age = 22;                        //type of age is int32
var name = "Ali Asad";               //type of name is string
var math = 10 / int.Parse("10");     //type of math is int32
```

■ **Note** Always initialize the var variable with a value. Otherwise the compiler will generate an error.

Array in C#

Array is a **collection or series** of elements of the same type. Each element stores data which can be accessed by calling its **index** number with an array name. An array can have three types:

- Single Dimension Array
- Multi Dimension Array
- Jagged Array

Single Dimension Array

In single dimension, an array stores elements in **linear** fashion. In most times of development, we use a single dimension array.

Syntax

```
type[] nameOfArray;
```

- **type** specifies what kind of data array can store
- **[]** specifies it's an array
- **nameOfArray** specifies name of the array

Code Snippet

Listing 1-9. Declare an array of string

```
string[] friends;
```

Initialize an Array

```
type[] nameOfArray = new type[size];
```

- new **type[size]**, helps to initialize series of elements of an array in memory. Size tells total length of an array.

Code Snippet

Listing 1-10. Declare a string array of size 4

```
string[] friends = new string[4];
```

Initialize an Array with Values (a)

```
type[] nameOfArray = new type[size];
nameOfArray[index] = value;
```

- **nameOfArray[index] = value**; tells to store value in specific index of an array.
- **Index** of an array cannot go out of the bounds.

Code Snippet

Listing 1-11. Declare and initialize string array of size 4 with values

```
string[] friends = new string[4];
friends[0] = "Ali";
friends[1] = "Mubashar";
```

Initialize an Array with Values (b)

```
type[] nameofArray = {values};
```

- **type[] nameofArray = {values}**; tells to store values directly without specifying length of an array. Length of an array depends upon number of values written inside {} curly braces.

Code Snippet

Listing 1-12. Declare and initialize a string array with values

```
string[] friends = { "Ali", "Mubashar" };
```

Initialize an Array with Values (c)

```
type[] nameOfArray = new int[size]{values};
```

- **type[] nameofArray = new int[size]{values};** tells to store values of 4 size.

Code Snippet

Listing 1-13. Declare and initialize string array of size 4 with values

```
string[] friends = new string[4] {"Ali", "Mubashar", "Lakhtey", "Hamza"};
```

Initialize an Array with Values (d)

```
type[] nameOfArray = new int[]{values};
```

- **type[] nameofArray = new int[]{values};** tells to initialize an array with no fixed size. Its size depends on number of values written inside {} curly brace.

Code Snippet

Listing 1-14. Declare and initialize an array with values

```
string[] friends = new string[] {"Ali", "Mubashar", "Lakhtey", "Hamza"};
```

Multi Dimension Array in C#

2D array is the most common kind of multi dimension array that we use in C#. In the real world, 2D array is used to store more complex data in a system (for example: digital image and board game). 2D array can be thought of as a table, which has rows and columns.

Syntax

```
type[,] my2dArray = new int[rowSize, colSize];
```

- **type[,]** tells array is 2D.
- **int[rowSize, colSize]** tells size of row and size of column.

Code Snippet

Listing 1-15. Declare 2D array of int, having 2 rows and 5 columns

```
int[,] numbers = new int[2,5];
```

Above code declares "numbers" array with 2 rows and 5 columns.

Initialize 2D Array with Values (a)

```
type[,] my2dArray = new int[rowSize,colSize]
{
        {values},
        {values}
};
```

11

Code Snippet

Listing 1-16. Initialize 2D array with values in sub arrays

```
int[,] numbers = new int[2, 5]
                        {
                            {2,4,6,8,10},
                            {1,3,5,7,9}
                        };
```

Above code snippet tells that "numbers" is a 2D array which has row size of 2 and column size of 5, which means it stores two single-dimension arrays of 5 size.

Access 2D Array

We use **loops** to access values of a 2D array. Loops are discussed with much detail later in this chapter. Following is a code snippet which explains how to access values of a 2D array.

Code Snippet

Listing 1-17. Display 2D array data

```
int[,] numbers = new int[2, 5]
                        {
                            {2,4,6,8,10},
                            {1,3,5,7,9}
                        };

for (int row = 0; row < numbers.GetLength(0); row++)
{
    for (int col = 0; col < numbers.GetLength(1); col++)
    {
        Console.Write(numbers[row, col]);
    }
    Console.WriteLine();
}

//Output
246810
13579
```

■ **Note** **GetLength(int32)** returns total number of elements in a specific dimension of an array.

Jagged Array in C#

It's an array of an array, which means it's a kind of array whose elements are also an array. Each element of a jagged array may have a different size.

Syntax

```
type[][] jaggedArray = new type[rowSize][];
```

- **type[][]** tells it's a jagged array.
- **type[rowSize][]** tells size of row is fixed but size of column is not fixed, because each element has a different size of array.

Code Snippet

```
int[][] jagged = new int[4][];
```

Declare a Jagged Array

Each index of a jagged array is initialized with a new size of array.

Code Snippet

Listing 1-18. Declare a jagged array having 4 rows

```
int[][] jagged = new int[4][];
```

Listing 1-19. Declare each row with a new size of array

```
jagged[0] = new int[2];
jagged[1] = new int[3];
jagged[2] = new int[4];
jagged[3] = new int[5];
```

- **int[4][]** tells jagged array has 4 rows but number of columns is not specified.
- **Jagged[0] = new int[2]**; tells row 0 has 2 columns.
- **Jagged[3] = new int[5]**; tells row 3 has 5 columns.

Initialize Jagged Array with Values (a)

Listing 1-20. Initialize value on the jagged array index

```
jagged[0][0] = 4;
jagged[0][1] = 5;
```

- **jagged[0][0] = 4**; store value in jagged array of row 0 and column 0.
- **jagged[0][1] = 5**; store value in jagged array of row 0 and column 1.

Initialize Jagged Array with Value (b)

Listing 1-21. Initialize jagged array of int with values

```
jagged[0] = new int[] { 4, 5 };
jagged[1] = new int[] { 6, 7, 8 };
```

- **jagged[0] = new int[] {4,5}**; initialize an array on row 0 with values {4,5}.
- **jagged[1] = new int[]{6,7,8}**; initialize an array on row 1 with values {6,7,8}.

Initialize Jagged Array with Values (c)

Listing 1-22. Initialize jagged array of int with values inside sub arrays

```
int[][] jagged =
        {
            new int[]{4,5},
            new int[]{6,7,8},
            new int[]{9,10,11},
            new int[]{12,13,14,15}
        };
```

- Initialize a jagged array with multiple arrays. The size of the jagged array's rows depends upon the number of arrays. In this case, the number of rows is 4.

Access Jagged Array

The values in a jagged array are accessed by specifying the index of both rows and columns.

Code Snippet

Listing 1-23. Display value of jagged array index

```
Console.WriteLine(jagged[0][0]);
Console.WriteLine(jagged[0][1]);
```

Loop Over Jagged Array

Listing 1-24. Use for loop to display each value in a jagged array index

```
//Initialize Jagged Array with Values
int[][] jagged =
        {
            new int[]{4,5},
            new int[]{6,7,8},
            new int[]{9,10,11},
            new int[]{12,13,14,15}
        };

//Loop over each index of jagged array
for (int i = 0; i < jagged.Length; i++)
{

        for (int j = 0; j < jagged[i].Length; j++)
        {
            Console.Write(jagged[i][j]);
        }

        Console.WriteLine();
}
```

- **jagged.Length**: Get total number of rows in a jagged array.

- **jagged[int].Length**: Get total number of columns of a specific row.

Implement Program Flow

Normally all statements of a program execute from **top to bottom**. But in a real application, we **control** the flow of execution by introducing:

- Decision Structure
- Decision Operators
- Loops
- Jump Statements

Control flow helps our program to **execute or skip** a code block, helps us to **repeat** a code until a condition is satisfied, and helps our control to **jump** anywhere in the code.

Decision Structure

Decision structures lets a program run only in certain **conditions**. Normally our program runs in a simple flow which executes all code from **top to bottom** without skipping any code. But in the real world, our application helps us **decide** what code to execute in certain conditions. For example, you're making a program that checks a person's age and decides whether or not a person has reached his retirement age. In such a case, we introduce decision structures to let the application decide whether a person has reached his retirement age or not.

C# has some decision structures that we can use listed below.

- If {}
- if-else{}
- if-else if{}
- switch {}

If {} Structure in C#

If statement helps us to control the flow of a program. It executes a program only when a certain condition returns **true**.

Syntax

```
if(condition)
{
        //TODO: Execute Program When Condition Returns True
}
```

- If (condition) returns true it will execute statements written inside {} curly brace. If condition returns false it will skip code written inside {} curly brace.

Example

Let's write a code that prints a message "Even Number" only when a number is even.

Listing 1-25. Write C# code to check if number is even

```
int number = 16;

if(number % 2 == 0)
{
    Console.WriteLine("Even Number");
}

//Output
Even Number
```

If Else {} Structure in C#

In real application, we find ourselves in a right or wrong situation. For example, if we enter a right username the system will log in. But if we enter an invalid username the system will pop an error. In such situations, we write code inside if-else statements.

Code written inside **if{}** block will execute when conditions satisfy. However, if a condition **doesn't satisfy**, code written inside **else{}** block will execute.

Syntax

```
if(condition)
{
    //TODO: Execute Code When Condition Satisfy
}
else
{
    //TODO: Execute Code When Condition Do Not Satisfy
}
```

- **If (condition)** returns true it will execute statements written inside {} curly brace.

- **Else {}** block will get executed when if(condition) returns false.

Example

To understand if-else, let's write a basic login code. The following code will check if a username is **correct**, it will print a message "Login Successful". But if a user name **isn't** correct, it will print "Invalid user name" message on output screen.

Listing 1-26. Check username is correct

```
string username = "dev";
if(username == "dev")
{
    Console.WriteLine("Login Successful");
}
else
{
    Console.WriteLine("Inavlid username, please try again");
}
```

```
//Output
Login Successful
```

■ **Note**   If username is other than "dev", in that case "Invalid username, please try again" message will print on screen.

If Else If {} Structure

Chain of multiple if and else makes if else-if. It helps a program to look into **multiple** conditions (options) to execute a specific block of code.

Syntax

```
if(condition)
{
        //TODO: run if condition satisfy
}
else if(condition)
{
        //TODO: run if condition satisfy
}
else if(condition)
{
        //TODO: run if condition satisfy
}
.
.
.
else
{
        //TODO: run if no condition is satisfied
}
```

- **If (condition)** returns true it will execute statements written inside {} curly brace.

- **Else If(condition)** control will check condition of else if only when if condition returns false. When else if condition returns true it will execute code written inside its body.

- When **else-if(condition)** returns false, control will then move to the next else-if(condition). When next else-if(condition) returns false, it will move to further next else-if(condition) and it will continue to do so until it finds else block of final else-if structure.

- When **any condition satisfied**, control will execute code statement written inside its block and skip the remaining else-if and else structure in its chain.

- **Else {}** will only get executed when no condition satisfies in its chain.

Example

Let's make a program that checks your age and prints on output screen whether you're a child, teenager, adult, or an old man.

Listing 1-27. Check user age and display a nice message

```
int age = 20;
if (age < 11)
{
    Console.WriteLine("You're a child!");
}
else if (age < 18)
{
    Console.WriteLine("You're a teenager!");
}
else if (age < 50)
{
    Console.WriteLine("You're an adult!");
}
else
{
    Console.WriteLine("You're an old person");
}
```

In the above example, the first and second conditions do not satisfy but the third condition else if (age < 50) satisfies, and the application will then print "You're an adult" on screen. After executing the code block, the control will then skip the remaining else if and move out of the if-else structure.

Switch {} Structure in C#

Switch is another decision structure, highly recommend when we have given **constants to compare with** an expression. If none of the constants matches with the expression, the default block will then execute.

Syntax

```
switch(expression)
{
        case constant:
                //case block
        break;

        case constant:
                //case block
        break;

        .
        .
        .

        default:
                //default case block
        break;
}
```

Example

Suppose we're making an application that helps us decide whether a number is even or odd.

Listing 1-28. Check if number is even or odd

```
int i = 3;

switch(i%2)
{
        case 0:
                Console.WriteLine("{0} is an even number", i);
        break;

        case 1:
                Console.WriteLine("{0} is an odd number", i);
        break;
}
```

■ **Note**   Use switch-case only when we have a **defined list of constants** that we can compare with the result of an expression. Otherwise, use if-else structure.

Decision Operators

There are some operators in C# which help us to return a data only when a certain condition satisfies. These are:

- Conditional Operator (? :)
- Null Coalescing Operator (??)

Conditional Operator (? :)

Conditional operator checks a condition and returns a value. If a condition satisfies, it returns a value that lies in the "True" block. But if it doesn't satisfy the condition, it returns a value that lies in the "False" block.

Syntax

```
(Condition) ? True_Statement : False_Statement;
```

Example

Suppose we're making an application that tells us whether a number is even or odd.

Listing 1-29. Check if number is even or odd

```
int num = 2;
string result = (num % 2 == 0) ? "Even" : "Odd";
Console.WriteLine("{0} is { 1}", num, result);
```

■ **Note**   Use a conditional statement only when you want to return a value. Otherwise, use an if-else statement.

Explanation

Let's understand how a conditional operator works in the above example.

- **((num % 2) == 0)** It's a Boolean expression or a condition to be satisfied.

- **?** It's a conditional operator. That helps to decide which statement to return. If a condition satisfies, it returns a True statement; and if it doesn't satisfy a condition, it returns a False statement.

- **"Even":"Odd"** These are two statements, separated by colon (:). A true statement is before a colon (:) and a false statement is after colon (:)

Null Coalescing Operator (??)

There are many cases when we make sure that we don't store a **Null** value in a variable. We can achieve this by using a Null Coalescing operator. It returns a left-hand variable (operand) if it's not null; otherwise, it returns a default value stored in a right-hand variable (operand).

Syntax

```
leftOperand ?? rightOperand;
```

Code Snippet

Listing 1-30. Set value "user" in username if "name" is null

```
string name = null;

//set username = name, if name is not null.
//set username = "user", if name is null.

string username = name ?? "user";
```

Loops in C#

In a real application we sometimes execute same a block of code **multiple** times. In such a case, we use loops to iterate over the same code statements for **x number** of times.

In C# we have four kinds of loops that we can use to iterate a code statement for multiple times.

- while loop
- do-while loop
- for loop
- foreach loop

While Loop

While loop helps to iterate over code statements till a condition written inside while() returns true.

Syntax

```
while(condition)
{
        //Execute Code: as long as condition returns true.
}
```

Code Snippet

Listing 1-31. Use while loop to print hello world for 20 times

```
bool isFound = false;
int value = 0;
while (isFound != true)    //check whether or not run code inside its block
{
    If(value == 99)
    {
        isFound = true;
    }
    value = value + 3;

}
```

■ **Note** Use while loop when you know a condition to be true and you don't know how many times it is going to iterate over a code block.

Do-while Loop

Do-while loop helps to iterate over code statements. It works the **same as while** loop; the only difference is the **condition always checks** at the **end**.

Syntax

```
do
{
        //Run Code: till condition is true

}while(condition);
```

Code Snippet

Listing 1-32. Use do-while loop to print Hello World for 5 times

```
int count = 1;
do                         //Do not check condition on first iteration
{
    Console.WriteLine("Hello World");
    count++;

} while (count <= 5); //check condition: if true, do block execute
```

Explanation

When do-while runs for the first time, it doesn't check the condition; instead it runs the code inside it. When the first iteration is complete, it then checks the condition to run the iteration for the second time. It will continuously repeat it so as long as the condition is true.

For Loop

For loop is used in a case when we have fixed numbers to iterate a code block for multiple times.

Syntax

```
for(variable_initialization; condition; increment/decrement)
{
        //Run Code: till condition is true
}
```

Explanation

Let's understand the syntax of for loop.

- **variable_initialization**: In this part of loop, the variable is declared and initialized or only initialized and this statement (first part of loop) is executed once when the controls enter the loop.

- **Condition**: Condition gives a green signal to loop to iterate over the code block only when a condition returns true.

- **Increment/decrement**: Increment/decrement helps to control the iteration of loop.

Code Snippet

Listing 1-33. Use for loop to print "Hello World" for 5 times

```
for(int count = 1; count <= 5; count++)
{
        Console.WriteLine("Hello World");
}
```

Explanation

int count = 1; here's a count value initialized with the value 1; afterward, a condition will be checked if it's satisfied, then a control can enter into it for the loop body to run all the statements written inside it. After executing an iteration of loop, a control will then move to a for loop signature to run count++; this allows a count variable to remember how many times it has executed. Afterward, it checks a condition and if it satisfies again, it goes into a loop body to run all statements. It repeats the same cycle (check condition ➤ run loop body ➤ increment value of count) as long as a condition is true.

■ **Note** For loop is useable when a number of iterations and conditions for termination is defined.

Foreach loop

Foreach loop always works on **collection**; the number of iterations depends upon the **length** of its collection. On each iteration, foreach loop gets a value of the **next index** of a collection.

Syntax

```
foreach(var item in collection)
{
        //Run Code
}
```

Code Snippet

Listing 1-34. Use foreach loop to iterate over an array

```
int[] array = { 1, 2, 3, 4, 5 };      //Collection of int

foreach (int item in array)           //iterating over each index of collection
{
    Console.WriteLine(item);          //print value stored in that index
}
```

Explanation

Let's break down a code snippet of foreach and understand its working step by step.

- **int item**: is a placeholder variable that stores a value that particular index of array has.
- **in** is a keyword, which gets the value of an array[index], until it gets all the index values in a continuous iteration over an array.
- **array** it's the name of an int[] collection defined above a foreach loop.

■ **Note**   We cannot modify the value of a collection while iterating over it in a foreach loop.

Jump Statements in C#

Jump statements allow program controls to move from **one point to another** at any particular location **during the execution of a program**.

Below are the jump statements that we can use in C#:

- Goto
- Break
- Continue
- Return
- Throw

Goto

A goto statement is a jump statement which transfers its controls to a **labeled statement**. The goto statement requires the label to identify the place where control will go. A label is any valid identifier and must be followed by a **colon**. The label is placed before the statement where control is to be transferred.

A common use of goto statement is in switching transfer control to specific switch-case or nested loops to change the control when work is done or depends on the scenario.

Syntax

```
label:
//some code
goto label;
```

OR

```
goto label;
label:
//some code
```

Goto Statements in Switch Case

Listing 1-35. Use "goto" in switch-case

```
char character = 'e';

switch (character)
{
    case 'a':
    {
        Console.WriteLine("Character is a vowel.");
        break;
    }
    case 'e':
    {
        goto case 'a';
    }
    case 'i':
    {
        goto case 'a';
    }
    case 'o':
    {
        goto case 'a';
    }
    case 'u':
    {
        goto case 'a';
    }
    case 'y':
    {
        Console.WriteLine("Character is sometimes a vowel.");
        break;
    }
    default:
    {
        Console.WriteLine("Character is a consonant");
        break;
    }
}
```

```
//Output:
Character is vowel.
```

Explanation

In the above code example, control jumps into case "e". Inside case "e" goto case "a" statement executes and control will then jump into case "a" block and print "Character is vowel." on output screen.

Goto Statements in Loops

Let's take another simple example to understand goto more clearly:

Listing 1-36. Use goto in for loop

```
int[] numbers = new int[] { 1, 2, 3, 4, 5, 6, 7, 8, 9, 10 };

for (int i = 0; i < 10; i++)
{
    if (numbers[i] == 8)
    {
        goto Control;
    }
}

Console.WriteLine("End of Loop");

Control:
Console.WriteLine("The number is 8");
```

```
//Output
//The number is 8
```

Explanation

In the above example, whenever the compiler detects the value of numbers[i] and if there is an 8, then the compiler will move to label "Control" and start executing the code after label "Control". So the output will just be "The number is 8".

■ **Note** There are two forms of goto statements: **Forward Jump** and **Backward Jump**. Figure 1-4 shows the flow of **goto** statement in forward and backward manner.

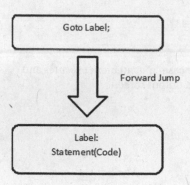

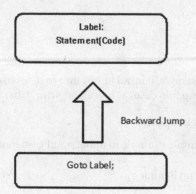

Figure 1-4. *Goto Statement's flow*

- Goto Statements with Loop example shows forward jump
- Goto Statements with Switch shows backward jump of goto statement.

■ **Note** Avoid goto statements in such scenarios which lead to the unreachable code.

Break

Break is a keyword that is also a jump statement, which **terminates** the program flow in loop or in switch statement (i.e., skips the current block and moves to outer block or code if any).

Use break statement in loop

Listing 1-37. Use break in for loop

```
int[] numbers = new int[] { 1, 2, 3, 4, 5, 6, 7, 8, 9, 10 };

for (int i = 0; i < 10; i++)
{
    if (numbers[i] == 3)
    {
        break;
    }
    Console.Write(numbers[i]);
}

Console.WriteLine("End of Loop");
```

Explanation

When above code snippet executes, output will be "End of Loop". Let us understand how.

When an if condition written inside for loop satisfies, break keyword will then execute. It terminates the remaining iteration of loop and jumps the control out from the loop and will start executing code which is written outside the loop, i.e., "Console.WriteLine("End of Loop");".

Continue

Continue statement is also a jump statement, which **skips the current iteration** and moves the control to the **next** iteration of loop.

Continue is a **keyword, the** same as break but with the above said behavior.

Use continue statement in loop

Listing 1-38. Use "continue" in for loop

```
int[] numbers = new int[] { 1, 2, 3, 4, 5, 6, 7, 8, 9, 10 };
for (int i = 0; i < 10; i++)
{
    if (numbers[i] == 5)
    {
        continue;
    }
    Console.Write(numbers[i]);
}
Console.WriteLine("End of Loop");
```

Explanation

In this example, the for loop will work normally as it works, but when the value numbers[i] becomes 5, it will skip the iteration, which means it will stop executing the current iteration further and move for the next iteration.

```
//Output
  1234678910 End of Loop
```

Return

Return is also a jump statement, which **moves back** the program **control to calling method**. It returns a value or nothing depending on the nature of method (i.e., return type of method).

Return is also a **keyword** with above said behavior.

Use return in method (a)

Listing 1-39. Use "return" in method

```
static int getAge()
{
    return 20;
}
static void Main(string[] args)
```

```
{
    Console.WriteLine("Welcome to Exam 70-483 Certification");
    int age = getAge();
    Console.WriteLine("Age is: " + age);
}
```

Explanation

In this example, the method getAge() is a type of int, so method returns the value of type int and control automatically goes to where it is calling, i.e., int age=getAge() in main method. So the value returned by the method getAge is stored in the "age" variable.

Use return Statement in Main Method (b)

Listing 1-40. Return statement in main method

```
static void Main(string[] args)
{
    Console.WriteLine("Welcome to Exam 70-483 Certification");
    return;
    Console.WriteLine("This Statement will never executed!");
}
```

Explanation

In the second above example, method has returned type void, meaning nothing, therefore it has no need to return value. In such a case, we use "return" statement without a value, which helps to skip the remaining statements of method and jumps the control back to where the method was called. **Note:**

- If return statement is used in try/catch block and this try/catch has finally block, then finally block will execute in this condition also and after it control will be returned to calling method.

- Tip: code after return statement is unreachable. Therefore it is wise to use the return statement inside the if-else block, if we are willing to skip the remaining statement of method only when a certain condition satisfies. Otherwise execute the complete method.

Methods in C#

Method contains a series of code statements that perform a certain functionality. It helps to **organize** code better, **eliminates** duplication of code, and helps to **re-use** it over and over again.

Syntax

```
Return_Type      Method_Name      (Parameter_List)
{
        //TODO: Method Body
}
```

- **Method_Name:** Method has a unique name, which helps to re-use the functionality of code whenever it is called.

- **Return_Type:** Method contains a series of code statements that manipulate data and generate results. If that result has to be used somewhere else in code, then data has to return where it is called. Return_Type helps us to describe, what type of data a method will return. If a method doesn't return any value, then use "*void*" for its return type.

- **Parameter_List:** We can pass values in methods through parameter_list. The type of value must match with the method's parameter type.

- **Method Body:** Here we write code statements that a method must contain. It executes only when method is called by its name in code.

Code Snippet

Suppose we want to make a method that takes two int values, adds them and returns a result.

Listing 1-41. Return a result

```
int Sum (int a, int b)
{
        int add = a + b;
        return add;
}
```

Now, method has a list of parameters. These parameters are adding up in the "add" variable; in the next statement, value stored in the variable "add" is returned. Note, the type of return variable must match with the return_type (int) of the method.

▪ **Note**   All variables defined inside method's body are **local** variables.

Named Argument

A named argument in methods helps us to pass values in **random order**. All we need to do is use a parameter name with a colon (:) and pass value there. For example, in the previous method example we made "Sum" method, which takes two parameters "(int a, int b)". Now, with the named argument we can pass "b" value first and "a" value last.

Listing 1-42. Use named arguments to pass value during method calling

```
Sum (b: 5, a: 10);
```

Optional Argument

When we define a list of parameters in method's signature, it becomes compulsory and required to pass values for all parameters. Optional argument gives us an edge to mark a parameter as optional, so we can call a method without passing value in optional parameter.

All we need to do is to give some **default values** to parameters which should be marked as optional. Doing that allows a user to call a method without passing values to an optional parameter.

Listing 1-43. Define optional parameter

```
int Sum(int a, int b = 1)
{
    int add = a + b;
    return add;
}
```

Now, look at parameter int b; it has a default value = 1, which helps the user to call Sum method without passing the value of "int b". In that case, "int b" would have a default value = 1. If the user passes a value of "int b", then the default value will be overridden with the newest value provided by the user. For example,

Listing 1-44. Use feature of optional argument during method calling

```
Sum (10);       //a = 10, b = 1
Sum (10, 5);    // a = 10, b = 5
```

Pass by Reference with ref Keyword

ref keyword helps us to pass an argument by reference. Any **change to the parameter's value** in the method would reflect the **same changes to the original variable's value**, where the method's argument was being called.

Syntax

The syntax of passing argument by reference with "ref" keyword is extremely simple. Just write "ref" keyword before defining a parameter in method's signature and when passing an argument while calling a method.

```
myMethod(ref data);
//use "ref" with parameter value when method is called

void myMethod(ref int d)
{
        //TODO:
}
//use "ref" with parameter definition in method's definition
```

Example

In below code we're incrementing value of ref parameter by one. The same changes would reflect to the original variable where method is called.

Listing 1-45. Change variable original value by passing it in method argument by refernce

```
class Program
{
        static void PassByRef(ref int i)
        {
            i = i + 1;
        }
```

```
static void Main(string[] args)
{
    int j = 0;
    PassByRef(ref j);
    Console.WriteLine(j);    //j = 1
}
}
```

In above code, see definition of PassByRef() method, "ref" keyword is written before int i, which tells us that this parameter would take reference, not its value. Now also see inside Main () method, where PassByRef() is being called. Here we also wrote "ref" before variable "j", which we're passing as an argument. It tells to pass a reference of "j" (not the value of "j"), which is basically a **memory address**. In the next statement we print the value of "j". Then every change that happens in PassByRef() would affect the same change in "j", which means "j" value is now 1.

Pass by Reference with out Keyword

out keyword works same as ref keyword works. The difference is, we can pass a **non-initialized variable** to method's argument by using out keyword. Also, it is used to get more than one return parameter from a method. Out signifies a **reference parameter**, whichs mean out keyword passes an argument by reference.

■ **Note**   The value of an **out** variable must be **initialized** in method's body.

Syntax

The syntax of out keyword is the same as ref keyword. We write "out" keyword before a parameter before defining a parameter in method's signature and before passing an argument while calling a method.

```
MethodName(out variableName);
//use out keyword with paremeter when method is called.

void MethodName(out v)
{
        //TODO:
}
//use out keyword with parameter when method is defined
```

Example

In below code, we're initializing a parameter value in method. The same changes would affect the variable, which was passed as an argument of the method.

Listing 1-46. Pass empty variable in method argument via out keyword and initialize it in method's body

```
class Program
{
        static void outMethod(out int i)
        {
            i = 1;
        }
```

```
    static void Main(string[] args)
    {
        int j;
        outMethod(out j);
        Console.WriteLine(j);   // j = 1
    }
}
```

In main method, see that the variable "j" is not initialized and passed to outMethod. When passing it to outMethod we must write the "out" keyword. Inside the outMethod body, the value of "I" is initialized with 1. The same changes will affect the original variable in main method "j", because the value of j is not 1.

Use Params Array to Pass Unlimited Method Argument

The number of arguments of a method depends upon the length of a parameter list in method's signature. For example, in our previous example of "Sum" method, we cannot pass more than two values in its arguments. But with param array we can pass an **unlimited** number of arguments.

Syntax

The syntax of using params array is simple; just write "params" before an array type in the method's parameter list.

```
void myMethod ( params int[] args )
{
        //TODO:
}
```

Example

Suppose we are required to make a method which takes unlimited arguments and returns a sum of all the arguments' values.

Listing 1-47. Add unlimited arguments and return its result

```
int Sum(params int[] args)
{
    int add = 0;

    foreach (int item in args)
    {
        add = add + item;
    }

    return add;
}
```

In the above code snippet, see that "params" keyword is used before int array. The code written in method body is simple and straightforward. It is iterating over all arguments and adding each one of them with the next value. In the end it returns the sum of all arguments.

```
Sum (1, 2, 3, 4, 5);     // return 15
```

In the above line, Sum method is being called, passed 5 arguments, and it returns a sum of 5 arguments (which is 15).

■ **Note**   **1 -** A method shouldn't have more than one param array.

2 - If there is more than one parameter, params array shoud be the last one.

Summary

- var is an implicit type; it can store data of any type at compile time.
- Operators are special symbols that manipulate data to produce a required result.
- C# is a strongly typed language.
- No data loss in implicit type conversion. No special syntax required for implicit type conversion.
- Data may be lost in explicit type conversion. Special syntax required for explicit type conversion.
- Jagged array is an array of an array, which means number of rows in jagged array is fixed but number of columns isn't fixed.
- Use "ref" keyword in method's parameter to pass data by its reference.
- Use "params array" to pass unlimited arguments in methods.
- Use switch when we have given constants to compare with.
- To repeat statements again and again use loops.
- To iterate over collection use foreach loop.
- Use jump statements (i.e., goto, break, continue, and return) to change normal flow of program.

Code Challenges

Challenge 1: Develop an Arithmetic Calculator Application

Develop a calculator application that helps users to add, subtract, multiply, or divide two values.

Output should be like:

Press any following key to perform an arithmetic operation:

```
1 - Addition
2 - Subtraction
3 - Multipliation
4 - Division

1
Enter Value 1: 10
Enter Value 2: 20

10 + 20 = 30
```

Do you want to continue again (Y/N)?

Tips:

- Use **separate** method for +, - , *, /
- Use **switch-case** structure to select user choice.
- Use **while** loop to repeat the program until user presses "N".

Challenge 2: Develop a Student Report Card Application

Develop a report card application that saves students' marks information; show position and report card of each student in descending order.

Requirements

- Each student has three subjects (English, Math and Computer).
- Application will save each student's marks along with student's name.
- Application will calculate total marks.
- Application will show position and report card in descending order.

Output should be like:

Press any following key

```
Enter Total Students : 2

Enter Student Name : Lakhtey

Enter English Marks (Out Of 100) : 50

Enter Math Marks (Out Of 100) : 60

Enter Computer Marks (Out Of 100) : 30
```

```
***********************************************
Enter Student Name : Ali Asad

Enter English Marks (Out Of 100) : 60

Enter Math Marks (Out Of 100) : 70

Enter Computer Marks (Out Of 100) : 30

***************Report Card*******************

****************************************
Student Name: Ali Asad, Position: 1, Total: 160/300

****************************************

Student Name: Lakhtey, Position: 2, Total: 140/300

****************************************
```

Tips:

- Use **multi-dimension** array to store student's information.
- Use **loops** to iterate over each student's information to generate report.

Practice Exam Questions

Question 1

Which of the following methods help us to convert string type data into integers? Select any two.

    A)   Convert.toInt32();

    B)   Convert.Int32();

    C)   int.parse();

    D)   parse.int();

Question 2

Suppose you're implementing a method name "Show" that will be able to take an unlimited number of int arguments. How are you going to define its method signature?

    A)   void Show(int[] arg)

    B)   void Show(params int[] arg)

    C)   void Show(int a)

    D)   void Show(ref int a)

Question 3

You're developing an application that saves user's information. The application includes the following code segment (line numbers included for reference).

```
01      public bool IsNull(string name)
02      {
03          return true;
04      }
```

You need to evaluate whether a name is null.
Which code segment should you insert at line 03

A)
```
if (name = null)
{
    return true;
}
```

B)
```
if (name == null)
{
    return true;
}
```

C)
```
if (null)
{
    return true;
}
```

D)
```
if (!name)
{
    return true;
}
```

Question 4

You need to use null-coalescing operator to make sure "name" variable must have a value not null. Select the right way to use null-coalescing operator in C#.

A) string name = n ?? "No Name";

B) string name = "No Name" ?? null;

C) string name = "No Name" ? null;

D) string name = null ? "No Name";

Question 5

Which jump statement will you use to start the next iteration while skipping the current iteration of loop?

- **A)** Break
- **B)** Continue
- **C)** Goto
- **D)** Return

Answers

1. A, C
2. B
3. B
4. A
5. B

CHAPTER 2

■ ■ ■

Types in C#

C# is a **strongly-typed** language. It says, data must have a type that defines its nature and behavior. Type helps to manipulate data in a much **managed** way. We'll cover the following main objectives that help to create and consume types in C#.

1. Understand Types

2. Create Types

3. Types and Memory Management

4. Special Types in C#

5. Type Conversion

Understand Types

Types are the declaration of an object which stores information and actions, that an object uses to produce required results. Type also stores the following information:

- How much memory an object holds

- Memory location where object is stored in memory

- The base type it inherits from

This information helps the compiler to make sure everything is type safe. In the previous chapter, we learned how to create variables by using common **built-in types,** i.e., *int, float, and bool*.

Code Snippet

Listing 2-1. Built-in types in C#

```
int age = 22;
string name = "Ali Asad";
```

Create Types

C# allow users to create their own types by using:

1. Enum

2. Struct

3. Class

© Ali Asad and Hamza Ali 2017
A. Asad and H. Ali, *The C# Programmer's Study Guide (MCSD)*, DOI 10.1007/978-1-4842-2860-9_2

Enum

Enum, a.k.a enumeration, is a set of named integer constants. It is used to group similar logically named constants (for example, days of the week and rainbow colors, etc.).

Syntax

```
enum MyEnum
{
    //list of named constants
}
```

Code Snippet

Listing 2-2. Use enum inside switch-case structure

```
enum Status
{
    Alive,
    Injured,
    Dead
}

class Program
{
    static void Main(string[] args)
    {
        Status player = Status.Alive;

        switch (player)
        {
            case Status.Alive:
                //Do Alive Code
                break;

            case Status.Injured:
                //DO Injured Code
                break;

            case Status.Dead:
                //Do Dead Code
                break;
        }
    }
}
```

- **Status player = Status.Alive;** tells player is alive.

■ **Note** In decision structures, enums are mostly used with a switch statement that uses enum's constant value to quickly jump over to a specific case block.

- Enums are useable to use constant values.

- Enums are readable and to give just information that is required in code.

- Enums are strongly typed. Therefore, an enum of one type cannot be implicitly assigned to an enum of another type.

Enum and Integer

By default, the first value of enum's named constant is always "0" and the value of each successive enumerator is increased by "1".

For example, in following enum's constants, the value of Alive is 0, Injured is 1, and Dead is 2.

Listing 2-3. Default value of enum's constants

```
enum Status
{
    Alive, //0
    Injured, //1
    Dead //2
}
```

To get the integer value of each constant an explict cast is necessary.

```
int valueOfAlive = (int)Status.Alive;
```

valueOfAlive would store '0'.

Override Constant's Values

Use initializers to override the default value of enum's constants. Therefore, subsequent constants are forced to increment their values from the override value. In the following code snippet, Alive is initialized with the value 2. Therefore, injured will have 3 and Dead will have 4.

Listing 2-4. Initialize enum's constant values

```
enum Status
{
    Alive = 2,
    Injured, //3
    Dead //4
}
```

Supporting Types

Enum supports the following types for its constant's values:

- byte
- sbyte
- short
- ushort
- int
- uint
- long
- ulong

Enforce enum to store the value in the above type.

Listing 2-5. Change enum's constants type to "byte"

```
enum Status : byte
{
    Alive = 1,
    Injured,
    Dead
}
```

The value type of Alive would be byte. It helps to minimize the memory storage required to initialize an enum.

Struct

Struct is used to **encapsulate** the attribute and behavior of an entity. It's used to define those objects which hold small memory. Most primitive types (int, float, bool) in C# are made up from struct. Struct doesn't support all object-oriented principles.

Syntax

```
struct NameOfType
{
  //...
}
```

- ***struct*** is a keyword, used to declare a type.

Code Snippet

Listing 2-6. Define and use custom type "Vector" with struct

```
struct Vector
{
    public int x;
    public int y;
}
```

```
class Program
{
    static void Main(string[] args)
    {
        Vector vector = new Vector();
        vector.x = 5;
        vector.y = 10;

        Console.WriteLine("x = {0}", vector.x);
        Console.WriteLine("y = {0}", vector.y);
    }
}
```

- *Vector vector* = *new Vector();* declare and initialize custom type Vector with *new* keyword.

- *vector.x* = *5;* assign a value 5 to its attribute "x".

The data encapsulated by struct are its **data member**. The variables are known as fields and functions included in it are called **member functions.**

struct is not limited to fields, but it can also have **functions, constructors, indexers, events, nested types, and an implemented interface**.

Constructor in struct

Constructor is a method called and executed first by runtime soon after its type's instance is created on memory. It doesn't have a return type. It is used to initialize data members that protect the application from any garbage computation error.

- Default Constructor (parameter less) is not allowed in struct.

- Constructor is optional in struct but if included it must not be parameterless.

- Constructor can be overload but each overloaded constructor **must initialize** all data members.

- Data members or fields cannot be initialized in the struct body. Use constructor to initialize them.

- Creating the object (without a new keyword) would not cause constructor calling even though a constructor is present.

Syntax

```
struct TypeName
{
    public TypeName(parameterlist)
    {
        //initialize fields
    }
    //declare fields
}
```

43

Code Snippet

Listing 2-7. Define parameter constructor in struct

```
struct Vector
{
    //Constructor
    public Vector(int a, int b)
    {
        //Initialize Fields
        x = a;
        y = b;
    }

    //Fields
    public int x;
    public int y;
}

class Program
{
    static void Main(string[] args)
    {
        //Initialize Vector, by passing 5,10 value to its constructor
        Vector vector = new Vector(5, 10);

        Console.WriteLine("x = {0}", vector.x);
        Console.WriteLine("y = {0}", vector.y);
    }
}
```

- **new Vector(5, 10);** passed 5,10 values to its constructor. Therefore, it could initialize its fields.

■ **Note**   Don't use struct to define complex types.

---

this keyword

this keyword indicates **current instance**. It is a special **reference type** variable that is used to call an instance's member inside **non-static method** definition.

this keyword has many uses:

- To pass an object itself as a parameter to other methods.

- To return an object itself from a method.

- To declare an extension method.

- To eliminate the naming conflict of a parameter's variable name and instance field name.

Code Snippet

Listing 2-8. Use "this" operator to access the instance member of a Vector type

```
struct Vector
{
    //Constructor
    public Vector(int x, int y)
    {
        //Initialize Fields
        this.x = x;
        this.y = y;
    }

    //Fields
    public int x;
    public int y;
}
```

- **this.x** referred to instance variable x (public int x).
- **this.x = x;** here x is a local (method parameter) variable which stores the value in an instance variable "x" (public int x).

Class

Class is used to encapsulate the attribute and behavior of an entity. It supports object-oriented principles. Therefore, classes are helpful to define complex types.

Syntax

```
class <class_name>
{
    // Fields
    // properties
    // Constructors
    // methods
    // events
    // delegates
    // nested classes
}
```

Code Snippet

Listing 2-9. Define and use custom type with "class"

```
class Person
{
    public string name;
    public int age;
```

```
    public void Display()
    {
        Console.WriteLine("Name = {0} Age = {1}", name, age);
    }
}

class Program
{
    static void Main(string[] args)
    {
        Person person = new Person();
        person.name = "Hamza Ali";
        person.age = 20;

        person.Display();
    }
}
```

Constructor in Class

Constructor is a method, called and executed first by runtime soon after its type's instance is created on memory. It doesn't have a return type. It is used to initialize data members that protect the application from any garbage computation error.

Syntax

```
class TypeName
{
    public TypeName()
    {
        //initialize data member
    }
    //declare data member
}
```

Code Snippet

Listing 2-10. Define default constructor in class

```
class Person
{
    public string name;
    public int age;

    //Default Constructor
    public Person()
    {
        name = "NILL";
        age = -1;
    }
}
```

- Default constructor doesn't have a parameter.
- Class can also have a parameterized constructor as well.

Base Constructor

Class may have many derived classes. A derived class inherits attributes and methods of its base class. If a base class has a parameterized constructor, its derived class must pass values to initialize its base class's constructor.

Syntax

```
class DerivedClass : BaseClass
{

    public DerivedClass(type x):base(x)
    {
    }
}
```

- **base(..)** it calls and passes values to a parameterized constructor of BaseClass.
- Derived class constructor at least has same parameters of BaseClass's constructor. Therefore, it could pass value to its base class's constructor.

Code Snippet

Listing 2-11. Pass value to parent class's constuctor

```
class Person
{
    protected string name;
    protected int age;

    public Person(string name, int age)
    {
        this.name = name;
        this.age = age;
    }
}

class Employee : Person
{

    public Employee(string n, int a) : base(n, a)
    {
        //...
    }
}

class Program
{
```

```
static void Main(string[] args)
{
    Employee emp = new Employee("Hamza", 20);
}
}
```

- **Employee emp = new Employee("Hamza", 20);** it calls and passes values to a parameterized constructor of BaseClass.

Types and Memory Management

In the above topic, we learned how to create types by using *enum, struct, and class*. C# has a concept to define these terms in: **Value** and **Reference** type.

Value Type

A type that is defined by either *struct* or *enum* is known as a **value type**. It holds data in its own memory allocation.

Reference Type

A type that is defined by either *class, interface,* or *delegate* is known as a **reference type**. It holds a pointer to a memory location that contains data called reference type.

In a .NET framework, CLR manages instances of value and reference type on three memory locations:

1. Heap

2. Stack

3. Registers

Heap

It's a memory location where instances of reference type are stored. Instances of value type can also be stored on heap when:

- value type is part of a class;

- value type is boxed;

- value type is an array;

- value type is a static variable;

- value type is used in an async or iterator block;

- value type is closed-over locals of a lambda or anonymous method.

Instances of value type **live longer** only when any of the above cases is true. Heap is an ideal location for instances that have a longer lifetime.

For example, in the following code snippet, see how CLR manages memory allocation.

```
string address = "Sialkot, Punjab";
```

The following figure 2-1 shows managed memory Heap.

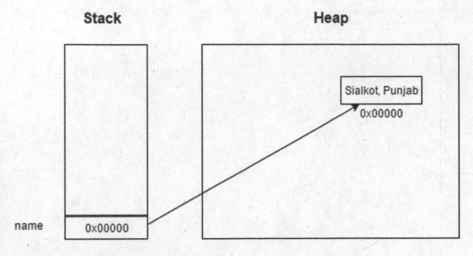

Figure 2-1. *Managed memory heap*

___

■ **Note**   The memory size of heap is larger than the Stack and register's size.

___

Stack

It's a memory location where short-lived temporary instances of value type and the memory address of an object can be stored. Temporary short-lived variables that Stack can store are:

- value types that are declared inside a method body or inside a parameter list;
- the memory address of an instance of a reference type.

It uses **LIFO** (Last In First Out) algorithm to manage the lifetime of each variable in a Stack. Its memory size is relatively smaller than heap, as shown in Figure 2-2.

For example, in the following code snippet, see how CLR manages memory allocation.

```
int age = 22;
```

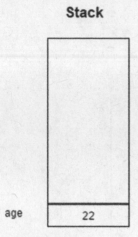

Stack

age   22

Figure 2-2. *Stack*

Register

It's a memory location where instances of short-lived temporary instances of value type or computation values of arithmetic operations are stored on register. Its memory size is relatively much smaller than Stack. Its up to CLR, which decides which short-lived memory instances are stored on either Stack or on Register.

Special Types in C#

C# provides special types which are syntactic sugar for users. These types help users to maximize their productivity by writing helper code inside them. These special types are listed below.

- System.Object type
- anonymous type
- dynamic type
- nullable type
- static type

System.Object Type

All value and reference types are derived from system.object type. In .NET, object is the base of all type hierarchy. The below Figure 2-3 shows system.object's type hierarchy.

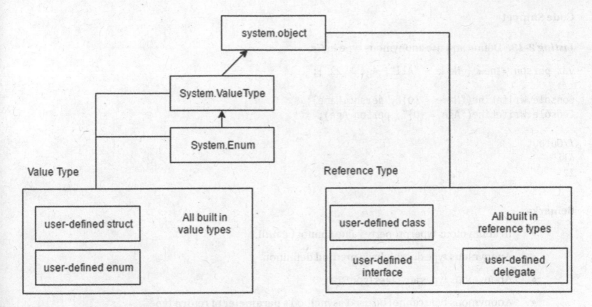

Figure 2-3. *System.object's type hierarchy*

Because all types in .NET are **derived** from system.object, it can handle values of all types. For example, in the following code snippet, object has stored both values of string and int.

Listing 2-12. Store any type's data in system.object type

```
object name = "Ali";
object age = 22;
```

Every type in .NET inherits methods of system.object type, which they can **override**. These methods are:

- **Equals** use to compare two objects.
- **Finalize** use to execute cleanup operations before object gets destroyed.
- **GetHashCode** use to get object's hash value from HashTable.
- **ToString** use to get object's information in text form.

Anonymous Type

Types that don't have names are called anonymous types. They are used to group temporary data into read-only properties. Unlike class, anonymous types don't have a blueprint to define property types. Therefore, each property must have a data to determine its property type.

Anonymous types are created by using a new operator with object initializer. The implicit type variable var is used to hold the reference of anonymous types.

Syntax

```
var variableName = new {/*object initializer*/};
```

Code Snippet

Listing 2-13. Define and use anonymous type in C#

```
var person = new { Name = "Ali", Age = 22 };

Console.WriteLine("Name = {0}", person.Name);
Console.WriteLine("Age = {0}", person.Age);

//Output
Ali
22
```

Remarks

- In anonymous type, property value cannot be **null**.

- Anonymous type doesn't have **method** definition.

- Anonymous types are **class** type.

- Anonymous type cannot be used as method's **parameter** of **return** type.

- Anonymous type is useful to store **query** result from **collection**.

Dynamic Type

Dynamic type is used to store and manipulate any data whose types definition and operation errors are determined at runtime. It ignores compile-time checks. Therefore, it is easy to access COM and DOM APIs with dynamic type.

It is defined by using a dynamic keyword.

Syntax

```
dynamic variableName = data;
```

Code Snippet

Listing 2-14. Use dynamic type

```
dynamic price = 20;
Console.WriteLine(price.GetType());

dynamic name = "Ali";
Console.WriteLine(name.GetType());

//Output
System.Int32
System.String
```

Unlike implicit type (var keyword), dynamic type can store values of different types with the same dynamic variable. Therefore, a dynamic variable can change its type at runtime.

Listing 2-15. Change dynamic variable's type at runtime

```
dynamic i = "Ali";
Console.WriteLine(i.GetType());

i = 22;
Console.WriteLine(i.GetType());
//Output
System.String
System.Int32
```

Remarks

- Dynamic type can be used for field, property, indexer, method parameter, and return **type**.

- **Exception** is thrown at runtime if data type or member name is not compatible.

Nullable Type

Normally, value type cannot be assigned with null value. But with nullable type, value type can be assigned with null value.

Value type can become nullable type by using "**?**".

Syntax

```
valueType? variableName = null;
```

Code Snippet

Listing 2-16. Nullable type of bool

```
bool? isMarried = null;
isMarried = true;
```

?? Operator

Use **null-coalescing** "**??**" with nullable type to non-nullable type.

Listing 2-17. Use null-coalaescing operator with nullable types

```
bool? isMarried = null;
bool married = isMarried ?? false;
```

Important Points

- Nullable<T> is an alternative of "?" operator. The above example can be written as **Nullable<bool> isMarried = null;**

- Value type is **boxed** whenever it becomes nullable.

Static Type

Unlike normal classes, static classes **cannot be instantiated**. They're useful to define helper static methods. Static class doesn't have any instance member. All **members must be static** in static class. Therefore, members of static classes can **access by using the class name itself**.

Static class is defined by writing a static keyword before the class definition.

Syntax

```
static class MyStaticClass
{
    //define static members
}
```

Code Snipeet

Listing 2-18. Define static method inside static class

```
static class Helper
{
    public static void MyMethod()
    {
        //...
    }
}
```

Listing 2-19. Access static method

```
To access MyMethod() use following code:
Helper.MyMethod();
```

Static Constructor

Unlike normal class, static class **doesn't contain a public instance constructor**. It **contains a private static constructor** to initialize static members. It is **called automatically** before the first instance is created or any static members are referenced.

Code Snippet

Listing 2-20. Define static constructor

```
static class Helper
{
    public static int age;

    static Helper()
    {
        age = 22;
    }

}
```

Extension Methods

Extension methods are special static methods. They inject addition methods without changing, deriving, or recompiling the original type. They are always called as if they were instance method.

- Extension methods are always defined inside **static class**.

- The first parameter of extension method must have **"this"** operator, which tells on whose instance this extension method should give access.

- The extension method should be defined in the same namespace in which it is used, or import the namespace in which the extension method was defined.

Syntax

```
public static class ExtensionClass
{
    public static void ExtensionMethod(this int origin)
    {
        //...
    }
}
```

Code Snippet

Listing 2-21. Define and use extension method

```
namespace Extension
{
    public static class ExtensionClass
    {
        public static bool isLessThan(this int origin, int compareValue)
        {
            //return true if origin value is less
            if (origin < compareValue)
                return true;
            else
                return false;
        }
    }

    class Program
    {
        static void Main(string[] args)
        {
            int age = 22;
            bool check = age.isLessThan(30);

            Console.WriteLine(check);
        }
    }

}
//output
True
```

age is an integer variable; it is called the **isLessThan** extension method. Remember, isLessThan is not defined by a .NET framework for integers. Its functionality is added by using the extension method.

Value **"30"** is passed on the isLessThan parameter as **compareValue**, whereas **this int origin** refers to the variable **age** itself.

Type Conversion

Conversion of one type to another is called type conversion. Type conversion has three forms:

1. Implicit Type Conversion
2. Explicit Type Conversion
3. User Defined Type Conversion

Implicit Type Conversion

If one type converts into another type automatically, it's called implicit type conversion. This is done by the compiler automatically. A common example is conversion of derived class to base class.

```
class A {...}
class B : A {...}
A a = new B();
```

Explicit Type Conversion

If one type **needs special syntax** to convert it into another type, it's called explicit type conversion. This is done by the **user**. A common example is conversion of base class to derived class.

Explicit type conversion is done by two ways:

1. **as** keyword
2. **(type)**value with **is** keyword

as operator

as is a keyword used to **explicitly** convert one type to another. If a type converts successfully, it would return value in that type. If a type doesn't convert properly, it returns **null** value.

Listing 2-22. Use "as" keyword for explicit type casting

```
class A {...}
class B : A {...}
A a = new B();

//convert explicitly from type A to B
B b = a as B;
```

is operator

It's a keyword that is used to **match a type**. If a type matches it returns true; otherwise it returns false. A common use of is keyword comes with (type) explicit type conversion.

(type)value is used to convert a type explicitly. If a type converts succesfully, it returns a value in that type. If a type doesn't convert properly, it throws an **exception**. To avoid this exception, it is common to check the type inside the sandbox of **is** operator.

Listing 2-23. Use is keyword to match a type with another type

```
class A {...}
class B : A {...}
A a = new B();

if(a is B)
{
    //convert explicitly from type A to B
    B b = (B)a;
}
```

■ **Note**   To prevent from any casting exception, we use is keyword to check whether a type can be convertible or not.

User Defined Type Conversion

C# allows users to provide the definition of **conversion for their custom type**. Its definition is similar to operator overloading's definition.

User defined conversion is of two kinds:

1. Implicit User Defined Conversion

2. Explicit User Defined Conversion

Implicit User Defined Conversion

A user can define an implicit conversion definition in a type that helps to convert it into another type. Implicit conversion occurs automatically.

For implicit conversion, a special **static method** is defined with an **implicit and operator keyword** inside the type definition.

Syntax

```
class MyClass
{
    public static implicit operator returnType(type t)
    {
        //...
    }
}
```

- **returnType** tells which type of data would get returned in implicit conversion.

- **type t** tells which type would get convert implicitly.

Code Snippet

Listing 2-24. Define implicit type conversion definition

```
class Byte
{
    public int  bits = 8;
    public static implicit operator int (Byte b)
    {
        return b.bits;
    }

}

class Program
{
    static void Main(string[] args)
    {
        Byte b = new Byte();
        int totalBits = b;
        Console.WriteLine(totalBits);
    }
}
//Output
8
```

Here, Byte "**b**" would get an implicit conversion into "**int**" by returning the total number of bits in a byte.

Explicit User Defined Conversion

A user can define an explicit conversion definition in a type that helps to convert it into another type. Casting is required to convert a type into another. Data can be lost in explicit conversion.

For explicit conversion, a special **static method** is defined with an **explicit and operator keyword** inside the type definition.

Syntax

Listing 2-25. Define explicit type conversion definition

```
class MyClass
{
    public static explicit operator returnType(type t)
    {
        //...
    }
}
```

- **returnType** tells which type of data would get returned in implicit conversion.

- **type t** tells which type would get converted implicitly.

Code Snippet

```
class Person
{
    public int Age { get; set; }
    public string Name { get; set; }

    public static explicit operator string (Person per)
    {
        return per.Name;
    }
}

class Program
{
    static void Main(string[] args)
    {
        Person per = new Person { Age = 22, Name = "Ali" };

        string name = (string)per;
        Console.WriteLine(name);
    }
}
//Output
Ali
```

where **(string)per**; casts a person's data into "string" explicitly by returning **Name** of person.

Summary

- Enum constant's values can **override** with integer value.

- Struct constructor **must initialize** all **data members**.

- Default value of reference type is always **Null**.

- Types defined with struct and enum are examples of value types.

- Types defined with class, interface, and delegates are examples of reference type.

- System.Object type is **base class** of all types in C# hierarchy.

- Anonymous types must have one or more **read only properties**.

- Dynamic types are useful for interacting with COM, DOM and Dynamic APIs.

- Value type **can store null** when it is declared as **nullable "?"**.

- Static types **cannot be instantiated**.

- Static types only have static members.

- Extension methods are only defined inside **static class** to **extend** the functionality of an **instance type**.

- Special casting is required for explicit type conversion.

- **as** operator is used to cast a type into another type.

- User can write their definition for type conversion by using **implicit** and **explicit** keyword with **special static methods**.

Code Challenges

Develop Temperature Converter Application

Application has two classes: FahrenheitTemperature and CelsiusTemperature. FahrenheitTemperature stores temperature in Fahrenheit and CelsiusTemperature stores temperature in Celsius. You have to define conversion methods in both classes to convert Fahrenheit to Celsius Implicitly and vice versa.

Practice Exam Questions

Question 1

Suppose you're developing an application that saves age value in integers.

```
int age = 22;
```

You're asked to select the right code snippet for defining the extension method for age.

A)
```
class Extension
{
    public static void ExtensionMethod(int i)
    {
        //...
    }
}
```

B)
```
static class Extension
{
    public static void ExtensionMethod(int i)
    {
        //...
    }
}
```

C)
```
static class Extension
{
    public static void ExtensionMethod(this int i)
    {
        //...
    }
}
```

D)
```
static class Extension
{
    public static void ExtensionMethod(int i)
    {
        //...
    }
}
```

Question 2

Which operator is used to compare types?

  A) as

  B) is

  C) this

  D) ?

Question 3

Choose the right code segment for defining implicit type conversion for a Person class.

A)
```
class Person
{
    public string name;
    public int age;

    public static implicit operator this[int i]
    {
        this.age = i;

        return this;
    }
}
```

B)
```
class Person
{
    public string name;
    public int age;

    public static implicit operator Person(string n)
    {
        Person person = new Person { age = 0, name = n };
        return person;
    }
}
```

C)
```
class Person
{
    public string name;
    public int age;

    public static implicit Person(string n)
    {
        Person person = new Person { age = 0, name = n };
        return person;
    }
}
```

D)
```
class Person
{
    public string name;
    public int age;

    public static implicit operator Person(this string n)
    {
        Person person = new Person { age = 0, name = n };
        return person;
    }
}
```

Question 4

Which operator is used to get instance data inside type definition?

    A)   as

    B)   is

    C)   this

    D)   ?

Question 5

Which type cannot be instantiated?

- **A)** enum type
- **B)** static type
- **C)** class type
- **D)** System.Object type

Answers

1. C
2. B
3. B
4. C
5. B

CHAPTER 3

■ ■ ■

Getting Started with Object Oriented Programming

C# provides full support of **object oriented programming**. In this chapter, you'll be walking through following OOP topics:

1. Introduction to Object Oriented Programming

2. OOP in a PIE

3. Encapsulation

4. Inheritance

5. Polymorphism

Introduction to Object Oriented Programming

Object oriented programming (OOP) is a software **design technique** that helps to organize **data** and **methods** in a single object. It helps objects to **talk** to each other by defining **relationships** among them.

In a 1994 "Rolling Stone" interview, **Steve Jobs** (CEO of Apple) explains object-oriented programming. His explanation still helps us to learn what OOP is in simple terms.

Jeff Goodell: *Would you explain, in simple terms, exactly what object-oriented software is?*

Steve Jobs: *Objects are like **people**. They're living, breathing things that have **knowledge** inside them about how to **do** things and have memory inside them so they can remember things. And rather than interacting with them at a very low level, you **interact** with them at a very high level of **abstraction**, like we're doing right here.*

Here's an example: *If I'm your **laundry** object, you can give me your dirty **clothes** and send me a message that says, "Can you get my clothes laundered, please." I happen to know where the best laundry place in San Francisco is. And I speak English, and I have dollars in my pockets. So I go out and hail a taxicab and tell the driver to take me to this place in San Francisco. I go get your clothes laundered, I jump back in the cab, I get back here. I give you your clean clothes and say, "Here are your clean clothes."*

© Ali Asad and Hamza Ali 2017
A. Asad and H. Ali, *The C# Programmer's Study Guide (MCSD)*, DOI 10.1007/978-1-4842-2860-9_3

*You have no idea how I did that. You have no knowledge of the laundry place. Maybe you speak French, and you can't even hail a taxi. You can't pay for one, you don't have dollars in your pocket. Yet I knew how to do all of that. And you didn't have to know any of it. All that complexity was hidden inside of me, and we were able to interact at a very high level of abstraction. That's what objects are. **They encapsulate complexity, and the interfaces to that complexity are high level.***

Source:

`http://www.edibleapple.com/2011/10/29/steve-jobs-explains-object-oriented-programming/`

OOP in a PIE

In a nuthshell OOP has three fundamental pillars: **P**olymorphism, **I**nheritance and **E**ncapsulation (**PIE**). These pillars define **flexibility** to communicate with other objects, **reusability** to avoid duplication, and **data protection** to hide the complexity of implementation from the outer world.

Encapsulation

Encapsulation is one of the three fundamental pillars of an object oriented program, which says, when data (attributes) and methods (behaviors) are defined in a single **entity,** it is called Encapsulation. It also refers to an object-oriented design principle called **Data Hiding**, which **restricts** the **accessibility** of data (attribute) and method (behavior) of an entity that are not necessary to its user.

Encapsulation is implemented through two ways:

1. Access Specifiers
2. Data Protection

Access Specifiers

Access specifiers are special keywords, used to define the accessibility level of a type (class, struct, enum) and all of the data members and methods defined inside it.

In C#, we have five kinds of access specifiers. Each access specifier defines a unique accessibility level. These access specifiers are:

1. Public
2. Private
3. Protected
4. Internal
5. Protected Internal

Public

Members defined with **public** access specifiers are accessible within the class as well as outside the class. Public data can also be accessible from outside the project.

Syntax

```
public Type MemberName;
```

Code Snippet

Listing 3-1. Define a method with public access specifier

```
class Access
{
    public void Method()
    {
        Console.WriteLine("Public Method");
    }
}

class Program
{

    static void Main(string[] args)
    {
        Access access = new Access();
        access.Method();
    }
}
```

Private

Members defined with **private** access specifiers are only accessible within the class and they cannot be accessed from outside the class.

Syntax

```
private Type MemberName;
```

Code Snippet

Listing 3-2. Define a field with a private access specifier

```
class Access
{
    private int age = 10;
    public int GetAge()
    {
        return age;
    }

    public void SetAge(int a)
    {
        age = a;
    }
}
```

```
class Program
{

    static void Main(string[] args)
    {
        Access access = new Access();
        int age = access.GetAge();
    }
}
```

■ **Note**   Use public methods to access a private member in the outer world.

Protected

Members defined with **protected** access specifiers are accessible within the class and also within its child classes. They cannot be accessible from outside the class.

Syntax

```
private Type MemberName;
```

Code Snippet

Listing 3-3. Define a field with protected access specifier

```
class Parent
{
    protected int age;
}
class Child : Parent
{
    public void Display()
    {
        Console.WriteLine("Age is = {0}",age);
        //Console.WriteLine("Age is = {0}", base.age);

    }
}
```

■ **Note**   **Base** is a keyword, used to access members defined as public/protected access specifiers in a parent/base class.

Internal

Within the project's assembly, members defined with **internal** access specifiers are accessible within the class as well as outside the class. But they are not accessible to any class which is defined outside the project's assembly.

Syntax

```
internal Type MemberName;
```

Code Snippet

Listing 3-4. Define a field with an internal access specifier

```
namespace Csharp
{
    class Access
    {
        internal int age = 10;
    }

    class Program
    {

        static void Main(string[] args)
        {
            Access access = new Access();
            int age = access.age;
        }
    }
}
```

■ **Note**   In C# classes by default are **internal**., which means no external assembly could access default classes. They could only be accessible to other assemblies if classes are marked with **public** access specifiers.

Internal Protected

Internal protected is a union of internal and protected behavior of access specifiers, which says, within the project's assembly, members defined with **internal protected** access specifiers are accessible within as well as outside the class and also to its child classes. But they aren't accessible to any class which is defined outside the project's assembly scope.

Syntax

```
internal protected Type MemberName;
```

Code Snippet

Listing 3-5. Define a field with an internal protected access specifier

```
namespace Csharp
{
    class Parent
    {
        internal protected int age = 10;

    }

    class Child : Parent
    {
        public void Display()
        {
            Console.WriteLine("age = {0}", base.age);
        }
    }

    class Program
    {

        static void Main(string[] args)
        {
            Parent parent = new Parent();
            int age = parent.age;

        }
    }
}
```

■ **Note**   **Internal protected** members aren't only accessible to their child classes but also accessible to other classes of the same project's assembly.

Data Protection

In C#, data is stored in a single variable or in an array. To protect this data from accidental damage, we have:

1. Properties
2. Indexers

Properties

Properties are used to encapsulate the value of a private field. They use access specifiers, which gives better control to read, write, or manipulate a field's value. It creates a sandbox over fields, which protects it from saving false data.

Properties are of two kinds:

1. Full Property
2. Auto Property

Full Property

In full property, we declare private fields and encapsulate them inside a property's definition.

Syntax

```
private Type field_name;
Access_Specifier Type Property_Name
{
        get { return field_name;}
        set { field_name = value;}
}
```

- **get** property accessors used to return the value of a field.

- **set** property accessors used to set a value in a field.

- **value** is a keyword that is used to assign a value to a field.

Code Snippet

Listing 3-6. Define and use full property

```
class Student
{
    private int age;
    public int Age
    {
        get { return this.age; }
        set { this.age = value; }
    }
}

class Program
{

    static void Main(string[] args)
    {

        Student std = new Student();
        std.Age = 10;
    }
}
```

■ **Note** **We can make a full property a read-only** property by two ways. Remove **set{}** block from full property's definition, or mark **set** block with a private access specifier. A read-only property is used to return the value of a field and a user cannot set its value from outside the class.

Auto Property

Auto property is a lot like full property. The only key difference is, it **doesn't** require any field or extra logic in its **get** and **set** to manipulate values, because a compiler creates its own private field automatically. It's just a syntactic sugar that C# gives to its developers.

Syntax

Access_Specifier Type Property_Name { get; set; }

Code Snippet

Listing 3-7. Define and use auto property

```
class Student
{
    public int Age { get; set; }
}

class Program
{

    static void Main(string[] args)
    {

        Student std = new Student();
        std.Age = 10;
    }
}
```

■ **Note** We can make an auto property a **read-only** property by two ways. Remove **set{}** block from auto property definition, or make **set** block private.

Indexers

Indexers are used to encapsulate the value of an array. It behaves and works like property. It also uses access specifiers, which give better control to read, write, or manipulate an array's value. It creates a sandbox over an array, which protects it from:

1. saving false data in an array;

2. using the wrong index value in an array;

3. changing the reference of an array from the outer world.

Syntax

```
Access_Specifier Type this[int index]
{
    get { /* return the value of specified index of array here */ }
    set { /* set the specified index to value here */ }
}
```

- **Type** defines the type of an array, i.e., (int[], object[]..)

- **this** defines an object's primary array.

- **[int index]** defines the index of an array; however, C# doesn't limit the type of index with integer. For example, we can use string as a type of index, which would be helpful to search a specific data from a collection (dictionary < string, object>).

Code Snippet

Listing 3-8. Define indexer

```
class Temprature
{
    //declare private array of float type.
    private float[] weekTemp =
        { 47.5F, 40.0F, 52.5F, 45.5F, 48.0F, 38.0F, 35.7F };

    //use float indexer, to encapsulate weekTemp
    public float this[int index]
    {
        get
        {
            return weekTemp[index];
        }
        set
        {
            weekTemp[index] = value;
        }
    }
}
```

Listing 3-9. Use indexer inside Main method

```
class Program
{

    static void Main(string[] args)
    {
        Temprature temp = new Temprature();
        float todayTemp = temp[1]; //read

        temp[1] = -5.0F; //Write

    }
}
```

73

Remember, we use indexer by calling the object name along with an array index, as in this case "temp[1]", which says get me the value of 1 index that the temp's indexer has encapsulated.

■ **Note**   In a class there should be only one indexer. However, you can overload a single indexer multiple times.

Validate Indexer Data

Data can be validated when it has been set or gotten by using if-else statements. For example, we can check if a value is greater than 0; then it can be set into memory. Similarly, we can check if the index value must be less than its array length and greater than or equal to 0.

Listing 3-10. Validate values of indexer

```
private float[] weekTemp =
    { 47.5F, 40.0F, 52.5F, 45.5F, 48.0F, 38.0F, 35.7F };

        //use float indexer, to encapsulate weekTemp
        public float this[int index]
        {
            get
            {
                if (index >= 0 && < weekTemp.Length)
                {
                    return weekTemp[index];
                }
                else
                {
                    return 0;
                }
            }
            set
            {
                if (value > 0)
                {
                    weekTemp[index] = value;

                }
                else
                {
                    Console.WriteLine("Please set value greater than 0");
                }

            }
        }
```

■ **Note**   You can **validate** index data and its value inside a **get** and **set** block with a simple **if-else** statement.

Inheritance

Inheritance is one of the three fundamental pillars of object-oriented programming. It allows new classes to **reuse or inherit** properties and methods from an existing class.

The class whose members are inherited is called **base** class and the class which inherited those members is called **derived** class (Figure 3-1).

Inheritance

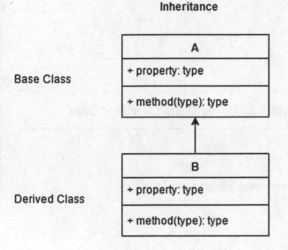

Figure 3-1. Inheritance

Syntax

```
Access_Specifier BaseClassName
{
        //TODO: Base class code
}

Access_Specifier DerivedClassName : BaseClassName
{
        //TODO: Derived class code
}
```

Code Snippet

Listing 3-11. Inherit Parent class in Child class

```
class Parent
{
    public string SurName { get; set; }
}

class Child : Parent
{
    private string _name;
```

```
    public string Name
    {
        get
        {
            return (_name + " " + base.SurName);
        }
        set
        {
            Name = value;
        }
    }
}
```

■ **Note**   In C#, a class cannot inherit from multiple classes, but it can be inherited at mulitple levels.

Multi Level Inheritance

When a class is derived from a derived class it's called multi-level inheritance.

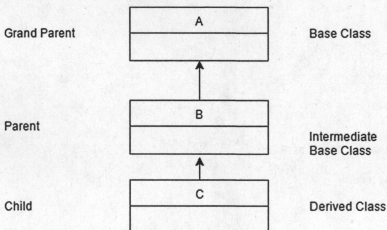

Multi- level inheritance

Grand Parent   Base Class

Parent   Intermediate
                        Base Class

Child   Derived Class

Figure 3-2. *Multi-level inheritance*

Code Snippet

Listing 3-12. Use multi-level inheritance

```
class GrandParent
{
    public GrandParent()
    {
```

```
        Console.WriteLine("Grand Parent");
    }
}

class Parent : GrandParent
{
    public Parent()
    {
        Console.WriteLine("Parent");
    }
}

class Child : Parent
{
    public Child()
    {
        Console.WriteLine("Child");
    }
}

class Program
{

    static void Main(string[] args)
    {
        Child child = new Child();

    }
}
```

Output
```
Grand Parent
Parent
Child
```

In the above code snippet, Child class has inherited from Parent class and the same Parent class has inherited from GrandParent class. This is called multi-level inheritance.

Remember, in inheritance while creating an object of a derived class, the compiler always executes its base/parent class's constructor first and then executes its child class's constructor. If the same parent class has inherited from another class, that class's constructor will execute first and then it will come down to its child and grandchild level to execute their constructor one after the other.

■ **Note**   A class **cannot inherit** multiple classes but it **can implement** multiple **interfaces** at the same time.

Abstract Class

Abstract classes **cannot be instantiated**. It is used as base class, where it provides common members to all its derived classes. It is either overridden partially or not at all. It is also used to declare **abstract methods** (method without definition) that when it inherits, it must be overridden by its derived classes.

Syntax

```
abstract class Class_Name
{
    //TODO: Code
}
```

Code Snippet

Listing 3-13. Define and use abstract class

```
abstract class Vehicle
{
    protected int wheels;
    public int Wheels
    {
        get { return wheels; }
    }
}

class Bike : Vehicle
{
    public Bike()
    {
        base.wheels = 2;
    }

}

class Program
{

    static void Main(string[] args)
    {
        Vehicle vehicle = new Bike();
        Console.WriteLine(vehicle.Wheels);

    }
}
```

■ **Note**   Vehicle class cannot be instantiated but it can store reference to its child object Bike. This is called polymorphism. You'll learn more on polymorphism and abstract methods in coming topics.

Interface

Interface **cannot be instantiated**. Its members have **no implementation detail**. All implementation detail is defined by classes which implement (inherit) interfaces. Interface provides the highest level of abstraction.

Syntax

```
interface IName
{
    //TODO:

}
```

In C#, class can implement interface by two ways:

1. Implement interface implicitly
2. Implement interface explicitly

Implement interface implicitly

Implicit interfaces are **implemented publicly**. It is implemented when explicit definition of each interface's members isn't required.

Code Snippet

Listing 3-14. Define and use interface

```
interface IVehicle
{
    int Wheels { get; }
}

class Bike : IVehicle
{
    private int wheels;
    public int Wheels
    {
        get
        {
            return wheels;
        }
    }

}

class Program
{

    static void Main(string[] args)
    {
        IVehicle vehicle = new Bike();
        Console.WriteLine(vehicle.Wheels);

    }
}
```

Key Points

1. Do not use access specifiers with interface's members.

2. Do not define definition of interface members.

3. Auto-property, indexer, method, and event can be used as a member of an interface.

4. Class must implement full definition of interface's members. Otherwise error may occur at compile/run time.

5. Class can implement more than one interface.

Implement interface explicitly

Explicit interfaces are implemented privately. We implement them explicitly when a separate definition of each interface's member is required. For example, when a class implements more than one interface which share a common member's name, explicit implementation of interface is required to separate the definition of each member.

Code Snippet

Listing 3-15. Define and use explicit implimentation of interfaces

```
interface IEnglish
{
    int Marks { get; }
}

interface IMath
{
    int Marks { get; }
}

class Student : IEnglish, IMath
{
    int english = 10;
    int math = 9;

    int IMath.Marks
    {
        get
        {
            return english;
        }
    }

    int IEnglish.Marks
    {
        get
```

```
        {
            return math;
        }
    }
}

class Program
{

    static void Main(string[] args)
    {
        Student std = new Student();

        int english = ((IEnglish)std).Marks;
        int math = ((IMath)std).Marks;

        Console.WriteLine("English Marks = {0} Math Marks = {1}",
                            english, math);

    }
}
```

Explanation

1. **IMath.Marks** used to implement interface explicitly by defining name of writing name of interface before member name.

2. **No Access specifier** used to implement explicit interfaces.

3. **((IEnglish)std).Marks**; used to access "Marks" property of "IEnglish" interface.

Polymorphism

Polymorphism is all about changing behaviors; in other words, it is different forms of one object.

In C#, polymorphism is of two types:

1. Static Polymorphism
2. Dynamic Polymorphism

Static Polymorphism

Polymorphism in programming is all about changing behavior. While static polymorphism means changing behavior of methods at compile time, it is also known as early binding.

In C#, static polymorphism can be implemented with two ways:

1. Method Overloading
2. Operator Overloading

Method Overloading

Inside type (class, struct) definition we can have multiple methods of the same name but with different parameters; this is called method overloading.

In C#, we can overload a method by two ways:

1. By parameter types

2. Dy length of parameters

Overload Method by Parameter Type

A method can be overloaded by defining different parameter types for each method which share the same method's name.

For Example

In the following code snippet, we have *"Add"* method, overloaded by defining different parameter types.

Listing 3-16. Define method overloading by parameter type

```
class Calculator
{
    public void Add(int a, int b)
    {
        int result = a + b;

        Console.WriteLine("Sum of ints = {0}",result);
    }

    public void Add(string a, string b)
    {
        string result = a + b;

        Console.WriteLine("Sum of strings = {0}", result);
    }
}

class Program
{
    static void Main(string[] args)
    {
        Calculator cal = new Calculator();
        cal.Add(1, 2);
        cal.Add("C", "Sharp");
    }
}
//Output
Sum of ints = 3
Sum of strings = CSharp
```

Explanation

- *cal.Add(1, 2);* when it is called, control will go and execute an overloaded Add method, which has two *int* parameters.

- *cal.Add("C", "Sharp");* when it is called, control will go to an overloaded Add method which has two *string* parameters

Overload Method by length of parameter

A method can be overloaded by defining a different parameter length for each method which shares the same method's name.

For Example

In the following code snippet, we have *"Show"* method overloaded by a different parameter length.

Listing 3-17. Define method overloading by parameter length

```
class Program
{
    public void Show(string name)
    {
        Console.WriteLine("Name = {0}", name);
    }

    public void Show(string name, int age)
    {
        Console.WriteLine("Name = {0} - Age = {1}", name, age);
    }
    static void Main(string[] args)
    {
        Program program = new Program();
        program.Show("Ali");
        program.Show("Ali", 22);

    }
}
```

//Output
```
Name = Ali
Name = Ali - Age = 22
```

Explanation

- *program.Show("Ali");* when it is called, control will go and execute an overloaded Show method, which has a single parameter of *string* type.

- *program.Show("Ali", 22);* when it is called, control will go and execute an overloaded Show method, which has two parameters of *string* and *int* type.

■ **Note**   Methods with the same name but different return types aren't considered overloaded.

Operator Overloading

In C#, we can overload the definition of an operator for custom types (class, struct). To overload the definition of an operator, we define special methods inside a custom type. These methods help the compiler to distinguish among different meanings of an operator that produce different results for a different type.

Generally, in C# we can overload three kinds of operators:

1. Unary Operators

2. Binary Operators

3. Comparison Operators

Overload Unary Operators

Unary operator operates on a single operand (+, -, !, ++, --, true, false). These are unary operators which can be overloaded in C#.

Syntax

```
public static return_type operator op (Type t)
{
    // TODO:
}
```

- *Static* operator overloaded method must be static.

- *operator* is a keyword used to define an operator overloaded method.

- *op* use special operator symbol, describe which operator definition is going to be overloaded, i.e., (+, -, ..).

- *Type* where type must be *struct* or *class.*

Code Snippet

Listing 3-18. Define and use unary operator overloading

```
class Distance
{
    public int meter { get; set; }

    public static Distance operator ++ (Distance dis )
    {
        dis.meter += 1;
        return dis;
    }
}

class Program
{
    static void Main(string[] args)
    {
        Distance distance = new Distance();
        distance.meter = 5;

        distance++;
        Console.WriteLine(distance.meter);

    }
}
```

Explanation

distance++; it's called operator ++ method; it passed its own object to operator ++ parameter.

Overload Binary Operator

Binary operator operates on two operands (+, -, *, /, %, &, |, ^, <<, >>). These are Binary operators which can be overloaded in C#.

Syntax

```
public static return_type operator op (Type1 t1, Type2 t2)
{
      //TODO:
}
```

- *Type t1* is left side operand
- *Type t2* is right side operand

Code Snippet

Listing 3-19. Define and use binary operator overloading

```
class Student
{
    public int Marks { get; set; }
  // + Operator Overloading Method

    public static Student operator + (Student s1, Student s2)
    {
        Student std = new Student();

        std.Marks = s1.Marks + s2.Marks;

        return std;
    }
}

class Program
{
    static void Main(string[] args)
    {
        Student s1 = new Student { Marks = 10 };
        Student s2 = new Student { Marks = 20 };

        Student s3 = s1 + s2;
        Console.WriteLine(s3.Marks);

    }
}
//Output
30
```

Explanation

Student s3 = s1 + s2; when it is called, operator + method will get executed, which takes s1 and s2 for its parameter values.

Overload Comparison Operator

Comparison operator operates on two operands and returns Boolean value when it compares left-sided operand's value with right-sided operand's value (==, !=, <, >, <=, >=). These are comparison operators which can be overloaded in C#.

Syntax

```
public static bool operator op (Type1 t1, Type2 t2)
{
    //TODO:
}
```

Code Snippet

Listing 3-20. Define and use comparison operator

```
class Distance
    {
        public int meter { get; set; }

        public static bool operator < (Distance d1, Distance d2 )
        {
            return (d1.meter < d2.meter);
        }
        public static bool operator > (Distance d1, Distance d2)
        {
            return (d1.meter > d2.meter);
        }

    }

    class Program
    {
        static void Main(string[] args)
        {
            Distance d1 = new Distance { meter = 10 };
            Distance d2 = new Distance { meter = 20 };

            if(d1 < d2)
            {
                Console.WriteLine("d1 is less than d2");
            }
            else if(d2 < d1)
            {
                Console.WriteLine("d2 is less than d1");
            }

        }
    }
```

Explanation

if(d1 < d2): When this code is executed, operator < method will get executed, which takes d1 and d2 as its parameter. It returns true if d1's meter value is less than d2's meter value.

■ **Note** Always overload opposite operator of comparison operator. For example, whenever we overload less than operator we must overload greater than operator as well. The same applies to ==, != operator.

Dynamic Polymorphism

Polymorphism in programming is all about changing behavior, while dynamic polymorphism means **changing behavior of an object at runtime** by overriding the definition of a method. It is also known as **late binding**.

In C#, method is overridden by two ways:

1. Virtual method
2. Abstract method

Virtual Method

Virtual is a keyword used with method in base class to define a virtual method. Virtual method has a definition of its method; its derived class can inherit or override its definition. Thus, when calling the method name the runtime will determine which method to invoke.

Syntax

```
virtual return_type methodName()
{
    //TODO:
}
```

Code Snippet

Listing 3-21. Define virtual method

```
class Vehicle
{
    public virtual void Run()
    {
        Console.WriteLine("Run Vehicle");
    }
}
```

Listing 3-22. Override virtual method

```
class Bike : Vehicle
{
    public override void Run()
    {
        Console.WriteLine("Bike Run");
    }
}

class Program
{

    static void Main(string[] args)
    {
        Vehicle vc = new Bike();
        vc.Run();

    }
}
```

Output
Bike Run

Explanation

1. public virtual void Run(){..} define a virtual method in base class.

2. public override void Run(){..} override Run method in derived class by defining its own implementation of Run() method.

3. Vehicle vc = new Bike(); vc holds object of its child class "Bike".

4. vc.Run(); control will first move to base "Run" method. When runtime is encountered, it's a virtual method; it will then move to its derived class "Bike" definition to find implementation of "Run()" method. If it finds the method it will invoke it; otherwise it will come back to base class to run virtual Run() method.

Abstract method

abstract is a keyword used with method in abstract class to declare an abstract method. Unlike virtual method, abstract method doesn't have its definition of method. Thus, its derived class **must implement the definition** of abstract method, otherwise compile time error will generate. Abstract methods always declare inside an abstract class.

Syntax

```
abstract class_Name
{
    public abstract Type Method();
}
```

Code Snippet

Listing 3-23. Define and override abstract method

```
abstract class Vehicle
{
    public abstract void Run();
}

class Bike : Vehicle
{
    public override void Run()
    {
        Console.WriteLine("Run Bike");
    }
}

class Program
{

    static void Main(string[] args)
    {
        Vehicle vc = new Bike();
        vc.Run();

    }
}
```

Explanation

1. public abstract void Run(); declare abstract method without implementing its definition.

2. public override void Run(); override the definition of Run method in derived class "Bike". Thus, when Run() method is called, the always derived method will invoke.

Summary

- C# has **five access specifiers,** i.e., Public, Private, Protected, Internal, Internal Protected.

- Properties and Indexers both are used to **encapsulate** data.

- Derived class can inherit all data from its base class, except one which is mentioned with **private access specifier**.

- C# doesn't allow **multiple** inheritance, but it allows **multi-level** inheritance.

- A class **must implement** all members of an interface and all abstract methods of an abstract class.

- Abstract method can only be written **inside** of an abstract class.

Code Challenges

Challenge 1: Develop a Transformer

We all have watched the *Transformers* film. They're intelligent vehicles which can transform into jets, cars and boats. Your job is to make an application where a transformer could change its behavior into the following vehicles.

Vehicle	Condition to transform	Attributes
Jet	When transformer is on air	Wheels = 8 Max Speed = 900
Car	When transformer is on road	Wheels = 4 Max Speed = 350
Boat	When transformer is on water	Wheels = 0 Max Speed = 200

Your job is to implement a Run method for each vehicle that transformer runs whenever the landscape changes.

Tip

1. Use Enum to store landscape, i.e., air, road, water.

2. Follow OOP principle of Polymorphism.

Challenge 2: Develop Steve Jobs Laundry System

Steve Jobs described OOP in a very simple example. Your job is to use that example to develop an application that uses Object Oriented Principle. The example that Steve Jobs gave us is given below:

> *If I'm your **laundry** object, you can give me your dirty **clothes** and send me a message that says, "Can you get my clothes laundered, please." I happen to know where the best laundry place in San Francisco is. And I speak English, and I have dollars in my pockets. So, I go out and hail a taxicab and tell the driver to take me to this place in San Francisco. I go get your clothes laundered, I jump back in the cab, I get back here. I give you your clean clothes and say, "Here are your clean clothes."*

Practice Exam Questions

Question 1

Suppose you are developing an application that includes the following code segment:

```
interface ICricket
{
    void Play();
}

interface IFootball
{
    void Play();
}
```

You need to implement both *Play*() methods in a derived class named Player that uses the *Play*() method of each interface.

Which two code segments should you use?

A)
```
class Player : ICricket, IFootball
{
    void ICricket.Play()
    {
        //TODO:
    }

    void IFootball.Play()
    {
        //TODO:
    }
}
```

B)
```
Player player = new Player();
((ICricket)player).Play();
((IFootball)player).Play();
```

C)
```
Player player = new Player();
player.Play();
```

D)
```
Player player = new Player();
player.Play(ICricket);
player.Play(IFootball);
```

```
E)
class Player : ICricket, IFootball
{
    public void ICricket.Play()
    {
        //TODO:
    }

    public void IFootball.Play()
    {
        //TODO:
    }
}
```

Question 2

Suppose you are developing an application. The application has two classes named Player and Person.
The Player class must meet the following requirements:

1. It must **inherit** from the Person class.

2. It must **not** be **inheritable by other classes** in the application.

Which code segment should you use?

```
A)
sealed class Player : Person
{
   //TODO:
}
```

```
B)
abstract class Player : Person
{
   //TODO:
}
```

```
C)
private class Player : Person
{
   //TODO:
}
```

```
D)
partial class Player : Person
{
   //TODO:
}
```

Question 3

Suppose you're creating a class named Player. The class exposes a string property named HitSpeed. Here is the code snippet of Player class.

```
01. class Player
02. {
03.    public int HitSpeed
04.    {
05.        get;
06.        set;
07.    }
08. }
```

The HitSpeed property must meet the following requirements:

1. The value must be accessed by code **within the Player** class.

2. The value must be accessed to **derived** classes of Player.

3. The value must be **modified** only by code within the Player class.

You need to ensure that the implementation of the EmployeeType property meets the requirements. Which code segment you should replace at line 05. And 06.?

A) Replace line 05. with "public get;".

   Replace Line 06. With "private set;".

B) Replace line 05. with "protected get;".

   Replace Line 06. With "private set;".

C) Replace line 05. with "internal get;".

   Replace Line 06. With "internal protected set;".

D) Replace line 05. with "internal protected get;".

   Replace Line 06. With "internal set;".

Question 4

Is the following method "Display" considered to be overloaded?

```
class Person
    {
        public void Display()
        {
            //
        }
        public int Display()
        {
            //
        }
    }
A) Yes.
B) No.
```

Question 5

How do you encapsulate an array of integers into an indexer?
    You must choose the right code segment.

A)
```
private int[] array;
public int this[int index]
{
    get { return array[index]; }
    set { array[index] = value; }
}
```

B)
```
private int[] array;
public int this(int index)
{
    get { return array[index]; }
    set { array[index] = value; }
}
```

C)
```
private int[] array;
public int[] this[int index]
{
    get { return array; }
    set { array[index] = value; }
}
```

D)
```
private int[] array;
private int index;

public int this
{
    get { return array[index]; }
    set { array[index] = value; }
}
```

Answers

1. A, B
2. A
3. B
4. B
5. A

CHAPTER 4

■■■

Advance C#

C# is a very rich language that provides too much sugar code that developers can take leverage from. In this chapter, we'll look into some of the most popular features of C#, such as:

1. Boxing/Unboxing

2. Generics

3. Collection

4. Framework Interfaces

5. Manipulating Strings

Boxing and Unboxing

Boxing and unboxing are important concepts in a C# type's system. They were introduced in C# 1 when there was no defined concept for generalization of types.

Boxing

Boxing refers to implicit conversion of a value type into an object type, or to any interface that it implements, e.g., int to IComparable<int>. Further, the conversion of an underlying value type to a nullable type is also known as boxing.

During boxing, value type is being allocated on a managed heap rather than a Stack.

Syntax

```
object boxedVariable = valueType_variable;
```

Code Snippet

Listing 4-1. Boxed int value

```
int age = 22;
object boxedAge = age;        //Boxing
```

Explanation

In the above example (Listing 4-1), the integer value age is *boxed* and assigned to object boxedAge.

© Ali Asad and Hamza Ali 2017
A. Asad and H. Ali, *The C# Programmer's Study Guide (MCSD)*, DOI 10.1007/978-1-4842-2860-9_4

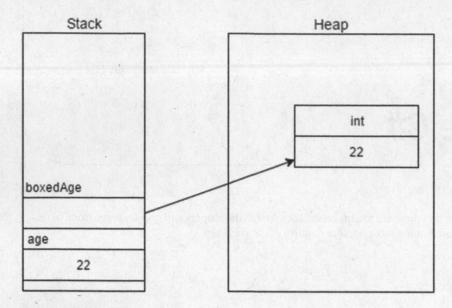

Figure 4-1. Boxing

Unboxing

Unboxing refers to an explicit conversion of object type to non-nullable-value type or the conversion of an interface type to a non-nullable-value type, e.g., IComparable<int> to int. Further, the conversion of nullable type to the underlying value type is also known as unboxing.

During unboxing, boxed value is unboxed from the managed heap to a value type which is being allocated on a Stack.

Syntax

```
valueType unboxedVariable = (valueType)boxedVariable;
```

Code Snippet

Listing 4-2. Unboxed, boxed value

```
int age = 22;
object boxedAge = age;           //Boxing

int unboxedAge = (int)boxedAge;  //Unboxing
```

Explanation

In the above example (Listing 4-2), the boxed value *object boxedAge* is being unboxed into *int unboxedAge*. During unboxing, CLR does the following operation:

- Check the boxed value is of the given value type.

- Assign a value to a value type variable from the boxed value.

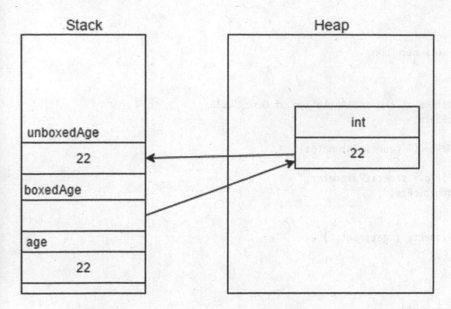

Figure 4-2. Unboxing

Performance of Boxing & Unboxing

Boxing and Unboxing are very expensive in terms of computation operations for a processor. Therefore, it is best to avoid using value types where they must be boxed and unboxed many times, for example, in ArrayList (ArrayList stores everything as a collection of objects). When a value is boxed, a new instance must be created in heap. This could take up to **20 times** longer than a simple reference assignment. When a boxed value is unboxed, it takes **4 times** longer than a simple reference assignment. Therefore, it is always preferable to use generics over boxing and unboxing.

Generics

Generics were introduced in C# 2. It gave the concept of **type-safe**. Generics defines a class in a way that its fields, methods, parameters, etc., can be able to work with any actual data-type. It performs **compile-time checks** for type safety and it is much **faster** than boxing/unboxing for type generalization.

Syntax

```
class ClassName <T>
{
    //TODO:
}
```

- Generic class: define by using "<>" angle brackets.

- **T** is a generic type parameter; refers to any compile-time type that is given when a class is instantiated.

- In the same way, we can define generic structs and generic interfaces, too.

Code Snippet

Listing 4-3. Define and use generic class

```
class GenericClass<T>
{
    //type 'T' will define at the instantiation of GenericClass
    private T genericField;

    public T GenericMethod(T genericParameter)
    {
        this.genericField = genericParameter;
        return this.genericField;
    }

    public T GenericProperty { get; set; }

}
class Program
{
    static void Main(string[] args)
    {
        //Here <T> type become string
        GenericClass<string> genStr = new GenericClass<string>();
        string strData = genStr.GenericMethod("C#");
        genStr.GenericProperty = "Certification Exam: ";
        Console.WriteLine("{0} {1}", strData, genStr.GenericProperty);

        //Here <T> type become int
        GenericClass<int> genInt = new GenericClass<int>();
        int intData = genInt.GenericMethod(70);
        genInt.GenericProperty = 483;
        Console.WriteLine("{0} - {1}",intData, genInt.GenericProperty);

    }
}

//Output
C# Certification Exam:
70 - 483
```

■ **Note** You can create more than one generic type paramter inside <> angle brackets i.e., <T, M>.

Constraints on Generic Type Parameters

Constraints on generic type parameters are useful to restrict the kinds of types that can be used for type arguments to instantiate a generic class. Compile time error will generate if client code tries to instantiate a generic class by using a type that is restricted for type parameter.

where keyword is used to apply constraints on generic type parameters.

Syntax

```
class ClassName<T> where T: specifyConstraint
{
    //TODO:
}
```

Kind of Constraints

There are **6 kinds** of constraints that we can apply on generic type parameters. The following table (Table 4-1) lists the kinds of constraints.

Table 4-1. *List of constraints for generic type parameters*

Constraints	Explanation
where T : struct	Type "T" must be a value type
where T : class	Type "T" must be a reference type
where T : new()	Type "T" must has a definition of public default constructor
where T : U	Type "T" must be or child of type "U"
where T : interfaceName	Type "T" must be or implement a specified interface

Code Snippet

Listing 4-4. Constraint "where T: struct"

```
class GenericClass<T> where T: struct
{
    //Where T: struct says, 'T' can only be a value type.
    private T genericField;

    public T GenericMethod(T genericParameter)
    {
        this.genericField = genericParameter;
        return this.genericField;
    }

    public T GenericProperty { get; set; }

}
class Program
{
    static void Main(string[] args)
    {
```

```
        //Here <T> type become int which is a value type
        GenericClass<int> genInt = new GenericClass<int>();
        int intData = genInt.GenericMethod(70);
        genInt.GenericProperty = 483;
        Console.WriteLine("{0} - {1}",intData, genInt.GenericProperty);

    }
}
```

Listing 4-5. Constraint "where T: class"

```
class GenericClass<T> where T: class
{
    //type 'T' will be a reference type
    private T genericField;

    public T GenericMethod(T genericParameter)
    {
        this.genericField = genericParameter;
        return this.genericField;
    }

    public T GenericProperty { get; set; }

}

class Program
{
    static void Main(string[] args)
    {
        //Here <T> type become string. Which is a reference type
        GenericClass<string> genStr = new GenericClass<string>();
        string strData = genStr.GenericMethod("C#");
        genStr.GenericProperty = "Certification Exam: ";
        Console.WriteLine("{0} {1}", strData, genStr.GenericProperty);

    }
}
```

Listing 4-6. Constraint "where T: new()"

```
class MyClass
{
    //Public Default Constructor
    public MyClass()
    {

    }
}
```

```
class GenericClass<T> where T : new()
{

    //TODO:
}

class Program
{
    static void Main(string[] args)
    {
        //Here 'T' is Myclass. Which has public default constructor
        GenericClass<MyClass> genMC = new GenericClass<MyClass>();
    }
}
```

Listing 4-7. Constraint "where T: BaseClass"

```
class Person
{

}
class Student : Person
{

}

class GenericClass<T> where T : Person
{
        //TODO:
}

class Program
{
    static void Main(string[] args)
    {

        GenericClass<Person> genPer = new GenericClass<Person>();

        //Student is also a Person. This is also valid.
        GenericClass<Student> genStd = new GenericClass<Student>();
    }
}
```

Listing 4-8. Constraint "where T: interfaceName" interface IPerson

```
{

}

class Person : IPerson
{
    //Implement Iperson
}
class Student : Person
{
    //TODO:
}

class GenericClass<T> where T : IPerson
{
    //TODO:
}

class Program
{
    static void Main(string[] args)
    {
        //Here 'T' is IPerson
        GenericClass<IPerson> genIPer = new GenericClass<IPerson>();

        //Here 'T' is Person which has implement 'IPerson'
        GenericClass<Person> genPer = new GenericClass<Person>();

        //Here 'T' is Student it inherit 'Person' which implement 'IPerson'.
        GenericClass<Student> genStd = new GenericClass<Student>();
    }
}
```

Listing 4-9. Constraint "where T: U"

```
class Person
{
    //TODO
}

class Student : Person
{
    //
}
class GenericClass<T, U> where T : U
{
    //TODO
}
```

```
class Program
{
    static void Main(string[] args)
    {
        //Here 'T' and 'U' types are same
        GenericClass<Person, Person> genPP =
            new GenericClass<Person, Person>();

        //Here 'T' inherit 'U' type
        GenericClass<Student, Person> genSP =
            new GenericClass<Student, Person>();
    }
}
```

Similarly, we can apply **more than one constraint** on type arguments.

Listing 4-10. Constraint "where T: BaseClass, new()"

```
class Person
{
    public string Name { get; set; }
    public Person()
    {
        this.Name = "default";
    }
}
class Student : Person
{
    //TODO:
}

class GenericClass<T> where T : Person, new()
{
    //Where T can only be Person which has a default constructor
    //TODO:
}

class Program
{
    static void Main(string[] args)
    {

        GenericClass<Person> genPer = new GenericClass<Person>();

        //Student is also a Person. This is also valid.
        GenericClass<Student> genStd = new GenericClass<Student>();
    }
}
```

Generic Methods

Generic methods help to type-safe a method's argument type, which helps in calling a method's parameter for multiple types.

Syntax

```
returnType methodName <T>(T arg)
{
    //TODO:
}
```

- Generic method defines by using "<>" angle brackets.
- **T** is a generic type parameter; it refers to any compile-time type that is given when the generic method is called.

Code Snippet

Listing 4-11. Use generic methods

```
class Example
{
    public void GenericMethodArgs<T> (T first)
    {
        Console.WriteLine(first);
    }

    public T ReturnFromGenericMethodArgs<T> (T first)
    {
        return first;
    }
    public void MultipleGenericMethodArgs<T, U>(T first, U second)
    {
        Console.WriteLine("{0}: {1}", first, second);
    }

    public U ReturnFromMultipleGenericMethodArgs<T, U>(T first)
    {
        U temp = default(U);

        return temp;
    }

}
class Program
{

    static void Main(string[] args)
    {
        Example ex = new Example();
```

```
        //Call generic method which has single generic type
        ex.GenericMethodArgs<int>(10);
        int FromSingle = ex.ReturnFromGenericMethodArgs<int>(10);
        Console.WriteLine(FromSingle + "\n");

        //Call generic method which has multiple generic type
        ex.MultipleGenericMethodArgs<string, int>("Exam", 70483);
        int FromMultiple =
            ex.ReturnFromMultipleGenericMethodArgs<string, int>("Exam: ");
        Console.WriteLine(FromMultiple);
    }
}

//Output
10
10

Exam:   70483
0
```

Constraints on Generic Methods

Constraints can also be applied on generic methods to restrict the kinds of types used to pass values during method calling.

Listing 4-12. Constraint on generic method

```
class Example
{
    public void GenericMethod<T> (T arg) where T: struct
    {
        //TODO:
        Console.WriteLine(arg);
    }
}
class Program
{

    static void Main(string[] args)
    {
        Example ex = new Example();
        ex.GenericMethod<int>(5);

        //without <> calling generic method.
        ex.GenericMethod(10);

    }
}
//Output
5
10
```

- Generic method can also be called without <> angle brackets. Types of generic arguments depend upong the type of passing values in a generic method's parameter.

■ **Note**   Generics can also be used to define generic **delegates** and **events**, which we'll cover in the next chapter.

Collection

Collection helps to manage a group of related objects. In C#, collections are **data structures** that provide a flexible way to store and retrieve objects **dynamically**. Unlike arrays, a group of objects in a collection can **grow and shrink** anytime.

Collections are classes that instantiated to manage a group of related objects. In C#, there are three kind of collections:

1. System.Collections

2. System.Collections.Generic

3. System.Collections.Concurrent

System.Collections

System.Collections is a namespace which contains classes and interfaces that manages a group of data. It stores each data in the form of a **system.object** type. Therefore, a group of value type data always gets **boxed/unboxed**. It defines multiple **data structures** to **store** and **retrieve** data such as list, queue, and hashtable.

Table 4-2. *Frequently used classes in system.collections namespace*

Class	Explanation
ArrayList	Array of objects whose size can grow and shrink dynamically
Hashtable	Collection of key/value pair, organize on base of hash code
Queue	Manages group of data in First In, First Out (FIFO) order
Stack	Manages group of data in Last In, First Out (LIFO) order

ArrayList

It's an array of objects which can grow and shrink its size dynamically. Unlike arrays, an ArrayList can hold data of multiple data types. It can be accessed by its index. Inserting and deleting an element at the middle of an ArrayList is more costly than inserting or deleting an element at the end an ArrayList.

An ArrayList contains many methods and properties that help to manage a group of objects. The following is a list of some frequently used properties and methods defined in an ArrayList.

Table 4-3. *Frequently used methods and properties of ArrayList*

Method and Property	Explanation
Add()	Add an object to the end of ArrayList
Contains()	Return true if specific object is in ArrayList
Clone()	Create a shallow copy of ArrayList
Remove()	Remove the first occurance of specific object in ArrayList
RemoveAt()	Remove the object from specific index of ArrayList
Clear()	Remove all objects from the ArrayList
Count	Get the actual number of objects stored in ArrayList
Capacity	Get or Set number of objects that ArrayList can contain

Code Snippet

Listing 4-13. Use ArrayList to manage a group of objects

```
using System.Collections;

class Program
{

    static void Main(string[] args)
    {
        ArrayList arraylist = new ArrayList();

        //add objects in arraylist
        arraylist.Add(22);
        arraylist.Add("Ali");
        arraylist.Add(true);

        //Iterate over each index of arraylist
        for (int i = 0; i < arraylist.Count; i++)
        {
            System.Console.WriteLine(arraylist[i]);
        }

        arraylist.Remove(22);

        System.Console.WriteLine();
        foreach (var item in arraylist)
        {
            System.Console.WriteLine(item);
        }
    }
}
```

```
//Output
22
Ali
True

Ali
True
```

Hashtable

Hashtable stores each element of a collection in a pair of key/values. It optimizes the lookups by computing the hash key and stores it to access the value against it.

Below are some common methods and properties used in a Hashtable class.

Table 4-4. *Frequently used methods and properties of Hashtable*

Method and Property	Explanation
Add()	Add an element with the specified key and value
ContainsKey()	Return true if specific key is in Hashtable
ContainsValue	Return true if specific value is in Hashtable
Clone()	Create a shallow copy of Hashtable
Remove()	Remove the element with the specified key from ArrayList
Clear()	Remove all objects from the Hashtable
Count	Get the actual number of key/value pairs in Hashtable
Keys	Get list of keys contains in Hashtable
Values	Get list of values contains in Hashtable

Code Snippet

Listing 4-14. Manage company and its owner info in Hashtable

```
using System.Collections;
using System;

class Program
{
    static void Main(string[] args)
    {
        Hashtable owner = new Hashtable();

        //Add some values in Hashtable
        //There are no keys but value can be duplicate
        owner.Add("Bill", "Microsoft");
        owner.Add("Paul", "Microsoft");
        owner.Add("Steve", "Apple");
        owner.Add("Mark", "Facebook");
```

```
//Display value against key
Console.WriteLine("Bill is the owner of {0}", owner["Bill"]);

//ContainsKey can be use to test key before inserting
if (!owner.ContainsKey("Trump"))
{
    owner.Add("Trump", "The Trump Organization");
}

// When you use foreach to enumerate hash table elements,
// the elements are retrieved as KeyValuePair objects.
//DictionaryEntry is the pair of key & value
Console.WriteLine();
foreach (DictionaryEntry item in owner)
{
    Console.WriteLine("{0} is owner of {1}", item.Key, item.Value);
}

//Get All values stored in Hashtable
var allValues = owner.Values;
Console.WriteLine();
foreach (var item in allValues)
{
    Console.WriteLine("Company: {0}", item);
}

    }
}

//Output
Bill is the owner of Microsoft

Steve is the owner of Apple
Trump is the owner of The Trump Organization
Mark is the owner of Facebook
Bill is the owner of Microsoft
Paul is the owner of Microsoft

Company: Apple
Company: The Trump Organization
Company: Facebook
Company: Microsoft
Company: Microsoft
```

Queue

Queue is a class of System.Collections namespace. It stores and retrieves objects in FIFO (First In, First Out) order. In other words, it manages a collection of objects on a first come, first served basis.

Below are some common methods and properties used in Queue class.

Table 4-5. *Frequently used methods and properties of Queue*

Method and Property	Explanation
Enqueue()	Add an element to the end of the Queue
Dequeue()	Remove and return the object at the beginning of the Queue
Peek()	Return the object at the beginning of the queue without removing it
ToArray()	Copy the Queue elements to a new array
Contains()	Return true if a specified object is in the Queue
Clear()	Remove all objects from the Queue
Clone()	Create a shallow copy of the Queue
Count	Get the actual number of objects in Queue

Code Snippet

Listing 4-15. Manage weekday's name in a queue

```csharp
using System.Collections;
using System;

class Program
{
    static void Main(string[] args)
    {
        Queue days = new Queue();

        //Add(Enque) objects in queus
        days.Enqueue("Mon");
        days.Enqueue("Tue");
        days.Enqueue("Wed");
        days.Enqueue("Thu");
        days.Enqueue("Fri");
        days.Enqueue("Sat");
        days.Enqueue("Sun");

        // Displays the properties and values of the Queue.
        Console.WriteLine("Total elements in queue are {0}", days.Count);

        //Remove and return first element of the queue
        Console.WriteLine("{0}", days.Dequeue());

        //return first element of queue without removing it from queue
        //return 'Tue'
        Console.WriteLine("{0}", days.Peek());

        //Iterate over each element of queue
        Console.WriteLine();
```

```
        foreach (var item in days)
        {
            Console.WriteLine(item);
        }

    }
}
//Output
Total elements in queue are 7
Mon
Tue

Tue
Wed
Thu
Fri
Sat
Sun
```

Stack

Stack is a class of System.Collections namespace. It stores and retrieves objects in LIFO (Last In, First Out) order. In other words, elements pushed at the end will pop first, for example, a pile of plates.

Below are some common methods and properties used in Stack class.

Table 4-6. *Frequently used methods and properties of Stack*

Method and Property	Explanation
Push()	Insert the object at the top of the Stack
Pop()	Remove and return object at the top of the Stack
Peek()	Return the object at the top of the Stack without removing it
ToArray()	Copy the Stack elements to a new array
Contains()	Return true if a specified object is in the Stack
Clear()	Remove all objects from the Stack
Clone()	Create a shallow copy of the Stack
Count	Get the actual number of objects in Stack

Code Snippet

Listing 4-16. Manage browser history in Stack

```
using System.Collections;
using System;

class Program
{
    static void Main(string[] args)
```

```
    {
        Stack history = new Stack();

        //Insert browser history in stack
        history.Push("google.com");
        history.Push("facebook.com/imaliasad");
        history.Push("twitter.com/imaliasad");
        history.Push("youtube.com");

        // Displays the properties and values of the Stack.
        Console.WriteLine("Total elements in stack are {0}", history.Count);

        //Remove and return top element of the Stack
        Console.WriteLine("{0}", history.Pop());

        //return top element of Stack without removing it from Stack
        //return 'twitter.com/imaliasad'
        Console.WriteLine("{0}", history.Peek());

        //Iterate over each element of Stack
        Console.WriteLine();
        foreach (var item in history)
        {
            Console.WriteLine(item);
        }

    }
}
```

```
//Output
Total elements in stack are 4
youtube.com
twitter.com/imaliasad

twitter.com/imaliasad
facebook.com/imaliasad
google.com
```

System.Collections.Generics

System.Collections.Generics is a namespace which contains classes and interfaces to manage a **strongly-typed** collection. In a generic collection, data cannot be boxed/unboxed because data always gets type-safed. It is **faster** and better than classes and interfaces defined in System.Collections. It also defines multiple **data structures** to **store** and **retrieve** data such as List<T>, Queue<T>, Stack<T>, and Dictionary<TKey, TValue>.

Table 4-7. *Frequently used classes in System.Collections.Generic namespace*

Class	Explanation
List<T>	List of type-safe objects that can dynamically grow & shrink
Dictionary<Tkey,Tvalue>	Represents collection of type-safe keys and values
Queue<T>	Represents First In, First Out collection of type-safe objects
Stack<T>	Represents Last In, First Out collection of type-safe objects

List<T>

List<T> is a type-safe collection of objects. List can grow and shrink its size dynamically. With generics support, it can store a collection of any type in a type-safe way. Therefore, it is much faster and optimized than *ArrayList*.

List<T> contains many methods and properties that help to manage a group of data. The following is list of some frequently used properties and methods defined in List<T>.

Table 4-8. *Frequently used methods and properties of List<T>*

Method and Property	Explanation
Add()	Add an object to the end of the List<T>
Contains()	Return true if specified object is in List<T>
Sort()	Sort all the objects of List<T> by using comparer
Remove()	Remove the first occurance of specific object in List<T>
RemoveAt()	Remove the object from specified index of List<T>
Clear()	Remove all objects from the List<T>
Find()	Search the object by using specified predicate
Count	Get the actual number of objects stored in List<T>

Code Snippet

Listing 4-17. Manage objects of multiple types in list<T>

```
using System.Collections.Generic;
using System;

class Person
{
    public string Name { get; set; }
    public int Age { get; set; }
}
class Program
```

113

```csharp
{
    static void Main(string[] args)
    {
        List<Person> people - new List<Person>();

        //Add Person in list
        people.Add(new Person { Name = "Ali", Age = 22 });
        people.Add(new Person { Name = "Sundus", Age = 21 });
        people.Add(new Person { Name = "Hogi", Age = 12 });

        //Get total number of person in list
        Console.WriteLine("Total person are: {0}", people.Count);

        //Iterate over each person
        Console.WriteLine();
        foreach (var person in people)
        {
            Console.WriteLine("Name: {0} - Age: {1}", person.Name, person.Age);
        }

        //Instantiate and populate list of int with values
        List<int> marks = new List<int>
        {
            10,
            25,
            15,
            23
        };

        //Remove '25' from the list
        marks.Remove(25);

        //Get each element by its index
        Console.WriteLine();
        Console.Write("Marks: ");
        for (int i = 0; i < marks.Count; i++)
        {
            Console.Write(marks[i] + " ");
        }
    }
}
//Output
Total persono are: 3

Name: Ali - Age: 22
Name: Sundus - Age: 21
Name: Hogi - Age: 12

Marks: 10 15 23
```

Dictionary<TKey, TValue>

Dictionary<TKey, TValue> is a class of System.Collections.Generic. It's a type-safe collection of key/value pairs. Each key in dictionary must be unique and can store multiple values against the same key. Dictionary<TKey, TValue> is much faster than Hashtable.

Below are some common methods and properties used in Dictionary<TKey, TValue> class.

Table 4-9. Frequently used methods and properties of Dictionary<Tkey, TValue> class

Method and Property	Explanation
Add()	Add pair of type-safe key/value in Dictionary.
ContainsKey()	Return true if specific key is in Dictionary.
ContainsValue	Return true if specific value is in Dictionary.
Clear()	Remove all objects from the Dictionary.
Remove()	Remove the element with the specified key in Dictionary.
Count	Get the actual number of key/value pairs in Dictionary.
Keys	Get list of keys contained in Dictionary.
Values	Get list of values contained in Dictionary.

Code Snippet

Listing 4-18. Manage students in Dictionary

```
using System.Collections.Generic;
using System;

class Student
{
    public string Name { get; set; }
    public int Age { get; set; }
}
class Program
{
    static void Main(string[] args)
    {
        //Initialize Dictionary (int for roll# and assign it to student)
        Dictionary<int, Student> students = new Dictionary<int, Student>();

        //Adding student against their roll#
        students.Add(53, new Student { Name = "Ali Asad", Age = 22 });
        students.Add(11, new Student { Name = "Sundus Naveed", Age = 21 });
        students.Add(10, new Student { Name = "Hogi", Age = 12 });

        //Display Name against key
        Console.WriteLine("Roll# 11 is: {0}", students[11].Name);
```

```
        //ContainsKey can be use to test key before inserting
        if (!students.ContainsKey(13))
        {
            students.Add(13, new Student { Name = "Lakhtey", Age = 21});
        }

        // When you use foreach to enumerate elements of dictionary,
        // the elements are retrieved as KeyValuePairPair object.
        //KeyValuePair<TKey, TValue> is the pair of key & value for dictionary
        Console.WriteLine();
        foreach (KeyValuePair<int, Student> student in students)
        {
            Console.WriteLine("Roll#: {0} - Name: {1} - Age: {2}",
                student.Key, student.Value.Name, student.Value.Age);
        }

        //Get All values stored in Dictionary
        var allValues = students.Values;
        Console.WriteLine();
        foreach (var student in allValues)
        {
            Console.WriteLine("Name: {0} - Age: {1}",
                student.Name, student.Age);
        }

    }
}
//Output
Roll# 11 is: Sundus Naveed

Roll# 53 - Name: Ali Asad - Age: 22
Roll# 11 - Name: Sundus Naveed - Age: 21
Roll# 10 - Name: Hogi - Age: 12
Roll# 13 - Name: Lakhtey - Age: 21

Name: Ali Asad - Age: 22
Name: Sundus Naveed - Age: 21
Name: Hogi - Age: 12
Name: Lakhtey - Age: 21
```

Queue<T>

Queue<T> is a type-safe class of System.Collections.Generic namespace. It stores and retrieves data in FIFO (First In, First Out) order. In other words, it manages a collection of data on a first come, first served basis. It is much faster than Queue defined in System.Collections because value-type gets boxed/unboxed in Queue, whereas Queue<T> always type-safes it.

Below are some common methods and properties used in Queue<T> class.

Table 4-10. *Frequently used methods and properties of Queue<T>*

Method and Property	Explanation
Enqueue()	Add an element to the end of the Queue<T>.
Dequeue()	Remove and return an element at the beginning of the Queue<T>.
Peek()	Return an element at the beginning of the Queue<T> without removing it.
ToArray()	Copies the Queue<T> elements to a new array.
Contains()	Return true if a specified element is in the Queue<T>.
Clear()	Remove all elements from the Queue<T>.
Count	Get the actual number of objects in Queue.

Code Snippet

Listing 4-19. Manage weekdays in Queue<string>

```
using System.Collections.Generic;
using System;

class Program
{
    static void Main(string[] args)
    {
        Queue<string> days = new Queue<string>();

        //Add(Enque) string object in days
        days.Enqueue("Mon");
        days.Enqueue("Tue");
        days.Enqueue("Wed");
        days.Enqueue("Thu");
        days.Enqueue("Fri");
        days.Enqueue("Sat");
        days.Enqueue("Sun");

        // Displays the properties and values of the Queue.
        Console.WriteLine("Total elements in queue<string> are {0}",
            days.Count);

        //Remove and return first element of the queue<string>
        Console.WriteLine("{0}", days.Dequeue());

        //return first element of queue without removing it from queue
        //return 'Tue'
        Console.WriteLine("{0}", days.Peek());

        //Iterate over each element of queue
        Console.WriteLine();
        foreach (var item in days)
```

```
    {
        Console.WriteLine(item);
    }

  }
}
//Output
Total elements in queue<string> are 7
Mon
Tue

Tue
Wed
Thu
Fri
Sat
Sun
```

Stack<T>

Stack<T> is a class of System.Collections.Generic namespace. It stores and retrieves elements in LIFO (Last In, First Out) order. In other words, elements pushed at the end will pop up first, for example, a pile of plates. It is much faster than Stack defined in System.Collections because value-type gets boxed/unboxed in Stack, whereas Stack<T> always type-safes it.

Below are some common methods and properties used in Stack<T> class.

Table 4-11. *Frequently used methods and properties of Stack<T>*

Method and Property	Explanation
Push()	Insert the element at the top of the Stack<T>.
Pop()	Remove and return element at the top of the Stack<T>.
Peek()	Return the element at the top of the Stack<T> without removing it.
ToArray()	Copy the Stack<T> elements to a new array.
Contains()	Return true if a specified element is in the Stack<T>.
Clear()	Remove all elements from the Stack<T>.
Count	Get the actual number of elements in Stack<T>.

Code Snippet

Listing 4-20. Manage browser history in Stack<string>

```csharp
using System.Collections.Generic;
using System;

class Program
{
    static void Main(string[] args)
    {
        Stack<string> history = new Stack<string>();

        //Insert browser history in stack<string>
        history.Push("google.com");
        history.Push("facebook.com/imaliasad");
        history.Push("twitter.com/imaliasad");
        history.Push("youtube.com");

        // Displays the properties and values of the Stack<string>.
        Console.WriteLine("Total elements in stack<string> are {0}",
            history.Count);

        //Remove and return top element of the Stack<string>
        Console.WriteLine("{0}", history.Pop());

        //return top element of Stack<string> without removing it from Stack
        //return 'twitter.com/imaliasad'
        Console.WriteLine("{0}", history.Peek());

        //Iterate over each element of Stack<string>
        Console.WriteLine();
        foreach (var item in history)
        {
            Console.WriteLine(item);
        }

    }
}
//Output
Total elements in stack<string> are 4
youtube.com
twitter.com/imaliasad

twitter.com/imaliasad
facebook.com/imaliasad
google.com
```

119

System.Collections.Concurrent

System.Collections.Concurrent namespace was introduced in .NET 4 framework. It provides several thread-safe collections classes which protect a collection from being manipluated by multiple threads. Collection classes that are defined in a System.Collections.Concurrent can only be manipulated by a single thread. The .NET 4.0 Framework introduces several thread-safe collections in the System.Collections.Concurrent namespace.

Table 4-12. *Frequently used classes in System.Collections.Concurrent namespace*

Class	Explanation
ConcurrentBag<T>	Represents a thread-safe, unordered collection of objects.
ConcurrentDictionary<T,V>	Represents a thread-safe collection of key-value pairs.
ConcurrentQueue<T>	Represents a thread-safe First In, First Out (FIFO) collection.
ConcurrentStack<T>	Represents a thread-safe Last In, First Out (LIFO) collection.

We'll discuss more about System.Collections.Concurrent in Chapter 8: Multithread, Async, and Parallel Programming.

Implement Framework Interface

You can take advantage of .NET framework on custom types by implementing the following interfaces.

C# provides built-in interfaces that are useful to manage custom types for different useful purposes like defining custom collections and dispose resources that are no longer needed.

- IEnumerable & IEnemerable<T>
- IEnumerator & IEnumerator<T>
- ICollection & ICollection<T>
- IList & IList<T>
- IComparable & IComparable<T>
- IComparer & IComparer<T>
- IEquatable<T>

IEnumerable & IEnumerable<T>

.NET defined two base class libraries. There is non-generic IEnumerable interface to create a custom non-generic collection and and there is generic type-safe IEnumerable<T> interface to create a custom type-safe collection.

IEnumerable

IEnumerable interface is defined in System.Collections namespace. It helps to create a customized non-generic collection. It contains a single **GetEnumerator** method that returns an IEnumerator. We'll discuss IEnumerator in much detail in a later topic. But for now, IEnumerator is used to iterate over a collection, stores the information of a current index, its value, and whether or not a collection iteration has completed.

Foreach loop only iterate over those types which implemented IEnumerable interface, i.e., ArrayList and Queue.

Listing 4-21. Definition of IEnumerable

```
public interface IEnumerable
{
    IEnumerator GetEnumerator();
}
```

Listing 4-22. Define custom ArrayList

```
using System;
using System.Collections;

class myArrayList : IEnumerable
{
    object[] array = new object[4];
    int index = -1;

    public void Add(object o)
    {
        if(++index < array.Length)
        {
            array[index] = o;
        }
    }
    public IEnumerator GetEnumerator()
    {
        for(int i = 0; i < array.Length; i++)
        {
            yield return array[i];
        }
    }
}
class Program
{
    static void Main(string[] args)
    {
        myArrayList list = new myArrayList();

        //stores object data in myArraylist
        list.Add("Ali");
        list.Add(22);
        list.Add("Sundus");
        list.Add(21);
```

```
        foreach (var item in list)
        {
            Console.WriteLine(item);
        }
    }
}
//Output
Ali
22
Sundus
21
```

Explanation

Foreach loop called the GetEnumerator method of "list", which yields a return value of each array's index on every iteration. Therefore, myArrayList has now become a custom collection due to IEnumerable. In the following image, you can see a **yield** return value of each array's index on every iteration. The following figure (Figure 4-3) explains how *yield return* in a loop works.

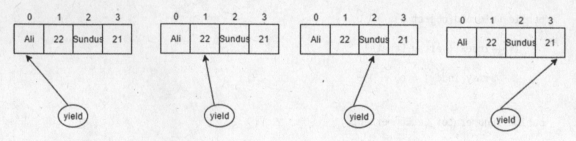

Figure 4-3. *Yield return in a loop*

■ **Note**   **Yield** returns an item; it saved us from writing the complete code to define IEnumerator.

IEnumerable<T>

IEnumerable<T> is a type-safe interface defined in System.Collections.Generic namespace. It is used to create a custom type-safe collection.

Listing 4-23. Definition of IEnumerable<T>

```
public interface IEnumerable<out T> : IEnumerable
{
    IEnumerator<T> GetEnumerator();
}
```

As you can see, IEnumerable<T> inherits an IEnumerable interface. Therefore, a type which implements IEnumerable<T> must implement IEnumerable, too.

Listing 4-24. Create a custom type-safe collection

```
using System;
using System.Collections;
using System.Collections.Generic;

class myList<T> : IEnumerable<T>
{
    List<T> list = new List<T>();

    //Get length of list<T>
    public int Length
    {
        get { return list.Count; }
    }
    public void Add (T data)
    {
        list.Add(data);
    }
    public IEnumerator<T> GetEnumerator()
    {
        foreach (var item in list)
        {
            yield return item;
        }
    }

    IEnumerator IEnumerable.GetEnumerator()
    {
        //return IEnumerator<T> GetEnumerator()
        return this.GetEnumerator();
    }
}

class Person
{
    public string Name { get; set; }
    public int Age { get; set; }
}
class Program
{
    static void Main(string[] args)
    {
        myList<Person> people = new myList<Person>();

        people.Add(new Person { Name = "Ali", Age = 22 });
        people.Add(new Person { Name = "Sundus", Age = 21 });
        people.Add(new Person { Name = "Hogi", Age = 12 });
```

```
        Console.WriteLine("Total person: {0} \n", people.Length);
        foreach (Person person in people)
        {
            Console.WriteLine("Name:{0} Age:{1}", person.Name, person.Age);
        }

    }
}
//Output
Total Person: 3

Name:Ali Age:22
Name:Sundus Age:21
Name: Hogi Age:12
```

IEnumerator & IEnumerator<T>

.NET defined two base class libraries. There are non-generic and generic IEnumerator interfaces to define the iteration of a collection.

IEnumerator

IEnumerator is non-generic interface defined in System.Collections namespace. It has methods and properties that a collection implements to define its iteration.

Listing 4-25. Definition of IEnumerator

```
public interface IEnumerator
{
    //Gets value of current index of collection
    object Current { get; }

    //Move to the next index of the collection
    bool MoveNext();

    //Move to the initial position of index = -1
    void Reset();
}
```

Listing 4-26. Define the iteration of your custom collection with IEnumerator

```
using System;
using System.Collections;
using System.Collections.Generic;

class People : IEnumerable
{
    Person[] people;
    int index = -1;
```

```csharp
    public void Add(Person per)
    {
        if (++index < people.Length)
        {
            people[index] = per;
        }
    }
    public People(int size)
    {
        people = new Person[size];
    }

    public IEnumerator GetEnumerator()
    {
        return new PersonEnum(people);
    }
}

//Implement IEnumerator
class PersonEnum : IEnumerator
{
    Person[] _people;
    int index = -1;

    public PersonEnum(Person[] people)
    {
        _people = people;
    }

    //Check whether foreach can move to next iteration or not
    public bool MoveNext()
    {
        return (++index < _people.Length);
    }

    //Reset the iteration
    public void Reset()
    {
        index = -1;
    }

    //Get current value
    public object Current
    {
        get
        {
            return _people[index];
        }
    }
}
```

```
class Person
{
    public string Name { get; set; }
    public int Age { get; set; }
}
class Program
{
    static void Main(string[] args)
    {
        People people = new People(3);

        people.Add(new Person { Name = "Ali", Age = 22 });
        people.Add(new Person { Name = "Sundus", Age = 21 });
        people.Add(new Person { Name = "Hogi", Age = 12 });

        foreach (var item in people)
        {
            //Cast from object to Person
            Person person = (Person)item;
            Console.WriteLine("Name:{0} Age:{1}", person.Name, person.Age);
        }

    }
}
//Output
Name:Ali Age:22
Name:Sundus Age:21
Name: Hogi Age:12
```

IEnumerator<T>

IEnumerator<T> is a generic interface defined in System.Collections.Generic namespace. It has methods and properties that a type-safe collection must implement to define its iteration.

Listing 4-27. Definition of IEnumerator<T>

```
public interface IEnumerator<out T> : IDisposable, IEnumerator
{

    //element in the collection at the current position of the enumerator.
    T Current { get; }
}
```

As you can see, IEnumerator<T> inherits IDisposable and IEnumerator interfaces. Therefore, a type which implements IEnumerator <T> must implement these interfaces too.

Listing 4-28. Write a type-safe iteration of a custom type-safe collection with IEnumerator<T>

```
using System;
using System.Collections;
using System.Collections.Generic;

class myList<T> : IEnumerable<T>
{
    T[] list;
    int index = -1;

    public void Add(T obj)
    {
        if (++index < list.Length)
        {
            list[index] = obj;
        }
    }

    public IEnumerator<T> GetEnumerator()
    {
        return new TEnum<T>(list);
    }

    IEnumerator IEnumerable.GetEnumerator()
    {
        return this.GetEnumerator();
    }

    public myList(int size)
    {
        list = new T[size];
    }

}

//Implement IEnumerator
class TEnum<T> : IEnumerator<T>
{
    T[] _list;
    int index = -1;

    public TEnum(T[] objs)
    {
        _list = objs;
    }

    //Return if foreach can iterate to next index or not
    public bool MoveNext()
    {
        return (++index < _list.Length);
    }
```

```csharp
    public void Reset()
    {
        index = -1;
    }

    //Get type-safe value of current array's index
    //Its the Implementation of IEnumerator<T>
    public T Current
    {
        get
        {
            return _list[index];
        }
    }

    //It's the implementation of 'IEnumerator'
    object IEnumerator.Current
    {
        get
        {
            //return T Current
            return this.Current;
        }
    }

    //It's the implementation of IDispose interface
    public void Dispose()
    {
        //Write code to dispose un-needed resource
    }

}

class Person
{
    public string Name { get; set; }
    public int Age { get; set; }
}

class Program
{
    static void Main(string[] args)
    {
        myList<Person> people = new myList<Person>(3);

        people.Add(new Person { Name = "Ali", Age = 22 });
        people.Add(new Person { Name = "Sundus", Age = 21 });
        people.Add(new Person { Name = "Hogi", Age = 12 });
```

```
        foreach (var item in people)
        {
            //No need to cast
            Console.WriteLine("Name:{0} Age:{1}", item.Name, item.Age);
        }

    }
}
//Output
Name:Ali Age:22
Name:Sundus Age:21
Name: Hogi Age:12
```

ICollection & ICollection<T>

ICollection and ICollection<T> are interfaces used to extend the definition of custom collection.

ICollection

ICollection is an interface defined in System.Collections to extend the definition of a custom non-generic collection.

It defines size, enumerators, and synchronization methods for all nongeneric collections.

Listing 4-29. Definition of ICollection

```
public interface ICollection : IEnumerable
{

    //     Gets the number of elements contained in the ICollection.
    int Count { get; }

    //     Gets a value indicating whether access to the ICollection
    //     is synchronized (thread safe).
    bool IsSynchronized { get; }

    //Gets an object that can be used to synchronize access to the ICollection.
    object SyncRoot { get; }

    //     Copies the elements of the ICollection to an Array,
    //     starting at a particular System.Array index.
    void CopyTo(Array array, int index);
}
```

ICollection inherits from IEnumerable. Therefore, all members of the IEnumerable interface must be implemented in all classes that implement the ICollection interface.

ICollection<T>

ICollection<T> is a type-safe interface defined in System.Collections.Generic. It extends the functionality of generic collections.

It defines methods to manipulate generic collections.

Listing 4-30. Definition of ICollection<T>

```
public interface ICollection<T> : IEnumerable<T>, IEnumerable
{

    //     Gets the number of elements contained in the `Generic.ICollection`.
    int Count { get; }

    //     Gets a value indicating whether the `Generic.ICollection`
    //     is read-only.
    bool IsReadOnly { get; }

    //     Adds an item to the `System.Collections.Generic.ICollection`.

    void Add(T item);

    //     Removes all items from the `Generic.ICollection`.
    void Clear();

    //     Determines whether the `System.Collections.Generic.ICollection`
    //     contains a specific value.
    bool Contains(T item);

    //     Copies the elements of the `Generic.ICollection` to an Array,
    //     starting at a particular System.Array index.
    void CopyTo(T[] array, int arrayIndex);

    // Removes the first occurrence of an object from the `Generic.ICollection`.

    bool Remove(T item);
}
```

It doesn't look exactly like a non-generic ICollection. The new definition of ICollection<T> has some more methods like Add, Remove, and Clear.

IList & IList<T>

IList and IList<T> are interfaces that extend the functionality of a custom collection type.

IList

IList is an interface defined in System.Collections. IList implementations fall into three categories:

1. read-only
2. fixed-size
3. variable-size

A read-only list cannot be modified. A fixed-size list cannot grow or shrink, but its elements can be editable, whereas a variable-size list allows addition, removal, and modification of elements.

IList represents a non-generic collection of objects that can be individually accessed by index.

Listing 4-31. Definition of IList

```
public interface IList : ICollection, IEnumerable
{

    //      Gets or sets the element at the specified index.
    object this[int index] { get; set; }

    //      Gets a value indicating whether the IList has a fixed size.
    bool IsFixedSize { get; }

    //      Gets a value indicating whether the IList is read-only.
    bool IsReadOnly { get; }

    //      Adds an item to the System.Collections.IList.
    int Add(object value);

    //      Removes all items from the System.Collections.IList.
    void Clear();

    //      Determines whether the IList contains a specific value.
    bool Contains(object value);

    //      Determines the index of a specific item in the IList.
    int IndexOf(object value);

    //      Inserts an item to the IList at the specified index.
    void Insert(int index, object value);

    //      Removes the first occurrence of a specific object from the IList.
    void Remove(object value);

    //      Removes the System.Collections.IList item at the specified index.
    void RemoveAt(int index);
}
```

IList inherits from ICollection and IEnumerable. Therefore, all members of the ICollection and IEnumerable interfaces must be implemented in all classes that implement the IList interface.

IList<T>

IList<T> is an interface defined in System.Collections.Generic. It is used to extend the custom generic collection. It doesn't look exactly like a non-generic IList. The new definition of IList<T> is a bit shorter than the non-generic equivalent. We only have some new methods for accessing a collection with specific positioning.

Listing 4-32. Definition of IList<T>

IList<T> represents a collection of objects that can be individually accessed by index.

```
public interface IList<T> : ICollection<T>, IEnumerable<T>, IEnumerable
{

    //      Gets or sets the element at the specified index.
    T this[int index] { get; set; }

    //      Determines the index of a specific item in the `Generic.IList`1.
    int IndexOf(T item);

    //      Inserts an item to the `IGeneric.IList`1 at the specified index.
    void Insert(int index, T item);

    //      Removes the `SGeneric.IList` item at the specified index.
    void RemoveAt(int index);
}
```

IList<T> inherits from ICollection<T>, IEnumerable<T>, and IEnumerable. Therefore, all members of the ICollection<T>, IEnumerable<T>, and IEnumerable interfaces must be implemented in all classes that implement the IList<T> interface.

IComparable & IComparable<T>

IComparable and IComparable<T> are interfaces used to define a comparison method for a type to order or sort its instances. The CompareTo method returns an Int32 that has one of three values which have following meaning:

- **Return zero**, current instance will occur in the same position.

- **Less than zero**, current instance precedes the object specified by the CompareTo method in the sort order.

- **Greater than zero**, current instance follows the object specified by the CompareTo in the sort order.

IComparable

IComparable is an interface defined in System namespace. It takes an object as its parameter and returns a result as an int32.

Listing 4-33. Definition of IComparable

```
public interface IComparable
{

    //      Compares the current instance with another object of the same
    //      type and returns
    //      an integer that indicates whether the current instance precedes,
    //      follows, or
    //      occurs in the same position in the sort order as the other object.

    int CompareTo(object obj);
}
```

Listing 4-34. Implement IComparable and sort list of persons

```
using System;
using System.Collections;

class Person : IComparable
{
    public string Name { get; set; }
    public int Age { get; set; }
    public int CompareTo(object obj)
    {
        Person next = (Person)obj;
        return this.Age.CompareTo(next.Age);
    }
}

class Program
{
    static void Main(string[] args)
    {
        ArrayList people = new ArrayList();

        people.Add(new Person { Name = "Sundus", Age = 21 });
        people.Add(new Person { Name = "Ali", Age = 22 });
        people.Add(new Person { Name = "Hogi", Age = 12 });

        //sort list of persons
        people.Sort();

        foreach(Person person in people)
        {
            Console.WriteLine(person.Age + " " + person.Name);
        }

    }
}
//Output
12 Hogi
21 Sundus
22 Ali
```

IComparable<T>

IComparable<T> is type-safe interface defined in System namespace. It takes a type-safe parameter and returns a result as an int32. Its implementation is the same as IComparable.

Listing 4-35. Definition of IComparable<T>

```
public interface IComparable<in T>
{

    //      Compares the current instance with another object of the same type
    //      and returns an integer that indicates whether the current instance
    //      precedes, follows, or occurs in the same position in the sort
            order                           //              as the other object.

    int CompareTo(T other);
}

using System;
using System.Collections.Generic;

class Person : IComparable<Person>
{
    public string Name { get; set; }
    public int Age { get; set; }

    public int CompareTo(Person other)
    {
        return this.Age.CompareTo(other.Age);
    }
}

class Program
{
    static void Main(string[] args)
    {
        List<Person> people = new List<Person>();

        people.Add(new Person { Name = "Sundus", Age = 21 });
        people.Add(new Person { Name = "Ali", Age = 22 });
        people.Add(new Person { Name = "Hogi", Age = 12 });

        //sort list of persons
        people.Sort();

        foreach(var person in people)
        {
            Console.WriteLine(person.Age + " " + person.Name);
        }

    }
}

//Output
12 Hogi
21 Sundus
22 Ali
```

IComparer & IComparer<T>

IComparer and IComparer<T> are interfaces used to implement in a separate class that helps to sort the objects according to its field or property values.

IComparer

IComparer is an interface defined in System.Collections.Generic namespace. It helps to compares two objects.

Listing 4-36. Definition of IComparer

```
public interface IComparer
{
    //     Compares two objects and returns a value indicating whether one is
    //     less than, equal to, or greater than the other.

    int Compare(object x, object y);
}
```

Listing 4-37. Sort person by age and name

```
using System;
using System.Collections;

class Person
{
    public string Name { get; set; }
    public int Age { get; set; }

}

class sortAge : IComparer
{
    public int Compare(object x, object y)
    {
        Person first = (Person)x;
        Person second = (Person)y;

        return first.Age.CompareTo(second.Age);
    }
}

class SortName : IComparer
{
    public int Compare(object x, object y)
    {
        Person first = (Person)x;
        Person second = (Person)y;
```

```
            return first.Name.CompareTo(second.Name);
    }
}

class Program
{
    static void Main(string[] args)
    {
        ArrayList people = new ArrayList();

        people.Add(new Person { Name = "Sundus", Age = 21 });
        people.Add(new Person { Name = "Ali", Age = 22 });
        people.Add(new Person { Name = "Hogi", Age = 12 });

        //sort list according to age
        people.Sort(new sortAge());

        foreach(Person person in people)
        {
            Console.WriteLine(person.Age + " " + person.Name);
        }

        Console.WriteLine();
        //sort list according to name
        people.Sort(new SortName());

        foreach (Person person in people)
        {
            Console.WriteLine(person.Name + " " + person.Age);
        }

    }
}
//Output
12 Hogi
21 Sundus
22 Ali

Ali 22
Hogi 12
Sundus 21
```

IComparer<T>

IComparer<T> is a type-safe interface defined in System.Collections.Generic. It helps to compares two objects. It takes type-safe parameters for its Compare method.

Listing 4-38. Definition of IComparer<T>

```
public interface IComparer<in T>
{
    //      Compares two objects and returns a value indicating
    //      whether one is less than, equal to, or greater than the other.

    int Compare(T x, T y);
}
```

Listing 4-39. Sort person by age and name

```
using System;
using System.Collections.Generic;

class Person
{
    public string Name { get; set; }
    public int Age { get; set; }

}

class sortAge : IComparer<Person>
{
    public int Compare(Person x, Person y)
    {
        return x.Age.CompareTo(y.Age);
    }
}

class SortName : IComparer<Person>
{
    public int Compare(Person x, Person y)
    {
        return x.Name.CompareTo(y.Name);
    }
}

class Program
{
    static void Main(string[] args)
    {
        List<Person> people = new List<Person>();

        people.Add(new Person { Name = "Sundus", Age = 21 });
        people.Add(new Person { Name = "Ali", Age = 22 });
        people.Add(new Person { Name = "Hogi", Age = 12 });

        //sort list according to age
        people.Sort(new sortAge());
```

```
        foreach(var person in people)
        {
            Console.WriteLine(person.Age + " " + person.Name);
        }

        Console.WriteLine();
        //sort list according to name
        people.Sort(new SortName());

        foreach (var person in people)
        {
            Console.WriteLine(person.Name + " " + person.Age);
        }

    }
}
//Output
12 Hogi
21 Sundus
22 Ali

Ali 22
Hogi 12
Sundus 21
```

IEquatable<T>

IEquatable<T> is an interface implemented by types whose values can be equated (for example, the numeric and string classes). But for most reference types using IEquatable is avoided because, if you do, you need to override Object.Equals(Object) and GetHashCode methods. Therefore, their behavior is consistent with the IEquatable.Equals method.

Listing 4-40. Definition of IEquatable<T>

```
public interface IEquatable<T>
{

    //      Indicates whether the current object is equal to
    //      another object of the same type.

    bool Equals(T other);
}
```

Listing 4-41. Equate two objects

```
using System;

class Person : IEquatable<Person>
{
    public string Name { get; set; }
    public int Age { get; set; }
```

```
    public bool Equals(Person other)
    {
        if(this.Name.CompareTo(other.Name) == 0 && this.Age == other.Age)
        {
            return true;
        }
        else
        {
            return false;
        }
    }

    public override bool Equals(object obj)
    {
        Person other = (Person)obj;
        return this.Equals(other);
    }

    public override int GetHashCode()
    {
        //custom implementation of hashcode
        string hash = this.Name + this.Age;
        return hash.GetHashCode();
    }

    public static bool operator ==(Person person1, Person person2)
    {
        if ((((object)person1) == null || ((object)person2) == null)
            return Object.Equals(person1, person2);

        return person1.Equals(person2);
    }

    public static bool operator !=(Person person1, Person person2)
    {
        if ((((object)person1) == null || ((object)person2) == null)
            return !Object.Equals(person1, person2);

        return !(person1.Equals(person2));
    }
}

class Program
{
    static void Main(string[] args)
    {
        Person person1 = new Person();
        person1.Age = 22;
        person1.Name = "Ali";
```

```
        Person person2 = new Person();
        person2.Age = 22;
        person2.Name = "Ali";

        Console.WriteLine(person1 == person2);
    }
}
//Output
True
```

Working with Strings

String is used to store text values. String is immutable, which means once a string variable stores some text it cannot edit it again; the text is stored as a read-only collection of Char objects. Therefore, whenever a string variable's value is updated, it re-creates an instance for string literals, which is not good in terms of memory and process consumption.

Listing 4-42. Record how much time it takes to append a string 1,000,000 times

```
using System;
using System.Diagnostics; //for stopwatch

class Program
{
    static void Main(string[] args)
    {
        Stopwatch watch = new Stopwatch();

        //Record how much time
        watch.Start();

        string mystring = "test";
        for(int i = 1; i <100000; i++)
        {
            mystring += i;
        }

        //Stop Recording time
        watch.Stop();

        float miliToSec = watch.ElapsedMilliseconds / 1000;
        Console.WriteLine("Total time: {0}s", miliToSec);

    }
}
//Output
Total time: 51s
```

In my machine, it took 51 seconds to append a string for 100,000 times, because every time CLR creates a new instance of string literals and reassigns its reference to a string variable.

StringBuilder

StringBuilder is a class of System.Text which provides better performance on manipulating text data in a much better way than a traditional System.String does. StringBuilder is mutable, which means text data can be editable. Its Append method helps to concatenate text data in a better way.

Listing 4-43. Record how much time it takes to append a StringBuilder's text for 100,000 times

```
using System;
using System.Diagnostics; //for stopwatch
using System.Text;

class Program
{
    static void Main(string[] args)
    {
        Stopwatch watch = new Stopwatch();

        //Record how much time
        watch.Start();

        StringBuilder mystring = new StringBuilder("test");
        for(int i = 1; i <100000; i++)
        {
            mystring.Append(i);
        }

        //Stop Recording time
        watch.Stop();

        Console.WriteLine("Total time: {0}ms", watch.ElapsedMilliseconds);

    }
}
//Output
Total time: 35ms
```

In my machine, it took **35 milliseconds** to append a text in StringBuilder, whereas in the previous example System.String took **51 seconds**. Hence **StringBuilder is faster** than System.String

StringReader

StringReader is a class of System.IO used to read lines from a string. With StringReader, we can read a character with *Read* or *ReadAsync* method, and an entire string with *ReadToEnd* or *ReadToEndAsync* method. This type helps to access string data through a stream-oriented interface.

Listing 4-44. Read line by line string with StringReader

```
using System;
using System.IO;

class Program
{
```

141

```
    static void Main(string[] args)
    {
        //'@' It's a verbatim string literal. It ignores escape sequence
        string text = @"Hi I'm Ali Asad.
I can help you in C# Certification Exam.
I've helped many individuals like you in their exam prep.
I believe if we work together, you can become:
Microsoft Certified Professional & Specialist in C#";

        StringReader reader = new StringReader(text);
        int currentLine = 0;
        string line = "";

        //return each line of string to 'line'
        while((line = reader.ReadLine())!= null)
        {
            Console.WriteLine("line{0}: {1}", ++currentLine, line);
        }


    }
}
//Output
Line1: Hi I'm Ali Asad.
Line2: I can help you in C# Certification Exam.
Line3: I've helped many individuals like you in their exam prep.
Line4: I believe if we work together, you can become:
Line5: Microsoft Certified Professional & Specialist in C#
```

StringWriter

StringWriter is a class of System.IO. It is used to write to a StringBuilder class. With StringWriter, we can write a character/string with *Write* or *WriteAsync* method, and an entire string line with *WriteLine* or *WriteLineAsync* method. It's an efficient way of using StringBuilder with StringWriter to manipulate string.

Listing 4-45. Write string data in StringBuilder by using StringWriter

```
using System;
using System.IO;
using System.Text;

class Program
{
    static void Main(string[] args)
    {
        StringBuilder builder = new StringBuilder();

        StringWriter swriter = new StringWriter(builder);

        swriter.Write("Ali Asad");
```

```
        Console.WriteLine(builder.ToString());

    }
}
//Output
Ali Asad
```

Enumerate String Methods

String used for text data. It has many methods and properties that help to maniuplate text data. Some of them are listed below.

Clone( )

Use to make clone of string in object type.

```
        string text = "Ali Asad";
        string cloned = text.Clone() as string;

        Console.WriteLine(cloned);
```
//Output
Ali Asad

CompareTo( )

Compare two string values and return integer value. It returns 0 for true.

```
        string text1 = "ali";
        string text2 = "asad";

        if((text1.CompareTo(text2)) == 0)
        {
            Console.WriteLine("both text are same");
        }
        else
        {
            Console.WriteLine("both text aren't same");
        }
```
//Output
both text aren't same

EndsWith( )

Return true if it finds a specified character is the last character of a string.

```
        string text1 = "ali";
        Console.WriteLine(text1.EndsWith("i"));
```
//Output
True

Equals( )

Compare two strings and return true if they're equal.

```
string text1 = "ali";
string text2 = "ali";

Console.WriteLine(text1.Equals(text2));
```

```
//Output
True
```

IndexOf( )

Return the index number of the first occurrence of a specified character.

```
string text1 = "ali";
Console.WriteLine(text1.IndexOf('l'));
```

```
//Output
1
```

ToLower( )

Return the lower case of string.

```
string text1 = "ALI";
Console.WriteLine(text1.ToLower());
```

```
//Output
ali
```

ToUpper( )

Return the upper case of string.

```
string text1 = "ali";
Console.WriteLine(text1.ToUpper());
```

```
//Output
ALI
```

Insert( )

Return a new string in which a new character/string is inserted at a specified index of a string.

```
string text1 = "Ali";
Console.WriteLine(text1.Insert(3, " Asad"));
```

```
//Output
Ali Asad
```

LastIndexOf( )

Return the last index of a specified character in a string.

```
string text1 = "ali asad";
Console.WriteLine(text1.LastIndexOf('a'));
```

```
//Output
6
```

Remove( )

Return a new string by deleting all the characters from a specified index to the end.

```
string text1 = "ali asad";
Console.WriteLine(text1.Remove(3));
```

```
//Output
ali
```

Replace( )

Return a new string in which the occurrence of specified characters are replaced with other specified characters.

```
string text1 = "ali asad";
Console.WriteLine(text1.Replace("ali", "asad"));
```

```
//Output
asad asad
```

Split( )

Split a string into an array of strings that are based on the characters that occur in a string.

```
string text1 = "ali asad";

string[] subString = text1.Split(' ');

foreach (var item in subString)
{
    Console.WriteLine(item);
}
```

```
//Output
ali
asad
```

StartsWith( )

Return true if the beginning of a string starts with a specified character/string.

```
string text1 = "ali asad";

Console.WriteLine(text1.StartsWith("al"));
```

```
//Output
True
```

145

Substring( )

Return a new string that contains characters from a specified start index to a specified length of characters.

```
string text1 = "ali asad";

Console.WriteLine(text1.Substring(2, 5));
```

```
//Output
i asa
```

ToCharArray( )

Return a new character array that contains a character of a string.

```
string text1 = "ali";

char[] chArray = text1.ToCharArray();

foreach (var item in chArray)
{
    Console.WriteLine(item);
}
```

```
//Output
a
l
i
```

Trim( )

Remove whitespaces from the beginning and ending of a string.

```
string text1 = "   ali   ";

Console.WriteLine("{0} {1}", text1.Trim().Length, text1.Trim());
```

```
//Output
3 ali
```

ToString( )

Converts an object to its string representation. It's a method that can be overridden in any custom type to get the object information as a string.

```
using System;

class Person
{
    public string Name { get; set; }
    public int Age { get; set; }

    public override string ToString()
    {
```

```
        string data = "Name = " + this.Name + " " + "Age = " + this.Age;

        return data;
    }
}

class Program
{
    static void Main(string[] args)
    {
        Person person = new Person { Name = "Ali", Age = 22 };

        //person & person.ToString() are same  in this case
        //Hence, both produce the same result at runtime.
        //person = person.ToString()
        Console.WriteLine(person);
        Console.WriteLine(person.ToString());
    }
}
Output
Name = Ali Age = 22
```

String.Format Method

String.Format helps to represent objects values in a specified format and return them as a string.
Its syntax is similar to Console.WriteLine method.

Syntax

```
string variable = string.Format("");
```

Code Snippet

```
        string name = "Ali";
        int age = 22;

        string info = string.Format("Name = {0} Age = {1}", name, age);

        Console.WriteLine(info);
//Output
Name = Ali Age = 22
```

Special Formats to Display Object Value

Objects are of multiple kinds. For each kind, data is stored or displayed in a different format. Some of the
formats are listed below:

- Standard Numeric Formats
- Control Spacing
- Control Alignment

147

Standard Numeric Formats

Standard numeric strings are used to format common numeric types. These are listed below in a table.

Table 4-13. *Numeric Format Specifier*

Format Specifier	Explanation
"C" or "c"	Used to format currency value
"D" or "d"	Used to format integer digit with optional negative sign
"E" or "e"	Used to format exponential notation
"F" or "f"	Used for precision specifier to define fixed floating value
"N" or "n"	Used to format numbers by group separators
"P" or "p"	Used to display percentage with number
"X" or "x"	Used to display Hexadecimal value

Listing 4-46. Use currency format

```
decimal price = 1921.39m;
Console.WriteLine(price.ToString("C"));
```

```
//Output
$1,921.39
```

Listing 4-47. Use integer digit format

```
int temp = 12;
Console.WriteLine(temp.ToString("D"));
//D3 = 3 digits will be display (012)
Console.WriteLine(temp.ToString("D3"));
```

```
//Output
12
012
```

Listing 4-48. Use exponential format

```
double value = 54321.6789;
Console.WriteLine(value.ToString("E"));
```

```
//Output
5.432168E+004
```

Listing 4-49. Use fixed-float format

```
double Number = 18934.1879;
Console.WriteLine(Number.ToString("F"));
```

```
//Output
18934.19
```

Listing 4-50. Use group separaters to format numbers

```
int Number = 12345678;
Console.WriteLine(Number.ToString("N"));
```

```
//Output
12,345,678,00
```

Listing 4-51. Show percentage value

```
int Number = 1;
Console.WriteLine(Number.ToString("P"));
```

```
//Output
100.00%
```

Listing 4-52. Display Hexadecimal value of a number

```
int Number = 2154;
Console.WriteLine(Number.ToString("X"));
```

```
//Output
86A
```

Control Spacing

Spacing is helpful to format the output. String can help to format the spacing.

Listing 4-53. Create 10 spaces

```
string name = "Ali";
int age = 22;

Console.WriteLine("Name {0,10} | Age {1, 10}", name, age);
```

```
//Output
Name          Ali | Age          22
```

Control Alignment

By default strings are right-aligned. To create a left-aligned string in a field, you need to use a negative sign, such as {0, -5} to define a 5-character right-aligned field.

Listing 4-54. Control text alignment

```
string name = "Ali";

Console.WriteLine("- {0,-8} |end", name);
```

```
//Output
- Ali      |end
```

Summary

- **Boxing** refers to implicit conversion of a value type into an object type or to any interface that it implements.

- **Unboxing** refers to an explicit conversion of an object type to a non-nullable-value type or the conversion of an interface type to a non-nullable-value type.

- Boxing could take up to **20 times** longer than a simple reference assignment. When a boxed value is unboxed, it takes **4 times** longer than a simple reference assignment.

- Generics perform **compile-time checks** for type safety and it is much **faster** than boxing/unboxing.

- **where** keyword is used to apply constraints on generic type parameters.

- C# defines data-structure in a collection (i.e., ArrayList, Stack, Queue).

- User can create a custom collection by implementing **IEnumerable** or **IEnumerable<T>.**

- **StringBuilder** provides better performance on manipulating text data in a much better way than traditional System.String does.

- **StringReader** is usually used to read lines from a string.

- **StringWriter** is used to write text to a StringBuilder.

- **String.Format** helps to represent objects values in a specified format and return them as a string.

Code Challenges

Challenge 1: Develop a Custom Generic Collection.

Create a custom generic collection which implements the following interfaces.

- IList<T>
- ICollection<T>
- IEnumerable<T>

Practice Exam Questions

Question 1

You are developing a game that allows players to collect from 0 through 1,000 coins. You are creating a method that will be used in the game. The method includes the following code. (Line numbers are included for reference only.)

```
01 public string FormatCoins(string name, int coins)
02 {
03
04 }
```

The method must meet the following requirements:

- Return a string that includes the player name and the number of coins.
- Display the number of coins without leading zeros if the number is 1 or greater.
- Display the number of coins as a single 0 if the number is 0.

You need to ensure that the method meets the requirements. Which code segment should you insert at line 03?

A)
```
return string.Format("Player {0}, collected {1} coins", name, coins.ToString("###0"));
```

B)
```
return string.Format("Player {0}, collected {1:000#} coins", name, coins.ToString());
```

C)
```
return string.Format("Player {name}, collected {coins.ToString('###0')} coins");
```

D)
```
return string.Format("Player {0}, collected {1:D3} coins", name, coins);
```

Question 2

The following code is boxed into object o.

```
double d = 34.5;
object o = d;
```

You're asked to cast "object o" into "int "".

A)
```
int i = (int)o;
```

B)
```
int i = (int)(double)o;
```

C)
```
int i = (int)(float)(double)o;
```

D)
```
int i = (float)o;
```

Question 3

Suppose you're developing an application which stores a user's browser history. Which collection class will help to retrieve information of the last visited page?

A)
ArrayList

B)
Queue

C)
Stack

D)
HashTable

Answers

1. D
2. C
3. C

CHAPTER 5

■ ■ ■

Implementing Delegates & Events

In any modern language, event-driven development is used to structure a program around various events. These events perform a certain functionality when a certain condition satisfies, for example, close the application when a user clicks on the "Exit" button. Or shut down the system when the heat Temperature rises, etc.

In this chapter, we'll learn everything we need to know about event-driven development in C#.

Delegate

Delegate is a type, similar to function pointers in C/C++. It stores the reference of a method inside a delegate object, to invoke the referenced method anywhere in the code. It also allows the method to be passed as an argument of another method. Unlike function pointers in C++, delegates are type-safe function pointers.

Delegate declaration determines a type that can refer to a method, which has the same set of arguments and returns a type. A single delegate object can hold the reference of multiple methods that can be called on a single event.

Syntax

```
access_specifier delegate retun_type delegateName(argument_list);
```

Code Snippet

Listing 5-1. Declare, instantiate, and use a delegate

```
//declare a delegate
public delegate void delegateName(string msg);

// Declare a method with the same signature as the delegate.
static void display(string msg)
{
     Console.WriteLine(msg);
}

static void Main(string[] args)
{
   // Create an instance of the delegate
   delegateName del = new delegateName(display);

   //Calling the delegate
   del("Ali Asad");

}
```

© Ali Asad and Hamza Ali 2017
A. Asad and H. Ali, *The C# Programmer's Study Guide (MCSD)*, DOI 10.1007/978-1-4842-2860-9_5

- **new delegateName(display);** pass "display" method's reference in the delegateName constructor.

- **del("Ali Asad");** call "del" which invokes the "display" method.

Delegate can also store a method's reference directly. See the following code snippet.

Listing 5-2. Store reference of a method directly

```
// Create an instance of the delegate
delegateName del = display;
```

Delegate can also be invoked by using the .invoke method. See the following code snippet.

Listing 5-3. Use the .invoke method

```
//call method by using .invoke() and pass string msg
del.Invoke("Ali Asad");
```

Multicast Delegate

Delegate holds the reference of more than one method called multicast delegate. It helps to invoke the multiple methods.

- By using +=, delegate can add a new method's reference on top of an exisiting stored reference.

- By using -=, delegate can remove a method's reference from a delegate's instance.

Listing 5-4. Add multiple method's reference

```
using System;

//declare a delegate
public delegate void delegateName(string msg);
class MyClass
{
    // Declare a method with the same signature as the delegate.
    static void display(string msg)
    {
        Console.WriteLine("display: {0}", msg);
    }

    static void show(string msg)
    {
        Console.WriteLine("show: {0}", msg);
    }

    static void screen(string msg)
    {
        Console.WriteLine("screen: {0}", msg);
    }
```

```
    static void Main(string[] args)
    {
        delegateName del = display;

        //Multicast delegate
        del += show;
        del += screen;

        //calling delegate
        del("Ali");

    }
}
//Output
display: Ali
show: Ali
screen: Ali
```

- del += add reference of method on top of existing reference of method.
- **del("Ali Asad");** invoke all methods one-by-one in the same order they were added.

Listing 5-5. Remove method's reference from a delegate's instance

```
using System;

//declare a delegate
public delegate void delegateName(string msg);
class MyClass
{
    // Declare a method with the same signature as the delegate.
    static void display(string msg)
    {
        Console.WriteLine("display: {0}", msg);
    }

    static void show(string msg)
    {
        Console.WriteLine("show: {0}", msg);
    }

    static void screen(string msg)
    {
        Console.WriteLine("screen: {0}", msg);
    }

    static void Main(string[] args)
    {
        delegateName del = display;
```

```
        //Multicast delegate
        del += show;
        del += screen;

        //remove method's reference
        del -= show;

        //calling delegate
        del("Ali");

    }
}
//Output
display: Ali
screen: Ali
```

- **del -=show;** removes the reference of a show method from a delegate instance.

Listing 5-6. Loop over each method by using getinvocationlist method

```
using System;

//declare a delegate
public delegate int delegateName();
class MyClass
{
    static int Get20()
    {
        Console.Write("Get20(): ");
        return 20;
    }
    static int Get30()
    {
        Console.Write("Get30(): ");
        return 30;
    }
    static int Get15()
    {
        Console.Write("Get15(): ");
        return 15;
    }

    static void Main(string[] args)
    {
        delegateName del = Get20;

        //add method reference
        del += Get30;
        del += Get20;
        del += Get15;
```

```
        foreach (delegateName item in del.GetInvocationList())
        {
            //invoke each method, and display return value
            Console.WriteLine(item());
        }

    }

}
//Output
Get20(): 20
Get30(): 30
Get20(): 20
Get15(): 15
```

- **del.GetInvocationList();** returns a list of all referenced methods stored in "del".

Common Built-in Delegates

C# provides many built-in delegates that are useful for common purposes. These built-in types provide a shorthand notation that virtually eliminates the need to declare delegate types.

Some common built-in delegates are:

- Action
- Action<>
- Func<>
- Predicate<>

Action

Action is a built-in delegate type available in System namespace. It can be used with methods that don't return a value and have no parameter list.

Syntax

```
public delegate void Action()
```

Code Snippet

Listing 5-7. Use Action delegate

```
using System;

class MyClass
{
    static void voidMethod()
    {
        Console.WriteLine("Void Method");
    }
```

```
    static void emptyMethod()
    {
        Console.WriteLine("Empty Method");
    }

    static void Main(string[] args)
    {

        Action act = voidMethod;
        act += emptyMethod;

        act();
    }

}
//Output
Void Method
Empty Method
```

Action<>

Action<> is a generic delegate. It can be used with methods that at least have one argument and don't return a value. Action<> delegate comes with 16 generic overloads, which means it can take up to 16 arguments of void method.

Code Snippet

Listing 5-8. Use Action<> delegate

```
using System;

class MyClass
{
    static void myintMethod(int i)
    {
        Console.WriteLine("myintMethod: i = {0}", i);
    }

    static void myintStringMethod(int i, string s)
    {
        Console.WriteLine("myintStringMethod: i = {0} s = {1}", i, s);
    }
    static void Main(string[] args)
    {

        Action<int> myIntAct = myintMethod;
        Action<int, string> myIntStringAct = myintStringMethod;

        myIntAct(22);
        myIntStringAct(22, "Ali");

    }

}
```

158

```
//Output
myintMethod: i = 22
myintStringMethod: i = 22 s = Ali
```

- **Action<>** delegate is type-safe, which means it can take arguments of any type and the argument type will be type-safe at compile time.

Func<>

Func<> is a generic delegate. It can be used with methods that return a value and may have a parameter list. The last parameter of Func<> determines the method's return type and the remaining parameters are used for a method's argument list. Func<> delegate comes with 17 generic overloads, which means it uses the last parameter as a method's return type and the remaining 16 can be used as a method's argument list. Also, if the Func<> has only one parameter, then its first parameter would be considered as a method's return type.

Code Snippet

Listing 5-9. Use Func<> delegate

```
using System;

class MyClass
{
    static int Add(int x, int y)
    {
        Console.Write("{0} + {1} = ", x, y);
        return (x + y);
    }

    static int Min(int x, int y)
    {
        Console.Write("{0} - {1} = ", x, y);
        return (x - y);
    }

    static int Mul(int x, int y)
    {
        Console.Write("{0} * {1} = ", x, y);
        return (x * y);
    }

    static string Name()
    {
        Console.Write("My name is = ");
        return "Ali Asad";
    }

    static string DynamicName(string name)
    {
        Console.Write("My name is = ");
        return name;
    }
```

159

```csharp
    static void Main(string[] args)
    {

        //return string value
        Func<string> info = Name;
        Console.WriteLine(info());

        //return string, and take string as parameter
        Func<string, string> dynamicInfo = DynamicName;
        Console.WriteLine(dynamicInfo("Hamza Ali"));

        //return int, and take two int as parameter
        Func<int, int, int> calculate = Add;
        calculate += Min;
        calculate += Mul;

        foreach (Func<int, int, int> item in calculate.GetInvocationList())
        {
            Console.WriteLine(item(10,5));
        }

    }

}
//Output
My name is = Ali Asad
My name is = Hamza Ali
10 + 5 = 15
10 - 5 = 10
10 * 5 = 50
```

- First parameter in func<> determines the method return type and the remaining are considered as a list of the argument type of method.

Predicate<T>

A predicate delegate represents a method that takes one input parameter and returns a bool value on the basis of some criteria.

Syntax

```csharp
public delegate bool Predicate<T>()
```

Code Snippet

Listing 5-10. Use Predicate to determine if a number is even or not

```csharp
using System;

class MyClass
{
```

160

```
    static bool Even (int i)
    {
        return (i % 2 == 0);
    }
    static void Main(string[] args)
    {

        Predicate<int> isEven = Even;

        Console.WriteLine(isEven(7));
    }

}
//Output
False
```

Variance in Delegate

With variance in delegates, the method doesn't need to match the delegate type. Because variance provides a degree of flexibility when matching a delegate type with the method signature, we can use variance in the following two ways.

1. Covariance
2. Contravariance

Covariance

Covariance is applied on a method's **return type**. With covariance, a delegate can hold a reference of a method, whose return value is a derived type of the return type in the delegate signature.

Code Snippet

Listing 5-11. Covariance in Delegate

```
using System;

class  Parent { }
class  Child : Parent { }

delegate Parent CovarianceHandle();

class Program
{
    static Child CovarianceMethod()
    {
        Console.WriteLine("Covariance Method");
        return new Child();
    }

    static void Main(string[] args)
```

```
    {
        //Covariance
        CovarianceHandle del = CovarianceMethod;

        del();
    }
}
//Output
Covariance Method
```

Contravariance

Contravariance is applied on a method's **parameter type**. With contravariance, a delegate can hold a reference of a method whose parameter value is a base type of the delegate signature parameter type.

Code Snippet

Listing 5-12. Contravariance in Delegate

```
using System;

class  Parent { }
class  Child : Parent { }

delegate void ContravarianceHandle(Child c);

class Program
{
    static void ContravarianceMethod(Parent p)
    {
        Child ch = p as Child;
        Console.WriteLine("Contravariance Method");
    }

    static void Main(string[] args)
    {

        ContravarianceHandle del = ContravarianceMethod;

        Child child = new Child();

        //Contravariance
        del(child);
    }
}
//Output
Contravariance Method
```

Problems with Delegate

Delegates have a few problems which events have overcome. These problems are:

1. Anyone can use an assignment operator which may overwrite the references of methods.

Listing 5-13. Overwrite the references of methods in Delegate

```
using System;

class Program
{
    static void Display()
    {
        Console.WriteLine("Display");
    }

    static void Show()
    {
        Console.WriteLine("Show");
    }
    static void Main(string[] args)
    {
        Action act = Display;
        act += Show;

        act = Display;

        act();
    }
}
//Output
Display
```

2. Delegate can be called anywhere in code, which may break the rule of Encapsulation.

Listing 5-14. Alert on high room Temperature

```
using System;

class Room
{
    public Action<int> OnHeatAlert;

    int temp;
    public int Temperature
    {
        get { return this.temp; }
        set
```

```
            {
                temp = value;
                if (temp > 60)
                {
                    if (OnHeatAlert != null)
                    {
                        OnHeatAlert(temp);
                    }
                }
            }
        }
    }
}
class Program
{
    static void Alarm(int temp)
    {
        Console.WriteLine("Turn On AC, Its hot. Room temp is {0}", temp);
    }
    static void Main(string[] args)
    {
        Room room = new Room();
        room.OnHeatAlert = Alarm;

        //OnHeatAlert will be called
        room.Temperature = 90;

        room.Temperature = 15;
        //OnHeatAlert will be called
        //Which shouldn't be called becaust room is not hot
        room.OnHeatAlert(room.Temperature);
        //Delegate is called outside the Room class
    }
}

//Output
Turn On AC, Its hot. Room temp is 90
Turn On AC, Its hot. Room temp is 15
```

Anonymous Method

An anonymous method is a method without a name. These are methods that are defined with a delegate keyword. An anonymous method doesn't have a return type in its signature. Its return type depends on the type of delegate variable which holds its reference.

Syntax

```
delegate_type delegate_variable = delegate (parameter_list)
{
    //Method Body
};
```

Code Snippet

Listing 5-15. Implement anonymous method(s)

```
using System;

class Program
{
    static void Main(string[] args)
    {
        //Anonymous method that doesn't return value
        Action act = delegate ()
        {
            Console.WriteLine("Inside Anonymous method");
        };

        //Anonymous method that does return value
        Func<int, int> func = delegate (int num)
        {
            Console.Write("Inside Func: ");
            return (num * 2);
        };

        act();
        Console.WriteLine(func(4));
    }
}
//Output
Inside Anonymous method
Inside Func: 8
```

Listing 5-16. Pass anonymous method as a method argument

```
using System;

class Program
{
    public static void TestAnonymous(Action act)
    {
        act();
    }
    static void Main(string[] args)
    {
        TestAnonymous(delegate ()
        {
            Console.WriteLine("Pass anonymous method in method's perameter");
        });
    }
}
//output
Pass anonymous method in method's perameter
```

165

Lambda Expression

Lambda expression is a better version of implementing the anonymous method.

Syntax

```
delegate_type delegate_variable = (parameter_list) =>
{
    //Method Body
};
```

OR

```
delegate_type delegate_variable = (parameter_list) => expression;
```

To create a lambda expression, we specify input parameters (if any) on the left side of the lambda operator =>, and put the expression or statement block on other side.

Code Snippet

Listing 5-17. Implement anonymous method with lambda expression

```csharp
using System;

class Program
{
    static void Main(string[] args)
    {
        //Lambda Expression that doesn't return value
        Action act = () =>
        {
            Console.WriteLine("Inside Lambda Expression");
        };

        //Lambda Expression that does have return value
        Func<int, int> func = (int num) =>
        {
            Console.Write("Inside Func: ");
            return (num * 2);
        };

        act();
        Console.WriteLine(func(4));
    }
}

//Output
Inside Anonymous method
Inside Func: 8
```

If an anonymous method's body contains only single statement, then mentioning curly braces "{}" and a return keyword with the value being returned is optional. See the following code snippet:

Listing 5-18. Implement inline anonymous method

```
using System;

class Program
{
    static void Main(string[] args)
    {
        //Lambda Expression that doesn't return value
        Action act = () => Console.WriteLine("Hello World");

        //Lambda Expression that does have return value
        Func<int, int> func = (int num) => num * 2;

        act();
        Console.WriteLine(func(4));
    }
}
//Output
Hello World
Inside Func: 8
```

Lambda expression also gives the ability to not specify a parameter type. Its parameter type will depend on the parameter type of the delegate type which holds its reference. See the following code snippet.

Listing 5-19. Anonymous method without specifying parameter type

```
        //type of name will be string
        Action<string> actName = (name) => Console.WriteLine(name);

        //for single parameter, we can neglect () paranthese
        Action<string> actName2 = name => Console.WriteLine(name);

        Func<int, int> mul = (x) => x * 2;

        actName("Ali");
        actName2("Ali");

        Console.WriteLine(mul(10));
//Output
Ali
Ali
20
```

Listing 5-20. Pass lambda expression on a method parameter

```
using System;

class Program
{
    static void TestLambda(Action act)
    {
        Console.WriteLine("Test Lambda Method");
        act();
    }
    static void Main(string[] args)
    {
        //Pass Lambda expression as parameter
        TestLambda(() =>
        {
            Console.WriteLine("Inside Lambda");
        });
    }
}
//Output
Test Lambda Method
Inside Lambda
```

Event

Event is an action that executes when a specified condition satisfied. It notifies all its subscribers about the action that is going to be executed. For example, when a Windows 10 event was launched, Microsoft notified every customer to update their OS for FREE. So in this case, Microsoft is a publisher who launched (**raised**) an event of Windows 10 and **notified** the customers about it and customers are the **subscribers** of the event and attended (**handled**) the event.

Similarly, in C# event is used in class to provide notifications to clients of that class when something happens to its object. Events are declared using delegates. Therefore, a class that contains the definition of an event and its delegate is called **Publisher**. On the other hand, a class that accepts the event and provides an event handler is called **Subscriber**.

Syntax

```
event delegate_type OnEventName;
```

CodeSnippet

Listing 5-21. Declare an event

```
delegate void DieEventHandler();
class Person
{
    //Declare an event
    public event DieEventHandler Die;
}
```

- **Event** always is a data member of a class or struct. It cannot be declared inside a method.

- It is good naming convention to postfix a custom delegate name with **"EventHandler"** only when it is going to be used with event.

Listing 5-22. Handling and raising an event

```
using System;

class Room
{
    public event Action<object> Alert;

    private int Temperature;
    public int Temperature
    {
        get { return this.Temperature; }
        set
        {
            this.Temperature = value;

            if(Temperature > 60)
            {
                if(Alert != null)
                {
                    Alert (this);
                }
            }
        }
    }
}

class Program
{
    static void Main(string[] args)
    {
        Room myRoom = new Room();

        //Subcribe to an event
        myRoom.Alert += OnAlert;

        //Alert Event will invoke
        myRoom.Temperature = 65;
    }

    private static void OnAlert(object o)
    {
        Room room = (Room)o;
        Console.WriteLine("Shutting down. Room temp is {0}", room.Temperature);
    }
}
```

```
//Output
Shutting down. Room temp is 65
```

- Event always gets subscribed by using +=, for example, **myRoom.Alert += OnAlert;.** It cannot be subscribed by using a single assignment operator.

- Event gets **unsubscribed** by using object.EventName -= MethodName;.

- **myRoom.Temperature = 65;** Alert event will invoke because room's temperature is greater than 60. Hence the condition satisfies and the event shall invoke.

- For naming convention, it is good to prefix a method's name with **On** only when it is going to be used with event, for example, **On**Alert.

- Event shall always be invoked inside a class where it is defined. Unlike delegates, events cannot be invoked outsite the class where they are defined.

Use Built-in Delegates to Implement Events

C# provides some important delegates to implement events. These delegates are useful under certain situations. Some of these delegates are:

- EventHandler
- PropertyChangedEventHandler

EventHandler

EventHandler is a delegate defined in the System namespace. This delegate defines a method of void return type.

1. Its first parameter is of a System.Object type that refers to the instance (where the event was defined) that raises the event.

2. Its second parameter is of an EventArgs type that holds event data. If the event doesn't have any data to pass, the second parameter is simply the value of the EventArgs.Empty field. However, if it does have a value to pass, it will be encapsulated into a derived type of EventArgs.

Syntax

```
namespace System
{
    public delegate void EventHandler(object sender, EventArgs e);
}
```

Code Snippet

Listing 5-23. Handling & Raising an Event by using EventHandler

```
using System;

class Room
{
    public event EventHandler Alert;
```

```
    private int Temperature;
    public int Temperature
    {
        get { return this.Temperature; }
        set
        {
            this.Temperature = value;
            if (this.Temperature > 60)
            {
                if (Alert != null)
                {
                    Alert(this, EventArgs.Empty);
                }
            }
        }
    }
}

class Program
{
    static void Main(string[] args)
    {
        Room room = new Room();
        room.Alert += OnAlert;

        room.Temperature = 75;
    }

    private static void OnAlert(object sender, EventArgs e)
    {
        Room room = (Room)sender;
        Console.WriteLine("Shutting down, Room temp = {0}", room.Temperature);
    }
}
//Output
Shutting down, Room temp = 75
```

Listing 5-24. Pass event data by using EventHandler

```
using System;

class HotelData : EventArgs
{
    public string HotelName { get; set; }
    public int TotalRooms { get; set; }
}
class Room
{
    public event EventHandler Alert;
```

171

```
    private int Temperature;
    public int Temperature
    {
        get { return this.Temperature; }
        set
        {
            this.Temperature = value;
            if (this.Temperature > 60)
            {
                if (Alert != null)
                {
                    HotelData data = new HotelData
                    {
                        HotelName = "5 Star Hotel",
                        TotalRooms = 450
                    };

                    //Pass event data
                    Alert(this, data);
                }
            }
        }
    }
}

class Program
{
    static void Main(string[] args)
    {
        Room room = new Room();
        room.Alert += OnAlert;

        room.Temperature = 75;
    }

    private static void OnAlert(object sender, EventArgs e)
    {
        Room room = (Room)sender;
        HotelData data = (HotelData)e;

        Console.WriteLine("Shutting down, Room temp = {0}", room.Temperature);
        Console.WriteLine("{0} has total {1} rooms", data.HotelName, data.TotalRooms);
    }
}

//Output
Shutting down, Room temp = 75
5 Star Hotel has total 450 rooms
```

PropertyChangedEventHandler

PropertyChangedEventHandler is a delegate defined in the System.ComponentModel namespace. It is used with event to refer a method that will invoke whenever a Property is changed on a component.

Syntax

```
public delegate void PropertyChangedEventHandler(
        object sender,
        PropertyChangedEventArgs e
)
```

PropertyChanged event uses a **PropertyChangedEventHandler** delegate in the **INotifyPropertyChanged** interface. Class, which implements the INotifyPropertyChanged interface, must define the event definition PropertyChanged.

Code Snippet

Listing 5-25. Implement INotifyPropertyChanged

```
using System.ComponentModel;
using System;

public class Person : INotifyPropertyChanged
{
    private string name;
    // Declare the event
    public event PropertyChangedEventHandler PropertyChanged;

    public Person()
    {
    }

    public Person(string value)
    {
        this.name = value;
    }

    public string PersonName
    {
        get { return name; }
        set
        {
            name = value;
            // Call OnPropertyChanged whenever the property is updated
            OnPropertyChanged("PersonName");
        }
    }

    // Create the OnPropertyChanged method to raise the event
    protected void OnPropertyChanged(string name)
    {
        PropertyChangedEventHandler handler = PropertyChanged;
```

```
        if (handler != null)
        {
            handler(this, new PropertyChangedEventArgs(name));
        }
    }
}

class Program
{
    static void Main(string[] args)
    {
        Person person = new Person();

        person.PropertyChanged += OnPropertyChanged;

        person.PersonName = "Ali";
    }

    private static void OnPropertyChanged(object sender, PropertyChangedEventArgs e)
    {
        Person person = (Person)sender;

        Console.WriteLine("Property [{0}] has a new value = [{1}]",
            e.PropertyName, person.PersonName);
    }
}
//Output
Property [PersonName] has a new value = [Ali]
```

Advantages of Events

1. Event encapsulates a delegate; it avoids overwriting of a method reference by restricting the use of assignment = operator.

2. Unlike delegate, event cannot be invoked outside the class, which makes sure event will only invoke when a certain codition satisfies.

Summary

- Delegates are **function pointers**. They store the reference of method(s) inside a delegate object.

- Delegate can be called anywhere in code to invoke method(s).

- Action delegate stores the reference of a method(s) that **doesn't return a value.**

- Func delegate stores the reference of a method(s) that **does return a value.**

- Predicate delegate stores the reference of a method(s) that takes one input parameter and returns a bool value.

- Covariance in delegate is applied on a method's **return type.**

- Contravariance in delegate is applied on a method's **input parameter.**

- Lambda expression is used to create an anonymous method.

- Event encapsulates a delegate and executes referred methods when a certain condition satisfies.

Code Challenges

Challenge1: Student Report Card Application

Write an application that handles a student report card. The application shall save the marks of computer science, math and english. Each subject has a total of 50 marks. If a student obtains at least 75/150 marks, an event will trigger and show a congratulation message on passing the exam. Otherwise, it will display an "F" grade.

Practice Exam Questions

Challenge 1: Invoke an event if a person's name is changed

Create a class Person which has a property "Name". Your task is to invoke an event that checks if a person's name has changed or not and assign a new value to a person name.

Question 1

Suppose you're writing a class that needs a delegate who can refer a method(s) of two input string parameters and return an integer value. Choose the right delegate from the following options.

A)
```
Action<int, string, string>
```

B)
```
Func<string, string, int>
```

C)
```
Predicate<int, string, string>
```

D)
```
EventArgs<int, string, string>
```

Question 2

You are implementing a method that creates an instance of a class named Person. The Person class contains a public event named Die. The following code segment defines the Die event:

```
Public event EventHandler Die;
```

You need to create an event handler for the Die event by using a lambda expression.

A)
```
Person person = new Person();
person.Die = (s, e) => { /*Method Body*/};
```

B)
```
Person person = new Person();
person.Die -= (s, e) => { /*Method Body*/};
```

C)
```
Person person = new Person();
person.Die += (s, e) => { /*Method Body*/};
```

D)
```
Person person = new Person();
person.Die += () => { /*Method Body*/};
```

Question 3

Suppose you're writing a method that has one input string parameter and it returns True if the value of the string input parameter is in upper case. Which of the following delegate(s) will you use to refer this method?

A)   Action<bool, string>

B)   Func<bool, string>

C)   Predicate<string>

D)   EventHandler

Answers

1.   B
2.   C
3.   C

CHAPTER 6

■ ■ ■

Deep Dive into LINQ

LINQ is a feature of C# introduced in .NET 3.5. It lets you work with different types of data and provides an easy and powerful way to write and maintain queries.

In this chapter, we will meet the following objectives:

1. Understand LINQ

2. Understand LINQ Operators

3. Understand LINQ Syntaxes

4. Working with LINQ Queries

5. Working with LINQ to XML

Introduction to LINQ

LINQ (Language Integrated Query) is a way to query different types of data sources that support *IEnumerable<T>* or *IQueryable<T>*. It offers an easy and elegant way to access or manipulate data from a database object, XML document, and in-memory objects.

Why we use LINQ

LINQ usually is more important than other query structures due to its way of working with different data sources. According to **MSDN**:

> *Queries are usually expressed in a specialized query language. Different languages have been developed over time for the various types of data sources, for example SQL for relational databases and XQuery for XML. Therefore, developers have had to learn a new query language for each type of data source or data format that they must support. LINQ simplifies this situation by offering a consistent model for working with data across various kinds of data sources and formats. In a LINQ query, you are always working with objects. You use the same basic coding patterns to query and transform data in XML documents, SQL databases, ADO.NET Datasets, .NET collections, and any other format for which a LINQ provider is available.*

© Ali Asad and Hamza Ali 2017
A. Asad and H. Ali, *The C# Programmer's Study Guide (MCSD)*, DOI 10.1007/978-1-4842-2860-9_6

Types of LINQ

LINQ operates with a different data source and, due to its working with these data sources, it is classified into the following types:

LINQ to Object

LINQ to Object provides the support for interaction with in-memory .NET objects that are implemented by an *IEnumerable<T>* interface. We will use LINQ to object for explanation of LINQ queries.

LINQ to Entities

LINQ to Entities provides the support for interaction with a relational database using an ADO.NET Entity Framework. It's more flexible than LINQ to SQL, but complex. It facilitates different data providers, such as Oracle, My SQL, MS SQL, etc.

LINQ to Dataset

LINQ to Dataset provides the support for interaction with an in-memory cache of data in an easy and faster way.

LINQ to SQL

LINQ to SQL, also known as DLINQ, provides the support for interaction with a relation database as objects.

LINQ to XML

LINQ to XML, also known as XLINQ, provides the support for interaction with XML documents, i.e., to load XML documents, and to perform queries like read, filter, modify, add node, etc., in XML data.

Parallel LINQ

Parallel LINQ, also known as PLINQ, provides the support for Parallel working of LINQ.

We will use LINQ to Object to elaborate the topic "Working with LINQ Queries" and for explicit elaboration of "LINQ to XML" as a topic.

Understanding LINQ Operators

LINQ Operators are actually a set of extension methods. These operators form the LINQ pattern. These operators offer flexibility to query data, such as filtering of data, sorting, etc.

The following LINQ query Operators we will discuss:

1. Filtering Operator

2. Projection Operator

3. Joining Operator

4. Grouping Operator

5. Partition Operator

6. Aggregation

In this topic, we will understand the purpose of these operators in LINQ.

Filtering Operator

Filtering Operator is used to filter a collection or sequence of data based on the predicate or some particular condition. We will discuss the following Filtering operator in this chapter:

Table 6-1. *Filtering Operator*

Operator	Description	Syntax
Where	Filter data based on predicate or condition	Where

Projection Operator

Projection Operator is used when an object is transformed into a new form based on some condition or not. We will discuss the following Projection operator in this chapter:

Table 6-2. *Projection Operator*

Operator	Description	Syntax
Select	Select an obtained result from a data source	Select

Joining Operator

Joining Operator is used to join two or more sequences or collections based on some key and produce a result. We will discuss the following Joining operator in this chapter:

Table 6-3. *Joining Operator*

Operator	Description	Syntax
Join	Join sequence on the basis of a matching key	join..in..on.equals

Grouping Operator

Grouping Operator is used to organize elements based on a given key. We will discuss the following Grouping operator in this chapter:

Table 6-4. *Grouping Operator*

Operator	Description	Syntax
GroupBy	Return a sequence of items in groups as an IGroup<key,element>	group.....by <or> group...by..into <or> GroupBy(<predicate>)

■ **Note** *GroupBy* and *ToLookup* both are Grouping operators and are supported by Query and Method Syntax, except *ToLookup( )* which is just supported in Method Syntax. Query Syntax is discussed in the next topic.

Partition Operator

Partition Operator is used to split up the collection or sequence into two parts and return the remaining part (record) left by the implication of these partition operators. We will discuss the following Partition operator in this chapter:

Table 6-5. *Partition Operator*

Operator	Description	Syntax
Skip	Skip the supplied number of records and return the remaining ones.	Skip<T>(<count>)
Take	Take the supplied number of records and skip the remaining ones.	Take<T>(<count>)

Aggregation

Aggregation means applying aggregate functions on LINQ. Aggregate function is a function that computes a query and returns a single value. We will discuss the following Aggregate function in this chapter:

Table 6-6. *Aggregate Functions*

Operator	Description	Syntax
Average	Take the average of a numeric collection.	Average<T>(<param>)
Count	Count the number of elements in a collection.	Count<T>(<param>)
Max	Return the highest value from the collection of numeric values.	Max<T>(<param>)
Min	Return the highest value from the collection of numeric values.	Min<T>(<param>)
Sum	Compute the sum of numeric values in a collection.	Sum<T>(<param>)

The use of these operators is defined in the "Working with LINQ Queries" topic.

Understand LINQ Syntax

LINQ provides different ways to interact with data sources to query them. It facilitates SQL developers to interact with different data sources for query using C# by giving them LINQ Query syntax and also facilitates C# developers who don't have a strong background in SQL to query the data by giving them the facility of LINQ Method Syntax.

These two ways or syntaxes of LINQ query are:

1. Method Syntax

2. Query Syntax

These two syntaxes of LINQ query are semantically identical but it is assumed that writing a query using Query syntax is easier and simpler.

Method Syntax

LINQ provides Method Syntax to interact with different data sources to query them. Basically, it uses extension methods to query data. It is also known as **Lambda Syntax Query,** as the extension method uses lambda syntax for predicate. It is also called **Fluent** or **Method Extension Syntax**.

Syntax

```
result=DataSource.Operator(<lambda expression>);
```

   OR

```
result=DataSource.Operator(<lambda expression>).Operator(<optional>);
```

where *result* must be of a type of returned data. You can also use *var* type when you are unsure about the returned data type.

■ **Note**   Method Syntax is also called Fluent Syntax because it allows a series of extension methods to call.

Listing 6-1 shows the Method Syntax example.

Code Snippet

Let's take an example of a collection of fruits as:

Listing 6-1. Array of fruits

```
string[] fruits = new string[]
{
    "Apple","Mango","Strawberry","Date",
    "Banana","Avocado","Cherry","Grape",
    "Guava","Melon","Orange","Tomato"
};
```

Now we want to get fruits whose name starts with "A". Therefore, we make a query on *fruits* (data source) to get the required result.

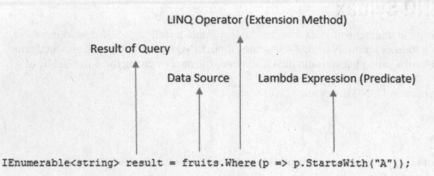

```
IEnumerable<string> result = fruits.Where(p => p.StartsWith("A"));
```

Figure 6-1. *Method Syntax Query*

Now the *result* holds all the fruits whose names start with "A". As the query will return all fruits starting with "A", so it would be a collection of fruits, and variables receiving these collections must be of the same type as the collection's type, which is a collection of strings. We can also further apply another operator (extension method) on the same query to count the number of fruits whose names started with "A".

```
int fruitsLength = fruits.Where(p => p.StartsWith("A")).Count();
```

The *where* operator filters the data source of *fruits* on the basis of the predicate provided (in *where*'s body) and gets all the fruits whose name started with "A" and, furthermore, *Count()* will count all the fruits returned by *Where()* and it returns the number of counted *fruits* to the *fruitsLength* variable.

Query Syntax

LINQ provides another way to perform a query on different data sources, which is Query Syntax. It is the same as using SQL for rational database. It is also known as **Query Comprehension** or **Query Expression Syntax**.

Syntax

```
<Returned result's Type> result = from <range variable> in Data Source
                                  <Query Operators> <lambda expression>
                          <select or groupBy operator> <result>
```

It is same as query in SQL, with little difference. Query in this syntax always ends with a *select* or *group..by* operator and starts with a from keyword.

Code Snippet

Let's take the above example of fruits and perform the same scenarios with this type of query syntax.

To get all the *fruits* whose name started with "A", a query with this type of syntax would be like:

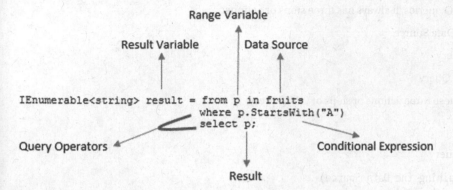

Figure 6-2. *Query Syntax*

where *from p in fruits* is the same as *foreach (var p in fruits)*. Here *p*, which is the Result, will return and store into the *result* variable.

Just as we did in Method Syntax for applying operator (extension method) further to filter out query, we can also do the same on this type of syntax. Taking the same example of counting the number of *fruits* whose name starts with "A", the query would be like:

```
int result = (from p in fruits
         where p.StartsWith("A")
         select p).Count();
```

Working with LINQ Queries

In this topic, we will discuss LINQ queries in detail. We have seen so far the ways to interact with different data sources. Now we will get to know more about LINQ queries and perform important LINQ operators to query data.

C# Features to Support LINQ

Some features are added into C# that support LINQ. Some features are necessary to create a query while some of them are to help you to create a query in a nice and easy way. These features are:

1. Implicitly Typed Variables

2. Object Initializers

3. Anonymous Types

4. Lambda Expressions

5. Extension Methods

These are the language features that make LINQ possible. All the features are explained in earlier chapters.

Parts of Query Operation

When working with LINQ queries, it always has three steps or actions:

1. Obtain the Data Source

2. Create a Query

3. Execute the Query

Listing 6-2 shows these three actions or steps of LINQ query.

Code Snippet

Listing 6-2. Steps of a query

```
//1- First Step (Obtaining the Data Source)
string[] fruits = new string[]
{
    "Apple","Mango","Strawberry","Date",
    "Banana","Avocado","Cherry","Grape",
    "Guava","Melon","Orange","Tomato"
};

//2- Second Step (Creation of Query)
var result = from p in fruits
 select p;

//3-Third Step (Execution of Query)
foreach (var item in result)
{
    Console.WriteLine(item);
}
```

Explanation

As shown from the code, three pain parts or actions of LINQ query are expressed. The details of these steps or actions are discussed below.

Data Source

In above code snippet, data source is an array which implicitly supports *IEnumerable<T>* so it can be queried. For queryable, a data source must be in the memory; that's why if there is an XML data source, then it must be loaded into memory. The data source may be different, i.e., in-memory objects, database objects, or XML data.

Creation of Query

The query tells the information to retrieve or to process whatever it needs to process from the data source. The query can be written with a different type of syntax offered by C#. Different types of LINQ operators can be performed in query to filter, sort, group, and shape data before it returns.

Query Execution

It is important to know that whenever a query is written, query execution is not done. The execution of query varies depending on your choice. By default, the execution of query is deferred until you iterate over the query variable, but you can force it to execute at the time of its creation.

Deferred Execution

The execution of a query when it is written is deferred by default and you cannot get the result of a query until you iterate over the *query variable* or perform aggregate methods (*Max()*, *Min()* and etc) or extension methods (*ToList()*, *ToArray()* and etc) to get the result. This concept is called deferred execution of query. Listing 6-3 shows this concept:

Listing 6-3. Deferred Execution

```
class Person
{
    public int ID { get; set; }
    public string Name { get; set; }
    public string Address { get; set; }
    public decimal Salary { get; set; }
}


    List<Person> persons = new List<Person>()
    {
        new Person() { ID=1,Name="Ali Asad"},
        new Person() { ID=5,Name="Hamza Ali"},

    };

    var query = from p in persons
                select p;

    int count = 0;
    count = query.Count();//Counts 2 records

    persons.Add(new Person() { ID = 3, Name = "John Snow" });

    count = query.Count();//Count 3 records

    Console.WriteLine(query);
```

The code is just counting the number of records. After a query is written, an operation of *Count()* is performed to get some result and, at that time, it will return the number of records, but not at the time the query is written. As there is addition in a data source after a query is written, so it should not have been added in the *count* variable; but this does not happen in deferred execution, as you will not get results until some kind of operation is performed. So again, after addition of a new element in data source, when *Count()* is called, it will get the latest result.

■ **Note**   Deferred Execution returns the latest data.

Immediate Execution

Immediate Execution of a query is the execution at the time a query is written. It forces the LINQ query to execute and returns the results immediately. By performing aggregate method/methods or calling *ToList<T>* or *ToArray<T>* (extension methods) on a query, you can force it to execute immediately. Immediate Execution returns the most recent data (result). Listing 6-4 shows this concept:

Listing 6-4. Force Execution

```
List<Person> persons = new List<Person>()
{
    new Person() { ID=1,Name="Ali Asad"},
    new Person() { ID=5,Name="Hamza Ali"},

};

var query = (from p in persons
             select p).ToList();

persons.Add(new Person() { ID = 3, Name = "John Snow" });

foreach (var item in query)
{
    Console.WriteLine(item.ID + "\t" + item.Name);
}
```

This code will not display the *ID* and *Name* of the last added person (person added after the query is written) as there is an immediate execution of the query by performing the extension method (*ToList()*) on it and, at that time, the written query performed on the *persons* variable contained just two records of *Person,* so the query will return those two persons.

■ **Note**   The execution of the Grouping Operator *GroupBy()* is deferred, whereas the execution of another grouping operator *ToLookup()* is immediate.

LINQ Operators to Query Data

The overview of LINQ standard operators is discussed earlier. The detailed use of those operators in LINQ queries are expressed below. Consider an example of Person with its ID, Name, Address, and Salary, and initialize all the persons using Object Initializer.

Listing 6-5. Initialization of Person object

```
class Person
{
    public int ID { get; set; }
    public string Name { get; set; }
    public string Address { get; set; }
    public decimal Salary { get; set; }
}
```

```
List<Person> persons = new List<Person>()
    {
        new Person() { ID=1,Name="Ali Asad",Address="Pakistan",Salary=10000},
        new Person() { ID=5,Name="Hamza Ali",Address="Pakistan",Salary=20000},
        new Person() { ID=3,Name="John Snow",Address="Canada",Salary=15000},
        new Person() { ID=2,Name="Lakhtey",Address="Pakistan",Salary=5000},
        new Person() { ID=4,Name="Umar",Address="UK",Salary=25000},
        new Person() { ID=6,Name="Mubashar",Address="Pakistan",Salary=8000},
    };
```

Now we will see the implementation of LINQ operators in this scenario.

Filtering Operator

This Operator is used to filter data on the basis of some criteria. Listing 6-6 shows the example of this operator:

Listing 6-6. Filtering Operator

```
IEnumerable<Person> result = from p in persons
                             where p.Name.Length > 4
                             select p;
    foreach (var item in result)
    {
        Console.WriteLine(item.ID + "\t" + item.Name + "\t" + item.Address);
    }
```

Projection Operator

Projection Operator is used to Project a source or an element other than a source based on the transform function. There are basically two Projection Operators: *Select* and *SelectMany*. Listing 6-7 and Listing 6-8 shows the example of these two operators:

Select

Listing 6-7. Select Operator

```
    IEnumerable<string> result = from p in persons
                                 where p.Name.Length > 4
                                 select p.Name;
foreach (var name in result)
{
    Console.WriteLine(name);
}
```

SelectMany

Listing 6-8. SelectMany Operator

```
var result = (from p in persons
            where p.Name.Length > 4
            select new
            {
                PersonID = p.ID,
                PersonName = p.Name,
                    PersonAddress=p.Address
            });

foreach (var item in result)
{
    Console.WriteLine(item.PersonID + "\t" + item.PersonName );
}
```

SelectMany query includes various properties which are not defined in any class and can retrieve the result of a query by accessing these properties of anonymous type. This type of query is called **Anonymous Type Query**.

Joining Operator

Joining Operator is used to join the sequences on the basis of matching keys. Take an example of a Class and its students and the aim is to know which student is of which class.

Listing 6-9 shows the example of this operator:

Listing 6-9. Joining Operator

```
class Class
    {
        public int ClassID { get; set; }
        public string ClassName { get; set; }
    }

    class Student
    {
        public int StudentID { get; set; }
        public string StudentName { get; set; }
        public int ClassID { get; set; }
    }

List<Class> classes = new List<Class>();
classes.Add(new Class { ClassID = 1, ClassName = "BSCS" });
classes.Add(new Class { ClassID = 2, ClassName = "BSSE" });
classes.Add(new Class { ClassID = 3, ClassName = "BSIT" });

List<Student> students = new List<Student>();
students.Add(new Student { ClassID = 1, StudentID = 1, StudentName = "Hamza" });
students.Add(new Student { ClassID = 2, StudentID = 2, StudentName = "Zunaira" });
students.Add(new Student { ClassID = 1, StudentID = 3, StudentName = "Zeeshan" });
```

```
var result = (from std in students
                join clas in classes on std.ClassID equals clas.ClassID
                select new
                {
                    _Student = std.StudentName,
                    _Class = clas.ClassName
                });

foreach (var item in result)
{
    Console.WriteLine(item._Student + "\t" + item._Class);
}
```

Grouping Operator

Grouping Operator is used to organize a sequence of items in groups as an *IGroup<key,element>*. Take a scenario to organize the students by address. Listing 6-10 shows this scenario:

Listing 6-10. Grouping Operator

```
var result = from p in persons
             group p by p.Address;

foreach (var student in result)
{
    Console.WriteLine("Address:" + student.Key);
    foreach (var st in student)
    {
        Console.WriteLine(st.ID + "\t" + st.Name);
    }
}
```

Partition Operator

Partition Operator is used to split up the collection or sequence into two parts and return the remaining one left by the implication of one of these partition operators. It contains *Take* and *Skip* Operators. Listing 6-11 and Listing 6-12 show the example of these two operators:

Take

Listing 6-11. Take Operator

```
var result = (from p in persons
             where p.Address.StartsWith("P")
             select p).Take(2);

foreach (var item in result)
{
    Console.WriteLine(item.ID + "\t" + item.Name);
}
```

Skip

Listing 6-12. Skip Operator

```
var result = (from p in persons
            where p.Address.StartsWith("P")
            select p).Skip(2);

foreach (var item in result)
{
    Console.WriteLine(item.ID + "\t" + item.Name);
}
```

Aggregation

Aggregate function is used to compute a query and return a single value. The following *Listing* of some aggregate functions are shown below:

Average

Listing 6-13. Average function

```
var averageSalary = (from p in persons
                   select p.Salary).Average();

Console.WriteLine(averageSalary);
```

Count

Listing 6-14. Count function

```
var noOfPersons = (from p in persons
                where p.Address.StartsWith("P")
                select p).Count();

Console.WriteLine(noOfPersons);
```

Max

Listing 6-15. Max function

```
var maximumSalary = (from p in persons
                   select p.Salary).Max();

Console.WriteLine(maximumSalary);
```

Min

Listing 6-16. Min function

```
var minimumSalary = (from p in persons
                select p.Salary).Min();

Console.WriteLine(minimumSalary);
```

LINQ to XML

To interact with XML in C#, XML query language is used (which is somehow complex) for developers to perform XML-based operations to XML data (add node, delete node, etc.) in C#, i.e., using XmlDocument, XmlWriter, and XmlReader classes. LINQ solves this type of problem as well as gives the support to interact with XML data using LINQ. You can load the XML document into memory, query, and modify the document in an easy way using LINQ. The main advantage of LINQ to XML is you can use the LINQ with XML in the same manner as you use LINQ with object (LINQ to Object) or other providers.

The namespace System.Xml.Linq provides the necessary classes to interact with XML document/data in C#. Some of the classes are:

1. XAttribute
2. XComment
3. XContainer
4. XDeclaration
5. XDocument
6. XElement
7. XNamespace
8. XNode
9. XObject
10. XText

Some of these classes will be used in the next topics to show different operations performed in XML data using LINQ.

Create XML data

LINQ to XML provides the facility to create an XML document in an easy way. You can use the above mentioned classes to create the XML document/data, i.e., *XElement* (used to create the Element (Node) in XML Document) or *XAttribute* (used to create the attribute of specific element). Listing 6-17 shows how to create XML data using the provided classes along with the help of LINQ.

Code Snippet

Listing 6-17. Creation of XML data

```
XElement rootElement = new XElement("RootElement");
rootElement.Add(new XElement("Name", "Hamza Ali"));
rootElement.Add(new XElement("Age", "21"));
rootElement.Add(new XElement("Address", "Pakistan"));
rootElement.Save("Sample.xml");
```

XElement's constructor is overloaded. It takes the name of the element as well as its value, etc., and you can further add sub-element (as added in code) by using the root or parent element's object.

The output of following code would look like:

```
<RootElement>
  <Name>Hamza Ali</Name>
  <Age>21</Age>
  <Address>Pakistan</Address>
</RootElement>
```

■ **Note** You can also add nodes wherever you want in XML data, i.e., append a node at a specific location in XML document.

Update XML data

Using LINQ to XML, you can update or delete a specific node or node value. Listing 6-18 shows how to update or delete some specific node or its value.

Code Snippet

Listing 6-18. Updating of XML data

```
string xmlData = @" <RootElement>
                        <Name>Hamza Ali</Name>
                        <Age>21</Age>
                        <Address>Pakistan</Address>
                    </RootElement>";

XDocument document = new XDocument();
document = XDocument.Parse(xmlData);
//this will read the Name's Node if the age is 21
var readNode = (from p in document.Descendants()
            where p.Element("Age").Value == "21"
            select p.Element("Name")).FirstOrDefault();
Console.WriteLine("The person's Name having age 21 is: "+ readNode.Value);

//Update Name (Node) with value "Ali Asad"
readNode.ReplaceWith("Ali Asad");

Console.WriteLine("Node's Value is Updated");
//You can now save this Xml in Docuemnt/File
document.Save("Sample.xml");
```

```
//this will delete  Address Node

document.Descendants().Where(s => s.Value == "Pakistan").Remove();

document.Save("Updated Sample 1.xml");
```

You can now read the saved XML document and will get updated contents.

Read XML data

We can also read the whole or specific XML data using LINQ. LINQ provides the lineate way to play with XML. You can read XML data by reading the XML file or XML string.

For example, we have XML in string format:

```
string xmlData = @" <RootElement>
                    <Name>Hamza Ali</Name>
                    <Age>21</Age>
                    <Address>Pakistan</Address>
                </RootElement>";
```

XML data from a file can also be read. The following code shows how to read XML data in string format from a file:

```
 //read xml from file
Stream xmlFromFile = File.Open("Sample.xml", FileMode.Open);
StreamReader reader = new StreamReader(xmlFromFile);
string xmlData= reader.ReadToEnd();
```

Listing 6-19 shows how to read the whole XML data using LINQ.

Code Snippet

Listing 6-19. Read XML data

```
    string xmlData = @" <RootElement>
                        <Name>Hamza Ali</Name>
                        <Age>21</Age>
                        <Address>Pakistan</Address>
                    </RootElement>";

XDocument document = new XDocument();
document = XDocument.Parse(xmlData);
var xml = (from p in document.Elements()
            select p).ToList();
foreach (var item in xml)
{
    Console.WriteLine(item.ToString());
}
```

XML data in string format needs to be parsed in XML document so that LINQ can be applied to perform further LINQ to XML operations. When the string formatted XML data is parsed, you can use its methods or properties. *Elements()* method gets all the elements of an XML document (obtained by parsing string formatted XML data).

We can also search through the XML data to find some specific element or element's value or attribute depending on our scenarios.

Listing 6-20 shows how to read some specific element (a Node) or element's value.

Code Snippet

Listing 6-20. Read Specific Node

```
//this will read the Name's Node
var readNode = (from p in document.Descendants()
         select p.Element("Name")).FirstOrDefault();
Console.WriteLine(readNode);

//this query will read Name (Node)'s Value
var readNodeValue = (from p in document.Descendants()
         select p.Element("Name").Value).FirstOrDefault();
Console.WriteLine(readNodeValue);
```

You can also read the XML on the basis of some criteria, i.e.,

```
//this will read the Name's Node if the age is 21
 var readNode = (from p in document.Descendants()
             where p.Element("Age").Value == "21"
             select p.Element("Name")).FirstOrDefault();

Console.WriteLine(readNode);
```

■ **Note**   In XML, there is a difference between Element and Node. A node can be an element node, an attribute node, a text node, etc., whereas element is everything including its start and end.

Summary

1. LINQ is a feature of C# that lets you work with different types of data and provides an easy and powerful way to write and maintain queries.

2. LINQ Operators operate on sequences and offer flexibility to query data, such as filtering of data, sorting, etc.

3. Aggregate functions are the functions that compute a query and return a single value.

4. LINQ has two basic syntaxes: Query Syntax and Method Syntax.

5. LINQ query consists of three main actions or steps: Obtaining of Data Source, Creation of Query and Execution of Query.

6. There are two types of execution of LINQ query: Deferred and Immediate.

7. LINQ to XML provides the facility to interact with XML data using LINQ query.

Code Challenges

Challenge 1: Perform CRUD Operation using LINQ to Object

Write a console application and make CRUD (Create, Read, Update and Delete) along with Search function. Take Countries as a Data Source (with its properties) and perform LINQ queries on this.

Practice Exam Questions

Question 1

You have the following code:

```
int[] Marks = new int[] { 59, 24, 40, 100, 35, 75, 90 };
```

You need to get all the marks that are greater than 60. Which code snippet should you use?

```
A)  var query = Marks.Take(60);
B)  var query = Marks.Where(s => s > 60);
C)  var query = Marks.Any(s => s > 60);
D)  var query = from p in Marks
                where p > 60
                select p;
```

Question 2

In order to perform a query, a data source must be implemented by:

A) Enumerable or Queryable

B) Enumerable and Queryable

C) IEnumerable or IQueryable

D) IEnumerable and IQueryable

Question 3

You have developed an application which displays the list of students. You need to display 10 students at a time, and so on. Which code snippet would you use for this purpose?

```
A) public static IEnumerable<int> Page(IEnumerable<int> source, int page, int pageSize)
    {
        return source.Skip((page - 1) * pageSize).Take(pageSize);
    }


B) public static IEnumerable<int> Page(IEnumerable<int> source, int page, int pageSize)
    {
        return source.Skip((page - 1) * page).Take(pageSize);
    }
```

```
C) public static IEnumerable<int> Page(IEnumerable<int> source, int page, int pageSize)
    {
        return source.Take((page - 1) * page).Skip(pageSize);
    }
```

```
D) public static IEnumerable<int> Page(IEnumerable<int> source, int page, int pageSize)
    {
        return source.Take((page - 1) * pageSize).Skip(pageSize);
    }
```

Answers

1. B & D
2. C
3. A

CHAPTER 7

■ ■ ■

Manage Object Life Cycle

In .NET, the "life cycle" of an object is the length of time between its creation and its destruction. In this chapter, we'll learn:

1. Fundamentals of Object Life Cycle

2. Fundamentals of .NET Garbage Collection

3. Management of Unmanaged Resources

4. Management of Memory Leaks

Fundamentals of Object Life Cycle

The life cycle of an object is simply the time between when an object is created in memory and when it is destroyed from it. Fundamentally, the life cycle of an object involves the following two steps:

1. Creation of an Object

2. Deletion of an Object

Creation of an Object

We use a **new** keyword to instantiate a new object.

```
Person Obj = new Person();
```

A block of memory is allocated. This block of memory is big enough to hold the object (CLR handles the allocation of memory for managed objects). The block of memory is converted to an object that is initialized in memory (we can control this step by implementing a **constructor**).

Deletion of an Object

We use destruction to reclaim any resources used by that object. The object is cleaned up, for example, by releasing any unmanaged resources used by the application, such as file handles and database connections (we can control this step by implementing a **destructor**). The memory used by the object is reclaimed.

With **Garbage Collection**, the **CLR** handles the release of memory used by managed objects; however, if we use unmanaged objects, we may need to manually release the memory by implementing **IDisposable**.

© Ali Asad and Hamza Ali 2017
A. Asad and H. Ali, *The C# Programmer's Study Guide (MCSD)*, DOI 10.1007/978-1-4842-2860-9_7

Fundamentals of .NET Garbage Collection

In a .NET framework, garbage collection (**GC**) is an automatic memory management service that takes care of the resource cleanup for all managed objects in the managed heap. It has the following benefits:

1. Enables developers to write applications with no worries about having to free memory manually.

2. Allocates memory on a managed heap.

3. Enables memory safety.

4. Reclaims unused objects from memory.

When Garbage Collection Run

Garbage collection is a very expensive process; it doesn't run all the time, it runs when any of following conditions is true:

1. When the system runs out of physical memory.

2. When the GC.Collect method is called manually.

3. When allocated objects in memory need more space.

Garbage Collector and Managed Heap

When garbage collector is initialized by CLR, it stores and manages objects by allocating a segment of memory called managed heap.

Each managed process in .NET has a managed heap. Each thread in a process shares the same managed heap to store and manage objects.

Garbage collector calls a win32 **VirtualAlloc** method to reserve a segment of memory in managed heap. When garbage collector needs to release a segment of memory, it calls a win32 **VirtualFree** method.

When garbage collector runs, it removes dead objects and **reclaims** their memory; it **compacts** the live objects together to preserve their **locality** and makes the managed heap smaller.

The volume of allocated memory objects and the amount of survived memory objects on a managed memory heap determines how many times and for how long a garbage collector will run.

The work of garbage collector depends on how many objects are allocated on a managed heap. For example, if fewer objects are allocated on a managed heap, the less work garbage collector has to do and vice versa. It is wise to not allocate managed objects on a managed heap more than you need. For example, do not allocate an array of 10 bytes when you only needed an array of 5 bytes. Heap is of two kinds: **large object heap** and **small object heap**. A large object heap usually contains objects whose size is 85,000 bytes and larger; these kinds of objects are usually arrays.

Generations

GC supports the concept of generations. It helps to organize short-lived and long-lived objects in a managed heap. There are three generations:

1. Generation 0

2. Generation 1

3. Generation 2

Generation 0

When an object is allocated on heap, it belongs to generation 0. It is the young generation, which contains short-lived objects like temporary variables. If newly allocated objects are larger in size, they will go on the large object heap in a generation 2 collection. GC occurs mostly in generation 0.

Generation 1

When objects survive from a garbage collection of generation 0, they go to generation 1. Objects in generation 1 serve as a buffer between short-lived and long-lived objects.

Generation 2

When objects survive from a garbage collection of generation 1, they go to generation 2. Objects in generation 2 serve as long-lived objects. If objects still survived in generation 2, they remain in generation 2 till they're alive.

Steps Involved in Garbage Collection

1. Suspend all managed threads except for the thread that triggered the garbage collection.

2. Find a list of all live objects.

3. Remove dead objects and reclaim their memory.

4. Compact the survived objects and promote them to an older generation.

Manage Unmanaged Resource

In a .NET framework, garbage collector automatically handle the life cycle of a managed resource. But it can't automatically handle the life cycle of an unmanaged resource; we must explicitly release resources of unmanaged resources to handle them manually. Some common unmanaged resources are: open a file, database connection, or network connection, etc.

Implement IDisposable to Release Unmanaged Resource

Types that use unmanaged resources must implement **IDisposable** to reclaim the unmanaged memory. **Dispose** method is used to release the unmanaged resource from the memory. To prevent garbage collector from calling an *object's finalizer (Destructor)*, dispose method uses **GC.SuppressFinalize** method.

Listing 7-1. IDisposable Definition

```
//Provides a mechanism for releasing unmanaged resources.
public interface IDisposable
{

    void Dispose();
}
```

Dispose method can be called by following two ways:

1. try/finally block

2. using statement

Call Dispose Inside try/finally Block

To dispose an unmanaged resource, dispose method can be called inside a try/finally block.

Listing 7-2. Implement IDisposable

```
using System;
using System.IO;

class myClass : IDisposable
{
    public StreamReader reader;
    public void Dispose()
    {
        //Cleanup unmanaged resources

        if (reader != null)
            reader.Dispose();

        GC.SuppressFinalize(this);
    }
}

class Program
{
    static void Main(string[] args)
    {
        myClass obj = null;
        try
        {
            obj = new myClass();

        }
        finally
        {
            //call dispose method
            obj.Dispose();

        }
    }
}
```

- **StreamReader** is a type that holds an unmanaged resource.

- **GC.SuppressFinalize(this)** prevents a finalizer from executing.

Call Dispose Inside Using Statement

When a type implements an IDisposable interface, its dispose method must call anywhere in the code to reclaim memory of an unmanaged resource. C# introduced using statement, which can only be used with types that implement an IDisposable interface; it automatically calls Dispose method after the **using** statement ends (when control goes out of the using block {}).

Syntax

```
using(type variableName = new type())
{
    //TODO:
}
```

Code Snippet

Listing 7-3. Implement IDisposable

```
using System;
using System.IO;

class myClass : IDisposable
{
    public StreamReader reader;
    public void Dispose()
    {
        //Cleanup unmanaged resources
        if (reader != null)
            reader.Dispose();

        GC.SuppressFinalize(this);

        Console.WriteLine("Disposed");
    }
}

class Program
{
    static void Main(string[] args)
    {
        using (myClass obj = new myClass())
        {

        }
        Console.WriteLine("End");
    }
}
//Output
Disposed
End
```

Disposable Pattern

Disposable pattern is a standard way to implement IDisposable interface. For example, see the following code snippet:

Code Snippet

Listing 7-4. Use Disposable Pattern

```
using System;
using System.IO;

class myClass : IDisposable
{
    // Flag: Check if dispose method has already been called?
    bool disposed = false;
    // type uses unmanaged resource
    StreamReader reader;

    // Public implementation of Dispose pattern callable by consumers.
    public void Dispose()
    {
        Dispose(true);
        GC.SuppressFinalize(this);
    }

    // Protected implementation of Dispose pattern.
    protected virtual void Dispose(bool disposing)
    {
        if (disposed)
            return;

        if (disposing)
        {
            if(reader != null)
            reader.Dispose();
            // Free any other managed objects here.
            //
        }

        // Free any unmanaged objects here.
        //
        disposed = true;
    }

    //Finalizer a.k.a Destructor
    ~myClass()
    {
        Dispose(false);
    }

}
```

Explanation

The above code snippet (Listing 7-4) is the general pattern for implementing the dispose pattern. The bool value *disposed* determines whether the dispose method was invoked. The parameterless Dispose method is used to free unmanaged resources and to indicate that there is a finalizer it doesn't have to run. The *Dispose(bool)* indicates whether the method was called from a parameterless *Dispose* method or it was called from a *finalizer* (destructor).

Memory Leaks

If an application doesn't free the allocated resource on memory after it is finished using it, it will create a memory leak because the same allocated memory is not being used by the application anymore.

If memory leaks aren't managed properly, the system will eventually run out of memory; consequently, the system starts giving a slow response time and the user isn't able to close the application. The only trick is to reboot the computer, period.

Manage Memory Leaks

Memory leaks must be managed. The following are a few common causes of memory leaks:

1. Holding references to managed objects for a long time.

2. Unable to manage unmanaged resource.

3. Static reference.

4. Event with missing unsubscription.

Holding References to Managed Objects for a Long Time

If a managed object's references stay longer than necessary, performance counters can show a steady increase in memory consumption and an OutOfMemoryException may arise. This may happen due to a variable global scope, because GC can't destroy an active variable even though it's not being used by an application anymore.

The developer needs to handle it by telling how long a variable can hold a reference and destroying it after it is no longer needed.

Unable to manage unmanaged resource

Garbage collector cannot release the memory of unmanaged resource. The developer needs to explicitly release resources of unmanaged resources. To do that, the developer needs to implement an IDisposable interface on types which use unmanage resource. Otherwise, memory leaks occur.

Static reference

If an object is referenced by a static field, then it will never be released. Such objects become long-lived. The developer needs to make sure unnecessary static field objects get destroyed when they're finished being used by the application.

Event with missing unsubscription

If an event handler is subscribed (+=), the publisher of the event holds a reference to the subscriber via the event handler delegate (assuming the delegate is an instance method). If the publisher lives longer than the subscriber, then it will keep the subscriber alive even when there are no other references to the subscriber. This is the cause of memory leak when unsubscription of an event isn't defined.

If the developer unsubscribes (-=) from the event with an equal handler, it will remove the handler and manage memory leaks.

Summary

- **Life cycle** of an object is simply a time between when an object is created in memory and when it is destroyed from it.

- **Garbage collection** is an automatic memory management service that takes care of the resource cleanup for all managed objects in the managed heap.

- Managed heap organizes objects into **generations.**

- Temporary and newly allocated objects are moved into **generation 0.**

- Generation 2 is a place where **long-lived** objects are compacted.

- **Dispose** method in IDisposable helps to release memory of an unmanaged resource.

Code Challenges

Challenge 1: Print Html Code of google.com

Write an application that gets the html code of www.google.com and print the html code on the console screen. You have to control the lifetime of unmanaged resources and ensure that they are disposed properly by using Disposable Pattern.

Practice Exam Questions

Question 1

An application includes an object that performs a long-running process. You need to ensure that the garbage collector does not release the object's resources until the process completes.

Which garbage collector method should you use?

- A) WaitForFullGCComplete()

- B) WaitForFullGCApproach()

- C) KeepAlive() // ans

- D) WaitForPendingFinalizers()

Question 2

Suppose you're writing an application that uses unmanaged resource. You've implemented an IDisposable interface to manage the memory of unmanaged resource. When implementing Dispose method, which method should you use to prevent garbage collector from calling the object's finalizer?

A) GC.SuppressFinalize(this)//ans

B) GC.SuppressFinalize(true)

C) GC.WaitForFullGCApproach()

D) GC.WaitForPendingFinalizers()

Question 3

You're instantiating an unmanaged resource; which of the following statements would you use to instantiate an unmanaged resource so that its Dispose method shall always call automatically?

A) if-else{}

B) try/catch

C) using()

D) switch()

Answers

1. C
2. A
3. C

CHAPTER 8

■ ■ ■

Multithreaded, Async & Parallel Programming

In this chapter, we'll learn how to increase the performance of complicated and time-consuming operations of an application by:

1. Working with Threads
2. Working with Task
3. Making UI Responsive (async and await)
4. Using Parallel Programming

Working with Threads

A **thread** controls the flow of an executable program. By default, a program has one thread called **Main Thread**. Main Thread starts when control enters in the Main method and it terminates when Main method returns.

If the execution of a program is controlled by more than one thread, it's called a **Multithreaded Application**. Such a program increases the performance and response time of an application. In C#, the **System.Threading** namespace is used for creating and managing thread(s) in a multithreaded application. A thread can be created by using *System.Threading.Thread* class. A thread can only be manipulated on a method. For example, MainThread needs a Main method to control the flow of a progam.

In a C# progarm, a thread can be found in any of the following states:

Table 8-1. *States of a Thread*

State	Explanation
Unstarted	Thread is created but not started yet
Running	Thread is executing a program
WaitSleepJoin	Thread is blocked due to Wait, Sleep or Join method
Suspended	Thread is suspended
Stopped	Thread is stopped, either normally or aborted

© Ali Asad and Hamza Ali 2017
A. Asad and H. Ali, *The C# Programmer's Study Guide (MCSD)*, DOI 10.1007/978-1-4842-2860-9_8

System.Threading.Thread class contains the following common methods and properties, which are helpful for managing a thread.

Table 8-2. *Common Methods and Properties of Thread Class*

Methods & Properties	Explanation
Start()	Changes state of thread to Running
Join()	Wait for finishing a thread before executing calling thread
Sleep()	Suspend a thread for specified number of miliseconds
Resume()	Resume the execution of suspended thread
Abort()	Terminates the execution of a thread
CurrentThread	Returns a reference of the current thread
IsAlive	Returns true if thread has not been terminated or aborted
IsBackground	Get or set to indicate a thread is or is not a background thread
Name	Get or set name of a thread
ThreadState	Returns the current state of thread

Create and Start a Thread

Inside the *MainThread,* a thread can be initialized by using the Thread class of the System.Threading namespace. A thread can start its execution when a *Thread.Start()* method is called.

Syntax

```
Thread variableName = new Thread(new ThreadStart(voidMethod));
```

- **ThreadStart** is a delegate; it represents the method that executes on a Thread.

OR

```
Thread variableName = new Thread(voidMethod);
```

- We can also reference "voidMethod" to thread without explicitly using "ThreadStart delegate".

Code Snippet

Listing 8-1. Create and start a thread

```
class Program
{

    static void MyThreadMethod()
    {
        Console.WriteLine("Hello From My Custom Thread");
        for (int i = 0; i < 10; i++)
        {
            Console.Write("{0} ", i);
        }
```

```
        Console.WriteLine();
        Console.WriteLine("Bye From My Custom Thread");
    }

    static void Main(string[] args)
    {
        //Instantiate a thread
        Thread myThread = new Thread(new ThreadStart(MyThreadMethod));

        //Start the execution of thread
        myThread.Start();

        //It's the part of Main Method
        Console.WriteLine("Hello From Main Thread");

    }
}

//Output
Hello From Main Thread
Hello From My Custom Thread
1 2 3 4 5 6 7 8 9
Bye From My Custom Thread
```

Explanation

(In Listing 8-1) Main Thread initializes "mythread" and prints "Hello From Main Thread". While "mythread" was being initialized, "myThread.Start()" changes its state to running and then executes "MyThreadMethod()". "Hello From Main Thread" was part of MainThread and displayed on the screen first, because "myThread" was taking time in changing its state to running.

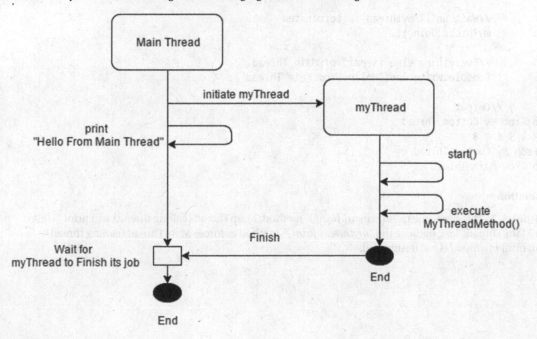

Figure 8-1. *Workflow of MainThread and myThread*

Thread.Join()

Thread.Join() method is used to keep the *calling thread* on wait until the *called thread* has not been stopped or its execution is terminated.

Thread.Join() changes the state of the calling thread to *ThreadState.WaitSleepJoin*. Also, the Thread.Join() cannot be invoked on a thread that is not in the *ThreadState.Unstarted* state.

Code Snippet

Listing 8-2. Use Thread.Join() to hold the execution of Main Thread

```
static void MyThreadMethod()
{
    Console.WriteLine("Hello From My Custom Thread");
    for (int i = 0; i < 10; i++)
    {
        Console.Write("{0} ", i);
    }
    Console.WriteLine();
    Console.WriteLine("Bye From My Custom Thread");
}

static void Main(string[] args)
{
    //Instantiate a thread
    Thread myThread = new Thread(new ThreadStart(MyThreadMethod));

    //Start the execution of thread
    myThread.Start();

    //Wait until mythread is terminated
    myThread.Join();

    //Everything else is part of Main Thread.
    Console.WriteLine("Hello From Main Thread");

} //Output
Hello From My Custom Thread
1 2 3 4 5 6 7 8 9
Bye From My Custom Thread
Hello From Main Thread
```

Explanation

(In Listing 8-2) This time, due to "*mythread.Join()*" method, MainThread (calling thread) will print "Hello From Main Thread" last, because the "*mythread.join()*" method enforces MainThread (calling thread) to wait until *mythread* is not terminated.

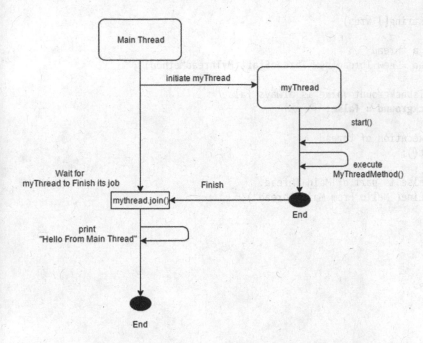

Figure 8-2. *Join method lets MainThread wait until myThread finishes*

Foreground & Background Thread

There are two kinds of threads in C#, i.e., **Foreground** thread and **Background** thread. By default, in C# all threads are initialized as *foreground thread*. An application cannot terminate its execution until all its foreground threads are completed.

A **background thread** is almost identical to a foreground thread. The one difference is that, if the *Main Thread* has completed its execution and the *background thread* is the only thread remaining in the application, the Main Thread **will terminate the application and not wait for the background thread to be completed**.

Code Snippet

Listing 8-3. Create and start a foreground thread

```
static void MyThreadMethod()
{
    Console.WriteLine("Hello From My Custom Thread");
    for (int i = 0; i < 10; i++)
    {
        Console.Write("{0} ", i);
    }
    Console.WriteLine();
    Console.WriteLine("Bye From My Custom Thread");
}
```

```
static void Main(string[] args)
{
    //Instantiate a thread
    Thread myThread = new Thread(new ThreadStart(MyThreadMethod));

    //by default Isbackgrount value is always false
    myThread.IsBackground = false;

    //Start the execution of thread
    myThread.Start();

    //Everything else is part of Main Thread.
    Console.WriteLine("Hello From Main Thread");

}

//Output
Hello From Main Thread
Hello From My Custom Thread
1 2 3 4 5 6 7 8 9
Bye From My Custom Thread
```

Explanation

(In Listing 8-3) By default, the value of *"Thread.IsBackground = false;"*, which makes it a foreground thread. Even though the MainThread has no other command after printing "Hello From Main Thread", it won't terminate until the foreground thread *"mythread"* is completed or terminated.

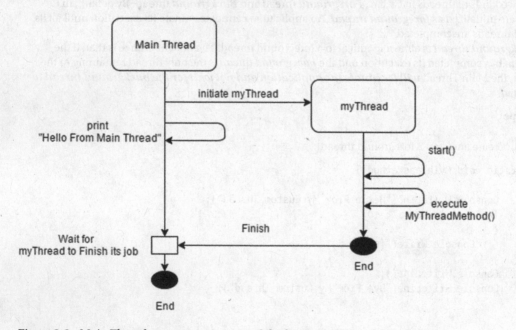

Figure 8-3. *Main Thread cannot terminate until the foreground thread terminates*

Code Snippet

Listing 8-4. Create and start a background thread

```
static void MyThreadMethod()
{
    Console.WriteLine("Hello From My Custom Thread");
    for (int i = 0; i < 10; i++)
    {
        Console.Write("{0} ", i);
    }
    Console.WriteLine();
    Console.WriteLine("Bye From My Custom Thread");
}

static void Main(string[] args)
{
    //Instantiate a thread
    Thread myThread = new Thread(new ThreadStart(MyThreadMethod));

    //now the thread become a background thread
    myThread.IsBackground = true;

    //Start the execution of thread
    myThread.Start();

    //Everything else is part of Main Thread.
    Console.WriteLine("Hello From Main Thread");

}
//Output
Hello From Main Thread
```

Explanation

(In Listing 8-4) *"Mythread"* is now a background thread because its ***Background property value is set to true***, which ***means MainThread terminates soon after it (Mythread) executes its last command to print*** "Hello From Main Thread" and won't wait for "*mythread*" to be completed or terminated.

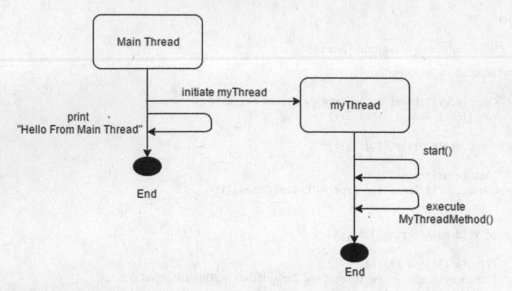

Figure 8-4. *Main Thread won't wait for background threads*

Pass a Parameterize Method to a Thread

What if we want a parameterize method to be executed on a separate thread? To do this, we need a "ParameterizedThreadStart" delegate inside the constructor of a Thread. It holds a reference of the method that takes an object as an input.

Code Snippet

Listing 8-5. Pass an argument to a thread method

```
static void MyThreadMethod(object number)
{
    int count = (int)number;
    Console.WriteLine("Hello From My Custom Thread");
    for (int i = 0; i < count; i++)
    {
        Console.Write("{0} ", i);
    }
    Console.WriteLine();
    Console.WriteLine("Bye From My Custom Thread");
}

static void Main(string[] args)
{
    //Instantiate a thread
    Thread myThread = new Thread(
        new ParameterizedThreadStart(MyThreadMethod));

    //Start the execution of thread
    myThread.Start(5);
```

```
        //Everything else is part of Main Thread.
        Console.WriteLine("Hello From Main Thread");


    }
//Output
Hello From Main Thread
Hello From My Custom Thread
1 2 3 4
Bye From My Custom Thread
```

Explanation

"ParameterizedThreadStart" is a delegate; it holds a reference of a method inside the Thread's constructor that takes an object as an input.

"Mythread.Start(5)," starts the execution of mythread and also passes *"5"* value as an object input to *"MyThreadMethod".*

Thread.Sleep(milliseconds)

It is used to suspend the execution of a current thread for a specified number of milliseconds.

Code Snippet

Listing 8-6. Block the execution of a thread for a specified period of time

```
static void MyThreadMethod()
{
    Console.WriteLine("Start of MyThread");
    for (int i = 0; i < 5; i++)
    {
        //suspend the thread for 100 milliseconds
        Thread.Sleep(100);
        Console.Write("{0} ", i);
    }
    Console.WriteLine();
    Console.WriteLine("End of MyThread");
}

static void Main(string[] args)
{
    Console.WriteLine("Start of Main Thread");

    //Instantiate a thread
    Thread myThread = new Thread(new ThreadStart(MyThreadMethod));

    //Start the execution of thread
    myThread.Start();

    //Main Thread wait until mythread terminated
    myThread.Join();
```

215

```
            Console.WriteLine("Main Method");
            for (int i = 0; i < 5; i++)
            {
                //Suspend the thread for 100 milliseconds
                Thread.Sleep(100);
                Console.Write("{0} ", i);
            }
            Console.WriteLine();
            Console.WriteLine("End of Main Thread");


        }
//Output
Start of Main Thread
Start of MyThread
1 2 3 4
End of MyThread
Main Method
1 2 3 4
End of Main Thread
```

ThreadPriority

Threadpriority defines how much CPU time a thread will have for execution. When a thread is created, initially it is assigned with Normal priority. A thread can be assigned with any of the following priorities:

Table 8-3. *Thread Priority Enums*

Priority	Explanation
High	Thread will schedule before threads with any priority
AboveNormal	Thread will schedule before Threads with Normal priority
Normal	Will schedule before Threads with BelowNormal priority
BelowNormal	Thread will schedule before Threads with Lowest priority
Lowest	Will schedule after Threads with BelowNormal priority

Code Snippet

Listing 8-7. Prioritize a thread

```
static bool stop = false;

static void Main()
{
    Thread thread1 = new Thread(new ThreadStart(myMethod));
    thread1.Name = "Thread 1";
    thread1.Priority = ThreadPriority.Lowest;
```

```
        Thread thread2 = new Thread(new ThreadStart(myMethod));
        thread2.Name = "Thread 2";
        thread2.Priority = ThreadPriority.Highest;

        Thread thread3 = new Thread(new ThreadStart(myMethod));
        thread3.Name = "Thread 3";
        thread3.Priority = ThreadPriority.BelowNormal;

        thread1.Start();
        thread2.Start();
        thread3.Start();

        Thread.Sleep(10000);
        stop = true;

    }

    private static void myMethod()
    {

        //Get Name of Current Thread
        string threadName = Thread.CurrentThread.Name.ToString();
        //Get Priority of Current Thread
        string threadPriority = Thread.CurrentThread.Priority.ToString();

        uint count = 0;

        while(stop != true)
        {
            count++;
        }

        Console.WriteLine("{0,-11} with {1,11} priority " +
            "has a count = {2,13}", Thread.CurrentThread.Name,
            Thread.CurrentThread.Priority.ToString(),
            count);
    }
//Output
Thread 3 with BelowNormal Priority has a count = 3990463114
Thread 2 with AboveNormal Priority has a count = 4151716090
Thread 1 with Normal Priority has a count = 4139585342
```

Explanation

The above example (Listing 8-7) shows the CPU time of a thread depends upon its priority. In the example, Thread 2 has a priority above the others, hence it increments more count value by using more CPU time. While Thread 3 has the least priority, hence it incremenents count value less than the other threads.

ThreadStatic

ThreadStatic is an attribute used on top of a static field to make its value unique (local) for each thread.

Code Snippet

Listing 8-8. Use ThreadStatic

```
using System;
using System.Threading;

class Program
{
    [ThreadStatic]
    static int _count = 0;

    static void Main()
    {
        Thread threadA = new Thread(() =>
        {
            for (int i = 0; i < 10; i++)
            {
                Console.WriteLine("ThreadA _count = {0} ", _count++);
            }
        });

        Thread threadB = new Thread(() =>
        {
            for (int i = 0; i < 10; i++)
            {
                Console.WriteLine("ThreadB _count = {0} ", _count++);
            }
        });

        threadA.Start();
        threadB.Start();

    }
}
//Output
ThreadA _count = 0
ThreadA _count = 1
ThreadA _count = 2
ThreadA _count = 3
ThreadA _count = 4
ThreadA _count = 5
ThreadA _count = 6
ThreadA _count = 7
ThreadA _count = 8
ThreadA _count = 9
ThreadB _count = 0
ThreadB _count = 1
```

```
ThreadB _count = 2
ThreadB _count = 3
ThreadB _count = 4
ThreadB _count = 5
ThreadB _count = 6
ThreadB _count = 7
ThreadB _count = 8
ThreadB _count = 9
```

Explanation

In the above code snippet (Listing 8-8), both threads have their unique local values of _count. Both threads have incremented the value of _count *10* times. The end result isn't 19, because *each thread has incremented the value of its local copy of the _count variable*.

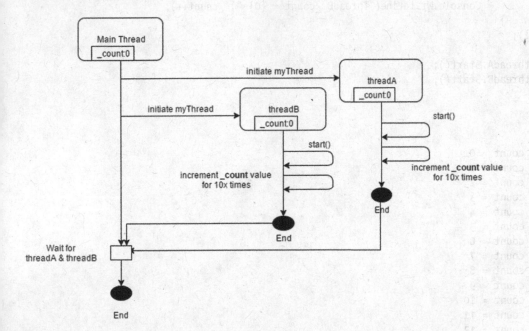

Figure 8-5. *Each thread has its own copy of the _count variable*

Code Snippet

Listing 8-9. Share a common resource to multiple threads

```
using System;
using System.Threading;

class Program
{
    static int _count = 0;
```

```
static void Main()
{
    Thread threadA = new Thread(() =>
    {
        for (int i = 0; i < 10; i++)
        {
            Console.WriteLine("ThreadA _count = {0} ", _count++);
        }
    });

    Thread threadB = new Thread(() =>
    {
        for (int i = 0; i < 10; i++)
        {
            Console.WriteLine("ThreadB _count = {0} ", _count++);
        }
    });

    threadA.Start();
    threadB.Start();

}
}
//Output
ThreadA _count = 0
ThreadA _count = 1
ThreadA _count = 2
ThreadA _count = 3
ThreadA _count = 4
ThreadA _count = 5
ThreadA _count = 6
ThreadA _count = 7
ThreadA _count = 8
ThreadA _count = 9
ThreadB _count = 10
ThreadB _count = 11
ThreadB _count = 12
ThreadB _count = 13
ThreadB _count = 14
ThreadB _count = 15
ThreadB _count = 16
ThreadB _count = 17
ThreadB _count = 18
ThreadB _count = 19
```

Explanation

In above code snippet (Listing 8-9), the _count variable didn't mark with the *"ThreadStatic"* attribute, hence both threads shared the same *_count* variable. When one thread increments the value of *_count*, it **affects the value of the _count variable which is used in the other thread**.

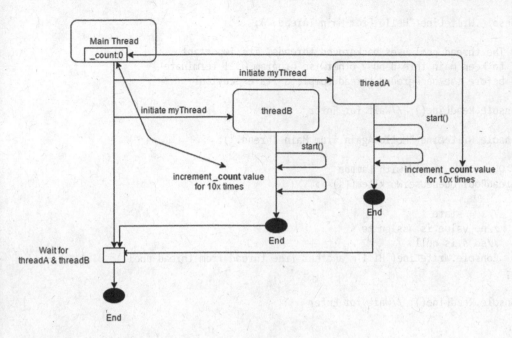

Figure 8-6. *Each thread share a common _count*

Thread Pool

The cost of instantiating a managed thread is higher than reusing a free thread. In .NET, a ***thread pool*** is helpful to reuse the *free threads*. *A thread pool is a collection of background threads* created by a *system* and are available to *perform any task* when required.

When a program requires an extra thread, it is more efficient to use available free threads from a thread pool because it can save the cost of creating a thread. And when a thread completes its execution, it can go back to the threadpool so other programs can reuse the same thread again.

.NET has implemented its own definition of thread pool through the ThreadPool class. It has a method, QueueUserWorkItem, which helps to queue the execution of available threads in a thread pool.
Code Snippet

Listing 8-10. Reuse a thread from ThreadPool

```
using System;
using System.Threading;

class Program
{

    static void Main()
    {
        // Queue the thread.
        ThreadPool.QueueUserWorkItem(new WaitCallback(ThreadProc));
```

```
        Console.WriteLine("Hello From Main Thread.");

        // The thread pool uses background threads, its important
        // to keep main thread busy otherwise program will terminate
        // before the background thread complete its execution

        Console.ReadLine(); //Wait for Enter

        Console.WriteLine("Hello Again from Main Thread.");

        // Queue the thread with Lambda
        ThreadPool.QueueUserWorkItem((s) =>
        {
            //s = state
            //no value is assign to s
            //so s is null
            Console.WriteLine("Hi I'm another free thread from thread pool");
        });

        Console.ReadLine(); //Wait for Enter
    }

    // This thread procedure performs the task.
    static void ThreadProc(Object stateInfo)
    {
        // No state object was passed to QueueUserWorkItem, so
        // stateInfo is null.
        Console.WriteLine("Hello from the thread pool.");
    }
}
//Output
Hello From Main Thread.
Hello from the thread pool.

Hello Again from Main Thread.
Hi I'm another free thread from thread pool.
```

Explanation

- **WaitCallback** is a delegate that represents a callback method to be executed by a thread pool thread. The method that it represents takes an object.

- **ThreadPool.QueueUserWorkItem** queues an available background thread for execution.

- **Console.ReadLine** keeps the main thread on wait until the user presses "Enter".

Limitation of Thread Pool

- It is hard to tell when a thread of a threadpool has finished its execution.

- There is no "Start" method, so we cannot tell when a thread of a thread pool has started its execution because it is being managed by the system.

- It can't manage a thread which returns a value.

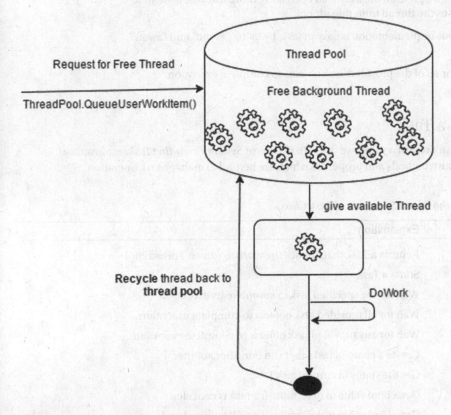

Request for Free Thread

ThreadPool.QueueUserWorkItem()

Thread Pool

Free Background Thread

give available Thread

Recycle thread back to thread pool

DoWork

Figure 8-7. Lifecycle of threads of thread-pool

Working with Tasks

Task is an important part of the Task Parallel Library. It is a lightweight object which asynchronously manages the unit of work. Task doesn't create new threads. Instead it efficiently manages the threads of a threadpool. Tasks are executed by TaskScheduler, which queues tasks onto threads.

Task provides the following powerful features over thread and threadpool.

1. Task allows you to return a result.

2. It gives better programmatical control to run and wait for a task.

3. It reduces the switching time among multiple threads.

4. It gives the ability to chain multiple tasks together and it can execute each task one after the other by using ContinueWith().

5. It can create a parent/child relationship when one task is started from another task.

6. Task can cancel its execution by using cancellation tokens.

7. Task leaves the CLR from the overhead of creating more threads; instead it implicitly uses the thread from threadpool.

8. Asynchronous implementation is easy in task, by using "async" and "await" keywords.

9. Task waits for all of the provided Task objects to complete execution.

Create and Run a Task

To create a task that doesn't return a value, we use a *Task* class of *System.Threading.Tasks* namespace. It contains some important methods and properties which are helpful to manage task operation.

Table 8-4. Common Methods and Properties of Task Class

Methods & Properties	Explanation
Run()	Returns a Task that queues the work to run on ThreadPool
Start()	Starts a Task
Wait()	Wait for the specified task to complete its execution
WaitAll()	Wait for all provided task objects to complete execution
WaitAny()	Wait for any provided task objects to complete execution
ContinueWith()	Create a chain of tasks that run one after another
Status	Get the status of current task
IsCanceled	Get a bool value to determine if a task is canceled
IsCompleted	Get a bool value to determine if a task is completed
IsFaulted	Gets if the Task is completed due to an unhandled exception.
Factory	Provide factory method to create and configure a Task

Task is an important part of asynchronous programming and it executes on a thread pool thread. Usually, a lambda expression is used to specify the work that the Task has to perform.

Syntax

```
Task mytask = new Task(actionMethod);
```

- **actionMethod** is a method that has a return type of void and takes no input parameter; in other words, there is an "Action" delegate in the parameter of the Task constructor.

- Task has a total of **8** overloaded constructors, but usually we work with the first overloaded constructor that has an "Action" delegate in its input parameter.

Code Snippet

Listing 8-11. Create and start a Task

```
using System;
using System.Threading.Tasks;

class Program
{

    static void Main()
    {
        //initialize mytask and assign
        //a unit of work in form of 'myMethod()'
        Task myTask = new Task(myMethod);
        myTask.Start();// Start the execution of mytask

        myTask.Wait(); //Wait until mytask finish its job

        //It's the part of Main Method
        Console.WriteLine("Bye From Main Thread");

    }

    private static void myMethod()
    {
        Console.WriteLine("Hello From My Task");
        for (int i = 0; i < 10; i++)
        {
            Console.Write("{0} ", i);
        }
        Console.WriteLine();
        Console.WriteLine("Bye From My Task");

    }
}
//Output
Hello From My Task
1 2 3 4 5 6 7 8 9
Bye From My Task
Bye From Main Thread
```

Explanation

We know Task performs on the background threads of a thread pool. Therefore (in Listing 8-11), it's important to write a *"wait()"* method, otherwise the program will shut down as soon the *Main Thread* finishes its exeeution.

Code Snippet

Listing 8-12. Reuse a Task by using Task.Factory.StartNew

```
using System;
using System.Threading.Tasks;

class Program
{

    static void Main()
    {
        //initialize and Start mytask and assign
        //a unit of work in the body of lambda exp
        Task mytask = Task.Factory.StartNew(new Action(myMethod));
        mytask.Wait(); //Wait until mytask finish its job

        //It's the part of Main Method
        Console.WriteLine("Hello From Main Thread");

    }

    static void myMethod()
    {
        Console.WriteLine("Hello From My Task");
        for (int i = 0; i < 10; i++)
        {
            Console.Write("{0} ", i);
        }
        Console.WriteLine();
        Console.WriteLine("Bye From My Task");
    }

}
//Output
Hello From My Task
1 2 3 4 5 6 7 8 9
Bye From My Task
Hello From Main Thread
```

Explanation

(In Listing 8-12) Create a task and start it immediately by calling the **StartNew** method. In .NET 4.0 it is preferable to use Task.Factory.StartNew for creating and starting a task because it saves performance cost, whereas Task(...).Start() consumes more performance cost for creating and starting a task.

Code Snipppet

Listing 8-13. Reuse a task by using Task.Run

```
using System;
using System.Threading.Tasks;

class Program
{

    static void Main()
    {
        //initialize and Run mytask and assign
        //a unit of work in form of 'myMethod()'
        Task mytask = Task.Run(new Action(myMethod));

        mytask.Wait(); //Wait until mytask finish its job

        //It's the part of Main Method
        Console.WriteLine("Hello From Main Thread");

    }

    private static void myMethod()
    {
        Console.WriteLine("Hello From My Task");
        for (int i = 0; i < 10; i++)
        {
            Console.Write("{0} ", i);
        }
        Console.WriteLine();
        Console.WriteLine("Bye From My Task");

    }
}
//Output
Hello From My Task
1 2 3 4 5 6 7 8 9
Bye From My Task
Bye From Main Thread
```

Explanation

(In Listing 8-13) Task.Run() returns and runs a task by assigning a unit of work in the form of a method ("myMethod"). In .NET 4.5, it is preferable to use Task.Run because it manages Task more efficiently than Task.Factory.StartNew.

Code Snippet

Listing 8-14. Use Lambda Expression to use Task.Run

```
using System;
using System.Threading.Tasks;

class Program
{

    static void Main()
    {
        //initialize and Run mytask and assign
        //a unit of work in the body of lambda exp
        Task myTask = Task.Run(()=>
        {
            Console.WriteLine("Hello From My Task");
            for (int i = 0; i < 10; i++)
            {
                Console.Write("{0} ", i);
            }
            Console.WriteLine();
            Console.WriteLine("Bye From My Task");

        });

        myTask.Wait(); //Wait until mytask finish its job

        //It's the part of Main Method
        Console.WriteLine("Hello From Main Thread");

    }

}
//Output
Hello From My Task
1 2 3 4 5 6 7 8 9
Bye From My Task
Bye From Main Thread
```

Explanation

(In Listing 8-14) *()=>{}* lambda expression is used to assign an anonymous method to *Task.Run()*. *myTask* will then execute the anonymous method on a separate task.

■ **Note**   Most commonly, lambda expression is used to assign a unity of work in Task.Run.

Create and Run a Task<Result>

Task<Result> is used with such asynchronous operations that return a value. Task<Result> class is found in the System.Threading.Task namespace and it inherits from Task class.

Syntax

```
Task<TResult> mytask = new Task<TResult>(funcMethod);
```

- **funcMethod** is a method that has a return type of TResult type and takes no input parameter; in other words, there is a "Func<TResult>" delegate in the parameter of Task constructor.

Code Snippet

Listing 8-15. Get a value from a method by using Task<T>

```
using System;
using System.Threading;
using System.Threading.Tasks;

class Program
{

    static void Main()
    {
        Task<int> myTask = new Task<int>(myMethod);
        myTask.Start(); //start myTask

        Console.WriteLine("Hello from Main Thread");

        //Wait the main thread until myTask is finished
        //and returns the value from myTask operation (myMethod)
        int i = myTask.Result;

        Console.WriteLine("myTask has a return value = {0}", i);
        Console.WriteLine("Bye From Main Thread");
    }

    static int myMethod()
    {
        Console.WriteLine("Hello from myTask<int>");
        Thread.Sleep(1000);

        return 10;
    }

}//Output
Hello from Main Thread
Hello from myTask<int>
myTask has a return value = 10
Bye From Main Thread
```

Explanation

- **Task<int>** tells the task operation to return an integer value.

- **myTask.Result;** is a property that returns a value when the task gets completed and blocks the execution of a calling thread (in this case, its main thread) until the task finishes its execution.

Code Snippet

Listing 8-16. Use Task<T>.Factory.StartNew to return a value from a Task method

```
using System;
using System.Threading;
using System.Threading.Tasks;

class Program
{

    static void Main()
    {
        Task<int> myTask = Task<int>.Factory.StartNew<int>(myMethod);

        Console.WriteLine("Hello from Main Thread");

        //Wait the main thread until myTask is finished
        //and returns the value from myTask operation (myMethod)
        int i = myTask.Result;

        Console.WriteLine("myTask has a return value = {0}", i);
        Console.WriteLine("Bye From Main Thread");
    }

    static int myMethod()
    {
        Console.WriteLine("Hello from myTask<int>");
        Thread.Sleep(1000);

        return 10;
    }
}
//Output
Hello from Main Thread
Hello from myTask<int>
myTask has a return value = 10
Bye From Main Thread
```

Explanation

(In Listing 8-16) Create a Task<T> and start it immediately by calling the **StartNew** method. In .NET 4.0 it is preferable to use Task<T>.Factory.StartNew for creating and starting a task because it saves performance cost, whereas Task<T>(...).Start() consumes more performance cost for creating and starting a task.

Code Snippet

Listing 8-17. Use Task.Run<int> to retun a value from Task's method

```
using System;
using System.Threading;
using System.Threading.Tasks;

class Program
{

    static void Main()
    {
        Task<int> myTask = Task.Run<int>(new Func<int>(myMethod));

        Console.WriteLine("Hello from Main Thread");

        //Wait for the main thread until myTask is finished
        //and return the value from myTask operation (myMethod)
        int i = myTask.Result;

        Console.WriteLine("myTask has a return value = {0}", i);
        Console.WriteLine("Bye From Main Thread");
    }

    static int myMethod()
    {
        Console.WriteLine("Hello from myTask<int>");
        Thread.Sleep(1000);

        return 10;
    }

}
//Output
Hello from Main Thread
Hello from myTask<int>
myTask has a return value = 10
Bye From Main Thread
```

Explanation

- **Task.Run<int>()** takes a Func<int> delegate to reference a method that returns an integer value. This method gets executed by a task and a value gets returned by using the **Result** property.

Code Snippet

Listing 8-18. Use Lambda Expression to return a value from a Task's method

```
using System;
using System.Threading;
using System.Threading.Tasks;

class Program
{
```

231

```
static void Main()
{
    Task<int> myTask = Task.Run<int>(()=>
    {
        Console.WriteLine("Hello from myTask<int>");
        Thread.Sleep(1000);
        return 10;
    });

    Console.WriteLine("Hello from Main Thread");

    //Wait for the main thread until myTask is finished
    //and return the value from myTask operation
    int i = myTask.Result;

    Console.WriteLine("myTask has a return value = {0}", i);
    Console.WriteLine("Bye From Main Thread");
}

}

//Output
Hello from Main Thread
Hello from myTask<int>
myTask has a return value = 10
Bye From Main Thread
```

Explanation

(In Listing 8-18) Lambda expression can be used to define a unit of work for Task<int>. And, inside lambda expression, its return value must match with the type of Task<T>.

Code Snippet

Listing 8-19. Use var & Task.Run<T> with Lambda Expression to return a value from Task's method

```
using System;
using System.Threading;
using System.Threading.Tasks;

class Program
{

    static void Main()
    {
        var myTask = Task.Run<int>(()=>
        {
            Console.WriteLine("Hello from myTask<int>");
            Thread.Sleep(1000);

            return 10;
        });
```

```
        Console.WriteLine("Hello from Main Thread");

        //Wait for the main thread until myTask is finished
        //and return the value from myTask operation
        int i = myTask.Result;

        Console.WriteLine("myTask has a return value = {0}", i);
        Console.WriteLine("Bye From Main Thread");
    }

}
//Output
Hello from Main Thread
Hello from myTask<int>
myTask has a return value = 10
Bye From Main Thread
```

Explanation

In the above code snippet (Listing 8-19) Task<int> didn't define; instead, var keyword is used. Var keyword detects the type of Task<T> by looking at the type of Task<T> written on the right side (which in this case is Task<int>).

Code Snippet

Listing 8-20. Use var & Task.Run with Lambda Expression to return a value from Task's method

```
using System;
using System.Threading;
using System.Threading.Tasks;

class Program
{

    static void Main()
    {
        var myTask = Task.Run(()=>
        {
            Console.WriteLine("Hello from myTask<int>");
            Thread.Sleep(1000);

            return 10;
        });

        Console.WriteLine("Hello from Main Thread");

        //Wait for the main thread until myTask is finished
        //and return the value from myTask operation
        int i = myTask.Result;

        Console.WriteLine("myTask has a return value = {0}", i);
        Console.WriteLine("Bye From Main Thread");
    }

}
```

```
//Output
Hello from Main Thread
Hello from myTask<int>
myTask has a return value = 10
Bye From Main Thread
```

Explanation

In the above code snippet (Listing 8-20) Task<int> didn't define on both sides. Instead, var keyword is used. Var keyword detects the type of Task<T> by looking in the return value of lambda expression.

Wait for One or More Task

Tasks asynchronously runs on a thread pool thread. Thread pool contains background threads, so when task is running, the main thread may terminate the application before the task is finished. To synchronize the execution of the main thread and the asynchronous tasks, we use a **Wait** method.

Wait method blocks the execution of a *calling thread* until the execution of a specified task has completed.

The following are important wait methods which help synchronize a main thread with Tasks.

1. Task.Wait()

2. Task.Wait(milliseconds)

3. Task.WaitAll()

4. Task.WaitAll(milliseconds)

5. Task.WaitAny

Task.Wait( )

To wait for a single task to complete, you can call its Task.Wait method. It blocks the calling thread until the specified task completes its execution.

Code Snippet

Listing 8-21. Use Task.Wait to hold the execution of Main Thread

```
using System;
using System.Threading;
using System.Threading.Tasks;

class Program
{

    static void Main()
    {
        Task myTask = Task.Run(() =>
        {
            Thread.Sleep(1000);
            Console.WriteLine("Task completed after 1 Sec");
        });
```

234

```
        Console.WriteLine("Hello From Main Thread");
        myTask.Wait();// wait until myTask get completed

        Console.WriteLine("Bye From Main Thread");
    }

}
//Output
Hello From Main Thread
Task completed after 1 Sec
Bye From Main Thread
```

Task.Wait(milliseconds)

Task.Wait(milliseconds) method blocks the execution of a calling thread until the specified task finishes or a timeout interval elapses.

Code Snippet

Listing 8-22. Use Task.Wait(millisec) to wait the Main Thread for a specific time

```
using System;
using System.Threading;
using System.Threading.Tasks;

class Program
{
    static void Main()
    {
        Task myTask = Task.Run(() =>
        {
            //Wait for 2 Sec
            Thread.Sleep(2000);
            Console.WriteLine("myTask completed after 2 Sec");
        });

        Task myTask2 = Task.Run(() =>
        {
            //Wait for half sec
            Thread.Sleep(500);
            Console.WriteLine("myTask2 completed after half Sec");
        });

        myTask.Wait(1000);// wait for 1 sec
        Console.WriteLine("Hello from Main Thread");

        myTask2.Wait(1000);// wait for 1 sec
        Console.WriteLine("Hello from Main Thread, again");

        Console.WriteLine("By From Main Thread");
    }

}
```

```
//Output
myTask2 completed after half Sec
Hello from Main Thread
Hello from Main Thread, again
By From Main Thread
```

Explanation

- **myTask.Wait(1000)** blocks the execution for 1 second; myTask didn't complete its execution in a given time, hence myTask was terminated.

- **myTask2.Wait(1000)** also blocks the execution for 1 second, but myTask2 completes its execution before 1 second. Hence, the main thread resumes its execution as soon myTask2 completed.

Task.WaitAll( )

Task.WaitAll method blocks the execution of a calling thread until all the specified tasks complete their execution. WaitAll is a static method of Task class.

All task objects must be referenced in a single array and WaitAll method needs that array to block the execution of a calling thread until all tasks specified in an array get completed.

Code Snippet

Listing 8-23. Use Task.WaitAll to wait for Main Thread until all specified Tasks are executing

```
using System;
using System.Threading;
using System.Threading.Tasks;

class Program
{

    static void Main()
    {
        Task tsk1 = Task.Run(() =>
        {
            Thread.Sleep(100);
            Console.WriteLine("tsk1 completed");

        });

        Task tsk2 = Task.Run(() =>
        {
            Thread.Sleep(500);
            Console.WriteLine("tsk2 completed");
        });

        Task tsk3 = Task.Run(() =>
        {
            Thread.Sleep(1000);
            Console.WriteLine("tsk3 completed");
        });
```

```
        //Store reference of all tasks in an array of Task
        Task[] allTasks = { tsk1, tsk2, tsk3 };

        //Wait for all tasks to complete
        Task.WaitAll(allTasks);

        Console.WriteLine("By from main thread");
    }

}
//Output
tsk1 completed
tsk2 completed
tsk3 completed
By from main 0   thread
```

Task.WaitAll(task[ ], milliseconds)

Task.WaitAll(task[], milliseconds) method blocks the execution of a calling thread until all the specified tasks finish or a timeout interval elapses.

Code Snippet

Listing 8-24. Use Task.WaitAll(task[], millisec) to wait for MainThread until all specified are executing for a specified period of time

```csharp
using System;
using System.Threading;
using System.Threading.Tasks;

class Program
{

    static void Main()
    {
        Task tsk1 = Task.Run(() =>
        {
            Thread.Sleep(500);
            Console.WriteLine("tsk1 completed");

        });

        Task tsk2 = Task.Run(() =>
        {
            Thread.Sleep(2000);
            Console.WriteLine("tsk2 completed");
        });

        Task tsk3 = Task.Run(() =>
        {
            Thread.Sleep(1000);
```

```
            Console.WriteLine("tsk3 completed");
        });

        //Store reference of all task in an array of Task
        Task[] allTasks = { tsk1, tsk2, tsk3 };

        //Wait for all tasks to complete
        Task.WaitAll(allTasks, 1200);

        Console.WriteLine("By from main thread");
    }

}
//Output
tsk1 completed
tsk3 completed
By from main thread
```

Task.WaitAny( )

Task.WaitAny is a static method of Task class. It blocks the execution of a calling thread until any first task from a collection of tasks completes its execution.

Code Snippet

Listing 8-25. Use Task.WaitAny to wait for a Main Thread, until any first thread completes its execution

```
using System;
using System.Threading;
using System.Threading.Tasks;

class Program
{

    static void Main()
    {
        Task tsk1 = Task.Run(() =>
        {
            Thread.Sleep(1000);
            Console.WriteLine("tsk1 completed");

        });

        Task tsk2 = Task.Run(() =>
        {
            Thread.Sleep(500);
            Console.WriteLine("tsk2 completed");
        });

        Task tsk3 = Task.Run(() =>
        {
```

```
            Thread.Sleep(2000);
            Console.WriteLine("tsk3 completed");
        });

        //Store reference of all task in an array of Task
        Task[] allTasks = { tsk1, tsk2, tsk3 };

        //Wait for all tasks to complete
        Task.WaitAny(allTasks);

        Console.WriteLine("By from main thread");
    }

}
//Output
Tsk2 completed
By from main thread
```

Task.WaitAny(task[ ], milliseconds)

Task.WaitAny(task[], milliseconds) method blocks the execution of a calling thread until any first task from a collection of tasks finishes or a timeout interval elapses.

Code Snippet

Listing 8-26. Use Task.WaitAny(task[], sec) to wait for a main thread for a specified time period

```
using System;
using System.Threading;
using System.Threading.Tasks;

class Program
{

    static void Main()
    {
        Task tsk1 = Task.Run(() =>
        {
            Thread.Sleep(500);
            Console.WriteLine("tsk1 completed");

        });

        Task tsk2 = Task.Run(() =>
        {
            Thread.Sleep(2000);
            Console.WriteLine("tsk2 completed");
        });

        Task tsk3 = Task.Run(() =>
        {
```

```
            Thread.Sleep(1000);
            Console.WriteLine("tsk3 completed");
        });

        //Store reference of all task in an array of Task
        Task[] allTasks = { tsk1, tsk2, tsk3 };

        //Wait for all tasks to complete
        Task.WaitAny(allTasks, 1200);

        Console.WriteLine("By from main thread");
    }

}
//Output
tsk1 completed
By from main thread
```

Chain Multiple Tasks with Continuations

Task.ContinueWith method is used to make chains of multiple tasks. Each next task in a chain will not be scheduled for execution until the current task has completed successfully, faulted due to an unhandled exception, or exited out early due to being canceled.

Code Snippet

Listing 8-27. Use Task.ContinueWith to chain one task after another.

```
using System;
using System.Threading;
using System.Threading.Tasks;

class Program
{

    static void Main()
    {
        Task tsk1 = Task.Run(() =>
        {
            Thread.Sleep(100);
            Console.WriteLine("tsk1");
        });

        //Run tsk2 as soon tsk1 get completed
        Task tsk2 = tsk1.ContinueWith((t) =>
        {
            Thread.Sleep(500);
            Console.WriteLine("tsk2");
        });

        tsk2.Wait();
    }
```

```
}
//Output
tsk1
tsk2
```

Explanation

- **tsk1.ContinueWith((t)=>{..});** execute and return a new task when tsk1 has **completed** its execution. Here "t" in the input parameter of ContinueWith method is the reference of tsk1. This "t" can be useable in the body of a lambda expression. For example, if tsk1 returns a value, by using "t" the return value can be useable in the body of a lambda expression.

- **Tsk2.Wait();** shall wait for tsk2 to complete its execution, and its execution shall start when tsk1 completes its execution. Therefore, tsk2.Wait() shall wait for all the tasks that were chained with it.

Use Task<TResult> with Continuation

Task<TResult> is a task that returns a value of the type TResult. Task<TResult> can be useable with continuation. Such a Task<TResult> returns a value so that a new task in a chain can use it.

Code Snippet

Listing 8-28. Return a result of first task in the body of a second task by using Task.Result;

```
using System;
using System.Threading;
using System.Threading.Tasks;

class Program
{

    static void Main()
    {
        Task<string> tsk1 = Task.Run(() =>
        {
            Thread.Sleep(100);
            return "Ali";
        });

        //Run tsk2 as soon tsk1 get completed
        Task tsk2 = tsk1.ContinueWith((t) =>
        {
            //Wait for tsk1 and return its value
            string name = t.Result;

            Console.WriteLine("My Name is: {0}", name);
        });

        tsk2.Wait();
    }
```

```
}
//Output
My Name is: Ali
```

Explanation

- **t.Result;** wait for tsk1 to complete its execution and return the value from it.

TaskContinuationOption

TaskContinuationOption is an enumeration that is used to specify when a task in a continuewith chain gets executed. The following are some of the most commong enums for TaskContinuationOption:

- **OnlyOnFaulted** Specifies that the continuation task should be scheduled only if its antecedent threw an unhandled exception.

- **NotOnFaulted** Specifies that the continuation task should be scheduled if its antecedent doesn't throw an unhandled exception.

- **OnlyOnCanceled** Specifies that the continuation should be scheduled only if its antecedent was canceled. A task is canceled if its Task.Status property upon completion is TaskStatus.Canceled.

- **NotOnCanceled** Specifies that the continuation task should be scheduled if its antecedent was not canceled.

- **OnlyOnRanToCompletion** Specifies that the continuation task should be scheduled if its antecedent ran to completion.

- **NotOnRanToCompletion** Specifies that the continuation task should be scheduled if its antecedent doesn't run to completion.

Code Snippet

Listing 8-29. Use TaskContinuationOption to run the chained task only if some condition satisfies

```
using System;
using System.Threading;
using System.Threading.Tasks;

class Program
{

    static void Main()
    {
        Task<string> tsk1 = Task.Run(() =>
        {
            throw new Exception();

            Console.WriteLine("tsk1 ran");
            Thread.Sleep(100);
            return "Ali";
        });
```

```
        Task tsk2 = tsk1.ContinueWith((t) =>
        {

            Console.WriteLine("tsk2 ran when tsk1 threw an exception");

        }, TaskContinuationOptions.OnlyOnFaulted);

        tsk2.Wait();
    }

}
//Output
tsk2 ran when tsk1 threws an exception
```

Explanation

In (Listing 8-29) the second parameter of **tsk1.ContinueWith method** (**TaskContinuationOptions**) was specified with **OnlyOnFaulted**, which says, tsk2 can only run if tsk1 threw an unhandled exception, otherwise it will skip the execution of tsk2.

Similarly, we can specify TaskContinuationOptions with other enums, i.e., OnlyOnCanceled, NotOnFaulted, etc.

The returned Task will not be scheduled for execution until the current task has completed. If the continuation criteria specified through the *continuationOptions* parameter are not met, the continuation task will be canceled instead of scheduled.

Options for when the continuation is scheduled and how it behaves:

Nested Task

A nested task is just a Task instance that is created in the user delegate of another task. A child task is a nested task that is created with the AttachedToParent option. A task may create any number of child and/or nested tasks, limited only by system resources. The following example shows a parent task that creates one simple nested task.

Detached Child Task

Every nested task is by default a detached child task. It runs independently of its parent.

Code Snippet

Listing 8-30. Create nested task

```
using System;
using System.Threading;
using System.Threading.Tasks;
class Program
{

    static void Main()
    {

        Task outer = Task.Run(() =>
        {
            Console.WriteLine("Hi I'm outer task ");
```

243

```
            Task inner = Task.Run(() =>
            {
                Console.WriteLine("Hi I'm inner task");
                Thread.Sleep(2000);
                Console.WriteLine("By from inner task");
            });

            Thread.Sleep(500);
            Console.WriteLine("By from outer task");
        });

        outer.Wait();
    }

}
//Output
Hi I'm outer task
HI I'm inner task
By from outer task
```

Explanation

(Listing 8-30) We can create an inner task as much as we want. But inner and outer tasks will run independantaly of each other. When an outer task completes its execution, it will move out and sync with the main thread.

Child Task Attached to Parent

A nested child task can attach to its parent by using the AttachedToParent option. The parent task cannot terminate its execution until all its attached child tasks complete their execution.

Code Snippet

Listing 8-31. Use AttachedToParent to create a nested child task

```
using System;
using System.Threading;
using System.Threading.Tasks;
class Program
{

    static void Main()
    {

        Task outer = new Task(() =>
        {
            Console.WriteLine("Hi I'm outer task ");

            //AttachedToParent only available with new Task()
            Task inner = new Task(() =>
```

```
    {
        Console.WriteLine("HI I'm inner task");
        Thread.Sleep(2000);
        Console.WriteLine("By from inner task");
    }, TaskCreationOptions.AttachedToParent);

    inner.Start();

    Thread.Sleep(500);
    Console.WriteLine("By from outer task");
    });

    outer.Start();
    outer.Wait();
}

}
//Output
Hi I'm outer task
Hi I'm inner task
By from outer task
By from inner task
```

Explanation

(In Listing 8-31) It's important to not use "Task.Run()" while making a child task that depends on its parent. In the above code snippet, a new nested task was created and it was attached to its parent by using the "*AttachedToParent*" property as the second argument of "*new task().*"

Synchronization of Variables in Multithreading

In a multithreading enviroment, the same variable can be accessed by two or more threads. If the operation performed on a shared variable is atomic or thread-safe, then it produces an accurate result. If the operation is non-atomic or not thread-safe, then it produces inaccurate results.

In atomic operation, only a single thread at a time can execute a single statement and produce accurate results; while, in a non-atomic operation, more than one thread is accessing and manipulating the value of a shared variable, which produces an inaccurate result (for example, if one thread is reading a value and the other thread at the same time is editing it).

Code Snippet

Listing 8-32. Multiple threads accessing the same resource "variable"

```
static void Main()
{
    int num = 0;
    int length = 500000;

    //Run on separate thread of threadpool
    Task tsk = Task.Run(() =>
    {
        for (int i = 0; i < length; i++)
```

```
        {
            num = num + 1;

        }
    });

    //Run on Main Thread
    for (int i = 0; i < length; i++)
    {
        num = num - 1;
    }

    tsk.Wait();
    Console.WriteLine(num);
}
//Output
-1500
```

Explanation

The above code snippet (Listing 8-32) gives inaccurate results because two threads are accessing and manipulating the value of *"num"* at the same time. The statement *"num = num + 1;"* is actually a combination of more than one statement; first it will read the current value of "num", add 1 to its current value, and assign it to "num".

Imagine if Main thread read the value of num = 6 but the other thread read the value of num = 3. When Main thread decrements the value of "num", it becomes 5. But the other thread already read the value of num = 3; when it increments it the value of num becomes "4", which is entirely wrong because the other thread must get the latest value of num and then increment it and the result should be "6". (The output of this program might be different if you run it on your machine, because it depends on the execution cycle of CPU.)

Handle Synchronization of Variables in Multithreading

The following are three common ways to handle synchronization variables in a multithreaded enviroment.

1. Lock

2. Monitor

3. Interlock

lock(object)

Lock is a C# keyword; it prevents a thread from executing the same block of code that another thread is executing. Such a block of code is called a locked code. Therefore, if a thread tries to enter a locked code, it will wait until the object is released. The lock keyword calls Enter at the start of the block and Exit at the end of the block.

The best practice is to use lock keyword with a private object, or with a private static object variable to protect data common to all instances.

Code Snippet

Listing 8-33. Use lock to thread-safe a shared resource

```
using System;
using System.Threading;
using System.Threading.Tasks;

class Program
{

}
//Output
0
```

Explanation

- **lock(thislock){...}** it will prevent other threads from manipulating the shared memory, i.e., "n". When control goes out of the block, the shared memory becomes useable for any thread.

- **thislock** is the same variable used in multiple threads, notifying other threads if someone already used it to lock a block of code.

- Hence shared memory becomes thread-safe and the program gives an accurate result.

Monitor

Monitor class also ensures that no other thread can execute the same section of code or a shared memory until it is being executed by its lock owner.

Code Snippet

Listing 8-34. Use Monitor.Enter to thread-safe a shared resource

```
using System;
using System.Threading;
using System.Threading.Tasks;

class Program
{
    //This object is use to lock a block
    private static object thislock = new object();

    static void Main()
    {
        int num = 0;
        int length = 500000;

        //Run on separate thread of threadpool
        Task tsk = Task.Run(() =>
        {
            for (int i = 0; i < length; i++)
```

247

```
        {
            //lock the block of code
            Monitor.Enter(thislock);

            num = num + 1;

            //unlock the locked code
            Monitor.Exit(thislock);

        }
    });

    //Run on Main Thread
    for (int i = 0; i < length; i++)
    {
        //lock the block of code
        Monitor.Enter(thislock);

        num = num - 1;

        //unlock the locked code
        Monitor.Exit(thislock);
    }

    tsk.Wait();
    Console.WriteLine(num);
    }

}
//Output
0
```

Explanation

- **Monitor.Enter** or **Monitor.TryEnter** method is used to lock a block of code for other threads and prevent other threads from executing it.

- **Monitor.Exit** method is used to unlock the locked code for another thread and allow other threads to execute it.

Interlocked

Interlocked class is used to synchronize the access of shared memory objects among multiple threads. Interlocked class provides the following useful operation on shared memory:

1. **Increment** and **Decrement** methods, used to increment or decrement a value of variable.

2. **Add** and **Read** method, used to add an integer value to a variable or read a 64-bit integer value as an atomic operation.

3. **Exchange** and **CompareExchange** methods, used to perform an atomic exchange by returnning a value and replacing it with a new value, or it will be contingent on the result of a comparison.

Code Snippet

Listing 8-35. Use Interlocked to thread-safe a shared resource

```
using System;
using System.Threading;
using System.Threading.Tasks;

class Program
{

    static void Main()
    {
        int num = 0;
        int length = 500000;

        //Run on separate thread of threadpool
        Task tsk = Task.Run(() =>
        {
            for (int i = 0; i < length; i++)
            {
                Interlocked.Increment(ref num);

            }
        });

        //Run on Main Thread
        for (int i = 0; i < length; i++)
        {
            Interlocked.Decrement(ref num);
        }

        tsk.Wait();
        Console.WriteLine(num);
    }

}
//Output
0
```

Explanation

- **Interlocked.Increment** takes the reference of a shared memory, i.e., "num" and increments it by thread-safing it.

- **Interlocked.Decrement** takes the reference of a shared memory, i.e., "num" and decrements it by thread-safing it.

Dead Lock

In a multithreaded enviroment, a dead lock may occur; it freezes the application because two or more activities are waiting for each other to complete. Usually it occurs when a shared resource is locked by one thread and another thread is waiting to access it.

Code Snippet

Listing 8-36. Create a dead lock

```csharp
using System;
using System.Threading;
using System.Threading.Tasks;

class Program
{
    //used as lock objects
    private static object thislockA = new object();
    private static object thislockB = new object();

    static void Main()
    {
        Task tsk1 = Task.Run(() =>
        {
            lock(thislockA)
            {
                Console.WriteLine("thislockA of tsk1");

                lock(thislockB)
                {
                    Console.WriteLine("thislockB of tsk2");
                    Thread.Sleep(100);

                }
            }
        });

        Task tsk2 = Task.Run(() =>
        {
            lock (thislockB)
            {
                Console.WriteLine("thislockB of tsk2");

                lock (thislockA)
                {
                    Console.WriteLine("thislockA of tsk2");
                    Thread.Sleep(100);
                }
            }
        });

        Task[] allTasks = { tsk1, tsk2 };
        Task.WaitAll(allTasks); // Wait for all tasks

        Console.WriteLine("Program executed succussfully");
    }

}
```

```
//Output
thislockA of tsk1
thislockB of tsk2
/* Application Freezed */
```

Explanation

Here is how the application got frozen.

1. Tsk1 acquires lock "thislockA".

2. Tsk2 acquires lock "thislockB".

3. Tsk1 attempts to acquire lock "thislockB", but it is already held by Tsk2 and thus Tsk1 blocks until "thislockB" is released.

4. Tsk2 attempts to acquire lock "thislockA", but it is held by Tsk1 and thus Tsk2 blocks until "thislockA" is released.

At this point, both threads are blocked and will never wake up. Hence, the application froze.

To prevent an application from freezing, it's important to use a lock statement carefully; otherwise, you will shoot your own foot.

CancellationToken

CancellationToken propagates a cancel notification to operations like *threads, thread pool work items, or task objects.*

Cancellation occurs when requesting a code calling the CancellationTokenSource.Cancel method, and then the user delegate terminates the operation. However, an operation can be terminated:

1. by simply **returning** from the delegate;

2. by calling the **CancellationTokenSource.Cancel** method.

The following are general steps for implementing the cancellation model:

1. Instantiate a **CancellationTokenSource**.

2. Get a **CancellationToken** from CancellationTokenSource.Token property.

3. **Pass** the CancellationToken to each task or thread that listens for cancellation.

4. Provide a mechanism for each task or thread to **respond to cancellation**.

5. Call the **CancellationTokenSource.Cancel** method to provide notification of cancellation.

Code Snippet

Listing 8-37. Request a thread to cancel its execution

```
using System;
using System.Threading;
using System.Threading.Tasks;

class Program
{
```

```csharp
static void Main()
{
    //1 - Instantiate a cancellation token source
    CancellationTokenSource source = new CancellationTokenSource();

    //2 - Get token from CancellationTokenSource.Token property
    CancellationToken token = source.Token;

    //3 - Pass token to Task
    Task tsk = Task.Run(()=>
    {
        Console.WriteLine("Hello from tsk");
        while(true)
        {

            Thread.Sleep(1000);

            Console.WriteLine("*");

            if(token.IsCancellationRequested == true)
            {
                Console.WriteLine("Bye from tsk");
                return;
            }

        }

    }, token);

    Console.WriteLine("Hello from main thread");

    //Wait
    Thread.Sleep(4000);

    //4 - notify for cancellation
    source.Cancel(); //IsCancellationRequested = true;

    //Wait
    Thread.Sleep(1000);

    Console.WriteLine("Bye from main thread");

}

}
//Output
Hello from main thread
Hello from tsk
*
*
*
*
```

```
Bye from tsk
Bye from main thread
```

Explanation

- **Tsk.Run()** shall continue its operation until IsCancellationRequested becomes true.

- **IsCancellationRequested** becomes true when **source.Cancel()** method is called in main thread after 4 seconds.

Making UI Responsive

In any .NET GUI Application (Windows Form, WPF, ASP.NET, etc.), the User Interface (UI) becomes unresponsive when a complex and time-consuming operation is executed during an event.

A **UI** (user-interface) thread manages the life cycle of UI controls (buttons, textbox, etc.), and it is commonly used to handle user inputs and respond to user events.

Before we dive into the topic, we must do the following steps:

1. Create an empty C# Windows Form Project. (You can create any GUI App i.e., WPF, ASP.NET, etc.)

2. From toolbox, drag a button and a label to the main form.

3. Double click on the button to generate the code for the click event.

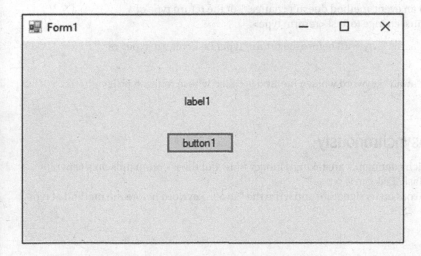

Figure 8-8. Drag button and label on empty windows form app

In the button click event, we simulated a time-consuming operation by using a Thread.Sleep method.

Listing 8-38. Execute a time-consuming operation in a UI Thread

```
private void button1_Click(object sender, EventArgs e)
{
    //Wait for 5 seconds
    Thread.Sleep(5000);

    label1.Text = "Hello World";

}
```

When we run the above code and click button1, the application hangs up. Until the UI thread is busy in executing time-consuming commands, it cannot respond to any additional user commands, for example, dragging the application window and clicking on the close button, etc.

How to Make UI Responsive with Async and Await

In .NET Framework 4.5, async and await keywords were introduced. They make asynchronous programming much simpler and provide a simpler way to make UI responsive.

In order to make UI responsive, it is essential to not execute complicated and time-consuming operations on a UI thread. Instead, these time-consuming operations must run on separate tasks, controlled by async and await keywords. Doing this, the UI thread becomes free and available to respond to any user input.

The following steps are essential to execute any method asynchronously:

1. The return type of an event-method doesn't change. But the return type of a normal method must change to Task<return_type>.

2. You must use the "async" keyword before the return_type/Task<return_type> of any method.

3. You must use the "await" keyword when a method is called whose return type is "Task/Task<T>".

Execute Click Event Asynchronously

It's important to figure out which commands are taking a longer time. Put those commands on a separate method whose return type is Task/Task<int>.

Next, use the "async" keyword on its signature and write the "await" keyword before the method of type "Task" is called.

Syntax

```
private async void button1_Click(object sender, EventArgs e)
{

    await DoComplicatedTaskAsync();
}
```

Code Snippet

Listing 8-39. Use async and await on an event-method

```
private async void button1_Click(object sender, EventArgs e)
{
    label1.Text = "Hello World";

    await DoComplicatedTaskAsync();

    label1.Text = "Bye World";

}

private Task DoComplicatedTaskAsync()
{
    Task task = Task.Run(() =>
    {
        Thread.Sleep(5000);
    });

    return task;
}
```

Explanation

(Listing 8-39) The UI thread will display "Hello World" on a label and wait until *DoComplicatedTaskAsync()* is executing. Meanwhile, the UI thread remains responsive to any user input. Once *DoComplicatedTaskAsync()* is completed, the UI thread will display "Bye World" on the label.

   DoComplicatedTaskAsync() is a method that returns a task which runs a time-consuming operation. The name of an async method, by convention, ends with an "Async" suffix.

   async is used to qualify a method as an asynchronous method.

   await is similar to Wait method, but it does not hang the UI thread and it can return a value if a Task has any value to return. It's important to note that the await keyword cannot work in a method that is not marked with an async keyword.

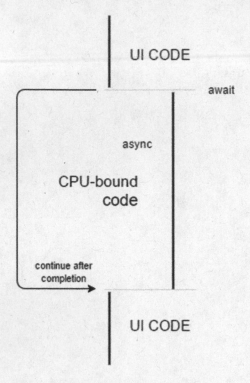

Figure 8-9. *Workflow of async method*

Execute Normal Method Asynchronously

In any normal method, it's important to figure out which operations are time-consuming and execute them on a separate task.

Code Snippet

Listing 8-40. Use async and await on a normal method

```
private async void button1_Click(object sender, EventArgs e)
{

    label1.Text = "Hello World";

    await normal_methodAsync();

    label1.Text = "Bye World";

}

private async Task normal_methodAsync()
{
    await DoComplicatedTaskAsync();

}
```

```
private Task DoComplicatedTaskAsync()
{
    Task task = Task.Run(() =>
    {
        Thread.Sleep(3000);

    });

    return task;
}
```

Explanation

(Listing 8-39) The UI thread will display "Hello World" on label1 and wait until **normal_methodAsync**()
is executing. Meanwhile, the UI thread remains responsive to any user input. **normal_methodAsync** is an
async method; it executes DoComplicatedTaskAsync on a separate task and waits for its completion. Once it
completes the execution, normal_methodAsync returns back to the click event where it was called. Then the
UI thread displays "Bye World" on label1.

Important Points

normal_methodAsync() doesn't return any value; use "Task" as a return type. When "async" is used with
normal methods, "void" cannot be used as a return type; we'll use "Task" instead.

DoComplicatedTaskAsync() method used "Task" as its return type. Therefore, in its body, the method
must return an object of type "Task".

normal_methodAsync and DoComplicatedTaskAsync Both methods have a return type of "Task".
But in their body, only DoComplicatedTaskAsync method returns an object of the type "Task" because its
signature doesn't mark with the "async" keyword.

Use Await to Get Value from Task<T>

Await keyword works like the Wait method, but it can also be used to get value from Task<T>.

Code Snippet

Listing 8-41. Use await to return a value from a Task<T> method

```
private async void button1_Click(object sender, EventArgs e)
{

    label1.Text = "Hello World";

    int value = await DoComplicatedTaskAsync();

    label1.Text = "Bye World" + value.ToString();
}

private Task<int> DoComplicatedTaskAsync()
{
    Task<int> task = Task.Run(() =>
    {
```

```
        Thread.Sleep(5000);
        return 15;
    });

    return task;
}
```

Explanation

await keyword waits for DoComplicatedTaskAsync to complete. The method signature of DoComplicatedTaskAsync has "Task<int>"; the method returns a task which returns a value "15" after waiting for 5 seconds. Await keyword returns the value "15" from the task of DoComplicatedTaskAsync() method. The UI thread will dispay "Bye World15" on label1.

Use Async Lambda

async lambda expression helps to create an anonymous async method. To use an async lambda expression, we need delegate. Its return type depends on the Delegate type.

Syntax

```
(async () =>
{
    await;
});
```

Code Snippet

Listing 8-42. Use async lambda

```
private async void button1_Click(object sender, EventArgs e)
{
    label1.Text = "Hello World";

    Func<Task> asyncLambda = (async () =>
    {
        await myWait(5000);
    });

    await asyncLambda();

    label1.Text = "Bye World";
}

private Task myWait(int milisec)
{
    Task task = Task.Run(() =>
    {
        Thread.Sleep(milisec);
    });

    return task;
}
```

Explanation

(Listing 8-42) In the body of async lambda it is essential to use an await keyword. To run the async lambda a delegate is required, such as Func<Task>. asynclambda delegate was called with an await keyword; until asynclambda is executing, the UI thread will wait and stay responsive.

Task.Delay(milisec)

Unlike Thread.Sleep, Task.Delay doesn't block the current thread. Instead it makes a logical delay for a specified period of time. Task.Delay is intended to run asynchronously. Await is used with Task.Delay because it returns a Task.

Code Snippet

Listing 8-43. Use Task.Delay to hold the execution of a Task

```
private async void button1_Click(object sender, EventArgs e)
{
    label1.Text = "Hello World";

    await Task.Delay(3000);

    label1.Text = "Bye World";
}
```

Explanation

(In Listing 8-43) After 3 seconds, the UI thread will display "Bye World" on label1.text but, meanwhile, it stays responsive.

Prevent Application from Cross Threading

In a multithreaded enviroment, only a UI thread can change the value of UI controls (button, label, textbox, etc.). If another thread tries to change the value of a UI control, then cross threading exception will arise because Runtime will not allow any thread to manipulate another thread data directly.

Listing 8-44. Cross threading example

```
private async button1_Click(object sender, EventArgs e)
{
    Task task = Task.Run((.) =>
    {
        label1.Text = "Hello World";
        Thread.Sleep(3000);

        label1.Text = "Bye World";
    });

    await task;
}
```

When the above code runs, an exception will arise which says, "Cross-thread operation not valid".

this.BeginInvoke

BeginInvoke method is used to change values of UI control from other threads. It does it in a thready-safe way. It requires a delegate; it tells which UI control needs to change its value.

Listing 8-45. Use lock to thread-safe a shared resource

```
private async void button1_Click(object sender, EventArgs e)
{
    Task task = Task.Run(() =>
    {
        this.BeginInvoke(new Action(() =>
        {
            label1.Text = "Hello";
        }));

    });

    await task;
}
```

The value of label1.Text shall be changed to "Hello" and no exception will arise because it's a thread-safe operation.

Parallel Programming

In the modern era, computers and workstations have at least two or four cores that help multiple threads to execute simultaneously. .NET provides easy ways to handle multiple threads on multiple cores.

In .NET, you can take advantage of parallelism by:

1. Concurrent Collection
2. Parallel.For & Parallel.Foreach
3. PLINQ

Concurrent Collection

In a multithreaded enviroment, multiple threads can access the same data at the same time to read/add/edit it. Such data aren't thread-safe and become vulnerable to multiple threads.

In C# we have Generic collections. These collections are type-safe, which means at compile time we can make a collection of any type. But these collections are not thread-safe. They become vulnerable when multiple threads can manipulate the same data at the same time.

Generic collections can also become thread-safe if they are used in a proper locking statement, but locking the entire collection for the sake of adding/removing an item could be a big performance hit. .NET has its own thread-safe collection called Concurrent collection. It was introduced in .NET 4.0. It contains the following thread-safe collections defined in the System.Collections.Concurrent namespace.

1. **ConcurrentDictionary<K,V>:** Thread-safe dictionary in key value pairs

2. **ConcurrentQueue<T>:** Thread-safe FIFO data structure

3. **ConcurrentStack<T>:** Thread-safe LIFO data structure

4. **ConcurrentBag<T>:** Thread-safe implementation of an unordered collection

5. **BlockingCollection<T>:** Provides a Classical Producer Consumer pattern

Code Snippet

Listing 8-46. Use generic collection in multiple threads

```
using System.Collections.Generic;
using System.Threading.Tasks;

class Program
{

    static void Main()
    {
        Dictionary<int, int> dic = new Dictionary<int, int>();

        Task tsk1 = Task.Run(() =>
        {
            for(int i = 0; i < 100; i++)
            {
                dic.Add(i, i + 1);
            }
        });

        Task tsk2 = Task.Run(() =>
        {
            for (int i = 0; i < 100; i++)
            {
                dic.Add(i + 1, i);
            }
        });

        Task[] allTasks = { tsk1, tsk2 };
        Task.WaitAll(allTasks); // Wait for all tasks

    }

}
//Output
/* System.AggregateException accur because 'an item with the same key has already been
added'. */
```

Explanation

(In Listing 8-46) Tsk1 and Tsk2 both tried to manipulate the key of dictionary, hence an error occurs.

Code Snippet

Listing 8-47. Use Concurrent Collection to prevent multiple threads from accessing a resource at the same time

```
using System.Collections.Concurrent;
using System.Threading.Tasks;

class Program
{

    static void Main()
    {
        ConcurrentDictionary<int, int> dic =
                                new ConcurrentDictionary<int, int>();

        Task tsk1 = Task.Run(() =>
        {
            for(int i = 0; i < 100; i++)
            {
                dic.TryAdd(i, i + 1);
            }
        });

        Task tsk2 = Task.Run(() =>
        {
            for (int i = 0; i < 100; i++)
            {
                dic.TryAdd(i + 1, i);
            }
        });

        Task[] allTasks = { tsk1, tsk2 };
        Task.WaitAll(allTasks); // Wait for all tasks

        System.Console.WriteLine("Program ran succussfully");
    }

}
//Output
Program ran succussfully
```

Explanation

ConcurrentDictionary<K,V> is a thread-safe collection; in the above code snippet, it prevents multiple threads from working on the same key value. If another thread tried to add a new key value which was already added by another thread, it would skip the iteration and move the control to the next iteration. This way, no conflict would occur and hence the program would run succussfully.

Similarly, there are other concurrent collections, like:

1. **ConcurrentQueue**<T>, it has *Enque*() method to enque an item and TryDeque() method to remove and return the first item.

2. **ConcurrentStack**< T> it has *Push*() method to push an item and *TryPop*() method to remove and return the last item.

3. **ConcurrentBack**<T> it has *Add*() method to add an item and *TryTake*() method to remove and return the item.

But Generics are not thread-safe it's a programmer's responsibility. Let's say you have a list collecting some objects. That list is shared amongst several threads; then it may work hazardously if two threads try to access the List at the same point in time, like adding/removing/iterating items from the same list at the same time.

Thread safety can be implemented with the help of locking the collection and other similar ways. But locking the entire list for the sake of adding/removing an item could be a big performance hit for an application based on the circumstances.

Parallel.For & Parallel.Foreach

Parallel.For and Parallel.Foreach are used in parallel programming to iterate statements over multiple threads.

Parallel.For

It is used to iterate a for loop upon multiple threads and processors. In most cases, Parallel.For loop is much faster than a normal for loop.

Syntax

```
Parallel.For(fromInclusive, toExclusive, Action<int> body);
```

Code Snippet

Listing 8-48. Use Parallel.For

```
using System;
using System.Threading.Tasks;

class Program
{
    static void Main()
    {
        Parallel.For(1, 5, (i) =>
        {
            Console.WriteLine(i);
        });

    }

}
```

```
//Output
1
3
4
2
/* output will be different when you run the same code, because in a multithreaded
enviroment, the scheduler decides which thread should run first */
```

Parallel.Foreach

It is used to iterate a foreach loop upon multiple threads and processors. In most cases, Parallel.Foreach loop is much faster than a normal foreach loop.

Syntax

```
Parallel.ForEach<T>(collection<T> data, Action<T> body);
```

Code Snippet

Listing 8-49. Use Parallel.Foreach

```
using System;
using System.Threading.Tasks;

class Program
{
    static void Main()
    {
        int[] data = { 1, 2, 3, 4, 5 };

        Parallel.ForEach<int>(data, (d) =>
        {
            Console.WriteLine(d);
        });

    }

}
//Output
1
3
4
2
5
/* output will be different when you run the same code, because in a multithreaded
enviroment the scheduler decides which thread should run first */
```

PLINQ

PLINQ is the parallel version of LINQ. It means queries can be executed on multiple threads by partitioning the data source into segments. Each segment executes on separate worker threads in parallel on multiple processors. Usually, parallel execution significantly runs faster than sequential LINQ. However, parallelism can slow down the execution on complicated queries.

It has the following common methods to help in parallelism:

1. **AsParallel**() Divide the data source in segments on multiple threads

2. **AsSequential**() Specify the query shall be executed sequentially

3. **AsOrdered**() Specify the query shall preserve the ordering of data

4. **AsUnordered**() Specity the query shall not preserve the ordering of data

5. **ForAll**() Process the result in parallel

Code Snippet

Listing 8-50. Run a LINQ query in parallel by using "AsParallel()"

```
using System;
using System.Linq;

class Program
{

    static void Main()
    {
        var data = Enumerable.Range(1, 50);

        //split source in segments on multiple threads
        //by using AsParalletl() with source 'data'
        var plinq = from d in data.AsParallel()
                    where d % 10 == 0
                    select d;

        foreach (var item in plinq)
        {
            Console.WriteLine(item);
        }

    }

}
//Output
10
20
30
40
50
```

Explanation

The above code snippet (Listing 8-50) tells how to make a sequential LINQ to a PLINQ by splitting the source into segments on multiple threads by using the **AsParallel()** method. No doubt its speed is faster than a sequential LINQ query.

Summary

- **Monitor.Enter** or **Monitor.TryEnter** method is used to lock a block of code for other threads and prevent other threads from executing it.

- A **thread** controls the flow of an executable program.

- By default, a program has one thread called **Main Thread**. Main Thread starts when control enters in the Main method and it terminates when Main method returns.

- Application has two kinds of threads: Background Thread and Foreground Thread.

- **Background** thread doesn't hold the main thread to finish its execution. If the main thread completes its execution it will terminate the progam.

- **Foreground** thread does hold the main thread to terminate the progam until foreground completes its execution.

- **Threadpriority** defines how much CPU time a thread will have for execution.

- **ThreadStatic** is an attribute used on top of a static field to make its value unique (local) for each thread.

- A **thread pool** is a collection of background threads, created by a system and is available to perform any task when required.

- **Task** doesn't create new threads. Instead it efficiently manages threads of a threadpool.

- **Task.Run** manages Task more efficiently than Task.Factory.StartNew.

- **Task.ContinueWith** method is used to run multiple Tasks in a chain only when a specified condition satisfies.

- **Lock** is a C# keyword; it prevents a thread from executing the same block of code that another thread is executing.

- **CancellationToken** propagates a notification that operations (threads, thread pool work items, or task objects) should be canceled.

- **UI** (user-interface) thread manages the life cycle of UI controls (buttons, textbox, etc.), and it is commonly used to handle user inputs and respond to user events.

- **async** and **await** keywords are used to make the UI of an application responsive.

- **async lambda** expression helps to create an anonymous async method.

- **Task.Delay** doesn't block the current thread. Instead it makes a logical delay for a specified period of time. It is better than using Thread.Sleep for an asynchronous operation.

- **this.BeginInvoke** method is used to send value to controls (button, textbox, etc.) of UI Threads.

- **Concurrent Collections** are thread-safe collections.

- **Parallel.For** and **Parallel.Foreach** are used to iterate loops upon multiple threads and processors.

- **PLINQ** is the parallel version of LINQ. By using **"AsParallel"** method, LINQ query divides its data source on multiple threads.

Code Challenges

Challenge 1: Develop a Windows Form Project to Display HTML

Develop a simple Windows Form Project in C# which gets the HTML of "google.com" and displays it on a label.

Application must have these UI Controls:

1. A Textbox to enter URL

2. A Label to display result

3. A button for downloading HTML and displaying it on a label

Your goals are:

1. The application must be responsive and use async and await.

2. Download the HTML of a URL and show it on a label.

Practice Exam Questions

Question 1

Suppose an application has a method name PrintAsterisk() that prints asterisks on a screen continuously. The method runs on a Task separate from the user interface. The application includes the following code. (Line numbers are included for reference only.)

```
01.    static void PrintAsterisk(CancellationToken token)
02.    {
03.        while(!token.IsCancellationRequested)
04.        {
05.            Thread.Sleep(100);
06.            Console.Write(" *");
07.        }
08.
09.    }
10.    private static void Main()
11.    {
12.        var tokenSource = new CancellationTokenSource();
13.        var task = Task.Run(() => PrintAsterisk(tokenSource.Token));
14.        Console.WriteLine("Press [Enter] to stop printing Asterisk");
15.        Console.ReadLine();
16.
17.        task.Wait();
18.    }
```

You need to ensure that the application stop printing the Asterisk on screen when the user presses the Enter key. Which code segment should you insert at line 16?

A)   tokenSource.Token.Register(() => tokenSource.Cancel());

B)   tokenSource.Cancel(); Ans

C)   tokenSource.IsCancellationRequested = true;

D)   tokenSource.Dispose();

Question 2

Suppose an application uses multiple asynchronous tasks to optimize performance. The application will be deployed in a distributed environment. You need to get the result of an asynchronous task from a web service.

The data will later be parsed by a separate task. Which code segment should you use?

A)
```
protected async void StartTask()
{
    string result = await GetData();
    ...
}

public Task<string> GetData()
{
    ...
}
```

B)
```
protected async void StartTask()
{
    string result = await GetData();
    ...
}

public async Task<string> GetData()
{
    ...
}
```

C)
```
protected async void StartTask()
{
    string result = GetData();
    ...
}

public Task<string> GetData()
{
    ...
}
```

```
D)
protected async void StartTask()
{
    string result = async GetData();
    ...
}

public Task<string> GetData()
{
    ...
}
```

Question 3

Identify a correct way to implement locking.

```
A)
//lockthis, is a private static variable of type object.
lock (lockthis)
{
    ...
}

B)
lock (new object())
{
    ...
}

C)
lock ()
{
    ...
}

D)
lock (this)
{
    ...
}
```

Question 4

An application uses multiple asynchronous tasks to optimize performance. You create three tasks by using the following code segment. (Line numbers are included for reference only.)

```
01.    private void MultipleTasks()
02.    {
03.        Task[] tasks = new Task[]
04.        {
05.            Task.Run(()=>Thread.Sleep(2000)),
06.            Task.Run(()=>Thread.Sleep(3000)),
07.            Task.Run(()=>Thread.Sleep(1000)),
08.        };
09.
10.        ...
11.    }
```

You need to ensure that the MultipleTasks () method waits until all three tasks complete before continuing. Which code segment should you insert at line 09?

A) task.WaitFor(3);

B) tasks.Yield();

C) tasks.WaitForCompletion();

D) Task.WaitAll(tasks);

Question 5

Which of the following methods is used to run a LINQ query in parallel?

A) AsParallel();

B) RunParallel();

C) ToParallel();

D) Parallel();

Answers

1. B

2. B

3. A

4. D

5. A

CHAPTER 9

■ ■ ■

Exception Handling and Validating Application Input

Introduction to Exception

Exception is an unexpected error that occurs at runtime (when an application is running). Sometimes a programmer doesn't know what and which exception could occur at runtime. For example, the code is reading a file but the file is missing from the location where it is read. It is accessing or reading data across the network but the Internet is not available, or it is loading some kind of data in memory but the system runs out of memory, etc. In all these cases, programmers write the code right but, due to unconditional ways, an exception could occur.

If exceptions are not handled properly, they can break the execution of a running program. To handle an exception, we write the suspicious code inside a try-catch block. When an exception is caught, its object can be use to read the detail of an exception, for example, error message and exception Stack, etc.

In terms of programming, an exception is a C# class (*System.Exception*). A developer can create a custom-exception by inheriting *System.Exception* class and can customize it accordingly. A custom-exception is useful when a developer wants to provide his own error messages to C# code.

The following is a list of some common .NET exceptions that may occur at runtime.

- **System.Exception**, is either thrown by a system or a running application to report an error.

- **InvalidOperationException**, is thrown when the state of an object cannot invoke a method or execute an expression.

- **ArgumentException**, is thrown when a method is invoked and one of its parameters doesn't meet the specification of a parameter.

- **ArgumentNullException**, is thrown when a method is invoked and one of its paremeter arguments is null.

- **ArgumentOutOfRangeException**, is thrown when the value of an argument is outside the range of values as defined by the type of the arguments of the invoked method.

- **NullReferenceException**, is thrown when you try to use a reference which is not initialized, or try to access a member of a type which is not initialized in memory.

- **IndexOutOfRangeException**, is thrown when an index of an array tries to access something which is outside of the array's range.

© Ali Asad and Hamza Ali 2017
A. Asad and H. Ali, *The C# Programmer's Study Guide (MCSD)*, DOI 10.1007/978-1-4842-2860-9_9

- **StackOverflowException**, is thrown when the Stack has too many nested methods and it cannot add more methods to execute it.

- **OutOfMemoryException**, is thrown when there is not enough memory to run a program.

- **ArithmeticException**, is thrown when there is an error in an arithmetic operation.

- **DivideByZeroException**, is thrown when there is an attempt to divide an integral or decimal value with zero.

- **OverflowException**, is thrown when an arithmetic operation returns a value that is outside the range of the data type.

- **IOException**, is thrown when there is an error in an IO operation.

- **DirectoryNotFoundException**, is thrown when there is an attempt to access a directory that is not found in the system.

- **FileNotFoundException**, is thrown when there is an attempt to access a file that is not found in the system.

- **SqlException**, is thrown when an sql server returns a warning or error.

Handling Exception

An exception can be handled by writing a code (that might throw an error at runtime) inside a try-catch or a try-catch-finally block.

try-catch

try-catch are two separate blocks that come together to handle an exception. In *try* block, we write the suspicious code that may throw an exception at runtime; use *catch* block to handle an exception thrown by the code written in try block as shown in the following Listing 9-1

Syntax

```
try
{
    //Write Suspicious Code
}
catch
{

    //Do something when exception occurs
}
```

Code Snippet

Listing 9-1. Use try-catch to handle an exception

```
using System;

namespace DemoProject
{
```

```
class Program
{
    static void Main(string[] args)
    {
        int[] numbers = new int[2];

        try
        {
            numbers[0] = 0;
            numbers[1] = 1;
            numbers[2] = 2;

            foreach (int i in numbers)
            {
                Console.WriteLine(i);
            }
        }
        catch
        {
            Console.WriteLine("An exception is thrown");
        }
    }
}
//Output
An exception is thrown
```

Explanation

The above code (Listing 9-1) handles the exception and didn't break the execution of the running program.

try-catch (ExceptionType ex)

try-catch are two separate blocks that come together to handle an exception. In *try* block, we write the suspicious code that may throw an exception at runtime; use *catch (ExceptionType ex)* block to handle the object of a specific type of exception.

Syntax

```
try
{
    //Write Suspicious Code
}
Catch (ExceptionType ex)
{

    //Do something when specified type of exception occurs
}
```

Code Snippet

Listing 9-2. Use try-catch (ExceptionType ex) to handle a specific exception instance

```
using System;

namespace DemoProject
{
    class Program
    {
        static void Main(string[] args)
        {
            int[] numbers = new int[2];

            try
            {
                numbers[0] = 0;
                numbers[1] = 1;
                numbers[2] = 2;

                foreach (int i in numbers)
                {
                    Console.WriteLine(i);
                }
            }
            catch (IndexOutOfRangeException ex)
            {
                Console.WriteLine("Error Message: {0}", ex.Message);
            }
        }
    }
}
//Output
Error Message: Index was outside the bound of the array.
```

Explanation

The catch block handled the object of IndexOutOfRangeException that was thrown by try block. ex.Message property is used to display the error message of the exception.

Code Snippet

Listing 9-3. Use try-catch (Exception ex) to handle an all exception instance

```
using System;

namespace DemoProject
{
    class Program
    {
        static void Main(string[] args)
        {
            int[] numbers = new int[2];
```

```
        try
        {
            numbers[0] = 0;
            numbers[1] = 1;
            numbers[2] = 2;

            foreach (int i in numbers)
            {
                Console.WriteLine(i);
            }
        }
        catch (Exception ex)
        {
            Console.WriteLine("Error Message: {0}", ex.Message);
            Console.WriteLine("ExceptionType: {0}", ex.GetType());
        }
    }
  }
}
//Output
Error Message: Index was outside the bound of the array.
ExceptionType: System.IndexOutOfRangeException
```

Explanation

System.Exception is a base class of an all exception type, so we can use *catch (Exception ex)* to handle those exceptions whose types are unknown to us. When the exception is handled in catch {}, we can use *ex. GetType()* method to get the type of exception. Also, it is the best practice is to write *Exception* class (in catch block) because Exception is something that can occur for many reasons.

try-catch (ExceptionType)

try-catch are two separate blocks that come together to handle an exception. In *try* block, we write the suspicious code that may throw an exception at runtime; in *catch (ExceptionType)* block we handle the specific type of exception. However, in *catch (ExceptionType)* we can't hold the reference of an exception object.

Syntax

```
try
{
    //Write Suspicious Code
}
Catch (ExceptionType)
{

    //Do something when specific type of exception occurs
}
```

Code Snippet

Listing 9-4. Use try-catch (ExceptionType) to handle a specific exception

```
using System;

namespace DemoProject
{
    class Program
    {
        static void Main(string[] args)
        {
            int[] numbers = new int[2];

            try
            {
                numbers[0] = 0;
                numbers[1] = 1;
                numbers[2] = 2;

                foreach (int i in numbers)
                {
                    Console.WriteLine(i);
                }
            }
            catch (IndexOutOfRangeException)
            {
                Console.WriteLine("Index out of bound exception is thrown");
            }
        }
    }
}
//Output
Index out of bound exception is thrown
```

Explanation

Catch block handles the exception of type IndexOutOfRangeException. The catch block cannot hold the reference of an IndexOutOfRangeException object. Under catch block we write the code to execute when a specific type of exception is raised.

try-catch-finally

try-catch-finally is a full version of handling exception in a better way. It comprises of three blocks:

- **try{}**, is used to write a block of code that may throw an exception. ·
- **catch{}**, is used to handle a specific type of exception.
- **finally {}**, is used to to clean up actions that are performed in a try block.

finally block is always run at the end, regardless of whether an exception is thrown or a catch block matching the exception type is found.

Syntax

```
try
{
    // Code to try goes here.
}
catch (ExceptionType ex)
{
    // Code to handle the exception goes here.

}
finally
{
    // Code to execute after the try-catch blocks
    // goes here.
}
```

Code Snippet

Listing 9-5. Use try-catch-finally to handle an exception gracefully

```
using System;

namespace DemoProject
{
    class Program
    {
        static void Main(string[] args)
        {
            int[] numbers = new int[2];

            try
            {
                numbers[0] = 0;
                numbers[1] = 1;
                numbers[2] = 2;

                foreach (int i in numbers)
                {
                    Console.WriteLine(i);
                }
            }
            catch (IndexOutOfRangeException)
            {
                Console.WriteLine("Index out of bound exception is thrown");
            }
            finally
            {
                numbers = null;
                Console.WriteLine("Program Ends");
            }
        }
```

```
        }
}
//Output
Index out of bound exception is thrown
Program Ends
```

Explanation

(In Listing 9-5) Finally block is executed right after the catch block finishes its execution. Usually finally block is used to free the resources.

try-finally

finally block can be used after try block to release the resources used by code written in try block.

Syntax

```
try
{
    // Code to try goes here.
}

finally
{
    // Code to execute after the try blocks
    // goes here.
}
```

Code Snippet

Listing 9-6. Use try-finally

```
using System;

namespace DemoProject
{
    class Program
    {
        static void Main(string[] args)
        {
            int[] numbers = new int[2];

            try
            {
                numbers[0] = 0;
                numbers[1] = 1;

                foreach (int i in numbers)
                {
                    Console.WriteLine(i);
                }
            }
```

```
        finally
        {
            numbers = null;
            Console.WriteLine("Program Ends");
        }
    }
  }
}
//Output
0
1
Program Ends
```

Use Multiple Catch Blocks to Handle Multiple Exceptions

After first try{} block, more than one catch block can be used to handle multiple types of exceptions that can be thrown by try block.

When stacking multiple catch blocks, we use the most specific exception type on the first catch block and use the least specific exception type at the last catch block.

Syntax

```
try
{
    // Code to try goes here.
}
catch (ExceptionType ex)
{
    // Code to handle the exception goes here.

}
catch (ExceptionType ex)
{
    // Code to handle the exception goes here.

}

finally
{
    // Code to execute after the try-catch blocks
    // goes here.
}
```

Code Snippet

Listing 9-7. Use multiple catch blocks to handle multiple exception types

```
using System;

namespace DemoProject
{
    class Program
```

```
{
    static void Main(string[] args)
    {
        try
        {
            Divide(1, 0, "Result = ");
        }
        catch (DivideByZeroException)
        {
            Console.WriteLine("Divide by zero exception");
        }
        catch (NullReferenceException)
        {
            Console.WriteLine("Null reference exception");
        }
        catch (Exception ex)
        {
            Console.WriteLine(ex.Message);
        }
        finally
        {
            Console.WriteLine("Program Ends");
        }
    }

    private static void Divide(int a, int b, string s)
    {
        int result = a / b;
        Console.WriteLine(s.ToUpper() + result);
    }
}
}
//Output
Divide by zero exception
Program Ends
```

Explanation

Multiple catch blocks are used to catch multiple exception types. When a specified exception type matches with catch (exceptiontype) it will execute the block and then jump to the finally block if it exists.

Throwing Exceptions

In C#, an object of exception can be explictly thrown from code by using the *throw* keyword. A programmer should throw an exception from code if one or more of the following conditions are true:

1. When method doesn't complete its defined functionality, for example, Parameters has null values, etc.

2. When an invalid operation is running, for example, trying to write to a read-only file, etc.

Syntax

```
throw exception;
```

Code Snippet

Listing 9-8. Throw a new exception instance

```
using System;

namespace DemoProject
{
    class Program
    {
        static void Main(string[] args)
        {
            try
            {
                Show(null, 10);
            }
            catch (ArgumentException ex)
            {
                Console.WriteLine(ex.Message);
            }
        }

        private static void Show(string fname, int age)
        {
            if (fname == null)
            {
                throw new ArgumentException("Parameter cannot be null", "fname");
            }

            Console.WriteLine(fname + " " + age);
        }
    }
}
//Output
Parameter cannot be null
Parameter name: fname
```

Explanation

Show method has a check statement; if parameter "fname" is null then it throws a new instance
of ArgumentException with a custom message passed to its constructor. The second parameter of
argumentexception shows the name of the parameter which causes the error, i.e., "fname".

When the exception caught is a catch block, it shows the message along with the name of the parameter
that causes the exception, i.e., "fname".

Re-throwing an Exception

If an exception is caught but still wants to throw to be caught again by the calling method, then use simple *throw;* for example, you may catch and log an exception and then re-throw it to be handled by the calling method.

By re-throwing an exception you can preserve the **stack trace**, which tells where the exception arised in the first place and where it was re-thrown.

Syntax

throw;

Code Snippet

Listing 9-9. Re-Throw an exception and preserve stack-trace

```
using System;

namespace DemoProject
{
    class Program
    {
        static void Main(string[] args)
        {
            try
            {
                Show(null, 10);
            }
            catch (NullReferenceException ex)
            {
                Console.WriteLine(ex.StackTrace);
            }

        }

        private static void Show(string fname, int age)
        {
            try
            {
                Console.WriteLine(fname.ToUpper() + " " + age);
            }
            catch (NullReferenceException)
            {
                //Log the exception message here!
                throw;
            }

        }
    }
}
//Output

    at DemoProject.Program.Show(String fname, Int32 age) in C:\Users\aliso\Source\Repos\demo\
DemoProject\DemoProject\Program.cs:line 29
```

at **DemoProject.Program.Main**(String[] args) in C:\Users\aliso\Source\Repos\demo\
DemoProject\DemoProject**Program.cs:line 12**\Call stack

Explanation

ex.StackTrace shows the exception first arised at Show method in Line 29 and then it was passed to the
Main Method, where it was handled again in line 12. Therefore, by using the *throw* keyword we can pass the
exception to the calling method to handle the exception.

Throwing an Exception with an Inner Exception

An exception can be thrown along with an inner exception by passing the inner exception in the second
parameter of the newly arised exception. Also, if you throw a new exception with the initial exception you
will preserve the initial stack trace too.

Code Snippet

Listing 9-10. Throw a new exception with an inner exception and preserve the stack-trace

```
using System;

namespace DemoProject
{
    class Program
    {
        static void Main(string[] args)
        {
            try
            {
                Show(null, 10);
            }
            catch (Exception ex)
            {
                Console.WriteLine(ex.Message);
                Console.WriteLine(ex.StackTrace);

                Console.WriteLine(ex.InnerException.Message);
            }

        }

        private static void Show(string fname, int age)
        {
            try
            {
                Console.WriteLine(fname.ToUpper() + " " + age);
            }
            catch (NullReferenceException ex)
            {
                //Null Reference passed in second parameter of new exception
                //so, null reference becomes the inner exception.
                throw new Exception("A new exception is arised",ex);
```

```
            }
        }
    }
}
//Output
A new exception is arised
    at DemoProject.Program.Show(String fname, Int32 age) in C:\Users\aliso\Source\Repos\demo\
DemoProject\DemoProject\Program.cs:line 34

    at DemoProject.Program.Main(String[] args) in C:\Users\aliso\Source\Repos\demo\
DemoProject\DemoProject\Program.cs:line 12
Object reference not set to an instance of an object.
```

Creating Custom Exceptions

In C#, a custom exception can be created by inheriting the System.Exception class. Generally, custom exceptions are useful in large-scale projects where multiple modules are talking to each other.

Syntax

```
class <ClassName> : System.Exception
{
    ...
}
```

Code Snippet

Listing 9-11. Create a custom exception

```
using System;

namespace DemoProject
{
    class MyCustomException : System.Exception
    {
        //Overload constructor if you want

        public MyCustomException(string message) : base(message)
        {
            //TODO: Provide definition if you want
        }
    }

    class Program
    {
        static void Main(string[] args)
        {
            try
            {
                Show();
            }
```

```
        catch (MyCustomException ex)
        {
            Console.WriteLine(ex.Message);
        }

    }

    private static void Show()
    {

        throw new MyCustomException("It's a custom exception!");
    }
}
}
//Output
It's a custom exception!
```

Explanation

Show method throws a custom exception with a custom message. Main method handled the custom exception and showed the custom message.

Validating Application Input

The output and result of an application or operation depends upon its input. The input data must be validated so the application can produce the right results. Most of the time, data can be validated through a simple if-else statement, but using if-else on each data wouldn't be easy to manage. For example, what if the huge list of email ids has to be validated? In that case .NET provides **Regular Expressions** to validate string values quickly.

Regular Expressions

.NET Framework provides a regular expression engine to validate a large amount of text by quickly parsing the text to find a specific character pattern. For example, a regular expression can be used to validate the pattern for email id, etc.

Character Pattern Cheatsheet

Character pattern defines how a string must be represented; patterns help to validate a string. The following are some commonly used characters for pattern matching a text in regular expression.

- *, matches the previous character for zero or more times. E.g.,"bo*" matches either "b" or "boo".

- +, matches the previous character for one or more times. E.g., "bo+" matches either "bo" or "boo".

- ?, matches the previous element zero or one time. E.g., "Al?i" matches either "Ai" or "Ali"

- ^, matches the character at the beginning of a string. E.g., "^\d{3}" matches "123-ali"

- **$**, matches the character at the end of a string. E.g., "\d{3}$" matches "ali-123"

- **{n}**, matches the previous element for "n" times. E.g., "\d{3}" matches "125"

- **x|y**, matches either x or y. E.g., "a|bc" matches "a" or "bc"

- **[xyz]**, matches any one of the enclosed characters. E.g., "[ali]" matches "a" in "Fart"

- **[^xyz]**, it's the negation of all enclosed characters. The matches string must not have those character sets. E.g., "[^ab]" matches "film"

- **\d**, matches a digit. Equivalent to **[0-9]**

- **\D**, matches a non-digit. Equivalent to **[^0-9]**

- **\s**, matches a whitespace, tab, form-feed, etc. Equivalent to **[\f\n\r\t\v]**

- **\S**, matches a non-white space. Equivalent to **[^\f\n\r\t\v]**

- **\w**, matches a word including an underscore. Equivalent to **[A-Za-z0-9]**

- **\W**, matches a non-word character. Equivalent to **[^A-Za-z0-9]**

Regex

In C#, we use the *Regex* class of *System.Text.RegularExpressions* namespace; it represents the .NET Framework's regular expression engine. The Regex class contains methods and properties to validate a text with a specific character pattern; some of them are listed below.

- **IsMatch(string input),** returns true if the regular expression specified in the Regex constructor matches with the specified input string.

- **IsMatch(string input, int startat),** returns true if the regular expression specified in the Regex constructor matches with the specified input string and begins at the specified starting position of the string.

- **IsMatch(string input, string pattern)**, returns true if the specified regular expression matches with the specified input string.

- **Matches(string input),** searches the specified input string for all occurrences of a regular expression.

- **Match(string InputStr, string Pattern)**, matches the input string with a string pattern.

- **Replace(string input, string replacement)**, in a specified input string, replaces all strings that match a regular expression pattern with a specified replacement string.

Code Snippet

Listing 9-12. Validate phone number with Regular Expression

```
using System;
using System.Text.RegularExpressions;

namespace DemoProject
{
    class Program
```

```
    {
        static void Main(string[] args)
        {
            //Pattern for Matching Pakistan's Phone Number
            string pattern = @"\(\+92\)\s\d{3}-\d{3}-\d{4}";

            //Ali's Phone Number
            string inputStr = "(+92) 336-071-7272";
            bool isMatched = Regex.IsMatch(inputStr, pattern);

            if(isMatched == true)
            {
        Console.WriteLine("Pattern for phone number is matched with inputStr");
            }
            else
            {
    Console.WriteLine("Pattern for phone number is not matched with inputStr");
            }

        }

    }
}
//Output
Pattern for phone number is matched with inputStr.
```

Explanation

Pattern string contains character set, which makes sure if the input string is according to Pakistan's phone number's pattern. Here is how it works:

@"\(\+92\)\s\d{3}-\d{3}-\d{4}";

Table 9-1. *Explain Phone number Pattern*

Pattern	Meaning
\('	\(' matches '('
\+'	\+' matches '+'
92'	92' matches '92'
\)'	\)' matches ')'
\s'	\s' matches a space ''
\d{3}'	\d{3}' matches numeric digits for 3 times, its equivalent to '456'
-'	-' matches '-'
\d{3}'	\d{3}' matches numeric digits for 3 times, its equivalent to '456'
-'	-' matches '-'
\d{4}	\d{4}' matches numeric digits for 4 times, its equivalent to '4561'

Code Snippet

Listing 9-13. Validate an Email ID with Regular Expression

```
using System;
using System.Text.RegularExpressions;

namespace DemoProject
{
    class Program
    {
        static void Main(string[] args)
        {
            //Pattern for Matching an email id
            string pattern =
                @"^\w+[a-zA-Z0-9]+([-._][a-z0-9]+)*@([a-z0-9]+)\.\w{2,4}";

            //Ali's email id
            string inputStr = "imaliasad@outlook.com";
            bool isMatched = Regex.IsMatch(inputStr, pattern);

            if(isMatched == true)
            {
            Console.WriteLine("Pattern for email id is matched with inputStr");
            }
            else
            {
            Console.WriteLine("Pattern for email isn't matched with inputStr");
            }

        }

    }
}
//Output
Pattern for email id is matched with inputStr.
```

Explanation

Pattern string contains chararacter set, which makes sure if the input string is according to the email ID pattern. Here is how it works:

@"^\w+[a-zA-Z0-9]+([-._][a-z0-9]+)*@([a-z0-9]+)\.\w{2,4}"

Table 9-2. *Explain Email ID Pattern*

Pattern	Meaning
^'	^' matches everything from start
\w+	\w+' tells there must be at least one or more alphabets
[a-zA-Z0-9]+	[a-zA-Z0-9]+' tells there must be one or more alphanumeric
[-._]	tells there can be any included special character i.e '-._'
([-._][a-z0-9]+)*	tells there can be a special character and alphanumeric values
@	@' matches '@'
\.	\.' matches a dot '.'
\w{2,4}	\w{2,4} tells there must be minimum 2 or maximum 4 words

Summary

- Exception is an error that occurs at runtime and may break the execution of an application.

- try-catch-finally blocks are useful to handle exception gracefully.

- Programatically, an exception can be thrown by using a **throw** keyword.

- A custom can be created by inheriting the Exception class.

- Regular Expression is useful to validate the large string values with certain patterns.

Code Challenges

Challenge 1: Validate Email, Phone Number, and Website

You're developing an application that asks the user to enter their

1. Email ID

2. Phone Number

3. Date of Birth

4. Zip Code

5. Website

Your application must validate their information by using regular expression and must handle exception in case the user enters invalid values.

Practice Exam Questions

Question 1

How do you throw an exception to preserve stack-trace information?

A)   throw;

B)   throw new Exception();

C)   throw e;

D)   return new Exception();

Question 2

You need to validate a string which has numbers in **333-456** format. Which pattern would you choose?

A)   @"\d\d-\d\d"

B)   @"\n{3}-\n{3}"

C)   @"[0-9]+-[0-9]"

D)   @"\d{3}-\d{3}"

Question 3

Suppose you're developing an application that require that need to define its own custom exceptions. Which of the following class you'd inherit to create a custom exception?

A)   Attribute

B)   Exception

C)   IEnumerable

D)   IEnumerator

Answers

1.   A

2.   D

3.   B

CHAPTER 10

■ ■ ■

File I/O Operations

Interacting with files is a common task when developing an application. Sometimes you need to store some kind of information into files and store that information in a different format (i.e., binary or text), or you need to send or access some kind of data over the network. In these scenarios, a .NET framework provides classes to deal with them.

This chapter will cover the main concepts used to interact with File System and give an understanding of the working of the following things:

1. Drives and Directories

2. Files and Streams

3. Interaction with Remote Files

4. Asynchronous File I/O

The .NET Framework gives the classes to interact with a File I/O that can be found in the *System.IO* namespace. This namespace is the collection of the base classes devoted to file-based and memory-based input and output services.

Working with Drive

Drive or Storage is important to know about when dealing with file system. The .NET framework provides a class (*DriveInfo*) to interact with a storage medium, which may be a hard drive or any other storage (i.e., removable disk). This class gives you information about the drives, such as the name, size, and free space of the drive. You can also get to know which drives are available and what kind they are.

Listing 10-1 shows how you can interact with Drives and get to know about them.

Code Snippet

Listing 10-1. Single Drive info

```
//Get the Drive
DriveInfo info = new DriveInfo(@"C:\");
Console.WriteLine("Name is: "+info.Name);
Console.WriteLine("Drive Type is: "+info.DriveType);
```

Explanation

DriveInfo is a class provided by .NET in *System.IO*, used to interact with Drives. In *DriveInfo*'s constructor, the Drive name is passed and you can access its information as shown in Listing 10-1.

© Ali Asad and Hamza Ali 2017
A. Asad and H. Ali, *The C# Programmer's Study Guide (MCSD)*, DOI 10.1007/978-1-4842-2860-9_10

You can also get all the drives and fetch their details using the *GetDrives()* method (static method of *DriveInfo* class). Listing 10-2 shows the use of the *GetDrives()* method.

Code Snippet

Listing 10-2. All Drive info

```
//Get the all the drive
DriveInfo[] driveInfo = DriveInfo.GetDrives();
foreach (var info in driveInfo)
{
    Console.WriteLine("Name is: " + info.Name);
    Console.WriteLine("Drive Type is: " + info.DriveType);
    Console.WriteLine("*******************");
}
```

Working with Directories

Drive contains directories and files. To work with them, *DirectoryInfo* or *Directory* (Static Class) is used. Both the classes can be used to access directory structure. You can access all the folders' files (or the subfolder), as well as the specific file in the folder or sub-folder using these classes. You can also create and perform other folder-related operations on a new folder or directory using these classes.

Directory and DirectoryInfo

Directory Class is a static class performing a single operation. It's usually used when performing single task, like just creating a folder. It is preferable to use in such cases.

DirectoryInfo is a non-static class performing multiple operations. It's usually used when performing multiple operations/tasks, like creating a folder, then creating sub-folders or moving them or getting files from that folder. It is preferable to use in such cases.

Listing 10-3 shows how you can create a new folder using these both classes.

Code Snippet

Listing 10-3. Create Directory

```
//Create new directory/folder using Directory Class
  DirectoryInfo directory = Directory.CreateDirectory("Directory Folder");

 //Create new directory/folder using DirectoryInfo Class
 DirectoryInfo directoryInfo = new DirectoryInfo("DirectoryInfo Folder");
 directoryInfo.Create();
```

Explanation

As shown from the code, you just need to give a full path along with a folder name where you want to create the folder as a parameter in the *CreateDirectory()* method of *Directory* Class. A new directory or folder with the name "Directory Folder" will be created. (As you can see, there is just the name of a folder, i.e., when the path is not given, then by default the folder will be created in the current directory where you are working). And a newly created directory returns *DirectoryInfo*'s object on which you can perform further operations given by a *DirectoryInfo* class on a newly created folder like the *Exist()* method (to check the existence of a folder), the *Delete()* method (to delete the folder), or the *CreateSubdirectory()* method (to create a subdirectory).

The code also shows the creation of a folder by *DirectoryInfo* Class. Give the name of a folder or path along with the folder name in *DirectoryInfo*'s constructor and it will catch the path where to create the folder and, later, its object's method: enter *Create()*, and a new folder named "DirectoryInfo folder" will be created. After creation, you can perform an operation on the newly created folder.

Listing 10-4 shows how you can check the existence of a created folder.

Code Snippet

Listing 10-4. checking the existence of specific directory

```
//Check Existence of created directory/folder using Directory Class
if(Directory.Exists("Directory Folder"))
{
    Console.WriteLine("Directory Folder Exists");
}
//Check Existence of created directory/folder using DirectoryInfo Class
if (directoryInfo.Exists)
{
    Console.WriteLine("DirectoryInfo Folder is Exists");
}
```

Explanation

As shown from code, if *Directory* Class is used, you have to give explicitly the path of the folder to perform any of the operations, but when *DirectoryInfo* Class is used, you just need to call its properties or functions as *DirecotoryInfo*'s object already knows where or what the folder is.

You can also delete the folder by using the *Delete()* method but if the directory is not found, you will encounter the following exception: **DirectoryNotFoundException.**

To move the directory from one location to another location is also a common task to use. Listing 10-5 shows how to move a folder using *Directory* and *DirectoryInfo* class.

Code Snippet

Listing 10-5. Move directory from one location to another

```
//Using Directory Class
Directory.Move("Directory Folder", "../Moved Directory Folder");

//Using DirectoryInfo Class
directoryInfo.MoveTo("../Moved DirectoryInfo Folder");
```

Explanation

Move() method is used with *Directory* Class (Static class), whereas *MoveTo()* method is used with *DirectoryInfo* Class. *Move()* method requires you to know the source directory path and the destination directory path, whereas the *MoveTo()* method just requires the destination directory path because the DirectoryInfo's object already constrains the reference of the source directory path.

■ **Note** When working with the huge directory structure, use the *EnumerateDirectories()* method instead of the *GetDirectories()* method to fetch the directories, as *EnumerateDirectories()* start enumerating directories before they have been completely retrieved (Lazy Loading or Deferred Execution); whereas in the *GetDirectories()* case, code would not move forward until all the list of directories have been retrieved (Immediate Execution).

Working with Files

As *Directory* and *DirectoryInfo* class allow you to interact with folder structure, *File* and *FileInfo* allow you to interact with files, for example, to create file or to delete a file or check its existence or the operations or properties provided by *File* or *FileInfo* Class.

Directory or *DirectoryInfo* class is also used to fetch all the files in a specific folder or its sub-folder or files with specific types (such as images), and *File* or *FileInfo* class is used to access the information of those files or to perform operations on those files.

Listing 10-6 shows how to fetch all the files from a folder/directory using these classes:

Code Snippet

Listing 10-6. get all files from a specific folder

```
//Get file from specific directory using Directory Class
string[] fileNames= Directory.GetFiles("Directory Folder");
foreach (var name in fileNames)
{
    Console.WriteLine("Name is:{0}",name);
}
//Get Files from specific directory using DirectoryInfo Class
DirectoryInfo directoryInfo = new DirectoryInfo("DirectoryInfo Folder");
FileInfo[] files= directoryInfo.GetFiles();
foreach (var file in files)
{
    Console.WriteLine("Name is:{0}",file.Name);
    Console.WriteLine("Directory Name:{1}",file.DirectoryName);
}
```

GetFiles() method is an overloaded method and you can use this accordingly.

■ **Note** *Directory* Class will just give you names of files in the provided directory, whereas *DirectoryInfo* will return a *FileInfo*(Class) object on which you can perform file-related operations.

File and FileInfo

Like *Directory* and *DirectoryInfo* class, .NET also provided *File* and *FileInfo* class to have the same working context but be used to interact with files.

Listing 10-7 shows some of the operations performed on a specific file.

Code Snippet

Listing 10-7. Some tasks performed on a specific file

```
//To Create a file in current location named "File" using File(Static Class)
File.Create("File.txt").Close();

//To Write content in a file named "File"
File.WriteAllText("File.txt", "This is file created by File Class");
```

```
//To Read the file named "File"
string fileContent= File.ReadAllText("File.txt");
Console.WriteLine(fileContent);

//To Copy "File" from current location to a new one (Previous folder)
File.Copy("File.txt", "../Copied File.txt");

//To Create file in current location named "FileInfo" using FileInfo Class
FileInfo info = new FileInfo("FileInfo.txt");
info.Create();

//To Move "FileInfo" from current location to a new one (Previous Folder)
info.MoveTo("../Moved FileInfo.txt");
```

As you noticed in the first line of code, *Create()* method is preceded by the *Close()* method. This is due to *File* (Static Class) performing a single operation which is, in this case, creation of a file and, after creation of a file, you must close the file before performing another operation on it. That's why *Close()* is called after creation: so that the file could be written.

These operations performed on a file are much like those performed on Directory. *Copy/CopyTo* (methods of *File/FileInfo*) should be used where you want to leave one copy at a previous location and another/others at a new location; whereas *Move/MoveTo* (methods of *File/FileInfo*) should be used where you do not want to leave a copy at a previous location but just copy it to a new location. It is just like cut and paste behavior.

When you need to update the content of a file or need to change the content of an already created file, then you can use the *AppendText()* method provided by both *File* and *FileInfo* Classes.

Basically, there are two different methods to create a file. These are given below with details:

1. **Create():** Create or override a file specified in a parameter as a Path and return *FileStream*'s object.

2. **CreateText():** Create or open a file for writing and return *StreamWriter*'s object.

Working with Stream

Stream is an abstract class used for writing and reading bytes. It is for File I/O operations. When working with files, it's important to know about Stream because a file is stored on your computer hard drive or DVD in a sequence of bytes. When communicating over the network, a file is transferred in the form of a sequence of bytes. Also, it is stored in memory in the form of a sequence of bytes.

Stream has three main tasks:

1. **Writing:** Writing means to convert the object or data into bytes and then store it in memory or a file, or it can be sent across the network.

2. **Reading:** Reading means to read the bytes and convert them into something meaningful, such as Text, or to deserialize them into an object.

3. **Seeking:** It is the concept of query for the current position of a cursor and moving it around. Seeking is not supported by all the streams, i.e., you cannot move forward or backward in a stream of bytes that is being sent over a network.

Stream has the following types:

1. FileStream

2. MemoryStream

3. BufferedStream

4. NetwrokStream

5. CryptoStream

The Stream offers you different kinds of operations, such as Create, Read, and Seek, etc.

FileStream

FileStream drives from the abstract class *Stream*, mainly used to write and read bytes in the file.

Using FileStream with File/FileInfo Class

Listing 10-8 shows how you can use *FileStream* when you can write content in a file when you interact with *File* Class.

Code Snippet

Listing 10-8. Use of FileStream with File to write content in a file

```
FileStream fileStream = File.Create("File.txt");
string content = "This is file content";
byte[] contentInBytes = Encoding.UTF8.GetBytes(content);
fileStream.Write(contentInBytes,0,contentInBytes.Length);
fileStream.Close();
```

Explanation

Basically, when you create the file using *File* or *FileInfo* Class, it returns an object of type *FileStream* or *StreamWriter* or another Stream (sequence of bytes), as the file is stored or transferred in the form of bytes. After getting the stream of a file, you can perform respective operations on a file depending on the type of Stream. As in this case, *File.Create()* returns a *FileStream* object so you can further perform FileStream's operations on the created file.

As mentioned, Stream works on bytes; therefore, to write something in the file, you need to convert the content in the form of bytes and then you can write into the file using *FileStream*'s *Write()* method.

The *Write()* method takes three parameters containing the bytes of contents to write, the starting, and the ending position of bytes to write.

When you are dealing with Files, it is important to release the resource as shown in the code for *File*; *Close()* method must be called to release the file resources so that it can be used for later operations to be performed in Files. If you don't release the resource, you will get the exception "A file is open/being used in another process" or something like this. You can also use block to release the resource.

■ **Note**   The process of converting characters into bytes and vice versa is called **Encoding** and **Decoding**.

Using FileStream Class

FileStream Class is used for the creation and writing of content in a file.

Syntax

```
FileStream <object_name> =new FileStream(<File_Name>,<FileMode>,<FileAccess>,<FileShare>)
```

Explanation

FileStream has some parameters to explain. The following details illustrate parameters that *FileStream* accepts:

Table 10-1. *FileStream Parameters*

Parameter	Description
File_Name	File_Name is the name of a file on which an operation will perform.
FileMode	FileMode is an enumeration that gives a different method to open the file: 1. **Append**: It Creates the file if the file does not exist and, if it exists, it puts the cursor at the end of the file. 2. **Create**: Creates a new file and, if the file already exists, it will override it. 3. **CreateNew**: Creates a new file and, if the file already exists, it will throw an exception. 4. **Open**: Opens the file. 5. **OpenOrCreate**: Opens the existing file; if it's not found, then it creates a new one. 6. **Truncate**: opens the existing file and truncates its size to zero bytes.
FileAccess	FileAccess is an enumeration that gives a different method to access a file: 1. **Read**: tells the file has just read access. 2. **ReadWrite**: tells the file has read and write access. 3. **Write**: tells the file has just write access.
FileShare	FileShare is an enumetation that gives different methods: 1. **Delete**: Allows subsequent deleting of a file. 2. **Inheritable**: Allows the file to handle child process inheritance. 3. **None**: Stops to share the file. File must be closed before access by another process. 4. **Read**: Allows file for reading. 5. **ReadWrite**: Allows file for reading and writing. 6. **Write**: Allows file to write.

Listing 10-9 shows how to write data in a file using FileStream Class.

Code Snippet

Listing 10-9. FileStream to write in the file

```
FileStream fileStream = new FileStream("File.txt",FileMode.Create,FileAccess.Write
,FileShare.Write);
string content = "This is file content";
byte[] contentInBytes = Encoding.UTF8.GetBytes(content);
fileStream.Write(contentInBytes, 0, contentInBytes.Length);
fileStream.Close();
```

MemoryStream

MemoryStream drives from the abstract class *Stream*; it's mainly used to write and read bytes from memory. Listing 10-10 shows how to write and read from *MemoryStream*.

Code Snippet

Listing 10-10. Use of MemoryStream

```
MemoryStream memoryStream = new MemoryStream();
string content = "This is file content";
byte[] contentInBytes = Encoding.UTF8.GetBytes(content);

//Write into file
memoryStream.Write(contentInBytes, 0, contentInBytes.Length);

//Set the position to the begninig of stream
memoryStream.Seek(0, SeekOrigin.Begin);

//Read from file
byte[] readContent = new byte[memoryStream.Length];

int count= memoryStream.Read(readContent, 0, readContent.Length);
for (int i =count; i < memoryStream.Length; i++)
{
    readContent[i] = Convert.ToByte(memoryStream.ReadByte());
}
string result= Encoding.UTF8.GetString(readContent);
Console.WriteLine(result);
```

BufferedStream

Buffer is a block of bytes in memory used to cache the data. *BufferedStream* needs stream to be buffered. Listing 10-11 shows how you can write and read from Buffer using *BufferStream*.

Code Snippet

Listing 10-11. Use of Buffer Stream

```
FileStream fileStream = File.Create("Sample.txt");
BufferedStream memoryStream = new BufferedStream(fileStream);
string content = "This is file content";
byte[] contentInBytes = Encoding.UTF8.GetBytes(content);

//Write into file
memoryStream.Write(contentInBytes, 0, contentInBytes.Length);

//Set the position to the begninig of stream
memoryStream.Seek(0, SeekOrigin.Begin);

//Read from file
byte[] readContent = new byte[memoryStream.Length];
```

```
int count= memoryStream.Read(readContent, 0, readContent.Length);
for (int i =count; i < memoryStream.Length; i++)
{
    readContent[i] = Convert.ToByte(memoryStream.ReadByte());
}
string result= Encoding.UTF8.GetString(readContent);
Console.WriteLine(result);
```

> ■ **Note** *NetworkStream* and *CryptoStream* are also common. It is recommended to explore them too, but these are not in exam 70-483.

Working with File Reader and Writer

To convert bytes into readable form or to write or read values as bytes or as string, .NET offers the following classes in such a case. For those purposes, we have:

1. StringRead and StringWriter

2. BinaryReader and BinaryWriter

3. StreamReader and StreamWriter

StringReader and StringWriter

These classes are used to read and write characters to and from the string. Listing 10-12 shows the use of *StringReader* and *StringWriter*.

Code Snippet

Listing 10-12. StringReader and StringWriter

```
//Write string or characters
 StringWriter stringWriter = new StringWriter();
 stringWriter.Write("String Writer example");
 stringWriter.Write(" Append Text");
 Console.WriteLine(stringWriter.ToString());
 //Read string
 StringReader stringReader = new StringReader("String Reader Example");
 Console.WriteLine(stringReader.ReadLine());
```

BinaryReader and BinaryWriter

These classes are used to read and write values as Binary Values. Listing 10-13 shows the example of *BinaryReader* and *BinaryWriter*.

Code Snippet

Listing 10-13. BinaryReader and BinaryWriter

```
//Write Data Types values as Binary Values in Sample.dat file
FileStream file = File.Create("Sample.dat");
```

```
BinaryWriter binaryWriter = new BinaryWriter(file);
binaryWriter.Write("String Value");
binaryWriter.Write('A');
binaryWriter.Write(true);
binaryWriter.Close();

//Read Binary values as respective data type's values from Sample.dat
FileStream fileToOpen = File.Open("Sample.dat", FileMode.Open);
BinaryReader binaryReader = new BinaryReader(fileToOpen);
Console.WriteLine(binaryReader.ReadString());
Console.WriteLine(binaryReader.ReadChar());
Console.WriteLine(binaryReader.ReadBoolean());
```

Explanation

BinaryReader has methods to read a specific data type's value. For example, if there is a string value in binary form then you use the *ReadString()* method and so on, but if there is no written value as binary and you want to read it then exception will be thrown. Also, it is important to read ordinally as values are written.

StreamReader and StreamWriter

StreamWriter drives from *TextWriter* class; it's used to write character/characters to the stream. *StreamReader* drives from *TextReader* class; it's used to read bytes or string. Listing 10-14 shows the example of *StreamReader* and *StreamWriter*.

Code Snippet

Listing 10-14. StreamReader and StreamWriter

```
StreamWriter streamWriter = new StreamWriter("Sample.txt");
streamWriter.Write('A');
StreamReader streamReader = new StreamReader("Sample.txt");
Console.WriteLine(streamReader.ReadLine());
```

Communication over the Network

System.Net namespace provides support for your applications to communicate across a network. Most commonly, the members of this namespace you use are *WebRequest* and *WebResponse* classes. Both of these classes are abstract and used to communicate over the network. *System.Net* namespace also provides specific implemented classes that depend on what the protocol is going to use for communication. For example, *HttpWebRequest* class and *HttpWebResponse* class are used when you are using Http Protocol.

In General, we use *WebRequest* class to send the request for information and *WebResponse* class to receive the response of the requested information.

Listing 10-15 shows how to use these classes when communicating over the network.

Code Snippet

Listing 10-15. WebRequest and WebResponse

```
WebRequest request = WebRequest.Create("http://www.apress.com");
WebResponse response = request.GetResponse();
```

```
StreamReader reader = new StreamReader(response.GetResponseStream());
string result = reader.ReadToEnd();

Console.WriteLine(result);
response.Close();
```

Explanation

WebRequest is created using the Create() method (static method of *WebRequest* class), which takes the address of the request in a string or Uri format. WebResponse is linked to WebRequest, so it gets the response of the requested information or data using its *GetResponse()* method.

The *Create()* method of *WebRequest* inspects the address and chooses the correct protocol implementation. In code, we passed http://www.apress.com, so it would choose Http protocol and return the *HttpWebRequest*. You can also use *WebRequest*'s method or properties to perform further operations on it.

After getting the response, *StreamReader* is used to get the response in stream so that it can be read.

Working with asynchronous File I/O

Reading and writing of the file might be a time-consuming task and you have to wait a long time to finish the operation. The code in this chapter is called synchronous code. The code is executed line by line and often waits till the task ends. This wait can be long enough to annoy the user and put a severe impact on the user experience.

For example, in desktop applications, you have one thread that is the main thread and which is responsible for all the tasks, i.e., updating the UI and processing other tasks as well. If you have a long task to process (i.e., waiting for the network stream to respond or reading a file from Internet), then the main thread will be busy in processing that task and, meanwhile, the UI of the application will be stuck and be unresponsive, which will be a bad experience for the user. In such scenarios, such a long-running task should be processed in another thread so that the main thread is not busy and the application stays responsive. In this way, your code will execute in an asynchronous manner.

■ **Note**   Details of Synchronous and Asynchronous code are discussed in Chapter 8.

Async and Await in File I/O

Async (*async*) and Await (*await*) are the keywords provided by .NET Framework in C# 5.0. They tell the compiler to execute code in an asynchronous manner.

According to MSDN:

> *An Async method contains async in its name, such as ReadAsync, WriteAsync, ReadLineAsync, and ReadToEndAsync, etc. These async methods are implemented on stream classes such as Stream, FileStream, MemoryStream, and on classes that are used for reading from or writing to streams such as TextReader and TextWriter.*

Listing 10-16 shows how to write and read a file asynchronously.

Code Snippet

Listing 10-16. Asynchronous File I/O

```
//Write to the File
FileStream file = File.Create("Sample.txt");
StreamWriter writer = new StreamWriter(file);
await writer.WriteAsync("Asynchronously Written Data");
writer.Close();

//Read From File
FileStream readFile = File.Open("Sample.txt", FileMode.Open);
StreamReader reader = new StreamReader(readFile);
string result = await reader.ReadToEndAsync();
Console.WriteLine(result);
```

■ **Note** You can find more on "Working with asynchronous File I/O" from the following link: `https://msdn.microsoft.com/en-us/library/kztecsys(v=vs.110).aspx`

Summary

1. DriveInfo class gives you support to interact with Drives.

2. C# gives Directory and DirectoryInfo Classes to interact with Directories. Directory class is static and preferable for single operations, whereas DirectoryInfo is preferable for multiple operations.

3. File and FileInfo: both classes are used to interact with Files. File Class is static and preferable for performing a single operation on a file, whereas FileInfo is for multiple operations.

4. Stream is an abstract class used for writing and reading bytes. It has three main tasks: Reading, Writing, and Seeking.

5. FileStream drives from the abstract class Stream; it's mainly used to write and read bytes in the file.

6. MemoryStream drives from the abstract class Stream; it's mainly used to write and read bytes from memory.

7. Buffer is a block of bytes in memory used to cache the data. BufferedStream needs stream to be buffered, i.e., a stream of bytes in memory for caching the data.

8. StringReader and StringWriter classes are used to read and write characters to and from the string.

9. BinaryReader and BinaryWriter classes are used to read and write values as Binary Values.

10. StreamWriter drives from TextWriter; it's used to write character/characters to the stream. StreamReader drives from TextReader; it's used to read bytes or string.

11. For communication over a network, we use WebRequest class to send the request for information and WebResponse class to receive the response of the requested information.

Code Challenges

Challenge 1: Download and Save Image

Download any of Image and convert in bytes and save those bytes in file named ImageData in your local space. Read those bytes from ImageData file and convert them into Image form and save obtained image in local drive as well.

Practice Exam Questions

Question 1

You have to develop an application for an organization which reads the file and displays the content of a file. Which code snippet will properly fulfill your requirement?:

A)
```
string fileContent = "";
StreamReader reader = new StreamReader("data.txt");
fileContent = reader.ReadToEnd();
reader.Close();
```

B)
```
string fileContent = "";
StreamReader reader = null;
using (reader = new StreamReader("data.txt"))
{
     fileContent = reader.ReadToEnd();
}
```

C)
```
string fileContent = "";
try
{
     StreamReader reader = new StreamReader("data.txt");
     fileContent = reader.ReadToEnd();
}
catch
{

}
```

D)
```
string fileContent = "";
StreamReader reader = new StreamReader("data.txt");
fileContent = reader.ReadToEnd();
```

Question 2

You need to read a file from a web server and save the content of the file locally. Which code snippet will more preferable?:

A)
```
WebRequest request = WebRequest.Create(remoteFileUri);
WebResponse response = request.GetResponse();
StreamReader reader = new StreamReader(response.GetResponseStream());
StreamWriter writer = new StreamWriter("localFile.txt");
writer.Write(reader.ReadToEnd());
```

```
B) WebRequest request = WebRequest.Create(remoteFileUri);
   WebResponse response = request.GetResponse();
   StreamReader reader = new StreamReader(response.GetResponseStream());
   StreamWriter writer = new StreamWriter("localFile.txt");
   writer.Write(reader.ReadToEnd());
   writer.Close();
   reader.Close();
   response.Close();


C) WebResponse response = null;
   WebRequest request = WebRequest.Create("");
   using (response = request.GetResponse())
   {
       StreamReader reader = new StreamReader(response.GetResponseStream());
       StreamWriter writer = new StreamWriter("localFile.txt");
       writer.Write(reader.ReadToEnd());
   }


D) WebResponse response = null;
   StreamReader reader = null;
   WebRequest request = WebRequest.Create("");
   using (response = request.GetResponse())
           reader = new StreamReader(response.GetResponseStream());
   StreamWriter writer = new StreamWriter("localFile.txt");
   writer.Write(reader.ReadToEnd());
```

Question 3

You are working on an application that reads the file named "sample.txt". Your application takes care of the following points when it reads the sample.txt file.

It does not make changes to the "sample" file.

It must allow other processes to access the "sample" file.

It must not throw an exception if the "sample" file does not exist.

Which code snippet should you choose to take care of said points about sample.txt?:

```
A) var read = File.Open("sample.txt", FileMode.Open, FileAccess.Read,      FileShare.Read);

B) var read = File.Open("sample.txt", FileMode.OpenOrCreate, FileAccess.Read, FileShare.
   ReadWrite);

C) var read = File.Open("sample.txt", FileMode.Open, FileAccess.ReadWrite, FileShare.Read);

D) var read = File.Open("sample.txt", FileMode.Open, FileAccess.Read, FileShare.ReadWrite);
```

Answers

1. A & B
2. B
3. B

CHAPTER 11

■■■

Serialization and Deserialization

When communicating with remote applications, you will often exchange data with other applications. Serialization and Deserialization of data is done before the exchange of data, when it's received or sent.

In this chapter, we will understand the following topics:

1. Serializations and Deserialization

2. Binary Serialization

3. XML Serialization

4. JSON Serialization

5. Custom Serialization

Serialization and Deserialization

Serialization and Deserialization are the processes of serializing and deserializing data. C# provides different techniques to perform these processes.

Serialization

The Process of converting an object or object graph into a stream of bytes is called **Serialization**. It is the process of transforming an object into bytes or text in order to store it into any kind of storage or exchange the object over the network.

Deserialization

The Process of converting a back stream of bytes into an object or object graph is called **Deserialization**.

Pictorial Representation

The process of serialization and deserialization is illustrated by a figure by which you can get to know how this is basically performed:

© Ali Asad and Hamza Ali 2017

A. Asad and H. Ali, *The C# Programmer's Study Guide (MCSD)*, DOI 10.1007/978-1-4842-2860-9_11

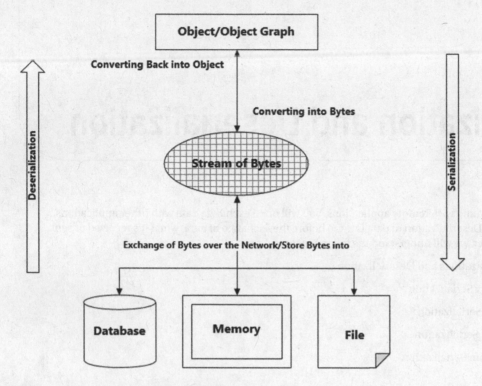

Figure 11-1. *Serialization and Deserialization*

Explanation

Serialization and Deserialization of data or an object is commonly used in those cases where you will often exchange data with other applications. For example, when data is going to be sent to a web service or over a network stream, you first have to convert data into a stream of bytes and, on the receiving side, you have to convert it back from a stream of bytes to an object that is your main concern. This is called Serialization and Deserialization, respectively.

The Serialized object carries an object's data in the form of a stream along with the information of object's type, i.e., its version, culture, and assembly name.

The .NET Framework provides classes to help you to serialize and deserialize the object and also offers you ways to configure your own objects.

By default, there are three serialization/deserialization mechanisms provided by .NET Framework:

1. BinaryFormatter

2. XmlSerializer

3. DataContractSerializer

BinaryFormatter is a serializer to serialize and deserialize the data in Binary format. *XmlSerializer* is used to serialize and deserialize the object in an XML document. This serializer enables you to control how objects are encoded into XML. DataContractSerializer is also used to serialize the object into an XML Stream by using a supplied data contract.

There are also other serializers which are used to serialize and deserialize the data according to their usage, such as:

1. DataContractJsonSerializer: Serialize the objects to the JavaScript Object Notation (JSON) and deserialize JSON data to objects.

2. JavaScriptSerializer: Serialize and deserialize the objects for AJAX-enabled application.

We'll explain these serialization mechanisms according to the Exam ref 70-483 point of view.

■ **Note** Methods are not serialized because serialization only serializes the data stored by an object.

Binary Serialization

Binary serialization serializes an object or data or object graph in binary format.

Binary serialization uses binary encoding for serialization to produce compact serialized data for uses as storage or socket-based network streams.

A binary sterilized object contains serialized data along with the object's Type information including version, public token, culture, and assembly name.

■ **Note** Binary serialization is dependent upon a .NET Platform, i.e., to exchange a binary serialized object or data from one application to another application, and both applications must be in a .NET platform.

Using Binary Serializer

Binary serializer uses a *BinaryFormatter* class to implement Binary Serialization. It is more secure than other serializations. To perform this type of serialization, you just need to mark an item with the *SerializableAttribute*. After that, you need to use the instance of Binary Serializer to serialize the object or object graph. The following are namespaces used in Binary Serialization:

1. System.Runtime.Serialization

2. System.Runtime.Serialization.Formatters.Binary

You can serialize the object into a file or memory or database according to your need.

Listing 11-1 shows how you can configure an object for binary serialization, serialize it into file, and then deserialize it into an object.

Code Snippet

Listing 11-1. Binary Serialization

```
[Serializable]
public class Teacher
{
    public int ID { get; set; }
    public string Name { get; set; }
    public decimal Salary { get; set; }
}
//Created the Instance and initialized
Teacher teacher = new Teacher()
```

```
{
    ID = 1,
    Name = "Ijaz",
    Salary = 1000
};

//Binary Serializer
BinaryFormatter formatter = new BinaryFormatter();

//Sample.bin(Binary File is Created) to store binary serialized data
using (FileStream file=new FileStream("Sample.bin",FileMode.Create))
{
   //this function serialize the "teacher" (Object) into "file" (File)
    formatter.Serialize(file,teacher);
 }

Console.WriteLine("Binary Serialization is Successfully Done!");
//Binary Deserialization
using (FileStream file=new FileStream("Sample.bin",FileMode.Open))
{
    Teacher dteacher=(Teacher)formatter.Deserialize(file);
}
Console.WriteLine("Binary Deserialization is Successfully Done!");
```

Explanation

In binary serialization, all the fields can be serialized, even those that are private. You can prevent fields from being serialized by using a *NonSerialized* attribute. For example, you don't want to serialize the field Salary of Teacher. You can do this:

```
[Serializable]
public class Teacher
{
    public int ID { get; set; }
    public string Name { get; set; }
    [NonSerialized]
    public decimal Salary;
}
```

Binary serialization is stricter than other serializations. When the Binary Serializer can't find a specific field, it throws an exception. You can use *OptionalFieldAttribute* to make sure that the binary serializer knows that the field is added in later versions and the current serialized object will not contain this field.

■ **Note**   Constructor does not execute during Binary deserialization.

XML Serialization

XML serialization serializes an object into XML format or an XML stream. In XML serialization, only public fields or properties can be serialized. Unlike Binary serialization, it does not include a serialized object's type information. For example, if you have a serialized object of type Teacher, then there is no guarantee that it would be deserialized into an object of type Teacher. That's why XML Serialization does not store an object's type information.

According to **MSDN**:

> *XML serialization does not convert methods, indexers, private fields, or read-only properties (except read-only collections). To serialize all of an object's fields and properties, both public and private, use the DataContractSerializer instead of XML serialization.*

Using XML Serializer

XML serialization uses *XmlSerializer* class to implement XML serialization. XmlSerializer is less strict than *BinarySerializer,* but it does not have best performance. It also does not maintain an object's information and you cannot serialize private fields.

To perform XML serialization, you mark your type with a *Serializable* attribute which tells the .NET framework that type should be serializable. It will check your object and object graph (all the objects it references) to make sure that it will serialize all the connected objects.

■ **Tip**   XML serialization can be done without specifying a *Serializable* attribute on the type, but it is bad approach.

Listing 11-2 shows how you can configure an object for XML serialization, serialize it into a file and then deserialize it into an object.

Code Snippet

Listing 11-2. XML Serialization using XmlSerializer

```
[Serializable]
public class Teacher
{
    public int ID { get; set; }
    public string Name { get; set; }
    public long Salary { get; set; }

}
XmlSerializer xml = new XmlSerializer(typeof(Teacher));
using (var stream = new FileStream("Sample.xml", FileMode.Create))
{
    xml.Serialize(stream, t);
}

Console.WriteLine("Data has been Serialized!");

Teacher teacher = null;
using (var stream = new FileStream("Sample.xml", FileMode.Open))
{
    XmlSerializer xml = new XmlSerializer(typeof(Teacher));
    teacher = (Teacher)xml.Deserialize(stream);
}
```

```
Console.WriteLine(teacher.ID);
Console.WriteLine(teacher.Name);
Console.WriteLine(teacher.Salary);

Console.WriteLine("Data has been Deserialized!");
```

Serialized object

The serialized object in XML format looks like:

```
<?xml version="1.0"?>
<Teacher xmlns:xsi="http://www.w3.org/2001/XMLSchema-instance"
xmlns:xsd="http://www.w3.org/2001/XMLSchema">
  <ID>2</ID>
  <Name>Ahsan</Name>
  <Salary>20000</Salary>
</Teacher>
```

Explanation

XML serialization can be configured to get more control over the type to be serialized using attributes provided by the *System.Xml.Serialization* namespace. The following are important attributes (with their use) that are commonly used:

1. **XmlRoot**: Applied on Type, which tells the compiler that this is going to be the main/parent Node of a Serialized object in XML.

2. **XmlAttribute**: Applied on any of the public fields mapped into an attribute on its parent node.

3. **XmlElement**: Applied on any of the public fields mapped into an element of a parent node.

4. **XmlIgnore**: Applied on any of the public fields which will not be serialized.

5. **XmlArray**, **XmlArrayItem**: These two (XmlArray and XmlArrayItem) can be applied on any of the public fields of the type collection for serialization.

By default, each public field of your type is serialized as *XmlElement*. Using these above-mentioned attributes, you can map your object into proper XML format.

Listing 11-3 shows how to configure your type more for XML serialization.

Code Snippet

Listing 11-3. Controlled XML serialization

```
[Serializable]
[XmlRoot("Teacher")]
 public class teacherClass
 {
     [XmlAttribute("ID")]
     public int id { get; set; }
     [XmlElement("Name")]
     public string name { get; set; }
     [XmlIgnore]
     public long salary { get; set; }
```

```
    [XmlElement("Students")]
    public studentClass st { get; set; }


}
[Serializable]
public class studentClass
{

    [XmlAttribute("RollNo")]
    public int rollno { get; set; }
    [XmlElement("Marks")]
    public int marks { get; set; }
}
//Serialization
teacherClass t = new teacherClass
{

    id = 2,
    name = "Ahsan",
    salary = 20000,
    st = new studentClass
    {
        rollno = 1,
        marks = 50
    }
};

XmlSerializer xml = new XmlSerializer(typeof(teacherClass));
using (var stream = new FileStream("Sample.xml", FileMode.Create))
{
    xml.Serialize(stream, t);
}
Console.WriteLine("Data has been Serialized!");

//Deserialization
teacherClass teacher = null;
using (var stream = new FileStream("Sample.xml", FileMode.Open))
{
    XmlSerializer xml = new XmlSerializer(typeof(teacherClass));
    teacher = (teacherClass)xml.Deserialize(stream);
}

Console.WriteLine(teacher.id);
Console.WriteLine(teacher.name);
Console.WriteLine(teacher.salary);
Console.WriteLine(teacher.st.rollno);
Console.WriteLine(teacher.st.marks);
Console.WriteLine("Data has been Deserialized!");
```

Serialized Object

The serialized object in XML format looks like:

```
<?xml version="1.0"?>
<Teacher xmlns:xsi="http://www.w3.org/2001/XMLSchema-instance"
xmlns:xsd="http://www.w3.org/2001/XMLSchema" ID="2">
  <Name>Ahsan</Name>
  <Students RollNo="1">
    <Marks>50</Marks>
  </Students>
</Teacher>
```

This is serialization of a teacherClass object and all the objects connected with it (object graph). As in code, you can also configure Attributes to grasp more control over the object to be serialized.

■ **Note**   Type must be public for XML serialization, as XmlSerializer serializes only public types or members.

Using DataContract Serializer

DataContractSerializer serialize an object into an XML format using a supplied data contract. When working with WCF, your types are serialized so that they can be sent to other applications. This serialization is done by *DataContractSerializer* or *DataContractJsonSerializer* (discussed next).

The main differences between **DataContractSerializer** and **XmlSerializer** are:

1. Instead of using *Serializable* Attribute, you use *DataContract* attribute.

2. Members are not serialized by default as in *XmlSerializer*.

3. All the members you want to serialize must be explicitly marked with a *DataMember* attribute.

4. To ignore a member to be serialized, you use the *IgnoreDataMember* attribute instead of *XmlIgnore*.

5. Private fields are also serializable by *DataContractSerializer*, which is not possible in *XmlSerializer*.

6. In *DataContractSerializer*, you use the *WriteObject()* method to serialize an object and *ReadObject()* method to deserialize the stream into an object.

■ **Note**   WCF uses *DataContractSerializer* as the default Serializer.

Listing 11-4 shows how to serialize and deserialize an object.

Code Snippet

Listing 11-4. XML Serialization using DataContractSerializer

```
[DataContract]
public class Teacher
{
```

```
    [DataMember]
     private int id = 1;
    [DataMember]
    public string name { get; set; }
    [IgnoreDataMember]
    public long salary { get; set; }


}
//Serialization
DataContractSerializer dataContract = new DataContractSerializer(typeof(Teacher));
using (var stream = new FileStream("Sample.xml", FileMode.Create))
{
    dataContract.WriteObject(stream, t);
}
Console.WriteLine("Data has been Serialized!");

//Deserialization
Teacher teacher = null;
DataContractSerializer dataContract = new DataContractSerializer(typeof(Teacher));

using (var stream = new FileStream("Sample.xml", FileMode.Open))
{
    teacher = (Teacher)dataContract.ReadObject(stream);
}
Console.WriteLine("Data has been Deserialized!");
```

You can use *DataContractSerializer* from the *System.Runtime.Serialization* namespace in the same way you used *XmlSerializer* and BinarySerializer (*BinaryFormatter*) with the difference of attributes or methods to serialize and deserialize.

■ **Note**   WCF (Windows Communication Foundation) is a framework for building a service-oriented application. This Topic is discussed in Chapter 13 "Accessing Remote Data."

JSON Serialization

JSON Serialization serializes an object into JSON (JavaScript Object Notation) format, an efficient encoding format that is specifically useful when sending a small amount of data between a Client (Browser) and AJAX-enabled Web services.

JSON Serialization is automatically handled by WCF when you use DataContract Types in service operations that are exposed over AJAX-enabled endpoints.

However, in some cases you may need to execute this serialization manually with JSON serialization, as this is a more lightweight medium to store data into some storage or send over the network.

Using DataContractJsonSerializer

DataContractJsonSerializer is used to convert an object into JSON data and convert back JSON data into an object. *DataContractJsonSerializer* is a class provided by .NET in the *System.Runtime.Serialization.Json* namespace.

Like *DataContractSerializer*, *DataContractJsonSerializer* provides a *WriteObject()* method for serialization and a *ReadObject()* method for deserialization. The rest of the procedure for JSON Serialization is the same as the others. It is mainly used with WCF.

Listing 11-5 shows JSON serialization using *DataContractJsonSerializer*.

Code Snippet

Listing 11-5. JSON Serialization using DataContractJsonSerializer

```
[DataContract]
public class Teacher
{
    [DataMember]
    private int id = 1;
    [DataMember]
    public string name { get; set; }
    [DataMember]
    public long salary { get; set; }

}

//Serialization
DataContractJsonSerializer dataContract = new DataContractJsonSerializer(typeof(Teacher));
    using (var stream = new FileStream("Sample.json", FileMode.Create))
    {
        dataContract.WriteObject(stream, t);
    }
    Console.WriteLine("Data has been Serialized!");
//Deserialization
Teacher teacher = null;
DataContractJsonSerializer dataContract = new   DataContractJsonSerializer(typeof(Teacher));
    using (var stream = new FileStream("Sample.json", FileMode.Open))
    {
        teacher = (Teacher)dataContract.ReadObject(stream);
    }
    Console.WriteLine("Data has been Deserialized!");
```

Serialized Object

```
{"id":1,"name":"Ahsan","salary":20000}
```

Private members are also serialized in Json Serialization.

■ **Note** *DataContractJsonSerializer* supports the same types as *DataContractSerializer*.

Using JavaScriptSerializer

JavaScriptSerializer is a class provided by .NET in the *System.Web.Script.Serialization* namespace found in the *System.Web.Extension* assembly used to serialize and deserialize an object into Json format for AJAX-enabled applications.

Listing 11-6 shows a basic example of how to serialize and deserialize an object using JavaScriptSerializer.

■ **Note**   There is no attribute required for the object's Type to be serialized when using JavaScriptSerializer.

Code Snippet

Listing 11-6.   JSON Serialization using JavaScriptSerializer

```
private class Teacher
{
    private int id { get; set; }
    public string name { get; set; }
    public long salary { get; set; }

}

//Serialization
JavaScriptSerializer dataContract = new JavaScriptSerializer();

string serializedDataInStringFormat = dataContract.Serialize(steacher);

Console.WriteLine("Data has been Serialized!");

//Deserialization
Teacher dteacher = null;

dteacher = dataContract.Deserialize<Teacher>(serializedDataInStringFormat);

Console.WriteLine("Data has been Deserialized!");
```

■ **Note**   Private members cannot be serialized using *JavaScriptSerializer* for Json Serialization.

Custom Serialization

Custom serialization allows an object to control its own serialization and deserialization. One of the ways to implement a custom serialization is to implement an *ISerializable* interface on an object's Type.

Using ISerializable

ISerializable is an interface that allows you to implement custom serialization. This interface involves the *GetObjectData()* method and a special constructor that is used when the object is deserialized.

Listing 11-7 shows custom serialization.

Code Snippet

Listing 11-7. Custom serialization using Iserializable interface

```
[Serializable]
public class Teacher : ISerializable
{
  public int ID { get; set; }
  public string Name { get; set; }
  public Teacher()
  {
  }
  protected Teacher(SerializationInfo info,StreamingContext context)
  {
    this.ID = info.GetInt32("IDKey");
    this.Name = info.GetString("NameKey");
  }

[SecurityPermissionAttribute(SecurityAction.Demand,SerializationFormatter = true)]
 public void GetObjectData(SerializationInfo info, StreamingContext context)
 {
    info.AddValue("IDKey", 1);
    info.AddValue("NameKey", "Hamza")
 }
}
```

Explanation

GetObjectData() method is called during serialization and you need to populate the *SerializationInfo* provided with the method call. Add the variable or value to be serialized with the name associated with it in the *AddValue()* method of *SerializationInfo*'s object. You can use any text as a name associated with a value or variable. You can add any or a few number of variables provided with the method call in *SerializationInfo*'s object. These provided variables or values will be serialized. With deserialization, a special constructor would call and serialized values deserialize by calling the *Get* method of the SerializationInfo's object.

Serialization Performance Comparison

The following table shows the rough idea of performance of serialization techniques by size of data (in bytes) and time (in milliseconds) taken to serialize and deserialize an object or object graph:

Table 11-1. *Performance Comparison of different Serialization techniques*

	Binary	XML	Data Contract
Size (Small)	669	298	370
Serialize	0.0210	0.0218	0.004
Deserialize	0.0194	0.0159	0.0127
Size (Large)	204,793	323,981	364,299
Serialize	13.7000	5.5080	4.4438
Deserialize	19.3976	7.8893	11.4690

Summary

1. The process of converting an object or object graph into a stream of bytes is called Serialization, and the reverse process is called Deserialization.

2. Binary Serialization is performed using a Serializable attribute. It is more secure than other serializations but restricted to a .NET Platform.

3. XML Serialization serialized only public members and is not restricted to a .NET Platform. An XML Serialized object is readable as compared to a Binary Serialized object, which is not readable to humans.

4. XmlSerializer and DataContractSerializer: both classes can be used for XML Serialization.

5. JSON serialization is considered a fast serialization approach. It is lightweight compared to XML and Binary Serialization. As with XML serialization, you can just serialize public members.

6. DataContractJsonSerializer and JavaScriptSerializer: both classes can be used for JSON serialization.

7. Custom Serialization can also be performed by implementing an ISerializable interface.

Code Challenges

Challenge 1: Perform Deserialization

You are given a sample file of serialized data in XML format (taken from MSDN); you need to deserialize the data using the appropriate deserialization technique.

Practice Exam Questions

Question 1

You are developing an application that retrieves Person type data from the Internet using JSON. You have written the following function for receiving the data so far:

```
serializer.Deserialize<Person>(json);
```

Which code segment should you use before this function?

A) `DataContractJsonSerializer serializer = new DataContractJsonSerializer(typeof(Person));`

B) `DataContractSerializer serializer = new DataContractSerializer(typeof(Person));`

C) `JavaScriptSerializer serializer = new JavaScriptSerializer();`

D) `NetDataContractSerializer serializer = new NetDataContractSerializer();`

Question 2

You need to store a large amount of data in a file. Which serializer would you consider better?

A)   XmlSerializer

B)   DataContractSerializer

C)   DataContractJsonSerializer

D)   BinaryFormatter

E)   JavaScriptSerializer

Question 3

You want to serialize data in Binary format but some members don't need to be serialized. Which attribute should you use?

A)   XmlIgnore

B)   NotSerialized

C)   NonSerialized

D)   Ignore

Answers

1.   C

2.   D

3.   C

CHAPTER 12

■ ■ ■

Consume Data

To work with data is an important part of developing an application. A normal application stores data in memory but when this application ends, data is lost. In this case, when you don't want to lose your data, the .NET framework gives you the interactive way to store your data in a persistent way. This can be achieved by interacting with a database or external web service to insert or retrieve data whenever you require.

In this chapter, we will learn about:

1. Working with a database

2. Consuming XML and JSON data

3. Working with a Web service

Working with a Database

The .NET framework provides the namespace System.Data.dll, using the classes to interact with relational database systems. These classes come under **ADO.NET**, in which there are three conceptual parts:

1. Connected Layer

2. Disconnected Layer

3. Entity Framework

ADO.NET

ADO.NET is a set of object-oriented libraries used to interact with a database. It enables you to connect with a database and perform different database-oriented operations on it, such as a CRUD operation (Create, Read, Update, and Delete data). According to MSDN:

> "**ADO.NET** is a set of classes that expose data access services for **.NET** Framework programmers. **ADO.NET** provides a rich set of components for creating distributed, data-sharing applications. It is an integral part of the **.NET** Framework, providing access to relational, XML, and application data."

System.Data provides different Types (Class or interface, etc.) that provide data access for different data providers.

© Ali Asad and Hamza Ali 2017
A. Asad and H. Ali, *The C# Programmer's Study Guide (MCSD)*, DOI 10.1007/978-1-4842-2860-9_12

Data Providers

The .NET framework allows you to work with different types of databases, for example, Microsoft SQL Server, Oracle, and MySQL database. System.Data.dll provides different Data providers to work with different databases. Data Providers are used for connecting to a database, executing a command, and retrieving a result. For example, if you want to work with an MS SQL server database, .NET gives you a Data Provider for this, i.e., the **System.Data.SqlClient** namespace (provides data access for Microsoft SQL server database) and the **System.Data.OleDb** namespace. For more information on Data Providers, visit:

```
https://msdn.microsoft.com/en-us/library/a6cd7c08(v=vs.110).aspx
```

We will discuss the interaction with an MS SQL server database in this chapter.

Connection

After deciding the data provider, connection to a specific database is important to work with. You must establish a connection with your database for further interaction. ADO.NET provides classes to establish connection with a specific database. A connection string is required which contains all the information to connect with a database including data location, database name, data provider, and authentication against database.

DbConnection class is a base class that provides the connection-related functionality. **SqlConnection** is derived with **DbConnection** class and can be used for connection with an SQL Server database. To connect with a specific database using a connection string, you must open the connection to proceed further.

The following steps show how to connect with an MS SQL server database:

Step 1:

Right-click on your project in Visual Studio and Click on Add ➤ **New Item**. Select **DataSet** and name it whatever you like (Sample.xsd in this example).

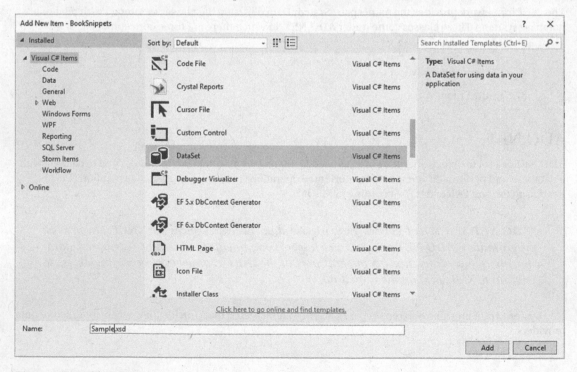

Figure 12-1. *Choose DataSet*

After this, the Sample.xsd window appears in front of you.

Step 2:

Add Data Connection by going to **Server Explorer**. In **Server Explorer**, right-click on Data Connections ➤ Add Connection; a wizard will open where you need to specify Server name and select a database which you made in SQL server. In this example, I have added **School** database, having two tables: **Student** (*StudentID*, StudentName) and **Class** (*ClassID*, ClassName, *StudentID*: as foreign key).

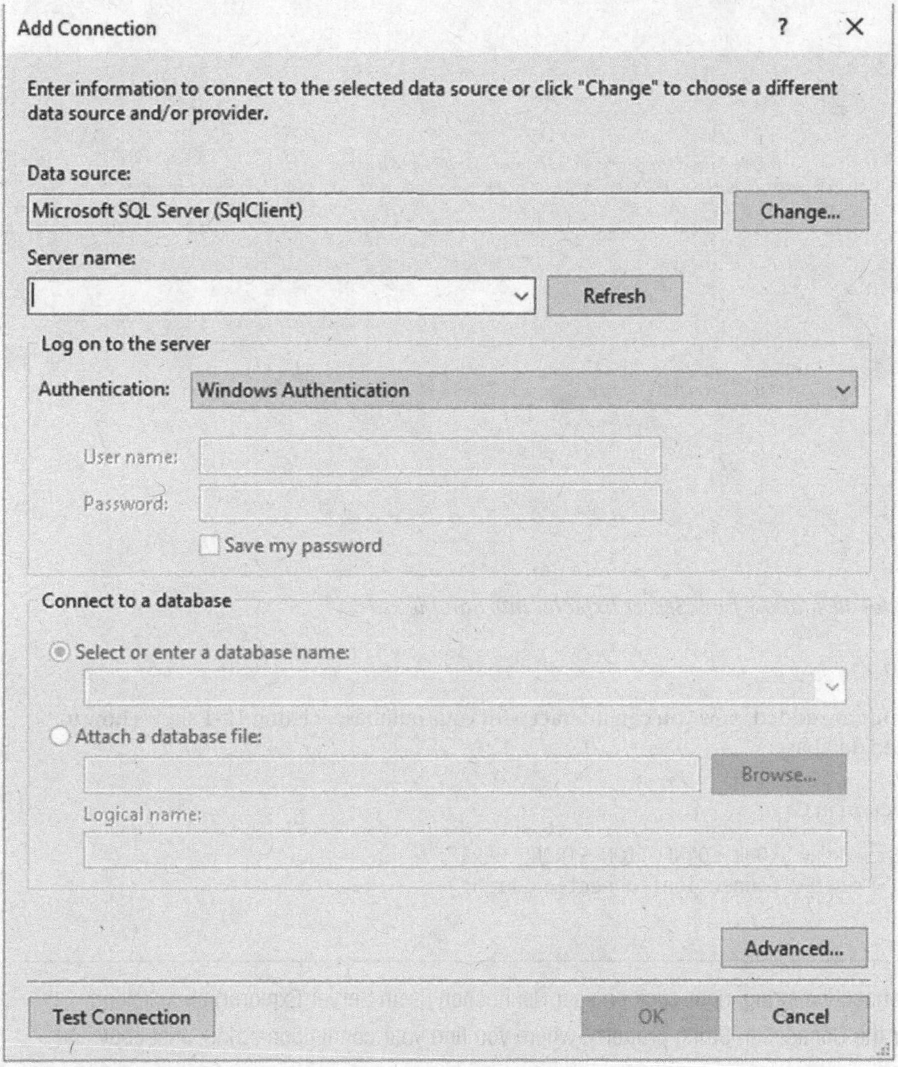

Figure 12-2. Choose Data Source after selecting DataSet

After selecting database, Click OK.

Step 3:

Drag the added connection (from the Server Explorer) in Sample.xsd (the window open in front of you) and Save the Sample.xsd.

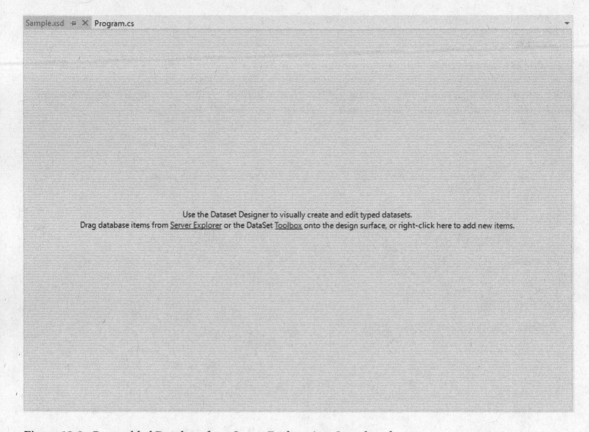

Figure 12-3. Drag added Database from Server Explorer into Sample.xsd

Step 4:

As the components are added, now you can interact with your database. Listing 12-1 shows how to connect with an added database:

Listing 12-1. Connection in C#

```
string connectionString = "YOUR CONNECTION STRING HERE";
SqlConnection con = new SqlConnection(connectionString);
con.Open();
```

■ **Note** To get a connection string, right-click on your Connection (from Server Explorer) and click on properties. Search for the Connection String property, where you find your connection string. Just copy and paste in your code.

You can also build your connection string dynamically by using the provided class **SqlConnectionStringBuilder**. Listing 12-2 shows dynamic building of a connection string:

Listing 12-2. Dynamic building of a connection string

```
SqlConnectionStringBuilder builder = new SqlConnectionStringBuilder();
builder.DataSource = "";
builder.InitialCatalog = "";
builder.IntegratedSecurity = true;

string connectionString = builder.ToString();
```

■ **Note** You must close the connection after performing the operation. Having connections open for too long is a problem, as other users can't connect . The server allows a specific number of connections and, if the limit is exceeded, it will not allow any other user to connect due to the busyness of the already allotted connections (that are still open).

Command

ADO.NET provides the class **SqlCommand,** used to execute statements (commands/queries) against the database. By using this class, you can execute insert, delete, update, or stored procedure commands. Listing 12-3 shows how to give command of a specify query:

Code Snippet

Listing 12-3. Command in C#

```
string command = "select *  from Student";
SqlCommand cmd = new SqlCommand(command,con);
```

SqlCommand requires a command (statement/query) to execute and a **connection** (connection string) on which a written command is going to execute. This code knows which command to execute on which connection (in other words, what to do using which path).

Conceptual parts of ADO. NET

Conceptually, ADO.NET consists of three layers, i.e., the different ways of interaction with a database. Each layer has its own suitability according to the scenario. The details of these layers are described below.

Connected Layer

In a connected layer, you connect to a database as a data source and execute queries by writing SQL. These queries are used by ADO.NET and forwarded to your database of choice.

In this way of interacting with a database, you normally use Connection, Command, and DataReader objects.

ExecuteNonQuery

ExecuteNonQuery is a method performed on a Command (**SqlCommand**) object used to execute the statement specified by a Command object and does not return result set(s) but a number of rows affected in a database by query execution. It is basically called on a Command object, having the query of insert, delete, and update. These queries do not return any record but a number of rows affected; that's why these types of queries are executed by **ExecuteNonQuery** Method.

Listing 12-4 shows the example of **ExecuteNonQuery**:

Code Snippet

Listing 12-4. ExecuteNonQuery on Insert Command

```
string connectionString = "YOUR CONNECTION STRING HERE";
SqlConnection con = new SqlConnection(connectionString);
con.Open();

string command = "Insert into Student values(1,'Hamza Ali')";
SqlCommand cmd = new SqlCommand(command, con);
int result = cmd.ExecuteNonQuery();
con.Close();
if (result > 0)
  Console.WriteLine("Data is Inserted");
else
  Console.WriteLine("Error while inserting");
```

This code basically inserts data in a Student table. **ExecuteNonQuery()** returns the number of affected rows.

■ **Tip**   When database related work is done, try to close the connection immediately. It is recommended to use a **Using** block in this case.

ExecuteScalar

The **ExecuteScalar** method is also performed on a Command's object in a case where you write queries that return a single value. This is the case in which you use aggregate functions in your queries.

Listing 12-5 shows how to use the **ExecuteScalar** method:

Code Snippet

Listing 12-5. ExecuteScalar on aggregate function

```
string con = "YOUR CONNECTION STRING HERE";

string command = "select count(*) from Student";
SqlCommand cmd = new SqlCommand(command, con);
var noOfStudents = cmd.ExecuteScalar();
con.Close();
Console.WriteLine(noOfStudents);
```

ExecuteScalar returns a single value of type Object which you can cast on the corresponding type.

ExecuteReader

The **ExecuteReader** method is also called on a Command's object where you need to retrieve the data, i.e., in the case of a "select" query. This method returns an **SqlDataReader** object that remains connected to a database the whole time the reader is open. **SqlDataReader** is a forward-only resultset, which means you cannot move to any previous record and can read one record at a time. You can read the specific column of a table by index number or column name. Listing 12-6 shows the use of the **ExecuteReader** method:

Code Snippet

Listing 12-6. ExecuteReader in Select Command

```
string con = "YOUR CONNECTION STRING HERE";

string command = "select * from Student";
SqlCommand cmd = new SqlCommand(command, con);

SqlDataReader reader = cmd.ExecuteReader();

int StudentID = 0;
string StudentName = null;
if (reader.HasRows)
{
  while (reader.Read())
  {
  StudentID = int.Parse(reader[0].ToString());//0 index means first clm in the table which
  is StudentID
  StudentName = reader["StudentName"].ToString();//it will fetch the value of provided clm
  name
  }
}
reader.Close();
con.Close();

Console.WriteLine("ID is: " + StudentID);
Console.WriteLine("Name is: " + StudentName);
```

SqlDataReader provides some properties like **HasRows** (to check if an SqlDataReader object has a row/rows or not), **FieldCount**, **IsClosed**, **Item[Int32]**, and **Item[string]**.

The last two properties are indexers which we have used in the above example. These are used to fetch a specific column value based on its name(string) or index number(int).

Read() method reads the record from a database and is ready to read for the next, while the loop iterates and execution takes place for the next record and so on until there is the last record and the loop ends.

You must close the reader object and then close the connection object. Forgetting to close the connection can hurt performance. You can use the **"Using"** block to avoid such things.

■ **Note**   You can use the **OleDbDataReader** class in place of the **SqlDataReader** class for retrieving data from Microsoft Access.

ExecuteXMLReader

The **ExecuteXmlReader** method is also called on a Command's object and is the same as **ExecuteReader** but the difference is that it returns an **XmlReader** object used to represent data as XML.

Disconnected Layer

In a disconnected layer, you normally use DataSets and DataTables that copy the structure of a relational database in memory. A **DataSet** is created in the result of an execution of a query against a connected database. It can be manipulated in memory and changes to a database take place using **DataAdapter**. DataTable and DataSets are another way to retrieve results from a database.

DataTable

DataTable is the same as **DataReader** except **DataTable** can also move forward and back. It is disconnected from a database and you can make changes to data in DataTable and commit or update a database with these changes

DataSet

DataSet is the container of DataTables. You can write a query that returns multiple resultsets and can be contained in a **DataSet**. You can then perform further operations on a received **DataSet,** such as filtering or sorting, etc. These updatings take place in memory.

DataAdapter

DataAdapter is the important object when you work with a disconnected layer. It acts like a bridge between data in memory and a database. **DataAdapter** populates a **DataTable** or **DataSets** and reconnects data in memory to a database. You can perform insert, update, delete, or read query while the data is in memory and then reconnect to a database to commit the changes.

Listing 12-7 shows how to perform database-oriented operations using a disconnected layer:

Code Snippet

Listing 12-7. Disconnected layer operations

```
string con = "YOUR CONNECTION STRING HERE";

string command = "select * from Student";
SqlDataAdapter ad = new SqlDataAdapter(command, con);

DataTable tbl = new DataTable();
ad.Fill(tbl);//Now the data in DataTable (memory)
con.Close();//connection closed

foreach (DataRow item in tbl.Rows)
{
  Console.WriteLine("ID is: " + item[0]);
  Console.WriteLine("Name is: " + item[1]);
}
```

When **DataAdapter's** Fill method is called, a query will be executed and the **Fill()** method will populate the DataTable(get the data and map into DataTable). DataTable doesn't need to keep open the connection to populate the data, which is not the case for DataReader (in a connected layer). This is the beauty of a disconnected layer, and it has better performance than a connected layer as it deals with the data present in memory, which is quickly accessible.

You can also use DataSet instead of DataTable when expecting multiple resultsets. The working is the same except it can return multiple tables. DataSet has the property of Table by which you can iterate over specific table data.

As stated, you can perform further operations on DataTable or DataSet, such as insert, delete, etc. (Data in memory), and these operations are fast in performance compared to operations performed in a Connected layer. As in a connected layer, database is connected and ADO.NET architecture takes the query and map into a database (which is time-consuming compared to map) or performs some function on the data which is present in memory but not at some external location (the case of a disconnected layer).

Listing 12-8 shows insertion of data in a DataTable and commits the changes to a database:

Code Snippet

Listing 12-8. Insertion of data (disconnected layer)

```
string connectionString = "YOUR CONNECTION STRING HERE";
SqlConnection con = new SqlConnection(connectionString);
con.Open();

string command = "select * from Student";//Currently has One Row(for example)
SqlDataAdapter ad = new SqlDataAdapter(command, con);

DataTable tbl = new DataTable();
ad.Fill(tbl);//Now the data in DataTable (memory)

//Data in Memory (One Row)
foreach (DataRow item in tbl.Rows)
{
  Console.WriteLine("ID is: " + item[0]);
  Console.WriteLine("Name is: " + item[1]);
}

//New Record to add in DataTable
DataRow newRow = tbl.NewRow();
newRow["StudentID"] = 2;
newRow["StudentName"] = "Ali Asad";
tbl.Rows.Add(newRow);

//Two Rows(As new row added to DataTable)
foreach (DataRow item in tbl.Rows)
{
  Console.WriteLine("ID is: " + item[0]);
  Console.WriteLine("Name is: " + item[1]);
}

//Now newRow has to add in Database(Pass newRow Parameters to this insert query)
string newCommand = @"Insert into Student(StudentID,StudentName)
                              Values(@StudentID,@StudentName)";
```

```
SqlCommand insertCommand = new SqlCommand(newCommand, con);

//Create the parameters
insertCommand.Parameters.Add(new SqlParameter("@StudentID", SqlDbType.Int, Int32.
MaxValue,"StudentID"));
insertCommand.Parameters.Add(new SqlParameter("@StudentName",  SqlDbType.VarChar,
40,"StudentName"));

//Associate Insert Command to DataAdapter so that it could add into Database
ad.InsertCommand = insertCommand;

ad.Update(tbl);

con.Close();
```

In this example, a Parameter property of a Command object is used, which takes new parameter-related data, such as column name, column size, and parameter name. "newRow" added in DataTable (new record in memory) but didn't add in database, but later used the **Update()** method of DataAdpater, which reconnects to a database to take changes (i.e., updated DataTable mapped to a database).

You can perform further operations likewise, i.e., to delete data, write a delete query, and associate it with a DataAdapter object like **da.DeleteCommand="";,** etc.

Entity Framework

The connected and disconnected layers force you to treat data in the manner of a physical schema of a database. These layers are tightly coupled with the relational database, as the user needs to use SQL to perform queries, and to keep in mind connection, command, DataReader, DataSet, and DataAdapter, etc. Unlike these layers, Entity Framework gives you the object-oriented way to interact with a database. Using this conceptual layer of ADO.NET, you don't need to worry about connection or command-like objects. This kind of stuff is automatically handled by Entity Framework.

Like ADO.NET, ADO.NET Entity Framework is also a set of libraries for interaction with a database in a different conceptual manner.

Entity Framework is an object relational mapping framework for ADO.NET. It has a graphical view on which you can drag and drop database objects and update this view whenever there is a change in the database. This is called the Object Relational Mapper (ORM). This is a preferable approach to interacting with a database for those who have/haven't weak knowledge of SQL, because it gives object-oriented interaction with a database as it maps the database schema into C# classes. It also makes the code short to interact with the database and handle a lot of things by itself.

LINQ is used instead of SQL and you can use one of LINQ's types with your data source provided by ADO.NET (Database).

■ **Note**   When you perform LINQ queries to your ADO.NET data source, the entity framework runtime generates a proper SQL statement on your behalf. But it slows down the performance as compared to the connected and the disconnected layer.

Entity Framework (EF) normally has four approaches to use:

1.   EF Designer from database

2.   Empty EF Designer model

3. Empty Code First model

4. Code first from database

These approaches can be used by using Entity Data Model Wizard but the "Code first from database" approach can also be used without the Entity Data Model Wizard.

Every approach has its own suitability. We will take "EF Designer from database" approach to interact with a database.

To use the Entity Framework approach (EF Designer from database) to interact with a database using the Entity Data Model Wizard:

Step 1:

Right-click on your project and click on Add ➤ New Item. Select "ADO.NET Entity Data Model", name it whatever you like (in this example I named it Sample), and click on the "Add" button.

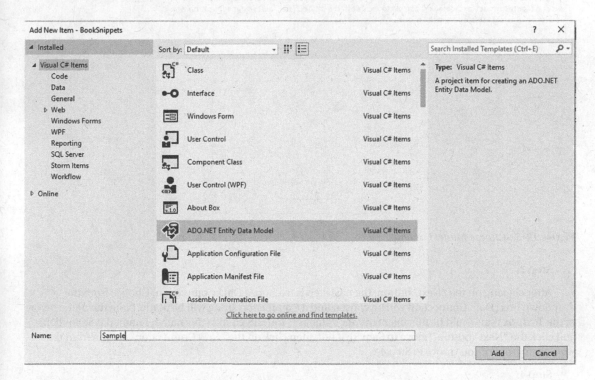

Figure 12-4. *Choose ADO.NET Entity Data Model*

Step 2:

After clicking the "Add" button, the next step is to choose Model Contents. Choose the first one, EF Designer from database, and click the "Next" button.

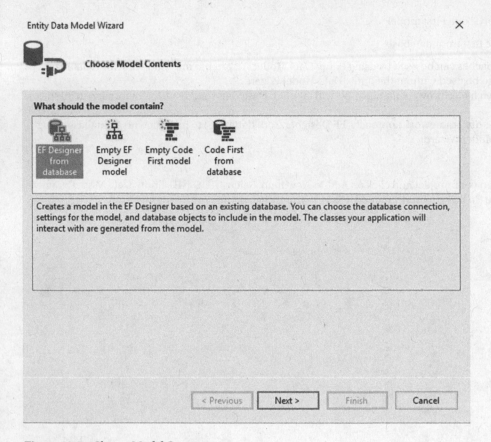

Figure 12-5. *Choose Model Contents*

Step 3:

After clicking on the "Next" button, the next step is to choose Data Connection. Choose from the dropdown box (Data Connection will be chosen and a Connection string will be made. Note the name below in the TextBox that would be the object of your database. You can change this name. I named it SchoolDB) and click the "Next" button, (move to Step 5); if not, then click on the "New Connection" button from the window in front of you (move to Step 4).

Step 4:

If you clicked on the "New Connection" button, then specify the server name and database and click the "OK" button.

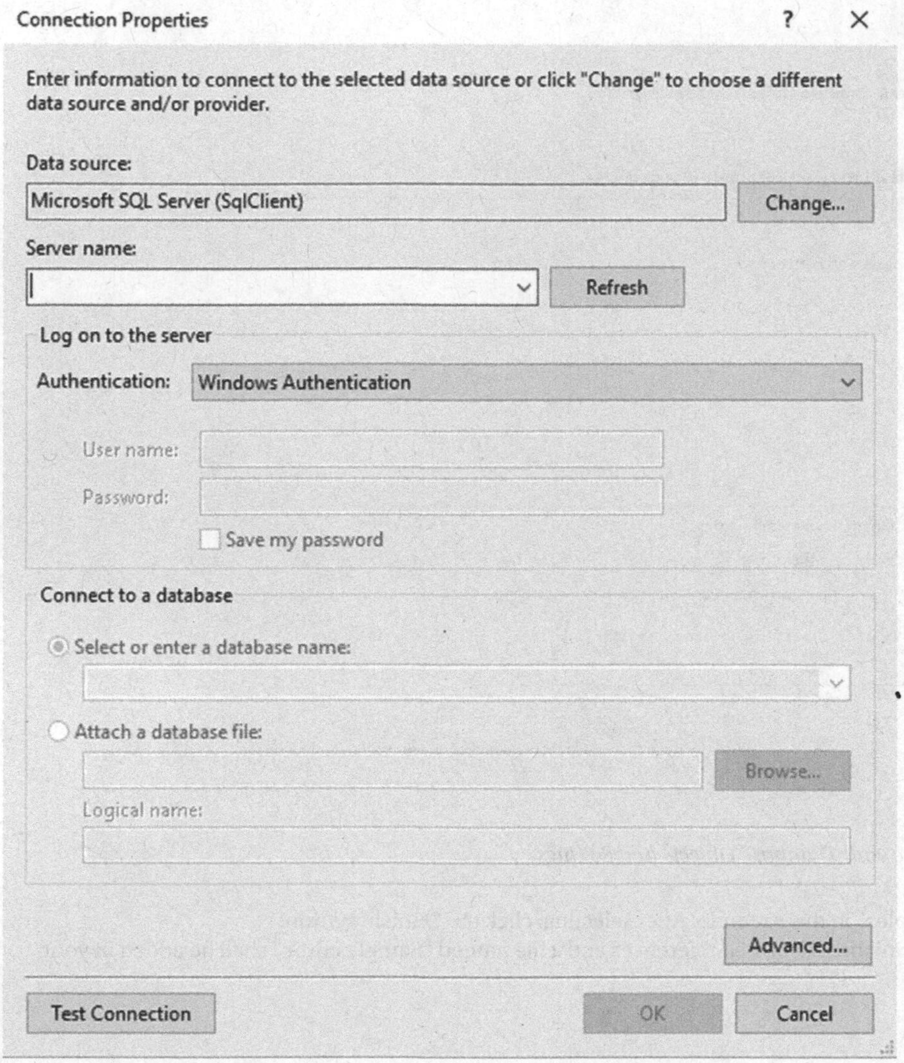

Figure 12-6. *Choose Data Source/Connection String*

(The "Connect to a database" panel will enable for entry when you specify the server name.) Data Connection will be selected and a connection string will be made. Click the "Next" button.

Step 5:

After clicking the "Next" button, choose your Database Objects and Settings. There are checkboxes of "Tables", "View", and "Stored Procedures and Functions". Select the checkbox or checkboxes on the Database Objects which you want to add.

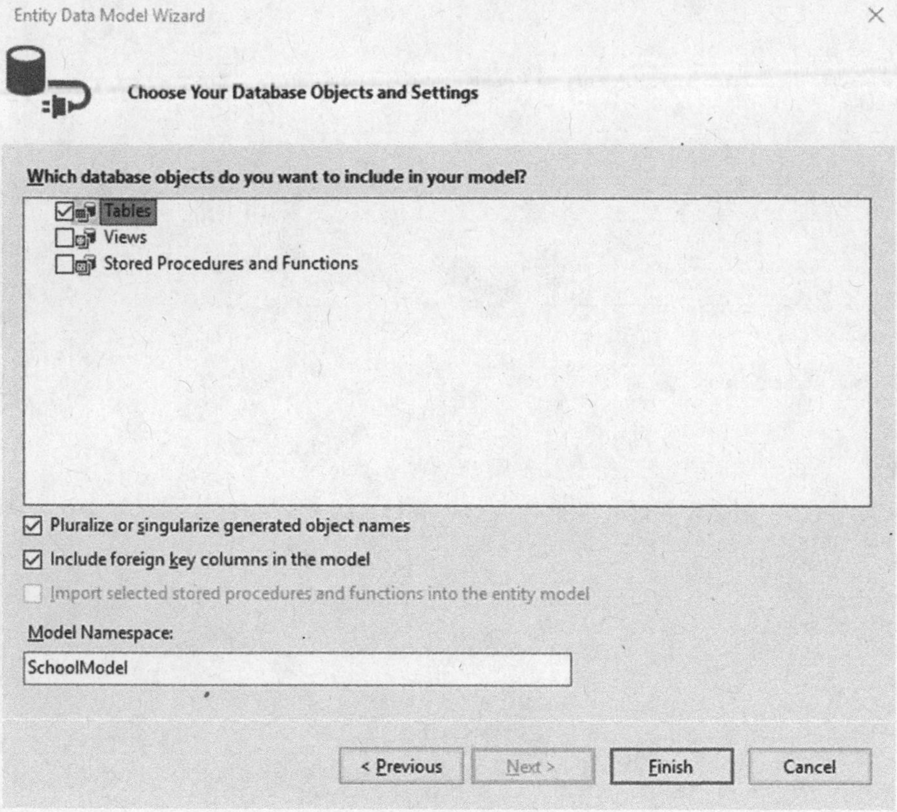

Figure 12-7. *Choose your Database Objects and Settings*

I select the "Tables" in this example. After selecting, click the "Finish" button.

Wizard is now finished. Required references and a file named "Sample.edmx" shall be added in your projects.

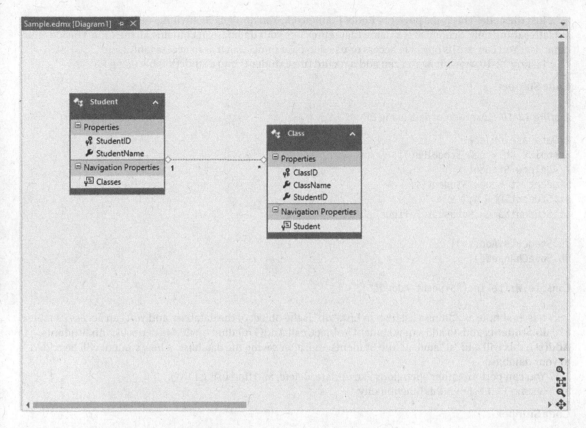

Figure 12-8. *The edmx file of added Database*

Now you are ready to interact with your database.

Listing 12-9 shows how you can get all the student data using Entity Framework:

Code Snippet

Listing 12-9. Read data using EF

```
//Database object
SchoolDB db = new SchoolDB();

//LINQ query to get students
var students = (from p in db.Students
select p).ToList();

foreach (var student in students)
{
  Console.WriteLine("ID is: " + student.StudentID);
  Console.WriteLine("Name is: " + student.StudentName);
}
```

Just the code! This is the power of Entity Framework. You don't need anything else except to work with a relative thing only. SchoolDB is a name that represents your database. It contains all the things inside your database. You can use its object to access or use database things, such as to access tables, etc.

Listing 12-10 shows how you can add a record (new student) into a student table using EF:

Code Snippet

Listing 12-10. Insertion of data using EF

```
//Database object
SchoolDB db = new SchoolDB();
//Add new Student
Student st = new Student();
st.StudentID = 3;
st.StudentName="Mubashar Rafique";

db.Students.Add(st);
db.SaveChanges();

Console.WriteLine("Student Added!");
```

It is as simple as adding a list item in List. "db" is the object of the database and you can access its tables like **db.Students** and, to add a new student's object, call **Add()** method on **db.Students** like **db.Students. Add(st);** this will add "st" student into Students and, after saving the database, a new student will be added to your database.

You can perform other operations like update, delete, and find using LINQ.

Listing 12-11 shows this functionality:

Code Snippet

Listing 12-11. Find, Update, and Delete using EF

```
//Database object
SchoolDB db = new SchoolDB();
//Find specific Studnet by ID (let say id is 2)
var std = (from p in db.Students
where p.StudentID == 2
select p).FirstOrDefault();

if (std != null)//if student is found
{
//Show the record
Console.WriteLine("ID is: " + std.StudentID + " Name is: " +  std.StudentName);
}

if (std != null)//if student is found
{
//update the record.
std.StudentName = "Updated Name";
db.SaveChanges();
}
```

```
if (std != null)//if student is found
{
//delete the record
db.Students.Remove(std);
db.SaveChanges();
}
```

These operations performed using other layers (connected and disconnected) are far easier to perform using this layer. And the developers who haven't much knowledge about SQL or are bothered by the connected or disconnected layer have a better choice to interact with a database using EF.

■ **Note**   Every layer has its own suitability and the choice of using it depends on the scenario and efficiency.

Consume XML and JSON Data

XML and JSON are mainly used for communication over the network between different applications or different platforms. We will discuss these two formats of passing messages/data over the Internet with a brief description.

XML Data

XML (Extensible Markup Language)is basically designed to store and transport data. The .NET Framework provides classes to work with XML. These classes are present in System.Xml.dll. You can read the XML documents as well as create them along with the implication of other operations like edit and parse, and store XML documents in memory or on disk.

We mainly use three classes to work with XML data:

1. **XmlDocument**: This class reads the entire XML into the memory and lets you navigate and edit XML.

2. **XmlReader**: This class reads the XML element vise, reads the current element, and moves for next. It holds the current element in memory instead of holding the entire document or XML in memory; that's why it is fast and less memory-consuming.

3. **XmlWriter**: This class is used to create XML. It is fast way to write XML data.

■ **Note**   LINQ to XML provides the flexible way to interact with XML data.

For example, we have a sample XML file and want to read this data:

```
<Student>
  <ID>1</ID>
  <Name>Hamza Ali</Name>
</Student>
```

Listing 12-12 shows how to read the above XML using XmlReader:

Code Snippet

Listing 12-12. Read XML using XmlReader

```
string xml = @"<Student>
                <ID>1</ID>
                <Name>Hamza Ali</Name>
                </Student>";

//to read xml string as a stream
StringReader sReader = new StringReader(xml);

//reader needs xml data as stream (xmlReader is ready)
XmlReader xReader = XmlReader.Create(sReader);

while (xReader.Read())//Read the entire xml
{
  Console.WriteLine(xReader.Value);
}
```

You can also use XmlDocument to read XML:

```
//to read xml string as a stream
StringReader sReader = new StringReader(xml);

XmlDocument doc = new XmlDocument();
doc.Load(sReader);
foreach (XmlNode item in doc.DocumentElement)
{
  Console.WriteLine(item.InnerText);
}
```

DocumentElement gets the root element of XML. If you want to create an XML document, XmlWriter will be used in this case. Listing 12-13 shows how you can write XML data using XmlWriter:

Code Snippet

Listing 12-13. Write XML data using XmlWriter

```
//Stream to store xml
StringWriter stream = new StringWriter();
using (XmlWriter writer = XmlWriter.Create(stream, new XmlWriterSettings() { Indent = true
}))//Indent to space between elements
{
  writer.WriteStartDocument();//Star Doc
  writer.WriteStartElement("Student");//write Elelment "Student"
  writer.WriteAttributeString("ID", "1");//Student's attribute "ID" with value 1
  writer.WriteElementString("Name", "Hamza Ali"); //"Name" element inside Student
with  inner text "Hamza Ali"
  writer.WriteEndElement();
}
Console.WriteLine(stream.ToString());//show written xml
```

You can further store the "stream" to a file.

JSON Data

JSON is another format used to transport data over the Internet. These types of formats (XML and JSON) are used by Web Services or Web APIs. It is lightweight and more human-readable than XML. You normally use those classes which are used for serialization of data in JSON format. Basically, use of JSON data is the same as JSON serialization which is discussed in Chapter 11. The .NET provides a JavaScriptSerializer class for JSON data parsing. Additionally, we use Newtonsoft.Json library to parse JSON data. You can visit the following link to consume JSON data using Newtonsoft.json:

```
http://www.newtonsoft.com/json
```

Working with Web Services

Web services are another way to store and retrieve data from a remote location. Data can travel through different applications using these services.

You just need to know the address of the web service and know how to call it. Implementation behind the calling is completely hidden from its consumers.

The .NET framework provides the facility to develop such services. You can develop this kind of service using .NET's technology WCF (Windows Communication Foundation) and using Visually Designed class for creating Web Service (ASMX Service). (This feature is included in .NET Framework 3.5 and below.) This is an old approach to create web services.

ASMX Web Service

There are two main steps to create a web service using "Visually Designed Class for web service":

1. Creating the Web Service
2. Creating Proxy and Consuming the Web Service

Creating the Web Service

The following steps show the way to create the web service:

Step 1:

Open VS, create a new project by navigating to "Web", then select ASP.NET Empty Web Application. Name it whatever you like (in this example, I named it WebServiceInCSharp) and click the "OK" button (the Framework selected should be ".NET Framework 3.5").

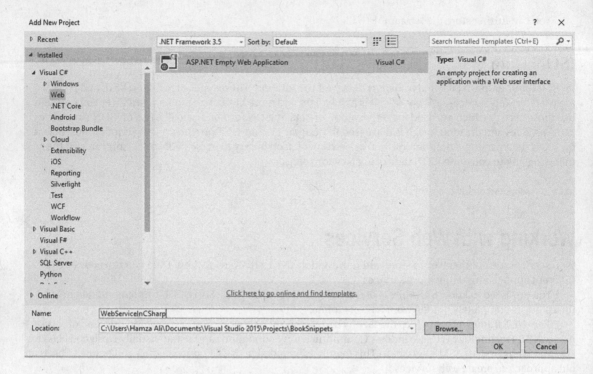

Figure 12-9. New ASP.NET Empty Web Application Project

Step 2:

After the creation of the project, right-click on project ➤ Add ➤ New Item. Select Web Service (ASMX) and name it whatever you like (in this example, I named it SampleService) and click the "Add" button.

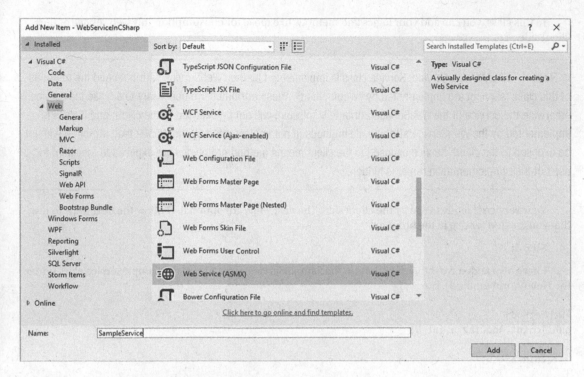

Figure 12-10. *Add ASMX Web Service*

Step 3:

After adding the SampleService, SampleService.asmx will be added in your project, which is a Visually Designed class, i.e., your web service. It looks like:

Listing 12-14. ASMX Web Service Class

```
namespace WebServiceInCSharp
{
    [WebService(Namespace = "http://tempuri.org/")]
    [WebServiceBinding(ConformsTo = WsiProfiles.BasicProfile1_1)]
    [System.ComponentModel.ToolboxItem(false)]
    // To allow this Web Service to be called from script, using ASP.NET AJAX, uncomment the
    following line.
    // [System.Web.Script.Services.ScriptService]
    public class SampleService : System.Web.Services.WebService
    {

        [WebMethod]
        public string HelloWorld()
        {
            return "Hello World";
        }

    }
}
```

339

In this class, you can add your logics and methods to expose for consumption this web service at the client side.

■ **Note** In ASMX Web Service, Service class is implemented by the "WebService" attribute and the methods of this class (service) are implemented by "WebMethod". These attributes are necessary to expose the service, otherwise the service (if the WebService attribute is missing) will not be exposed to the client; and if class is implemented by the WebService attribute, its methods (if not implemented by the WebMethod attribute) will not be exposed to the client. Service exposed to the client means method prototypes are exposed to the client for use but their implementation remains hidden.

Your service is ready to use by the client side. The next steps are optional. (Follow the next steps to test that you created service in the browser.)

Step 1:

I have also added two other functions in the SampleService.asmx file (in the SampleService class under the HelloWorld method), like:

```
[WebMethod]
public int Add(int a,int b)
{
  return a + b;
}

[WebMethod]
public int Subtract(int a,int b)
{
  return a - b;
}
```

To test this service, right-click on SampleService.asmx ➤ View in the Browser.

The list of methods written in your service are the list down in front of you. The view can give you access to use it as a client (it basically exposes the methods of the Web service).

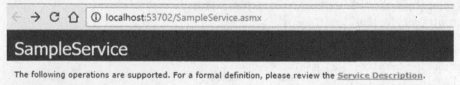

Figure 12-11. *List of Methods exposed by Service*

Step 2:

Click on any of one to test the method. (Click on Add.)

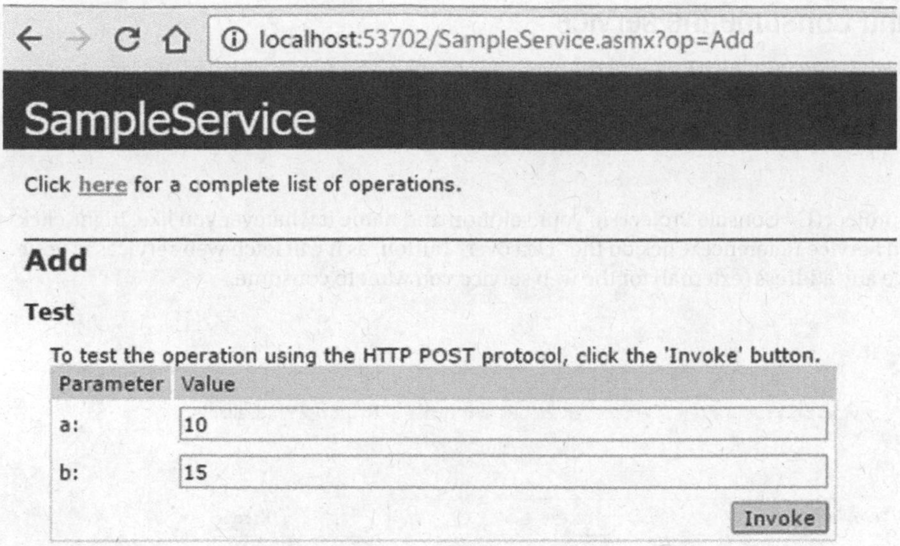

Figure 12-12. *Invoking Add Method of Service*

As you can see from your code, **add()** methods take two parameters with the names a and b and return a result. The same happens here.

Step 3:

After involving the method, the result would be viewed in the form of XML as described XML and JSON used to transport data over the network and mainly used by a Web Service or Web APIs.

```
← → C ⌂   ⓘ localhost:53702/SampleService.asmx/Add

This XML file does not appear to have any style information ass

<int xmlns="http://tempuri.org/">25</int>
```

Figure 12-13. *Respose of Add method in XML format*

These are the steps for creating and testing a created web service.

Create Proxy and Consume the service

Creation of Proxy is important, as it registers with the client application and allows web services' methods to be used as local methods at the client side.

For this you must follow the following steps:

Step 1:

Create another project (C# Console Project) in your solution and name it whatever you like. Right-click on References ➤ Add Service Reference. Click on the "Discover" button, as it will fetch web services in your solution. You can give any address (external) for the web service you want to consume.

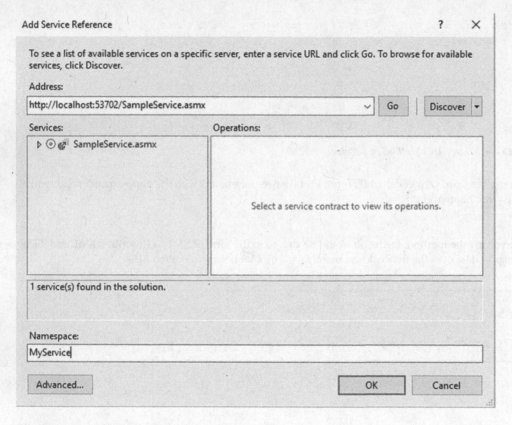

Figure 12-14. *Add Service Reference to Client Project*

You can change the namespace for your discovered web service. (I named it MyService, which it will use later in the code.)

Step 2:

After clicking the "OK" button, a folder of Service References is added with necessary DLLs. Now in your code file (Program file), simply write the following code snippet:

Listing 12-15. Creation of Proxy to consume Web Service

```
//Create the proxy for your service to use its methods
MyService.SampleServiceSoapClient proxy = new MyService.SampleServiceSoapClient();
```

```
int addResult = proxy.Add(5, 10);
int subtractResult = proxy.Subtract(100, 40);

Console.WriteLine("Addition Result is: " + addResult);
Console.WriteLine("Subtraction Result is: " + subtractResult);
```

MyService is the Namespace which you added while adding SampleService in this project. You can create a proxy with the written class (above in code).

When there is a change in Service, you just need to update your added reference to that service. This is done by just expanding the folder "Service Reference" in Client project. Right-click on your service and click "Update Service Reference".

■ **Note**   The class of your service is SampleService but, at the time of creating a proxy, you have to write SoapClient (suffix) with the class name as SampleServiceSoapClient. If the service class name is MyService the proxy class will be MyServiceSoapClient.

WCF Web Service

According to MSDN:

> *Windows Communication Foundation (WCF) is a framework for building service-oriented applications. Using WCF, you can send data as asynchronous messages from one service endpoint to another. A service endpoint can be part of a continuously available service hosted by IIS, or it can be a service hosted in an application.*

Modern web services are being created using WCF. You can follow the simple WCF getting started directions from the following link:

```
https://msdn.microsoft.com/en-us/library/ms734712(v=vs.110).aspx
```

■ **Note**   In WCF Web Service, Service class is implemented by the ServiceContract attribute (like WebService in ASMX) and its methods are implemented by the OperationContract (like WebMethod in ASMX).

WCF web service vs. ASMX Web Service

Table 1-1. *WCF vs. ASMX Web Service*

WCF Service	ASMX Service
1. WCF service can be hosted in IIS, WAS, Console, WCF Provided Host	1. ASMX service can just be hosted in IIS.
2. It supports multiple communication protocols i.e., HTTP, TCP, MSMQ, and NamedPipes.	2. It supports only HTTP.
3. It uses DataContractSerializer.	3. It uses XmlSerializer.

Summary

1. **ADO.NET** is a set of object-oriented libraries used to interact with a database.

2. In a **connected layer**, you connect to a database as a data source and execute queries by writing SQL. These queries are used by ADO.NET and forwarded to your database of choice.

3. In a **disconnected layer**, you normally use DataSets and DataTables that copy the structure of a relational database in memory. A DataSet is created as the result of an execution of query against a connected database.

4. **Entity Framework** is an object relational mapping framework for ADO.NET

5. **Web service** is imaginary software available on the Internet used by the client to expose its service in a standardized XML or JSON messaging system.

6. **ASMX web service** is a Visually Designed class (Service) that is available to create at .NET framework 3.5

7. **WCF web service** is the evolution of ASMX web service, and modern services are being developed using a .NET Framework through WCF.

Code Challenges

Challenge 1: Create ASMX Web Service

Create a database of School with one table, Student having required fields (StudentID as primary key and StudentName). Create a Web Service named SchoolService and include ADO.NET for databse interactivity. The service should include two methods to add and read all students (students should be returned to client in JSON format). Create a console project (Client) which exposes this service and consumes the written methods in service.

[Hint] Create an Asp.NET Empty Web Project with the name SchoolService and then add an ASMX web service named SchoolWebService. Write the Add() method for add student and the ReadAll() method for read all students. Add an ADO.NET component into this project to connect the service with a database. Make another class (Serializable) so that data can be sent in serialized form. Without making data serializable, it does not send back to the client.

Practice Exam Questions

Question 1

You want to retrieve data from Microsoft Access 2013, which should be read-only. Which class you should use?

A) SqlDataAdapter

B) DbDataAdapter

C) OleDbDataReader

D) SqlDataReader

Question 2

Suppose you created the ASMX Web Service named SampleService. Which class you would use to create the proxy for this service?

    A) SampleServiceSoapClient

    B) SampleService

    C) SampleServiceClient

    D) SampleServiceSoapProxy

Question 3

Choose the correct code snippet/snippets for insert query (insert code snippet of C#, syntax vise):

```
A) SqlConnection con=new SqlConnection("ConectionString");
   SqlCommand cmd=new SqlCommand(insertQuery,con);
   Con.open();
   Cmd.ExecuteNonQuery();
   Con.close();

B) Using(SqlConnection con=new SqlConnection("ConectionString"))
   {
      SqlCommand cmd=new SqlCommand(insertQuery,con);
      Cmd.ExecuteNonQuery();
   }

C) SqlConnection con=new SqlConnection("ConectionString");
   Using( SqlCommand cmd=new SqlCommand(insertQuery,con))
   {
      Con.open();
      Cmd.ExecuteNonQuery();
   }

D) Using(SqlConnection con=new SqlConnection("ConectionString"))
   {
      SqlCommand cmd=new SqlCommand(insertQuery,con);
      Con.Open();
      Cmd.ExecuteNonQuery();
   }
```

Answers

1. C

2. A

3. A, D

CHAPTER 13

■ ■ ■

Working with Cryptography

Security is an important part to cover when developing your application. You need to take care about data privacy, user authenticity, data travel security and that data is not be compromised.

The .NET Framework gives you a powerful way to secure your sensitive data. It gives several algorithms which you can use in development of your application. In this chapter, we will cover the following topics:

1. Cryptography and Cryptanalysis

2. Encryption and Decryption

3. Symmetric and Asymmetric Encryption

4. Digital Certificates

5. Key Management

6. Code Access Security

7. Hashing

8. Securing String Data

Cryptography

The word Cryptography is formed from two words: **"crypto"** means encrypted or hidden and **"graphy"** means designing or writing of the representation of something.

Cryptography deals with the study of secret communication. It is the technique to hide data or messages into a hidden or unreadable form.

Cryptography is mainly used to send data from an insecure channel so that data can reach its destination successfully. It is performed by doing **Encryption** on data.

Encryption

Encrypt is also formed from two words: **"en"** means to make and **"crypt"** means secret or unreadable or hidden. Therefore, encrypt means to make hidden or to make unreadable, and the process of making unreadable is called Encryption.

It is the process of transforming a plain text into an unreadable form of cipher text by performing some algorithms on it.

In ancient times, to do secure communication or send messages via an insecure channel to receivers, cryptography was used. This is done by sending a messenger with an encoded (Encrypted) message from the sender to the receiver. The receiver knew the pattern and performed the decoding called **Cryptanalysis** to decode (Decrypt) the message according to a pattern or rules set between the two parties for secret communication.

© Ali Asad and Hamza Ali 2017
A. Asad and H. Ali, *The C# Programmer's Study Guide (MCSD)*, DOI 10.1007/978-1-4842-2860-9_13

The set of rules or algorithm used for encryption is known to the receiver and the sender. This set of rules or algorithm should be kept secret from others or you can use a public way to send your message using a **key** (same like a password) which should be kept secret. The key for your algorithm controls the encryption process.

■ **Info**   Plain Text is a message or data that is human-readable and cipher text is such a text which is encrypted (meaningless, unreadable).

Cryptanalysis

Decrypt is also formed from two words: "**de**" means remove or opposite or transform and "**crypt**" means hidden or unreadable, so decrypt means transform a hidden or unreadable message, and the process of transforming cipher text into plain text is called Decryption.

Pictorial Representation

A pictorial representation of the general encryption and decryption process is as follows:

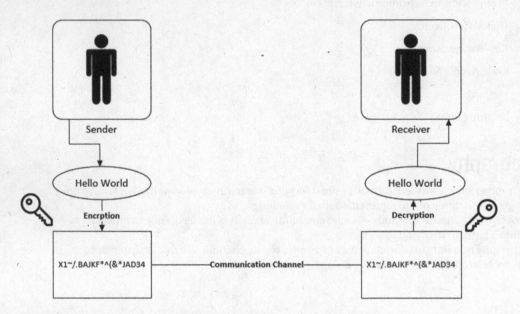

Figure 13-1. *Representation of Encryption and Decryption Process*

■ **Info**   Cryptography is the art or study of encryption and decryption.

Types of Encryption

There are two types of encryption which have their own suitability for use according to two scenarios. These are:

1. Symmetric Encryption
2. Asymmetric Encryption

Symmetric Encryption

Symmetric encryption is the encryption in which you send the key along with the data so that the user can decrypt the data with the same key. It is also called shared secret encryption.

Data is secure due to symmetric encryption but it should travel to an authorized person as a key also travels with the data. Once the data goes to an unauthorized person, data becomes compromised as the receiver could decrypt data with the received key.

The algorithm for symmetric encryption works in the following way: the data to be encrypted is transformed into blocks of cipher and each block has a specific size to contain ciphered data. This is called **cipher block chaining**. When the data is bigger than the size of the block (block size), data is split into multiple blocks. The block size depends on the algorithm used.

The first block contains encrypted value of some random value called Initialization Vector (IV) and encryption key, the next block contains encrypted value of previous block with key and so on. If the size of last block is less than the data resides on it, the block gets padded. Symmetric algorithm is fast than asymmetric encryption and suitable for large amount of data.

The .NET Framework gives five different symmetric algorithms to work with.

Table 13-1. Symmetric Algorithms

Algorithm	Description
AES	AES (Advanced Encryption Standard) is a symmetric algorithm. It was designed for both software and hardware. It has support for 128-bit data and 128,192,256-bit key.
DES	DES (Data Encryption Standard) is a symmetric algorithm published by National Institute of Standard and Technology (NIST).
RC2	RC2 (Ron's Code or Rivest Cipher) also known as ARC2 is a symmetric algorithm designed by Ron Rivest.
Rijndael	Rijndael is symmetric algorithm chosen by NSA as a Advanced Encryption Standard (AES).
TripleDes	TripleDes also known as 3DES (Triple Data Encryption Standard) applies DES algorithm three times to each data block.

These symmetric algorithm are defined in .NET and can be found their classes in **System.Security. Cryptography**.

For example, we have a secret data: "Secret Message", and want to encrypt it. You can use any of the above algorithms (classes). Listing 13-1 shows how you can perform symmetric encryption.

Code Snippet

Listing 13-1. symmetic encryption

```
//specify the data
string plainData = "Secret Message";
```

```
//convert into bytes of array
byte[] plainDataInBytes = Encoding.UTF8.GetBytes(plainData);

//Create a default cryptography object used to perform symmetric encryption
SymmetricAlgorithm symmetricAlgo = SymmetricAlgorithm.Create();

//Create encryptor with key and IV (Optional)
ICryptoTransform encryptor = symmetricAlgo.CreateEncryptor(symmetricAlgo.Key,
symmetricAlgo.IV);

byte[] cipherDataInBytes = encryptor.TransformFinalBlock(plainDataInBytes, 0,
plainDataInBytes.Length);

//get the bytes of encrypted data into string
string cipherData = Encoding.UTF8.GetString(cipherDataInBytes);

Console.WriteLine("Encrypted Data is: "+ cipherData);
```

■ **Info**   The algorithm and key used for encryption should be same while decrypting.

Data must be in bytes as **System.Security.Cryptography** works on bytes of data to encrypt.

SymmetricAlgorithm class is an abstract class of symmetric algorithms (**Aes**, **DES,** etc.). You can use its Create method to create the default object for cryptography. By default, it uses a **RijndaelManaged** algorithm (a managed version of **Rijndael** algorithm). You can give the name of any symmetric algorithm in Create method or can create the instance of them.

After specifying the algorithm, you specify the **key** and **IV** (which are optional) and create encryptor. **TransformFinalBlock** used to transform data in bytes to cipher text.

■ **Info**   Whenever the encryption performs, cipher text changes.

Listing 13-2 shows how to decrypt data.

Code Snippet

Listing 13-2.   Symmetric Decryption

```
//Create a default cryptography object used to perform symmetric encryption
SymmetricAlgorithm symmetricAlgo = SymmetricAlgorithm.Create();

ICryptoTransform decryptor = symmetricAlgo.CreateDecryptor(symmetricAlgo.Key,
symmetricAlgo.IV);

byte[] plainDataInBytes = decryptor.TransformFinalBlock(cipherDataInBytes, 0,
cipherDataInBytes.Length);

string plainData= Encoding.UTF8.GetString(plainDataInBytes);

Console.WriteLine("Decrypted Data is: " + plainData);
```

To decrypt data, create decryptor and call the same function on cipher text (TransformFinalBlock).

The output would be look like:

```
Encrypted Data is: 20917944468192702566763722515215199184
Decrypted Data is: Secret Message
```

Figure 13-2. Output

Asymmetric Encryption

Asymmetric encryption uses a pair of two keys instead of one for encryption. These two keys are mathematically related to each other. One of the keys is called **Public key** and other one is called **Private key**. You use one of the keys to encrypt data and other to decrypt data. The other key should be from the pair of keys you generated. The encryption you do with these keys is interchangeable. For example, if key1 encrypts the data then key2 can decrypt it and if key2 encrypt the data then key1 can decrypt it, because one of them can be given to everyone and the other one should be kept secret.

The data gets encrypted with the receiver's public key and can only be decrypted by the private key from the specific receiver because only that user should have access to the private key.

The public key transmits along the data while the secret key kept with the recipient.

Asymmetric encryption avoids sharing the encryption key; that's why it is more secure than a symmetric key. But, on the other hand, it is slower than symmetric encryption.

The .NET Framework provides several Asymmetric algorithms to work with.

Table 13-2. *Asymmetric Algorithms*

Algorithm	Description
RSA	RSA is an asymmetric algorithm commonly used by modern computers.
DSA	DSA (Digital Signature Algorithm), produced by NIST, is a standard to create digital signatures for data integrity.
ECDsa	ECDsa (Elliptic Curve Digital Signature) offers variant of the DSA.
ECDiffieHellman	Provides a basic set of operations that ECDH implementations must support.

These Asymmetric algorithms are defined in .NET and their classes can be found in **System.Security. Cryptography**.

Take the above used example in symmetric encryption and perform any of the asymmetric algorithm provided for encryption to show how it works.

Listing 13-3 shows how to generate keys used for DSA asymmetric encryption.

Code Snippet

Listing 13-3. DSA asymmetric enryption

```
//Creation of asymmetric algo object
RSACryptoServiceProvider rsa = new RSACryptoServiceProvider();

//saving the key information to RSAParameters structure
RSAParameters RSAKeyInfo = rsa.ExportParameters(false);
```

```
//generating both keys( public and private)
string publicKey = rsa.ToXmlString(false);
string privateKey = rsa.ToXmlString(true);
```

ToXmlString method returns the public or private key based on the Boolean value. To generate a private key make the value true, and for a public key the value shall be false.

Now we have two interlinked keys of an asymmetric algorithm. If A wants to send data to B then both parties should have an understanding about the pattern or keys used for communication between them.

The recipient (B) should have the private key for decryption and the sender (A) will encrypt data using the public key. The data that traveled to B will only be decrypted with the secret key which generated along with the public key (used for encryption).

Listing 13-4 shows how to encrypt data with the available or obtained public key and decrypt with the private key.

Code Snippet

Listing 13-4. encrypt and decrypt data with public key, private key

```
RSACryptoServiceProvider rsa = new RSACryptoServiceProvider();

//Encrypting Code (On Sender side)

//data to encrypt
string data = "Secret Message";
//convert into bytes
byte[] dataInBytes = Encoding.UTF8.GetBytes(data);

//Specify the public key obtained from receiver
rsa.FromXmlString(publicKey);

//Use Encrypt method for encryption
byte[] encryptedDataInBytes = rsa.Encrypt(dataInBytes, true);

//get the bytes of encrypted data into string
string encryptedData = Encoding.UTF8.GetString(encryptedDataInBytes);

Console.WriteLine("\nEncrypted Data is: "+ encryptedData);

//Decrpyting Code (on receiver side)

//Specify the private key
rsa.FromXmlString(privateKey);

//Use Decrypt method for encryption
byte[] decryptedDataInBytes= rsa.Decrypt(encryptedDataInBytes, true);

//get the bytes of decrypted data into string
string decryptedData = Encoding.UTF8.GetString(decryptedDataInBytes);

Console.WriteLine("Decrypted Data is: "+ decryptedData);
```

You can use a private key (instead of public) for encryption and public for decryption. One could be known to all and the other must be secret.

> ■ **Info** Combining a symmetric and an asymmetric algorithm can be more secure and help you to transmit a larger amount of data.

Implement Key management

The management of Keys used for encryption is an important part of cryptography process. In a Symmetric algorithm, a key and an IV are required to generate. The key must be secret and only known to the receiver so that others can not decrypt data. Asymmetric requires the creation of two keys where one should be public and the other must be private.

Symmetric Keys

In a symmetric algorithm, keys must be private, whereas there is no compulsion for an IV. Listing 13-5 shows how to create a symmetric key and an IV.

Code Snippet

Listing 13-5. Creation of symmetric key and IV

```
SymmetricAlgorithm symmetric = SymmetricAlgorithm.Create();
symmetric.GenerateIV();
symmetric.GenerateKey();
```

Asymmetric Keys

When the instance of an asymmetric algorithm created, a key pair of public and private key generated. ToXmlString method returns a key in XML form and ExportParameters returns RSAParameters that hold information of key.

The private key should be stored securely so that no unauthorized person can steal it. For this purpose, you should use a key container to manage the private key.

Listing 13-6 shows how to store a private key in a key container.

Code Snippet

Listing 13-6. store private key in key container

```
//Creating the container

CspParameters parameter = new CspParameters();
parameter.KeyContainerName = "KeyContainer";

//Creation of asymmetric algo object
RSACryptoServiceProvider rsa = new RSACryptoServiceProvider(parameter);

//saving the key information to RSAParameters structure
RSAParameters RSAKeyInfo = rsa.ExportParameters(false);

string privateKey = rsa.ToXmlString(true);

Console.WriteLine("Key is stored in Container"+ privateKey);
```

Listing 13-7 shows how to delete key from key container.

Code Snippet

Listing 13-7. delete key from key container

```
//Creating the container

CspParameters parameter = new CspParameters();
parameter.KeyContainerName = SET THE NAME OF THAT KEY CONTAINER USED TO STORE KEY;

//Creation of asymmetric algo object
RSACryptoServiceProvider rsa = new RSACryptoServiceProvider(parameter);

//saving the key information to RSAParameters structure
RSAParameters RSAKeyInfo = rsa.ExportParameters(false);

rsa.PersistKeyInCsp = false;
rsa.Clear();

Console.WriteLine("Key is Deleted");
```

You can also read the key from the container.

Encrypt Stream

Streams are covered in Chapter 10. Encrypting the data that goes through streams for privacy and integrity is also important.

C# provides a class, **CryptoStream,** for the encryption of data that travels through streams.

Listing 13-8 shows how you can encrypt data.

Code Snippet

Listing 13-8. encrypt stream

```
string message = "SECRET MESSAGE";

SymmetricAlgorithm symmetric = SymmetricAlgorithm.Create();

ICryptoTransform encryptor = symmetric.CreateEncryptor(symmetric.Key, symmetric.IV);

MemoryStream memoryStream = new MemoryStream();

//crptoStream know encrptor and stream in which data to written
CryptoStream crptoStream = new CryptoStream(memoryStream, encryptor, CryptoStreamMode.
Write);

//writer has reference of cryptoStream (what to encrypt and where)
using (StreamWriter streamWriter = new StreamWriter(crptoStream))
{
  //write the ecrypted message into memeory stream
  streamWriter.Write(message);
}
```

```
//close cryptoStream
crptoStream.Close();
//Close memoryStream
memoryStream.Close();
```

Listing 13-9 shows how to decrypt data.

Code Snippet

Listing 13-9. decrypt stream

```
ICryptoTransform decryptor = symmetric.CreateDecryptor(symmetric.Key, symmetric.IV);

MemoryStream memoryStream = new MemoryStream(CIPER_TEXT_HERE);

CryptoStream cryptoStream = new CryptoStream(memoryStream, decryptor, CryptoStreamMode.
Read);

using (StreamReader streamReader = new StreamReader(cryptoStream))
{
  string decryptedData = streamReader.ReadToEnd();
}
```

Working with ProtectedData Class

Without worrying about using the encryption algorithm (i.e., symmetric or asymmetric), you can still protect your data by using the **ProtectedData** class.

In a .NET framework, a ProtectedData class contains two static methods:

1. **Protect()**

2. **Unprotect()** to decrypt the data

The **ProtectedData** class is a part of the **System.Security.Cryptography** namespace; to add the namespace in a project you must add the *System.Security* assembly in the references folder.

Protect()

Protect method is the static method of ProtectedData class; it is used to encrypt the data. It contains the following method signature:

```
public static byte[] Protect(byte[] userData,byte[] optionalEntropy,
                        DataProtectionScope scope)
```

- **userData**: An array of bytes that contains data to be encrypted.

- **optionalEntropy**: Is an optional byte array that is used to increase the complexity of the encryption, or null for no additional complexity.

- **scope**: It takes the value of the DataProtectionScope enumeration that specifies the scope of encryption.

Code Snippet

Listing 13-10. encrypt by Protect method

```
string message = "Hello World";

//Convert data into a byte array
byte[] userData = Encoding.UTF8.GetBytes(message);

//encrypt the data by using ProtectedData.Protect method
byte[] encryptedDataInBytes = ProtectedData.Protect(userData, null, DataProtectionScope.
CurrentUser);

string encryptedData = Encoding.UTF8.GetString(encryptedDataInBytes);

Console.WriteLine("Encrypted Data is: " + encryptedData);
```

Explanation

The string data convert into a byte array and then the Protect method encrypts it, while DataProtectionScope.CurrentUser specifies only the current user can decrypt the encrypted data. DataProtectionScope is enumeration. **CurrentUser** means only the current user can encrypt the data and **LocalMachine** means all the users of a local machine can encrypt data.

Unprotect

Unprotect method is the the static method of the ProtectedData class; it is used to decrypt the encrypted data. It contains the following method signature:

```
public static byte[] Unprotect(byte[] userData,byte[] optionalEntropy,
                        DataProtectionScope scope)
```

- **userData**: An array of bytes that contains data to be encrypted.

- **optionalEntropy**: Is an optional byte array that is used to increase the complexity of the encryption, or null for no additional complexity.

- **scope**: It takes the value of DataProtectionScope enumeration that specifies the scope of encryption.

   The method signature of both Protect and Unprotect methods are the same.

Code Snippet

Listing 13-11. decrypt by UnProtect method

```
byte[] decryptedDataInBytes = ProtectedData.Unprotect(encryptedDataInBytes, null,
DataProtectionScope.CurrentUser);

string decryptedData = Encoding.UTF8.GetString(decryptedDataInBytes);

Console.WriteLine("Decrypted Data is: " + decryptedData);
```

Explanation

The encrypted data is decrypted by using the Unprotect method; it takes data that is encrypted (i.e., encryptedDataInBytes) and then decrypts it.

Manage and Create Digital Certificates

A digital certification uses hashing and asymmetric encryption to authenticate the identity of the owner (signed object) to others. An owner of the certificate contains both public and private keys. The public key is used to encrypt the sent message while the private key is used to decrypt it; only the owner of the certificate has access to the private key to decrypt the encrypted message. This way, digital certificates enable the integrity of data.

A digital certificate is part of a public key infrastructure (PKI). A public key infrastructure is a system of digital certificates, certificate authorities, and other registration authorities to verify and authenticate the validity of each involved party.

Create and Install Certificate

Certificate Authority (CA) is a third-party tool that is used to issue a certificate. Each certificate contains a *public key* and the data, such as, a *subject* to which the certificate is issued, a validity date for how long the certificate will remain validated, and the information about the *issuer* who issued the certificate.

We'll use a tool, *Makecert.exe*, that will help us to create an X.509 digital certificate, which is commonly used to authenticate clients and servers, encrypt, and digitally sign messages.

Follow the following steps to create a digital certificate:

1. Run Command Prompt as Administrator.

2. To create a digital certificate, enter the following command: makecert {Certificate_Name}.cer

3. **makecert myCert.cer**

The above command will create a certificate file of name "myCert.cer". To use the generated certificate file, you must install it in your machine to be able to use it. *Certificate Store* is a place where you stored the certificate after installation.

Follow the following steps to create and install a certificate.

1. Run Command Prompt as Administrator.

2. To create a digital certificate, enter the following command: makecert {Certificate_Name}.cer

```
makecert -n "CN=myCert" -sr currentuser -ss myCertStore
```

The above command will create and install a certificate file.

Working with System.Security Namespace

The System.Security namespace contains the fundamental building blocks of a .NET code access security framework. Child namespace **System.Security.Permissions** provides Code Access Security (CAS), which protects your computer from malicious code.

Code Access Security (CAS)

The CLR in .NET Framework enforces security restrictions to use third party resources. You must ask for permission to access and manipulate the protected resources of third party tools.

There are two ways to specify CAS in C# code:

1. Declarative
2. Imperative

Declarative

In a declarative way, we use attributes to apply security information.

Code Snippet

Listing 13-12. Declarative CAS

```
[FileIOPermission(SecurityAction.Demand,
AllLocalFiles = FileIOPermissionAccess.Read)]
public void MyDeclarativeCAS()
{
    // Method body
}
```

Imperative

In an imperative way, we explicitly ask for the permission in the code.

Code Snippet

Listing 13-13. Imperative CAS

```
FileIOPermission fp = new FileIOPermission(PermissionState.None);
fp.AllLocalFiles = FileIOPermissionAccess.Read;
fp.Demand();
```

FIleIOPermissionAccess.Read will explicitly allow the read-only file access.

Hashing

Hashing (performing hashing algorithms) is the process of converting data into short and fixed length unreadable form. This process is irreversible, i.e., you cannot convert hashed data back to the original one. Every time you generate hash for specific data, it will be the same output (hashed form). It is used to check the integrity of data, string comparison, Data authenticity and, most importantly for security, password storage. Unlike encryption, Hashing is a one-way process.

C# provides several algorithms of hashing to work with. Table 13-3 shows the hash algorithms provided in **System.Security.Cryptography**.

Table 13-3. *Hashing Algorithms*

Algorithm	Description
SHA1	SHA1 is a cryptography hash function, resulting in a 160-bit hash value.
SHA256	SHA256 is a cryptography hash function, resulting in a 256-bit hash value.
SHA512	SHA512 is a cryptography hash function, resulting in a 512-bit hash value.
SHA384	SHA384 is a cryptography hash function, resulting in a 384-bit hash value.
RIPEMD160	RIPEMD (RACE Integrity Primitives Evaluation Message Digest) 160 is a cryptography hash function, similar in performance to SHA1.

These algorithms (classes) are defined in .NET and can be used to perform hashing. You can use any of the above hashing algorithms. We use SHA256 in the example to understand how it is performed.

For example, you have a password and want to store it in your database so that if anyone ever stole the database, the hacker would not know the password as it would be in unreadable form.

Listing 13-14 shows how to perform hashing.

Code Snippet

Listing 13-14. Hashing

```
//password to be hashed
string password = "HelloWorld";

//password in bytes
var passwordInBytes = Encoding.UTF8.GetBytes(password);

//Create the SHA512 object
HashAlgorithm sha512 = SHA512.Create();

//generate the hash
byte[] hashInBytes = sha512.ComputeHash(passwordInBytes);

var hashedData = new StringBuilder();
foreach (var item in hashInBytes)
{
  hashedData.Append(item);
}

Console.WriteLine("Hashed Password is: " + hashedData.ToString());
```

You can save a hashed password into a database or compare a logged-in user by converting the password into hashed form and comparing its hash with an already stored hashed value of that specific user.

There is a problem in this process. Every time a request is being sent or a user logs in, the same hash is generated. So the hacker can track down the traffic through a communication channel and the hacker gets to know that each time the data is traveled, the password/message/hashed value is the same. Therefore, the hacker can send the same value without knowing what it is and can successfully enter in your system, which is a security breach.

To avoid such a problem, salt hashing comes in handy.

Salt Hashing

Salt is non-repetitive random data that is added with the hashed value to make it unique every time it is generated.

Listing 13-15 shows how to perform salt hashing.

Code snippet

Listing 13-15. Salt Hashing

```
//password to be hashed
string password = "HelloWorld";

//generate Salt (GUID is globally uniqe identifer)
Guid salt = Guid.NewGuid();

//Merge password with random value
string saltedPassword = password + salt;

//password in bytes
var passwordInBytes = Encoding.UTF8.GetBytes(password + salt);

//Create the SHA512 object
HashAlgorithm sha512 = SHA512.Create();

//generate the hash
byte[] hashInBytes = sha512.ComputeHash(passwordInBytes);

var hashedData = new StringBuilder();
foreach (var item in hashInBytes)
{
  hashedData.Append(item);
}

Console.WriteLine("Unique hashed Password is: " + hashedData.ToString());
```

NewGuid method created a global unique identifier, i.e., it changed a value concatenation with a password to generate a different hash every time the code runs; hence, salt hashing protects you from a security attack by hackers.

C# provides GetHashCode() method on every instance to generate its hash code, which is normally used for a string or value comparison .

■ **Tip** Use GetHashCode() method for comparing values instead of comparing values itself.

Choosing an appropriate Algorithm

When you have multiple algorithms for performing encryption or hashing, then it is important to choose the best algorithm with respect to the scenario. The following points illustrate the usage of different commonly used algorithms with respect to the scenario.

1. When there is a scenario to deal with more sensitive data, you should use Asymmetric encryption instead of symmetric encryption.

2. When there is a scenario for data privacy, use Aes (Symmetric algorithm).

3. When there is a scenario for Data Integrity, use HMACSHA256 and HMACSHA512 hashing algorithms.

4. When there is a scenario for digital signing (Digital Signature), use ECDsa and RSA.

5. When there is a scenario to generate a random number, use RNGCryptoServiceProvider.

■ **Info** You can read more about this topic from the following link:

https://msdn.microsoft.com/en-us/library/0ss79b2x(v=vs.110).aspx

---

Working with SecureString Class

When working with secure strings (data) such as passwords or credit card numbers (which are commonly in string formats), we normally use string class or type to store or work with them. This is inappropriate because string stores your data in plain text, so your sensitive data is open for attack. String class is also immutable, which leaves copies in memory on every change which could be compromised as it is impossible for a garbage collector to clear all the copies of data.

In such a situation, C# provides SecureString class to work with your sensitive strings. It can be found in the System.Security namespace. It makes your string more secure. SecureString automatically encrypts the string and stores it in a special memory location. It is mutable and implemented by IDisposable; that's why there is not a problem of multiple copies of data and the impossibility of a garbage collector to clear all copies. Whenever you are done working with SecureString, you can make sure its content is removed from memory, using IDisposable.

SecureString does not properly secure the data but minimizes the risk for data to be compromised. It takes string character by character, not the whole string at all. When necessary, you can make the string encrypted by SecureString as just read-only.

Listing 13-16 shows how you can secure the string using SecureString class.

Code Snippet

Listing 13-16. SecureString class to secure sensitive data

```
SecureString secureString = new SecureString();

Console.Write("Please enter your Credit Card Number: ");
while (true)
{
  ConsoleKeyInfo enteredKey = Console.ReadKey(true);
  if (enteredKey.Key == ConsoleKey.Enter)
    break;
  secureString.AppendChar(enteredKey.KeyChar);
  Console.Write("#");
}
secureString.MakeReadOnly();

//When done with SecureString, Dispose the content so that it does not remain in memory
secureString.Dispose();
```

You can also read the encrypted string (by SecureString) using the special class Marshal, which can be found in System.Runtime.InteropServices. Reading the encrypted string makes the string decrypted and returns it as a normal string (plain text) so you must clear the normal string from memory after reading; even these would be an exception. So encapulate **reading code** with try/catch/finally block.

Listing 13-17 shows how you can read the string as plain text.

Code Snippet

Listing 13-17. Read the data protected by SecureString

```
IntPtr plainTextAsIntPtr = IntPtr.Zero;
        try
        {
            //Decrypt string (as a IntPtr)
            plainTextAsIntPtr = Marshal.SecureStringToGlobalAllocUnicode(secureString);
            Marshal.PtrToStringUni(plainTextAsIntPtr);
        }
        catch (Exception ex)
        {
            Console.WriteLine(ex.Message);
        }
        finally
        {
            //This method CLeared dycrypted string from memory
            Marshal.ZeroFreeGlobalAllocUnicode(plainTextAsIntPtr);
            Console.WriteLine("Memory Cleared.");
        }
```

The Marshal class gives a method for decrypting string along with a method to clear the content of decrypted string from memory.

SecureStringToGlobalAllocUnicode() method is static and is used to read the secure string and return the address of a memory location which contains the value as IntPtr (pointer). That pointer contains the address of the memory location, and is converted to a string (value) that the pointer contains (points to).

ZeroFreeGlobalAllocUnicode() method is also static and is used along with SecureStringToGlobalAllocUnicode() method to free the content of the decrypted string from memory. Marshal class also provides other methods for reading the secure string along with their respective methods for disposing the decrypted content from memory. You can find out about them and more about SecureString from the following link:

https://msdn.microsoft.com/en-us/library/system.security.securestring(v=vs.110).aspx

Summary

1. Encryption is the process of converting plain text into cipher text.

2. Decryption is the process of converting cipher text into plain text.

3. Symmetric Encryption uses one key to encrypt and decrypt data.

4. Asymmetric Encryption uses two mathematically linked keys: public and private. One of them is used to encrypt the data and other is used to decrypt the data.

5. Digital Certificates are used for the authenticity of an author.

6. Hashing is the process of converting data into long unreadable form and it cannot be converted back.

Code Challenges

Challenge 1: Develop a simple window form application and perform Salt hashing

Create a simple database table of login to store username, hashed password, and GUID value (salt value). Use the Connected Layer approach to interact with the database. Make two forms: Registration and Login. Register the user (password should be inserted in hashed form) and then log in the user successfully.

Practice Exam Questions

Question 1

The application needs to encrypt highly sensitive data. Which algorithm should you use?

A) DES

B) Aes

C) TripleDES

D) RC2

Question 2

You are developing an application which transmits a large amount of data. You need to ensure the data integrity. Which algorithm should you use?

A) RSA

B) HMACSHA256

C) Aes

D) RNGCryptoServiceProvider

Question 3

Salt Hashing is done by:

A) Merging data with random value and perform cryptography.

B) Merging data with random value and perform cryptanalysis.

C) Merging data with random value and perform encryption.

D) Merging data with random value and perform hashing.

Answers

1. B
2. B
3. D

CHAPTER 14

■ ■ ■

Assembly and Reflection

Assembly is an important part in any .NET application development, while reflection is used to read all the information of an assembly at runtime. In this chapter, we'll learn:

1. Assembly

2. Creation and Use an Assembly

3. Installing an Assembly in a Global Assembly Cache

4. Reflection in C#

5. Creating and Using Custom Attributes

Introduction to Assemblies

An assembly is the output of the compiled code. It's a physical code that is used to deploy an application. In a .NET, assembly it is typically a Dynamic Link Library (DLL) or an Executable (EXE) file.

When Code is Compiled

When code is compiled, a compiler converts the source code into Microsoft Intermediate Language (**MSIL**) code; it is a CPU-independent code. The Common Language Runtime (CLR) uses Just In Time (**JIT**) compiler to convert MSIL code into a native code to the operating system. This MSIL code is available in a portable executable (**PE**) file, which helps in executing an assembly.

When a compiler converts the source code into MSIL code it also creates its **metadata**. Metadata stores information about the data stored in an assembly. For example, it contains information of the types available in that assembly, their containing namespaces, base class of each available type, the interfaces it implemented, its methods and their scope, each method's parameters, each type's properties, and so on. In other words metadata is the encrypted documentation of a source code.

When a code is compiled successfully, an **assembly manifest** file is generated. It's an XML file which contains information about assembly, like its name, version number, and an optional strong name that uniquely identifies the assembly. It also contains the names of other reference assemblies used in the code.

Types of Assembly

Assembly is typically divided into two types:

1. Private Assembly

2. Public Assembly

© Ali Asad and Hamza Ali 2017
A. Asad and H. Ali, *The C# Programmer's Study Guide (MCSD)*, DOI 10.1007/978-1-4842-2860-9_14

Private Assembly

A private assembly (.dll or .exe) can be used by only a single application. Generally private assembly is found in the application root folder.

   If another application tries to refer a private assembly, it must used store a copy of that private assembly in its root directory, otherwise the application won't be able to deploy succussfully.

Public/Shared Aseembly

A public assembly (.dll or .exe) can be used by multiple applications at a time. It is also known as a shared assembly, which is stored in Global Assembly Cache (**GAC**). This shared assembly also known as a strong name assembly.

   Generally, when an application is deploying, it doesn't need a public assembly to be referenced in the root folder of the application.

Uses of Assembly

Assembly has many uses; some of the important uses of assembly are given below:

1. Assembly allows component-based development, which means multiple assemblies can reuse each other's types, methods, and classes to build a software product.

2. Assemblies help in versioning, which is useful to archive previously built assemblies.

3. Assembly enables security, which can manage by specifying the level of trust for code from a particular site or zone.

4. Assembly supports culture and language, so when an application is deployed it can display results according to a specific culture or language.

Creating and Using Custom Assembly

An assembly is either a .DLL or an .EXE file.

Dynamic Link Library (.DLL)

Dynamic Link Library (.DLL) is a class library that contains namespaces, types, and methods to be reused by other applications. For example, "System" is a .dll, which is a Class library that contains namespaces, types, and methods that we reuse in our application, i.e., Console.WriteLine("");

Create a Custom .DLL

These steps will help you to create a .dll

1. Open Visual Studio

2. Select Visual C#

3. Select Class Library as a project template

4. Enter name for project

5. Click Ok

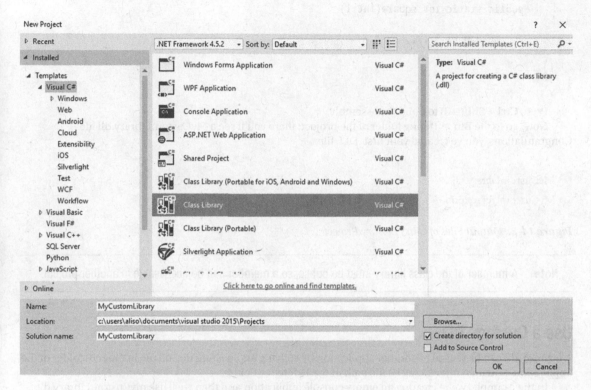

Figure 14-1. *Create an Empty C# Class Library Project*

The following code will be shown:

```csharp
using System;

namespace MyCustomLibrary
{
    public class Class1
    {
    }
}
```

You can clearly see that class library project doesn't have a Main Method. Therefore, a class library doesn't have an entry point.

Let's create a simple method inside Class1, which returns the square of an integer.

Listing 14-1. Create a Method Inside a Class Library

```csharp
using System;

namespace MyCustomLibrary
```

```
{
    public class Class1
    {
        public static int square(int i)
        {
            return (i * i);
        }
    }
}
```

Press **Ctrl + Shift + B** to build the assembly.

Now, go to the **Bin ➤ Debug** folder of the project; there you'll see a MyCustomLibrary.dll file. Congratulations, you've created your first .DLL file.

MyCustomLibrary.dll

MyCustomLibrary.pdb

Figure 14-2. Output Files of Class Library Project

■ **Note**   A member of the class library must be public, so a member can be accessable in another project.

Use a Custom .DLL

A custom .dll can be reused in another application by copying and pasting the .dll file in the root folder of the application, and then referencing its file path in the Reference Folder.

In the example, we're creating an empty console application and then we'll use myCustomLibrary.dll.

1. Create an Empty C# Console Application.

2. Copy the MyCustomLibrary.dll in the root directory of Console App.

3. Right-click on References Folder in Solution Explorer and click Add Reference.

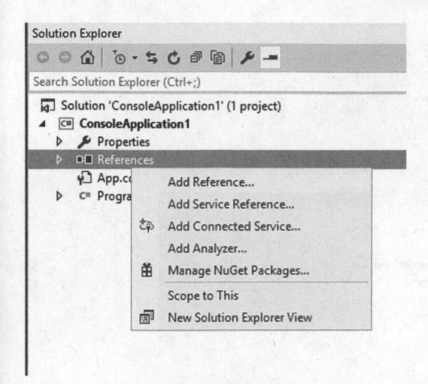

Figure 14-3. Add Custom .DLL File Reference

4. A new window will pop up; click on the "Browse" button to select the MyCustomLibrar.dll that you've copied in the root folder of the console app and then Click Okay.

Now, MyCustomLibrary.dll shall be available in the References folder of Console App.

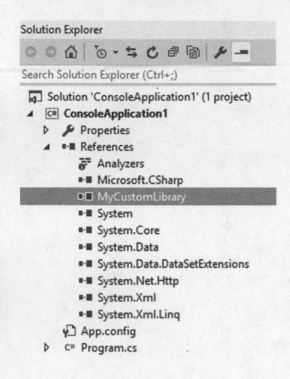

Figure 14-4. List of .DLL Files in References Folder

We can use all the public methods and types available in MyCustomLibrary in our console app. For example, we can write the following code in Main Method.

Listing 14-2. Read a Class Library Inside Main Method

```
        static void Main(string[] args)
        {
            int i = 4;
            int sqri = MyCustomLibrary.Class1.square(i);

            Console.WriteLine("Square of {0} = {1}",i, sqri);
        }
//Output
Square of 4 = 16
```

When code is compiled it matches all the types and methods with the assemblies referenced in the References folder; if the the types or method aren't defined in the project or in the reference assemblies, then an error will occur.

Executeable (.EXE)

Executeable assemblies are those assemblies which have a Main Method defined in it. Main Method is the entry point of executable assemblies to run. In an operating system, these executeable files take processor and memory (Stack, Heap) for running, for example, Console App, Windows Form App, WPF App, etc.

WinMD Assembly

The concept of WinMD Assembly was introduced when Windows 8 came out. WinMD stands for Windows Meta Data. It allows the communication between different programming languages. For example, WinMD library built with C# can be used in a C++ project. It removed the language barrier through Windows Runtime Component.

Create WinMD Assembly

WinMD Assembly is used in store apps; to make the WinMD Assembly, you must install Windows 8.1 SDK. At this point, I assume your Visual Studio has Windows 8.1 SDK installed.

Now, to create the WinMD Assembly, follow these steps:

1. Open Visual Studio.

2. Create a new project, select **Visual C#➤ Windows Store,** and then select **Windows Runtime Component** as a project template and select Okay.

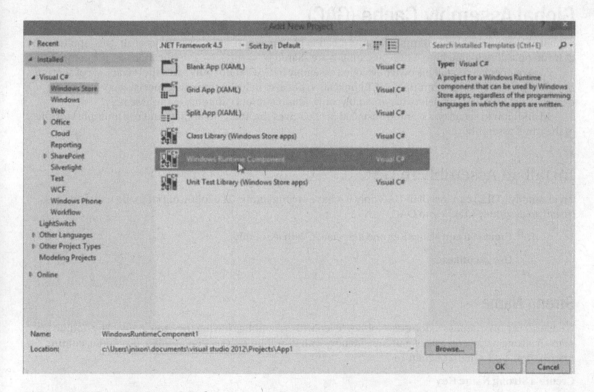

Figure 14-5. *Create an Empty Windows Runtime Component*

Now, create a static method that returns the square root of an integer value.

Listing 14-3. Create a Method Inside a Windows Runtime Component Project

```
public sealed class Class1
{
    public static int square(int i)
    {
        return (i * i);
    }
}
```

Build the assembly and now you can use it in any store app template of any language, i.e., VB.NET, F#, etc.

■ **Note**   In WinMD assemblies, all types must be sealed, and if polymorphism is required then use interface on the sealed classed to implement polymorphism.

Global Assembly Cache (GAC)

Global Assembly Cache is a common shared location of a system to store assemblies of all .NET applications that run on a certain machine. These assemblies are shared by several .NET applications on the computer.

A developer can install his own developed assembly in GAC. It not only gives the advantage of sharing the same assembly among multiple .NET application but also helps in providing special security. For example, not all users can delete the assembly; only administrators can remove the assembly.

In addition to security, assembly installed in GAC gives the ability to archive and use multiple versions of the same assembly.

Install an Assembly in GAC

An assembly (.DLL) can install in GAC only if it has a **strong name**. The following steps are required to install an assembly (.DLL) into GAC.

1. Create Strong Name Key and associate it with assembly.

2. Use gacutil.exe.

Strong Name

It ensures the uniqueness among assemblies (even with assemblies having the same names) by unqiue key pairs. A strong name consists of a unique identity with its public key, version number, text name, culture information, and a digital signature.

Create a Strong Name Key

Strong Name Key is file that needs to be associated with the assembly to make it a strong name assembly.

1. Open Visual Studio and create an empty C# Class Library Project (build the project by pressing ctrl+shift+B).

2. Goto StartMenu ➤ Find, Visual Studio Command Prompt ➤ Run it as Administrator.

3. Use Visual Studio Command Prompt to navigate to the root folder of class library project. e.g., cd "{PathLocation}" press enter (cd "C:\Users\aliso\Documents\ visual studio 2015\Projects\myClassLibrary"). OR **cd "{PathLocation}" press enter**.

4. Inside the project's root folder, create a strong name key by writing a command "'**sn -k {KeyName}.snk**" (for example, "sn -k myClassLibrarykey.snk"), and press Enter.

Associate Strong Name Key with Assembly

When a strong name key is generated, it must be associated with an assembly so that the assembly can become a strong name assembly. To do this, follow the following simple steps.

1. Open the **AssemblyInfo.cs** file in Visual Studio .NET Solution Explorer, (This file is underneath the Properties file of solution explorer.)

2. Associate a strong name key with the assembly by adding an assembly attribute and location of a strong name key, such as **[assembly: AssemblyKeyFile("myCl assLibrarykey.snk")]**

3. Press **ctrl + shift + B**. This will associate the strong name key pair with the assembly. Remember, Visual Studio must be runing as Administrator.

Use Gacutil.exe

Gacutil.exe is a tool that is used to install a strong name assembly into a global assembly cache. Follow the following steps to install a strong name assembly into GAC:

1. Run Visual Studio Command Prompt as Administrator.

2. Enter the following command to install a strong name assembly into GAC:

```
gacutil -i "{file path of strong name assembly}.dll"
```

for example, gacutil -i "C:\Users\aliso\Documents\Visual Studio 2015\Projects\ myClassLibrary\myClassLibrary\bin\Debug\myClassLibrary.dll"

OR

If the command prompt already navigated to the folder where a strong name assembly is stored, then you can directly enter the following command:

```
gacutil -i myClassLibrary.dll
```

AssemblyInfo.cs

Whenever a new .NET assembly project is created in Visual Studio, a file named AssemblyInfo is created that contains attributes used to define, name, description, version, etc.

The AssemblyInfo.cs file can be found in the solution explorer '**Properties➤AssemblyInfo.cs**'.

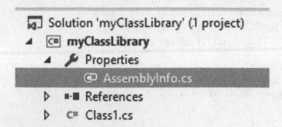

Figure 14-6. AssemblyInfo.cs

Versioning the Assembly

In the development lifecycle (e.g., Development, Test, Production), versioning the assembly helps team members to identify multiple versions of the same assembly, which helps in troubleshooting a problem or identifying which assembly to deploy.

In .NET, Versioning is done only on assemblies with strong names. An attribute "AssemblyVersion" is used to manage the versioning of the assembly.

```
[assembly: AssemblyVersion("{Major}.{Minor}.{Build Number}.{Revision}")]
OR
[assembly: AssemblyVersion("1.0.0.0")]
```

It consists of four important parts:

1. Major Version

2. Minor Version

3. Build Number

4. Revision

Major Version

An integer value, incremented for major releases, such as adding new features.

Minor Version

An integer value, incremented for minor releases, such as introducing small changes to existing features.

Build Number

An integer value, typically incremented automatically as part of every successful build performed on the Build Server. This allows each build to be tracked and tested.

Revision

An integer value, incremented on builds which is released with hotfixes or patches.

Reflection in C#

Reflection is used to read attributes (metadata) to obtain information of all assemblies, modules, and types of a running application.

Basically, reflection converts binary (Low-Level) information to human-readable (High-Level) language and allows humans (developers) to manipulate the data and behavior of an application at runtime.

In terms of processing, reflection costs a lot of processor power because, by using metadata, it reverse engineers all the binary data to readable data.

Working with Reflection

System.Reflection namespace contains tons of classes that dynamically allow you to create and use types, methods, and properties of a running application.

Use Reflection to Read Current Assembly

System.Reflection.Assembly class contains methods and properties used to read and manipulate information of an assembly at runtime.

Code Snippet

Listing 14-4. Use Reflection to Read Current Assembly

```
using System;
using System.Reflection;

namespace DemoAssembly
{
    class Program
    {
        static void Main(string[] args)
        {
            //Get current loaded assembly
            Assembly assembly = Assembly.GetExecutingAssembly();

            //Get Full Name of the current Assembly
            string assemblyName = assembly.FullName;

            Console.WriteLine(assemblyName);
        }
    }
}
//Output
DemoAssembly, Version = 1.0.0.0, Culture = neutral, PublicKeyToken = null
```

Explanation

(Listing 14-4) When an application is running, it gets the metadata of the current assembly and reads its full-name. Assembly Fullname always contains 4 parts, which describe the assembly name, assembly version number, and assembly culture, and tells if the asssembly is strong named (if it has a public key token associated with it).

Use Reflection to Read all Types of an Assembly

Reflection can also read all the types defined in a particular assembly at runtime.

Code Snippet

Listing 14-5. Use Reflection to Read all Types in Current Assembly

```csharp
using System;
using System.Reflection;

namespace DemoAssembly
{
    class Program
    {
        static void Main(string[] args)
        {
            //Get current loaded assembly
            Assembly assembly = Assembly.GetExecutingAssembly();

            //Get all types defined in an assembly
            Type[] types = assembly.GetTypes();

            //Get information of each type
            foreach (Type type in types)
            {
                //Return name of a type and its base type
                Console.WriteLine("Type Name:{0}, Base Type:{1}",
                        type.Name, type.BaseType);

            }
        }
    }

    class A { }
    class B : A { }

}
//Output
Type Name:Program, Base Type:System.Object
Type Name:A, Base Type:System.Object
Type Name:B, Base Type:DemoAssembly.A
```

Explanation

(Listing 14-5) *Type* is a class used to store information of any type. Type class contains methods and properties used to read and edit values of a specified type.

In the above example, assembly.GetTypes() returns an array of non-static Types. By using properties like *type.Name* and *type.BaseType* we can get the name of a type and its base type respectively.

Use Reflection to Read Metadata of Properties and Methods

During runtime, reflection can help to read all the information of a type in an assembly including its methods, properties, events, etc.

Code Snipppet

Listing 14-6. Use Reflection to Read Metadata of a Property

```
using System;
using System.Reflection;

namespace DemoAssembly
{
    class Program
    {
        public int Age { get; set; }
        public string Name { get; set; }

        static void Main(string[] args)
        {
            //Get current loaded assembly
            Assembly assembly = Assembly.GetExecutingAssembly();

            //Get all types defined in an assembly
            Type[] types = assembly.GetTypes();

            //Dig information of each type
            foreach (Type type in types)
            {
                //Return name of a type
                Console.WriteLine("Type Name:{0}, Base Type:{1}",
                    type.Name, type.BaseType);

                //Get all properties defined in a type
                PropertyInfo[] properties = type.GetProperties();

                foreach (PropertyInfo property in properties)
                {
                    Console.WriteLine("\t{0} has {1} type",
                        property.Name, property.PropertyType);
                }

            }
        }
    }

    class A
    {
        public int Random { get; set; }
    }
    class B { }
```

```
}
//Output
Type Name:Program, Base Type: System.Object
        Age has System.Int32 type
        Name has System.String type
Type Name:A, Base Type:System.Object
        Random has System.Int32 type
Type Name:B, Base Type:System.Object
```

Explanation

(Listing 14-6) *PropertyInfo* class is used to store information of a property. It contains the method and properties used to read and edit data of a property. By default, Type.GetProperties() returns all non-static public properties of a type.

    Property.Name returns the name of a property. *Property.PropertyType* returns the type of the property.

Listing 14-7. Use Reflection to Read Metadata of a Method

```
using System;
using System.Reflection;

namespace DemoAssembly
{
    class Program
    {
        public void Show() { }
        public int SqRoot(int i)
        {
            return (i * i);
        }

        static void Main(string[] args)
        {
            //Get current loaded assembly
            Assembly assembly = Assembly.GetExecutingAssembly();

            //Get all types defined in an assembly
            Type[] types = assembly.GetTypes();

            //Dig information of each type
            foreach (Type type in types)
            {
                //Return name of a type
                Console.WriteLine("Type Name:{0}, Base Type:{1}",
                    type.Name, type.BaseType);

                //Get all non-static methods of a type
                MethodInfo[] methods = type.GetMethods();

                foreach (MethodInfo method in methods)
                {
                    Console.WriteLine("\tMethod Name:{0}, Return Type:{1}",
```

```
                            method.Name, method.ReturnType);
                }
            }
        }
    }
}
//Output
Type Name:Program, Base Type:System.Object
        Method Name:Show, Return Type:System.Void
        Method Name:SqRoot, Return Type:System.Int32
        Method Name:ToString, Return Type:System.String
        Method Name:Equals, Return Type:System.Boolean
        Method Name:GetHashCode, Return Type:System.Int32
        Method Name:GetType, Return Type:System.Type
```

Explanation

MethodInfo is a class that stores information of a method. MethodInfo class contains methods and properties that are used to read and edit data of a method. By default, Type.GetMethods() returns all non-static public methods of a type.

method.Name returns the name of a method. *method.ReturnType* returns the return type of a method.

The output of a program also showed "ToString", "Equals", "GetHashCode", and "GetType" methods which aren't defined in Program class. These methods were defined in System.Object class. Since every class inherits System.Object class, the program showed these methods too.

Similarly, there are other methods and properties defined in System.Type class which are useful to get not only information about methods and properties but also about events, interfaces, fields, etc.

Use Reflection to Get and Set Value of Object's Property

Reflection can also be used to read and write actual value stored in a property of some class's instance at runtime.

Code Snippet

Listing 14-8. Use Reflection to Read Values of a Property

```csharp
using System;
using System.Reflection;

namespace DemoAssembly
{
    class Person
    {
        public int Age { get; set; }
        public string FirstName { get; set; }
    }

    class Program
    {
```

```
        static void Main(string[] args)
        {
            var personobj = new Person { FirstName = "Sundus", Age - 21 };
            var personobj2 = new Person { FirstName = "Ali", Age = 22 };

            //Store Metadata of Person Type in Type's Object
            //return Type of 'Person' class
            Type persontype = typeof(Person);

            //Specify which property information is required
            //Return metadata of specified property
            PropertyInfo nameproperty = persontype.GetProperty("FirstName");

            //Specify 'instance' (personobj) of 'Type' (Person)
            //Whose 'property' (nameproperty) value is required
            var value = nameproperty.GetValue(personobj);

            Console.WriteLine("{0} = {1}", nameproperty.Name, value);

        }
    }

}
//Output
FirstName = Sundus
```

Explanation

To get a value of a specified object's property, the following steps are required:

1. Return and store the type of Object by using typeof operator or GetType method.

2. Return and store metadata of specified property of a type.

3. Use GetValue() method. Specify the type's instance whose value is about to get.

Code Snippet

Listing 14-9. Use Reflection to Set and Read Values of a Property

```
using System;
using System.Reflection;

namespace DemoAssembly
{
    class Person
    {
        public int Age { get; set; }
        public string FirstName { get; set; }
    }

    class Program
    {
```

```
        static void Main(string[] args)
        {
            var personobj = new Person { FirstName = "Sundus", Age = 21 };
            var personobj2 = new Person { FirstName = "Ali", Age = 22 };

            //Store Metadata of Person Type in Type's Object
            //return Type of 'Person' class
            Type persontype = typeof(Person);

            //Specify which property information is required
            //Return metadata of specified property
            PropertyInfo nameproperty = persontype.GetProperty("FirstName");

            //Specify 'instance' (personobj) of 'Type' (Person)
            //Whose 'property' (nameproperty) value is about to change
            nameproperty.SetValue(personobj, "Lakhtey");

            //Specify 'instance' (personobj) of 'Type' (Person)
            //Whose 'property' (nameproperty) value is required
            var value = nameproperty.GetValue(personobj);

            Console.WriteLine("{0} = {1}", nameproperty.Name, value);

        }
    }

}
//Output
FirstName = Lakhtey
```

Explanation

To set a value of a specified object's property, the following steps are required:

1. Return and store the type of Object by using typeof operator or GetType method.

2. Return and store metadata of the specified property of a type.

3. Use SetValue() method. Specify the type's instance and value that is about to set.

Use Reflection to Invoke a Method of an Object

Reflection can also be used to invoke any defined method of an object anytime during runtime.

Code Snippet

Listing 14-10. Use Reflection to Invoke the Method of an Object

```
using System;
using System.Reflection;

namespace DemoAssembly
{
```

```csharp
    class Person
    {
        public int Age { get; set; }
        public string FirstName { get; set; }

        public int Show()
        {
            Console.WriteLine("FirstName = {0}", FirstName);

            return Age;
        }
    }

    class Program
    {
        static void Main(string[] args)
        {
            var personobj = new Person { FirstName = "Sundus", Age = 21 };
            var personobj2 = new Person { FirstName = "Ali", Age = 22 };

            //Store Metadata of Person Type in Type's Object
            //return Type of 'Person' class
            Type persontype = personobj.GetType();

            //Specify which method's information is required
            //Return metadata of specified method
            MethodInfo methodinfo = persontype.GetMethod("Show");

            //Provide instance (personobj) name whose method is about to invoke
            //pass parameter value 'null' if specified method has parameter
            var returnValue = methodinfo.Invoke(personobj, null);

            Console.WriteLine("Age = {0}", returnValue);

        }
    }

}
//Output
FirstName = Sundus
Age = 21
```

Explanation

To Invoke a specified method at runtime, the following steps are required:

1. Return and store the type of Object by using the typeof operator or GetType method.

2. Return and store metadata of a specified method of a type.

3. Use Invoke() method. Specify the type's instance and parameter values to invoke the method of a specified type's instance.

Use Reflection to Get Private Members

By default, reflection is used to get all public members, but with some code tweaking it can also be useful to find private members of a type. To get the private member, we specify the BindingFlags.NonPublic enum in the paremeter of Type.GetFields() and Type.GetMethods() methods, etc.

Code Snippet

Listing 14-11. Use Reflection to Read Private Members

```
using System;
using System.Reflection;

namespace DemoAssembly
{
    class Person
    {
        private int Age { get; set; }
        private string FirstName { get; set; }

        public Person(int age, string name)
        {
            this.Age = age;
            this.FirstName = name;
        }

    }

    class Program
    {
        static void Main(string[] args)
        {
            var personobj = new Person (21, "Sundus");
            var personobj2 = new Person(22, "Ali");

            //Store Metadata of Person Type in Type's Object
            //return Type of 'Person' class

            Type persontype = personobj.GetType();

            //Pass BindingFlags to specify what kind of
            //data member you want.
            //NonPublic = Private
            //Non-Static = Instance

            PropertyInfo[] props =
            props.GetProperties(BindingFlags.NonPublic | BindingFlags.Instance);

            foreach (PropertyInfo prop in props)
            {
            Console.WriteLine("{0} = {1}", prop.Name, prop.GetValue(personobj));
            }
```

```
            }
        }

}
//Output
Age = 21
FirstName = Sundus
```

Explanation

GetProperties() is used to return property information by using the BindingFlags enums; this method can return the specified type of properties. These enums tell a property should be non-public and non-static, etc. When passing bindingflags, use the vertical bar pipe '|' to add more than one BindingFlag in the GetProperties() method.

Use Reflection to Get Static Members

By default, reflection is used to get the public instance member of a type, but by using BindingFlags.Public and BindingFlags.Static together we can get the public static members of a type.

Code Snippet

Listing 14-12. Use Reflection to Read Static Member

```
using System;
using System.Reflection;

namespace DemoAssembly
{
    class Person
    {
        public static string company = "Microsoft";

    }

    class Program
    {
        static void Main(string[] args)
        {
            //Store Metadata of Person Type in Type's Object
            //return Type of 'Person' class

            Type persontype = typeof(Person);

            //Pass BindingFlags to specify what kind of
            //data member you want.
            //BindingFlags.Static = Static Member
            //BindingFlags.Public = Public Member

            FieldInfo[] fields =
                persontype.GetFields(BindingFlags.Public | BindingFlags.Static);
```

```
        foreach (FieldInfo field in fields)
        {
            Console.WriteLine("{0}", field.Name);
        }

    }
}

}
//Output
Company
```

Attributes in C#

Attributes are a kind of metadata for tagging C# code (types, methods, properties, and so forth). Attributes can be used with reflection to query down C# code at runtime, for code generation, or in editor at compile time in any number of ways (for example, to hide/seek windowsform controls from toolbar).

Syntax for Specifying an Attribute to C# Code

```
[attribute(parameter_name = value, ...)]
Element
```

Create a Custom Attribute

In term of programming, attributes are C# classes, inherited from the type "Attribute". When creating a custom attribute, it is a rule to suffix its class name with "Attribute". For example, see the below code snippet.

```
class MyCustomAttribute : Attribute
{

}
```

where MyCustomAttribute is the name of a custom attribute that inherits a class "Attribute".

Use Custom Attribute with Reflection

By using reflection, we can query down any C# code that was marked with a custom attribute.

Specify a Custom Attribute on a C# Code (Class, Method, etc)

In the example, a custom attribute is going to specify on Class, Method, and Properties, and then we'll use reflection to query it down.

Code Snippet

Listing 14-13. Use Custom Attribute on a C# Code

```
using System;
using System.Linq;
```

385

```csharp
using System.Reflection;

namespace DemoProject
{
    class MyCustomAttribute : Attribute
    {

    }

    [MyCustom] //Class, Marked with Custom Attribute
    class Person
    {

        //Property, Without Custom Attribute
        public int ID { get; set; }

        [MyCustom] //Property, Marked with Custom Attribute
        public int Age { get; set; }

        //Method, Without Custom Attribute
        public void Bye()
        {
            Console.WriteLine("Bye, world!");
        }

        [MyCustom] //Method, Marked with Custom Attribute
        public void Hi()
        {
            Console.WriteLine("Hi, world!");
        }
    }

    //Class, Without Custom Attribute
    class Machine
    {
        public int ID { get; set; }
    }

    class Program
    {
        static void Main(string[] args)
        {
            Assembly assembly = Assembly.GetExecutingAssembly();

            //Get all types that are marked with 'MyCustomAttribute'
            var types =
                from t in assembly.GetTypes()
                where t.GetCustomAttributes<MyCustomAttribute>().Count() > 0
                select t;

            foreach (var type in types)
            {
```

```csharp
        Console.WriteLine(type.Name);

        //Get all properties which are marked with 'MyCustomAttribute'
        var properties =
            from p in type.GetProperties()
            where p.GetCustomAttributes<MyCustomAttribute>().Count()> 0
            select p;

        foreach (var property in properties)
        {
            Console.WriteLine("\tProperty Name: {0}", property.Name);
        }

        //Get all methods  which are marked with 'MyCustomAttribute'
        var methods =
            from m in type.GetMethods()
            where m.GetCustomAttributes<MyCustomAttribute>().Count()> 0
            select m;

        foreach (var method in methods)
        {
            Console.WriteLine("\tMethod Name: {0}()", method.Name);
        }
            }
        }
    }
}
//Output
Person
        Property Name: Age
        Method Name: Hi()
```

Explanation

[MyCustom] = [MyCustomAttribute] because .NET framework already knows "Attribute" is a suffix, so it is a feature of C# which allows it to ignore suffix.

In above code snippet (Listing 14-13), a custom attribute of name "MyCustomAttribute" is created. This attribute [MyCustom] is marked on a class, property, and method.

In the main method, by using reflection, all the types, properties, and methods which were marked with "MyCustomAttribute" can be found by using the GetCustomAttributes<TAttribute>() method.

Declaring Properties in Custom Attribute Class

Properties can be declared in a custom attribute class. Values of these properties can be assigned when an instance of custom attribute is attached to any C# code element.

Only public property with get;set; can declare in attribute class.

Code Snippet

Listing 14-14. Read Attribute of a C# Code

```
using System;
using System.Reflection;

namespace demoProject
{
    class DeveloperAttribute : Attribute
    {
        public string Name { get; set; }
        public int Age { get; set; }
    }

    [Developer(Name = "Ali Asad", Age = 22)]
    class VehicleApp
    {
        public int Wheels { get; set; }
        public string Color { get; set; }
    }

    class Program
    {
        static void Main(string[] args)
        {
            //******Retrieve Property Values**********//

            //Get types
            Type vtype = typeof(VehicleApp);
            Type atype = typeof(DeveloperAttribute);

            //get the developerattribute attached with vehivle type
            DeveloperAttribute developer =
                (DeveloperAttribute)Attribute.GetCustomAttribute(vtype, atype);

            Console.WriteLine(developer.Age);
            Console.WriteLine(developer.Name);
        }
    }
}
//Output
22
Ali
```

Explanation

Only public property can be used in a custom attribute class. Its value can be assigned when the attribute is attached to any C# code. By using the Attribute.GetCustomAttribute() method, the value stored in properties of an attribute can be retrieved. To retrieve a custom attribute instance from a class, we need to specifiy what type of Attribute it is and what type of class it is attached to by using the typeof operator or getType() method.

Declaring Constructor in Custom Attribute Class

A constructor can be declared in a custom attribute class in the same way that it is declared in any C# class. Constructor can contain a parameter which can also be an optional parameter. Constructor is useful to assign values to properties defined in custom attribute class.

Code Snippet

Listing 14-15. Declare a Constructor in Custom Attribute Class

```
using System;

namespace demoProject
{
    class DeveloperAttribute : Attribute
    {
        public string Name { get; set; }
        public int Age { get; set; }

        public DeveloperAttribute(string name, int age = -1)
        {
            this.Name = name;
            this.Age = age;
        }
    }

    [Developer("Ali Asad")]
    class VehicleApp
    {
        public int Wheels { get; set; }
        public string Color { get; set; }
    }

    [Developer("Sundus", 21)]
    class Program
    {
        static void Main(string[] args)
        {
            //TO DO:
        }
    }
}
```

Explanation

By specifing an optional parameter in constructor we can have the advantage of either passing a value or discarding it. This feature of using constructor in custom attribute is helpful when providing optional information.

Use AttributeUsage on Custom Attribute Class

AttribtuteUsage tells on what C# code a custom attribute can be applied. In the parameter of AttributeUsage, we use AttributeTargets to restrict a custom attribute to only be applied on those enums (Class, Method, Property, etc). Use a vertical bar pipe '|' to add more than one AttributeTargets in the constructor of AttributeUsage.

The following are some commonly used enums of AttributeTargets that are useful for applying restrictions on C# Code.

Table 14-1. *AttributeTargets Enums List*

AttributeTargets Enums	Explanation
All	Attribute can be applied to any C# code element
Class	Attribute can be applied to C# class
Constructor	Attribute can be applied to constructor
Delegate	Attribute can be applied to a delegate
Enum	Attribute can be applied to an enumeration
Field	Attribute can be applied to a field
Interface	Attribute can be applied to an interface
Method	Attribute can be applied to a method
Property	Attribute can be applied to a parameter
Struct	Attribute can be applied to a struct

Syntax for Specifying an AttributeUsage to Custom Attribute Class

```
[AttributeUsage(AttributeTargets.Class, ...)]
Class SampleAttribute : Attribute{}
```

Code Snippet

Listing 14-16. Use Attribute Usage to Limit the Use of Custom Attribute Class for Only Certain C# Code

```
using System;
using System.Linq;
using System.Reflection;

namespace DemoProject
{
    //Tells MyCustomAttribute can only be use on a Class and Property
    [AttributeUsage(AttributeTargets.Class | AttributeTargets.Property)]
    class MyCustomAttribute : Attribute
    {

    }

    [MyCustom] //Class, Marked with Custom Attribute
    class Person
```

```
    {
        [MyCustom] //Property, Marked with Custom Attribute
        public int Age { get; set; }

        //[MyCustom] //Cannot use MyCustom on Method
        public void Hi()
        {
            Console.WriteLine("Hi, world!");
        }
    }

    class Program
    {
        static void Main(string[] args)
        {
            Assembly assembly = Assembly.GetExecutingAssembly();

            //Get all types that are marked with 'MyCustomAttribute'
            var types =
            from t in assembly.GetTypes()
            where t.GetCustomAttributes<MyCustomAttribute>().Count() > 0
            select t;

            foreach (var type in types)
            {
                Console.WriteLine(type.Name);

                //Get all properties which are marked with 'MyCustomAttribute'
                var properties =
                    from p in type.GetProperties()
                    where p.GetCustomAttributes<MyCustomAttribute>().Count() > 0
                    select p;

                foreach (var property in properties)
                {
                    Console.WriteLine("\tProperty Name: {0}", property.Name);
                }

            }
        }
    }

}
//Output
Program
        Property Name: Age
```

Explanation

By using AttributeUsuage and specifiying AttributeTargets, we restricted the use of MyCustomAttribute only for specified targets.

Use ILdasm.exe to View Assembly Content

Intermediate Disassembler (ILdasm) is a tool used to parse any .NET assembly into a human-readable format.

Such parsed information is useful to determine all the reference assemblies used in the specified assembly (.dll or .exe). It also displays the metadata, namespaces, types, and interfaces used within the assembly.

Use the following steps to parse any assembly in ildasm.exe:

1. Create and build an empty console C# application.

2. Go to Start Menu and open Visual Studio Command Prompt.

3. Use Visual Studio Command Prompt to navigate to the root folder of the C# console project that you just created. e.g., cd "{PathLocation}" press enter (cd "C:\Users\aliso\Documents\visual studio 2015\Projects\myConsoleApp\bin\Debug"). OR **cd "{PathLocation}" press enter**.

4. Inside the project's root folder, open .exe or .dll of the project file with ildasm.exe by entering a command **"ildasm {assemblyname}"**, for example "ildasm myConsoleApp.exe", and press enter.

In the following image you can see the application is parsed into human-readable format. It displays the application MANIFEST, myConsoleApp. The MANIFEST information can be readable by double clicking it. Similarly, every piece of file content can be readable in an intermediate language by double clicking it.

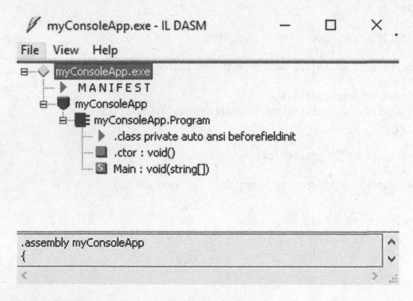

Figure 14-7. *Open an Assembly in IL-DASM*

Summary

- Exception is an error that occurs at runtime and may break the execution of an application.

- An assembly is the output of the compiled code. It can be either a .DLL or an .EXE file.

- Public Assembly is also known as a strong named assembly, which has a strong name key associated with it.

- Reflection is used to read attributes (Metadata) to obtain information of all assemblies, modules, and types of a running application.

- Attributes are a kind of metadata for tagging C# code (types, methods, properties, and so forth).

- Intermediate Disassembler (ILdasm) is a tool used to parse any .NET assembly into human-readable format.

Code Challenges

Challenge 1: Install a .DLL to Global Assembly Cache

It's not a code challenge, but rather a practice session in which you have to create a .dll file and install it to a Global Assembly Cache.

The solution is available in this chapter but don't look at it until you forget steps for installing an assembly to a GAC.

Practice Exam Questions

Question 1

Which of the following commands is required to create a strong name key?

- **A)** sn -k {assembly_name}.snk
- **B)** sn k {assembly_name}.snk
- **C)** gacutil -i {assembly_name}.snk
- **D)** gacutil i {assembly_name}.snk

Question 2

Which of the following methods is used for getting the information of the current assembly?

- **A)** Assembly. GetExecutingAssembly();
- **B)** Assembly.GetExecutedAssembly();
- **C)** Assembly.GetCurrentAssembly();
- **D)** Assembly.ExecutingAssembly();

Question 3

Which bindingflags are useful for getting the private data instance?

- **A)** BindingFlags.NonPublic | BindingFlags.Instance
- **B)** BindingFlags.Private | BindingFlags.Instance
- **C)** BindingFlags.NonPrivate | BindingFlags.NonStatic
- **D)** BindingFlags.Private | BindingFlags.NonStatic

Answers

1. A
2. A
3. A

CHAPTER 15

■ ■ ■

Debugging and Diagnostics

When you are working in the development of your application, you will normally encounter unexpected problems due to logical or runtime errors, even if the application is being tested or in production and you want to monitor the health of an application or to gather the extra information that you need to identify errors or bugs. To take care of such problems or identify and fix such errors or monitor an application's health, C# and Microsoft Visual Studio helps us out in this case to provide classes and tools for debugging and diagnostics.

In this chapter, we will learn about:

1. Debugging

2. Compiler Directives

3. Build Types

4. Diagnostics

5. Logging and Tracing

6. Profiling and Performance Counter

We will understand these main concepts along with sub-concepts (described below) that are useful for debugging and diagnostics.

Debugging

Debugging is the process of identifying and removing the errors from your application. It is just like a virtual execution of code in front of you and you can see the changes taking place in your code. Visual studio provides the facility to interact with such virtual execution of code where you can watch the execution and changes taking place, and perform other features provided like "Breakpoint", "Step over" and "Step into", etc. The changes taking place in front of you help to identify the error or logical mistake, as you can see the changing in value whether they are per requirement or not and then ultimately the error is identified and you can correct them after stopping the debugging process.

You can start the debugging process for your application by pressing **F11** from in Visual studio or make a breakpoint to start debugging from the specific point.

© Ali Asad and Hamza Ali 2017
A. Asad and H. Ali, *The C# Programmer's Study Guide (MCSD)*, DOI 10.1007/978-1-4842-2860-9_15

Figure 15-1 shows the debugging on simple code:

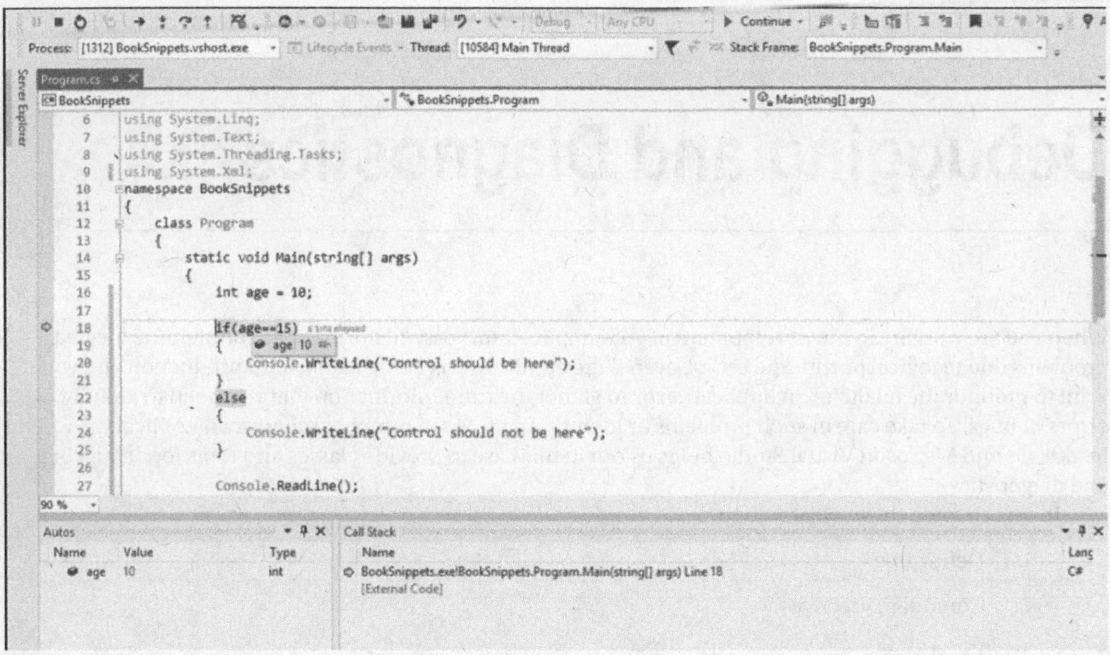

Figure 15-1. *Debugging*

For example, we have a scenario in which the line "Control should be here" must be printed. For this, the value of age must be 10 but the assigned value is 10, but the developer mistakenly makes a check on age for value 15 instead of 10; therefore, he/she is not getting any idea why "Control should be here" is not printed. In such a scenario, the developer will debug the code to find the error or mistake by pressing F11 or marking the breakpoint at a specific location by placing the cursor at that position and pressing F9 to identify where the problem is occurring, or for which condition the code is not behaving according to requirement. During debugging, he/she can watch the changes by hovering the cursor over the variables as mentioned in the picture above. In the above picture, when the developer hovers the cursor in the "age" variable (which gives age=10 and, on the spot, the developer tends to know that the value of age is 10), that's why the condition gets wrong. The error is identified now. After identification, he/she gets to know where is the problem and then is able to correct it.

Debugging is performed line by line (step by step). You can perform other functionalities to pass through code, such as step over, step into, and step out.

Visual Studio provides many debugging-related functionalities to perform. Their details are not in Exam-70-483. You can find more detail about them from the following link:

```
http://csharp.net-tutorials.com/debugging/introduction/
```

Choose appropriate Build Type

There are two default build configurations for a project in Visual Studio. When you build your project, a setting from a selected configuration is used. You can also define your own build configuration. Default configurations are:

1. **Debug Mode**: In this mode of configuration, extra information of code is created which helps for the debugging process. In this mode, the code does not optimize. This mode is generally used during development for debugging purposes.

2. **Release Mode**: In this mode of configuration, code is optimized and no extra code is generated for debugging purposes; that's why debugging cannot be done in this mode and generally is used for the final build of your project.

Listing 15-1 illustrates the difference between two configuration modes.

Code Snippet

Listing 15-1. A simple program illustrating the difference between two configurations.

```
int age = 10;
if (age == 10)
{
  Debug.Write("Condition is True");
  Console.WriteLine("Age is: " + age);
}
else
{
  Debug.Write("Condition is False");
  Console.WriteLine("Age is: " + 0);
}
```

When this code is executed in "Build" mode, "Condition is True" is outputted in the "Output Window" (a tool window in Visual Studio) and "Age is: 10" will be outputted in the Console screen. **Debug** is a class used in "Debug Mode" for debugging of code to report errors, and is available to execute or build under 'Debug' Mode. The detail of this class is explained in the "Diagnostics" topic.

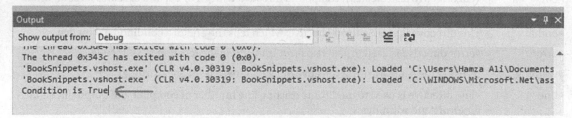

Figure 15-2. Result at OutputWindow

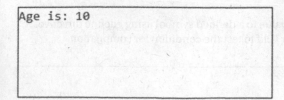

Figure 15-3. Output in Console

When the same code is executed in "Release" Mode, it will not output the "Condition is True" in the Output Window, as Debug class and its functions are ignored or removed by Release Mode and executed the renaming code by optimizing it. "Age is: 10" is outputted in Console Screen.

■ **Note** In release configuration, a lot of code could be removed or rewritten; that's why Release Mode is faster than Debug Mode and better regarding performance-vise. It's mainly used for a production environment.

Creating and Managing Compiler Directives

C# supports compiler directives or preprocessor compiler directives that are the instructions for the compiler, which helps in the compilation process. These directives tell the compiler how to process the code. Normally these are used to help in conditional compilation. In C#, they are not used to create macros (fragments of code) unlike in C or C++.

Directives start from "#" and do not end with a semicolon as they are not statements. There must be only one preprocessor directive on a line.

C# offers the following directives to work with:

Table 15-1. *Compiler Directives*

Directibes	Description
#define	#define directive is used to define a symbol which might be a character or sequence of characters.
#undef	#undef directive is used to undefine the defined symbol using #define directive or in compiler option. It must be on the top of non-directive code.
#if	#if directive is used to evaluate the symbol defined and execute its code if it finds the symbol defined. This directive is always followed by #endif directive.
#else	#else is used to create a compound directive with #if or #elif and execute its code when #if or #elif is false.
#elif	#elif directive also creates a compound directive with #if or elif and executes its code when it finds its condition or symbol to be true.
#endif	This directive is used with #if directive, which tells the end of a conditional directive.
#error	#error directive is used to generate error from a specific location in your code.
#warning	Its use is the same as #error directive but generates a level one warning.
#line	#line directive is used to modify the existing line number of compiler and output filename for errors and warnings.

#define

It is just used to define a symbol. You cannot assign any value to a defined symbol using #define directive. Symbols are normally conditions which are used in #if or #elif to test the condition for compilation.

■ **Note** #define directive must be on the top in the file.

The following code snippet shows how you can define a symbol:

```
#define Hamza
```

There should not be a conflict between the name of a symbol and a variable.

You can also define a symbol in compiler options by navigating to properties of Project and:

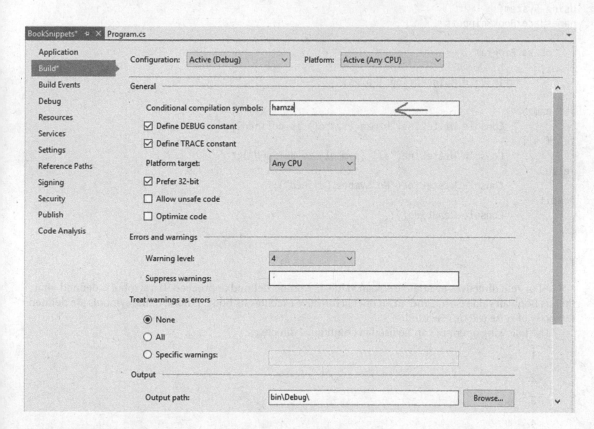

Figure 15-4. Project properties

■ **Note**   You cannot define the constants with #define directive in C# as possible in C++.

#if #elif #else and #endif

These directives are called conditional directives. #if or #elif is used to evaluate a symbol or condition that is defined using a #define directive or in a compiler option. #if directive operates on Boolean value and checks if the symbol or condition is defined (true) or not (false) and, based on this, its execution is performed. #if directive must end with an #endif directive.

Listing 15-2 shows how to use #if and #endif directives.

Code Snippet

Listing 15-2. #if and #endif directives

```
#define hamza
using System;
namespace BookSnippets
{
    class Program
    {
        static void Main(string[] args)
        {
#if hamza
            Console.WriteLine("hamza (Symbol) is defined");
#elif ali
            Console.WriteLine("ali (symbol) is defined");
#else
            Console.WriteLine("No Symbol Defined");
#endif
            Console.ReadLine();
        }
    }
}
```

#if or #elif directives evaluate Boolean value or symbols defined to proceed. If a symbol is defined, that means Boolean value is true and an #if or #elif directive executes its body. If none of the symbols are defined, the body of #else will be executed.

The following operator can be used in conditional directives:

1. ==

2. !=

3. &&

4. ||

You can view and learn about the complete list of preprocessor directives in C# from the following link: https://msdn.microsoft.com/en-us/library/ed8yd1ha.aspx

#error

#error is commonly used in a conditional directive. This directive generates a specific error at a specific location and shows in "Error List" (tool window in Visual Studio). The following code snippet shows how to use #error directive:

```
#if hamza
            Console.WriteLine("hamza (Symbol) is defined");
#else
            Console.WriteLine("No Symbol Defined");
#error No Symbol Defined
#endif
```

"Error list" window shows the error "No Symbol Defined" along with the line number and file name, etc.

Figure 15-5. *Error list*

This directive generates user-defined errors. #warning directive is also used in the same manner.

#line

You can renumber the compiler line number using this directive to give a line number and optionally rename the filename by giving the name (in string format) in which the code resides. You can also make the line number hidden by #line hidden (that will hide successive lines from debugger) and turn back to normal line number behavior by using #line default.

It can be used in debugging where you want to go to a specific line number or skip that line number. You can also show custom warnings with custom line numbers using this directive, i.e., if you have a value to validate and, when its validation fails, you output some message with a defined line number on your wish (supposed line number on which you think during development a warning should display).

Listing 15-3 shows how to use #line directive with its behaviors:

Code Snippet

Listing 15-3. #line directive

```
static void Main(string[] args)
{

        Console.WriteLine("Default/Normal Line No")
#line 100
        Console.WriteLine("Override Line No");
#line hidden
        Console.WriteLine("Hidden Line No");
#line default
        Console.WriteLine("Default/Noraml Line No");
}
```

Debug this code by pressing F11 and you will move line by line, but debugger will not encounter with the following statement "Console.WriteLine("Hidden Line No");" as its line number is hidden; that's why debugger will miss it and move to line number 101 (if any) and then navigate to default behavior.

Understand PDBs and Symbols

Program Database File (PDB) is a file created with the name of the Project you made, along with extension .pdb on the compilation of your code or project. A PDB file is a file containing information about your code or program which is used by debugger for debugging purposes. It stores a list of all symbols present in a module (DLL or EXE) along with the line number where they are declared and address where they stored. This information helps for debugging or throwing error at a specific location.

The information included in a PDB file can be controlled by using a Project's properties. To do this, right-click on the Project and select Properties. Click on the "Advance" button in Build Tab. A dialog will open where you can specify the information included in a PDB file; to use "Debug Info", drop down to select "full" or "pdb-only".

The choice "full" is the default selection for the PDB file in Debug Mode and "pdb-only" is for Release Mode. These two choices of "Debug Info" control the information to store in a PDB file about Program or code for debugging. One more option available for Debug Info is "none", which does not generate a PDB file and hence you cannot debug your code even in Debug Mode with a "none" selection.

When you select the "full" option for Debug Info (which is the default selection in Debug Mode), a PDB file is generated and an assembly has debug information; but for a "pdb-only" selection, a PDB file is generated with no modification in assembly and Visual Studio does not include a Debuggable attribute and hence debugging cannot perform in Release Mode or on a "pdb-only" selection.

The reason a PDB file is generated in Release Mode is to have information for exception messages about where the error occurred, i.e., stack trace or target of error, etc. Most importantly, you cannot trace your errors or message without having a PDB file.

■ **Note**   A PDB file is created for a specific build and it can only be used for that build. A PDB file cannot debug the code from a different build.

Diagnostics

How do you tackle such a situation in which an application is in a Production environment and the user faces some errors or performance-related issues regarding an application or how to trace down where the problem is occurring? Diagnostics helps you to tackle such a situation, because Debugging is not handy for a production environment.

Debugging helps you in Debug mode, which we normally use in a development phase where we can find out errors and correct them; but if the same thing happens after the release of an application or when an application is in real use, then we can diagnose our application to tackle such problems. Although remote debugging is possible (which you can do for your application, but the application must be hosted), it means you can't do debugging for your offline applications. Also, for remote debugging there must be a Debug Mode while publishing the application, which is not preferable for releasing the application.

To diagnose an application, we normally do Instrumenting of our application, in which different approaches can be used.

Instrumenting an Application

To instrument an application, features of diagnostics are added into it to study its behavior. Features of diagnostics means to add code for logging and tracing or to monitor applications' health. This makes you able to trace the program execution (i.e., what error occurred at which location in code) and gives the reason of performance-related problems without doing debugging.

There are some ways to instrument your application to perform diagnostics:

1.   Logging and Tracing

2.   Profiling the Application

Logging and Tracing

Tracing of an application means to track down the application to know what is going on in an application. You can get to know where the error is occurring by tracing your application and following the program's execution. You can follow the program's execution to know which methods it is going to call, which decision it is making, the occurrence of errors and warnings, etc. It provides the detailed information to instigate an issue when there is any problem in an application.

Logging gives you the facility to record the errors or report the errors. Normally it is applied on a running application (in real use) to receive information messages about the execution of an application.

Tracing has three main phases:

1. **Instrumenting**: Adding tracing code in your application.

2. **Tracing and logging**: The tracing code traces the issues and writes to a specified target. The target might be an output window, file, database, or event log.

3. **Analysis**: After getting the issues described in a specific format or written in a specific target, you analyze the details and identify the problem.

C# provides classes to trace and log errors: Debug and Trace.

Working with Debug and Trace Class

Debug and Trace classes can be used to trace and log the errors that occurred in an application. Normally, Debug and Trace classes use Listeners to log traced errors. These classes provide a couple of methods for tracing and put those traced errors into files, a database, or EventLogs.

Debug class is normally used in Debug Mode for tracing and logging, but what if you need to perform tracing and logging in an application which is in real use? Trace class comes in handy in such situations. It is used in Release Mode.

These classes provide some of the common functions with the same working:

Table 15-2. *Debug and Trace Common Methods*

Debug	Trace	Description
Assert	Assert	Checks the Boolean condition and throws an exception on a false condition with a call stack (traced information about error).
Flush	Flush	Flushes the buffers and puts the write-buffered data into Listeners.
Indent	Indent	Increases the Indent by one level.
UnIndent	UnIndent	Decreases the indent by one level.
Write	Write	Writes to message to trace listener.
WriteIf	WriteIf	Takes the condition and Writes the message to trace listener if the condition is true.
WriteLine	WriteLine	Writes the message to Debug's Listeners collection by line terminator. It is an overloaded function and provides more interactivity to log the traced error.
WriteLineIf	WriteLineIf	Behave same as WriteLine method but makes proceeding based on a condition.

■ **Tip**   Some other methods of these classes are also there. You should also work with them while practicing.

You can use these functions to trace and print out the errors(log) and use Listener instance (TraceListeners provided in C#) to log traced information to specific target.

Listing 15-4 shows how to use Debug class for tracing and basic logging:

Code Snippet

Listing 15-4. Debug class for tracing and logging

```
static void Main(string[] args)
{
  try
  {

    Debug.WriteLine("Tracing Start");

    int age = 10;
    Debug.WriteLineIf(age.GetType() == typeof(int), "Age is Valid");

    for (int i = 0; i < 5; i++)
    {
      Debug.WriteLine("Loop executed Successfully");
    }
    Debug.Print("Tracing Finished");
  }
  catch (Exception)
  {
    Debug.Assert(false);
  }
}
```

Debug class use Output window (Target Listener) of Visual Studio as Default trace listener.

You can also use Trace class for such a purpose. For example, we have two numbers and want to evaluate that they must be **int** and the divisor should not be zero, if zero changes the value and provides the information. Listing 15-5 explains this example.

Code snippet

Listing 15-5. Trace class to trace and log data

```
static void Main(string[] args)
{
  try
  {

    Trace.WriteLine("Tracing Start:Numbers must be Int");

    int num1 = 10;
    int num2 = 0;
```

```
Trace.WriteLineIf(num1.GetType() == typeof(int) && num2.GetType() == typeof(int), "Numbers
are valid");

    if (num2 < 1)
    {
        num2 = num1;
        Trace.TraceInformation("num2 has been changed due to zero value");
    }
    int result = num1 / num2;
    Trace.Indent();
}
catch (Exception ex)
{
    Trace.Assert(false);
    Trace.TraceError(ex.Message);
}

}
```

TraceInformation provides the information about the error which occurred or which you want to occur. The same code executes again without the **if** condition; the exception occurred due to the 0 value of the divisor and the Assert method gives you the call stack of error in a message box. But if you want to record such a traced error (to log your error), you would use the **TraceError** method in such a situation. It logs down the call stack to the output window (default listener).

■ **Note**   The Debug and Trace classes show their output in an output window (Visual Studio tool window) by default.

Another class which comes in handy is **TraceSource**, and it's more preferable to use than static Trace class. Listing 15-6 shows how to trace and log issues in your application with **TraceSource** class:

Code Snippet

Listing 15-6. TraceSource class to trace and log data

```
TraceSource ts = new TraceSource("TraceSource1", SourceLevels.All);
ts.TraceInformation("Tracing  the application..");
ts.TraceEvent(TraceEventType.Error, 0, "Error trace Event");
ts.TraceData(TraceEventType.Information, 1, new string[]{ "Info1","Info2" });
ts.Flush();//flush the buffers
ts.Close();//close the listeners (in this case listener is outout window)
```

TraceSource class has some extra functions. Some of them, like TraceEvent and TraceData, are used here. TraceEvent will write down the trace event message/error with the event type and numeric identifier to the trace listener, whereas TraceData will write down traced data to the listener along with the event type, event identifier, and trace data in an array form. The event type provided in TraceEvent and TraceData method is enumeration: **Critical, Error, Warning, Information, Verbose, Stop, Start, Suspend, Resume, Transfer**. TraceSource class has two overloaded constructors in which you can give the name of TraceSouce or name along with SourceLevel (tracing to which level). It is also an enumeration: **ActivityTracing, All, Critical, Error, Information, Off, Verbose, Warning**.

Trace or TraceSource class gives you more interactivity with the issues in an application when it is in real use, as opposed to Debug class.

■ **Note**   Trace class can be used in Release as well as in Debug Mode. It runs in a different thread, whereas Debug runs in the main thread.

Working with Trace Listeners

Trace listeners receive the traced information or errors by Debug, Trace, or TraceSource class. They are used to log the errors. They direct the traced data to a target such as EventLog, Console, Output window, or Text file. Besides Output window (which is the default trace listener), there are several other trace listeners.

The .NET framework provides the following listeners:

1.   ConsoleTraceListener

2.   DelimitedTraceListener

3.   EventLogTraceListener

4.   TextWriterTraceListener

5.   XmlWriterTraceListener

To work with such listeners, you must clear the default listener first. You can have as many listeners as you want.

The detail and use of some of these trace listeners (to log the errors or issues) are below:

ConsoleTraceListener

This listener logs the errors or outputs them to a console screen (Target), which is standard output.

Listing 15-7 shows how to log errors on Console.

Code Snippet

Listing 15-7. Use of ConsoleTraceListener

```
//specify the trace source
TraceSource ts = new TraceSource("ConsoleTraceSource", SourceLevels.All);

//Specify the listener (Console would be the Target)
ConsoleTraceListener listener = new ConsoleTraceListener();

//clear the default listener
ts.Listeners.Clear();

//adding the listener

ts.Listeners.Add(listener);

//tracing the information/issue which will log into added listener
ts.TraceInformation("Tracing  the application..");
ts.TraceData(TraceEventType.Error, 1, new string[] { "Error1", "Error2" });
ts.Flush();
ts.Close();
```

TextWriterTraceListener

This listener logs the debugged or traced data into text files (target). You can also read traced data from the file. Listing 15-8 shows how to use TextWriterTraceListener.

Code Snippet

Listing 15-8. Use of TextWriterTraceListener

```
//specify the trace source
TraceSource ts = new TraceSource("SampleTraceSource", SourceLevels.All);

//Specify the target for TextWriterTraceListener
Stream file = new FileStream("TraceFile.txt", FileMode.Append);

//Specify the listener
TextWriterTraceListener txtListener = new TextWriterTraceListener(file);

//clear the default listener
ts.Listeners.Clear();

//adding the listener

ts.Listeners.Add(txtListener);

//tracing the information/issue which will log into added listener
ts.TraceInformation("Tracing  the application..");
ts.TraceData(TraceEventType.Error, 1, new string[] { "Error1", "Error2" });
ts.TraceInformation("Tracing complete");
ts.Flush();
ts.Close();
```

The output of traced data is:

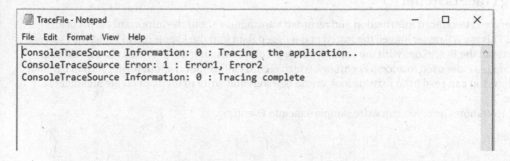

Figure 15-6. Output of Traced data in File

You can also specify the listeners in a configuration file, which is more beneficial than specifying in code because you can easily change them after the deployment of an application.

The following configuration code shows how to specify the listeners in a configuration file:

```
<sources>
      <source name="SampleTraceSource" switchName="defaultSwitch">
        <listeners>
          <add initializeData="TraceFile.txt" name="txtListener" type="System.Diagnostics.
          TextWriterTraceListeer">
            <filter type="System.Diagnostics.EventTypeFilter" initializeData="Error"/>
          </add>
          <add name="consoleListener" />
          <remove name="Default"/>
        </listeners>
      </source>
</sources>
<switches>
      <add name="defaultSwitch" value="All" />
</switches>
```

You can give the source of a trace listener inside the sources tag, where you specify the source of the listener. This source can use two trace listeners: text and console.

The switch tag is also defined, which is used by the trace source; this is what we also did in our code to specify the source label in the **TraceSource** constructor. Its value specifies how to deal with incoming messages: "All" means all types of messages. You can specify which type of message can be viewed this way. Switch works on the **TraceSource** level, so its impact will be on all the listeners defined under a trace source. To specify the type of message you can see, or determine which event is processed for a specific listener, you can apply a filter. This is commonly used in such cases where you have multiple listeners under a trace source.

■ **Note**   Add the above code in the system.diagnostics tag and place it inside the configuration tag.

EventLogTraceListener

Event Log received the traced information and recorded information about the important events of an application. This trace listener logged the traced or debugged data into the EventLogs of Windows (Target). You can also read the EventLogs with the administrative permission, using the provided class **EventLog**.

EventLog is a class used to access EventLogs, which records information about the important event of an application. You can read from existing logs, create new logs and write to them, or create and delete an event source.

Listing 15-9 shows how you can write sample data into EventLog:

Code Snippet

Listing 15-9. Create Event source

```
string sourceName = "Sample Log";
string logName = "Application";
string machineName = ".";// . means local machine
string entryTowritten = "Some random entry into Event Log";
if (!EventLog.SourceExists(sourceName, machineName))
```

```
{
    EventLog.CreateEventSource(sourceName, logName);
}

EventLog.WriteEntry(sourceName,entryTowritten,EventLogEntryType.Information);
```

CreateEventSource method is used to create the source of an event (creation of new EventLog) with the provided name. Log name, which is an application, is optional. Log is a category or something similar to a file in which source entries are to be written. There are three types of Logs: Application, System, or Custom log.

To write data or an entry into an EventLog, you use the WriteEntry method, in which you have to know what to write, where to write, and what should be the level of data to be written.

To view the created log, open the Event Viewer by going to "Start" in Windows ➤ search "Administrative Tools". When the window is open, open the "Event Viewer" application.

On the left side (menu panel) of Event Viewer, there is a folder ("Windows Logs"), which contains all the logs of type Application and System (log name which we specify in our code). The logs with a custom log name go in the "Application and Services Logs" folder.

Click on the "Application" log as we specified in the log name "Application" in code. Search through all logs with the given source name (the name given in the code, which is Sample Log). Click on it. It will look like this:

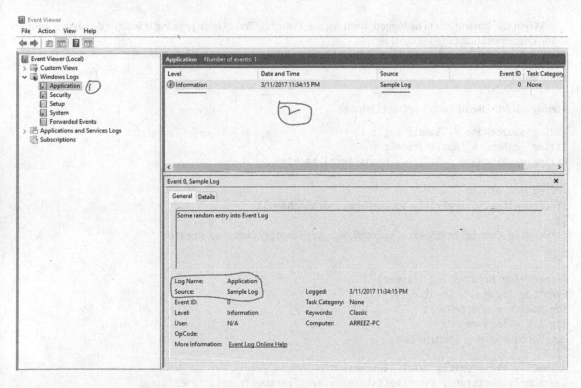

Figure 15-7. *Event viewer*

The marking on the above figure shows our information specified in code is in EventLog.

Whenever the code runs, a new entry is created with the specific message inside the given log.

You can also read the EventLog. For example, I need to read the latest information of Sample Log. The following code helps you out:

```
string sourceName = "Sample Log";
string logName = "Application";
string machineName = ".";// . means local machine

EventLog log = new EventLog(logName,machineName,sourceName);
Console.WriteLine("Total entries: " + log.Entries.Count);

EventLogEntry last = log.Entries[log.Entries.Count - 1];//last(latest) log with "Sample Log"
name

Console.WriteLine("Index: " + last.Index);
Console.WriteLine("Source: " + last.Source);
Console.WriteLine("Type: " + last.EntryType);
Console.WriteLine("Time: " + last.TimeWritten);
Console.WriteLine("Message: " + last.Message);
Console.WriteLine("Machine Name: " + last.MachineName);
Console.WriteLine("Category: " + last.Category);
```

When the tracing has to be logged, then we use EventLogTraceListener to log traced or debugged data in the corresponding target (EventLog).

Listing 15-10 shows how you can write information to EventLog using this listener:

Code snippet

Listing 15-10. Use of EventLogTraceListener

```
string sourceName = "Sample Log";
string logName = "Application";
string machineName = ".";// . means local machine

//Creation of log
if (!EventLog.SourceExists(sourceName, machineName))
{
  EventLog.CreateEventSource(sourceName, logName);//EventLog created
}

//Specifing created log (target)
EventLog log = new EventLog();
log.Source = sourceName;
log.Log = logName;
log.MachineName = machineName;

//specify the EventLog trace listener
EventLogTraceListener eventLogListener = new EventLogTraceListener();

//specify the target to listener
eventLogListener.EventLog = log;
```

```
//specifing the Trace class
TraceSource trace = new TraceSource("Sample Source",SourceLevels.Information);//just to
trace information

//Clearing default listener
trace.Listeners.Clear();

//assigning new listener
trace.Listeners.Add(eventLogListener);

//Start tracing

trace.TraceInformation("Tracing start to Event Log");

trace.Flush();
trace.Close();
```

You can read this traced information as we did above: Code to Read Event Logs.

■ **Note**   Visual Studio should start "Run as Administrator" in order to read Event Logs.

Profiling the Application

Profiling is an activity of collecting information about something in order to give a description or to analyze it.

Profiling in an application is to gather information about it to analyze or study its performance or health: the speed of an application, memory consumed, disk space usage or other performance-related characteristics.

There are two main ways to do profiling of an application:

1. Profiling using Visual Studio Tool

2. Profiling by Hand

Profiling using Visual Studio Tool

Visual Studio 2012 and above of version Ultimate, Premium or Professional includes several profiling-related tools like Memory Usage, CPU Usage, Performance Explorer, etc., which you can call Profilers. When working with Profiler, the easiest way is to use Performance Wizard (profiling tool in Visual Studio).

To work with Performance Wizard, click on Analyze menu ➤ select Launch Performance Wizard. The wizard looks like:

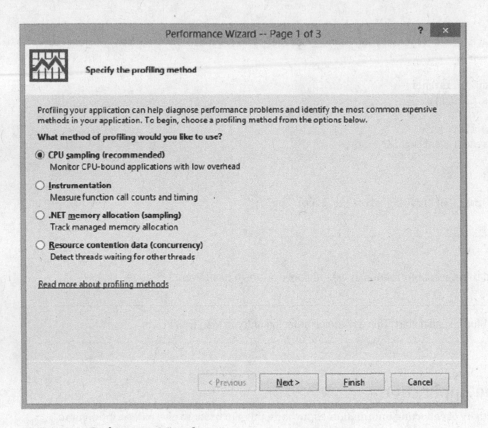

Figure 15-8. *Performance Wizard*

There are four ways to do profiling using Performance Wizard:

1. **CPU sampling**: It is the most recommended method to do profiling and is used for initial search for performance-related problems.

2. **Instrumentation**: As discussed earlier, instrumentation means to add code in your program. Basically, you add some code to gather timing information for each function called and examine it.

3. **.NET memory allocation**: This method gives you information when a new object is created or destroyed by a garbage collector.

4. **Resource contention data**: This method is useful for a multithreaded environment.

Select "CPU Sampling" and click "Next". In the next window, click on "Finish". After finishing the wizard, Profiler will launch. This may take a couple of seconds to start.

Profiler will analyze the data shown in the respective panels. The most often used calls and method paths are shown in those panels.

Profiling by Hand

Profiling by Hand is instrumenting, i.e., inserting some code to watch the performance of an application. Normally you work with **StopWatch** in this method and record a program's execution time. You capture timing information for every function that is called.

Listing 15-11 shows how to perform this:

Code snippet

Listing 15-11. Profiling by Hand

```
static void Main(string[] args)
{

  Stopwatch watch = new Stopwatch();

  //Time taken by LoadData method
  watch.Start();
  LoadData();
  watch.Stop();

  //Time Taken by FetchData method
  Console.WriteLine("Time Taken by LoadData method: " + watch.Elapsed);

  //Reset watch
  watch.Reset();

  //Time taken by FetchData method
  watch.Start();
  var data = FetchData();
  watch.Stop();

  Console.WriteLine("Time taken by FetchData method: " + watch.Elapsed);

  Console.WriteLine("Profiling by Hand is Done");
  Console.ReadLine();
}
static void LoadData()
{
  for (int i = 0; i < 100; i++)
  {
    Debug.Write("Loading");
  }
```

```
}
static int FetchData()
{
  int data-0;
  for (int i = 0; i < 10; i++)
  {
    for (int j = 0; j < 10; j++)
    {
      data = j;
    }
  }
  return data;
}
```

The output of this code looks like:

```
Time Taken by LoadData method: 00:00:00.1203933
Time taken by FetchData method: 00:00:00.0002119
Profiling by Hand is Done
```

Figure 15-9. Output (Profiling by Hand)

StopWatch has different methods and you can get time in milliseconds also.

Profiling using Performance Counter

Performance Counter lets you monitor the performance of an application. You can track what the computer is doing, i.e., the activity of the computer, CPU performance, etc. Keep an eye on the application or on the hardware. It is also another approach of Profiling by Hand.

Displaying of CPU usage is an example of Performance Counter as it displays the activity of the CPU and you can track down what is happing.

These performance counters are managed by Windows like EventLogs and you can view them by using the **Perfmon.exe** program.

To view Performance Monitor, hit the "Run" command by pressing window key +R, type perfmon and hit enter. This will bring Performance Monitor in front of you:

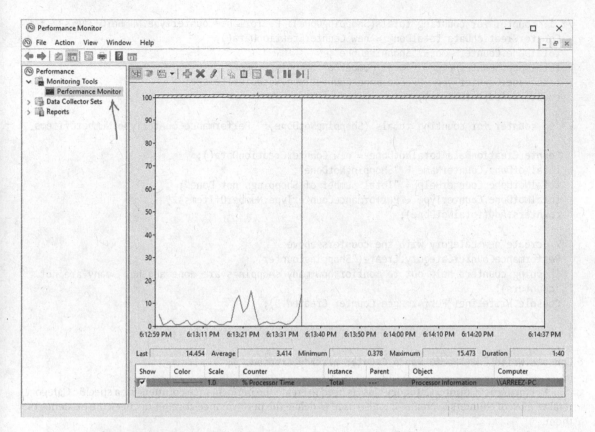

Figure 15-10. *Performance Monitor*

The figure shows the examining of data about CPU.

Creating the Performance Counter

There are two ways to create Performance Counter.

1. Using Server Explorer

2. Using Code

C# provides a class, **PerformanceCounterCategory** class, to create Performance Counter, and **PerformanceCounter** to interact with them. You can also create manual performance counters using Server-Explorer.

Listing 15-12 shows how to create Performance Counter in C#.

Code Snippet

Listing 15-12. Create Performance Counter

```
if (!PerformanceCounterCategory.Exists("ShoppingCounter"))
{
CounterCreationDataCollection counters = new  CounterCreationDataCollection();
```

```
/* 1. counter for counting totals(ShoppingDone): PerformanceCounterType.NumberOfItems32 */
  CounterCreationData totalDone = new CounterCreationData();
  totalDone.CounterName = "ShoppingDone";
  totalDone.CounterHelp = "Total number of Shoppings Done";
  totalDone.CounterType = PerformanceCounterType.NumberOfItems32;
  counters.Add(totalDone);

/* 2. counter for counting totals (ShoppingNotDone): PerformanceCounterType.NumberOfItems32
*/
  CounterCreationData totalNotDone = new CounterCreationData();
  totalNotDone.CounterName = "ShoppingNotDone";
  totalNotDone.CounterHelp = "Total number of Shoppings not Done";
  totalNotDone.CounterType = PerformanceCounterType.NumberOfItems32;
  counters.Add(totalNotDone);


  // create new category with the counters above
  PerformanceCounterCategory.Create("ShoppingCounter",
 "Shopping counters help out to montior how many shoppings are done and how  many are not.
", counters);
  Console.WriteLine("Performance Counter Created.");

}
else
Console.WriteLine("Performance Counter already Created.");
```

PerformanceCounterCategory class is used to create the performance counters for a specific Category. It takes a list of counters to create. It is also used to delete the performance counter or check the existence of them.

Performance counters are defined for a specific category using **CounterCreationData** class. **CounterCreationDataCollection** takes the instances of **CounterCreationData** class.

The above code will create Performance Category "ShoppingCounter" and add two counters, "ShoppingDone" and "ShoppingNotDone", into it.

You can view them by navigating to Server Explorer ➤ Servers ➤ Performance Counter and search down for the created category.

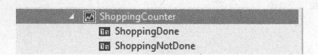

Figure 15-11. *Performance Counter Category*

Right-click on the "ShoppingCounter" and click Edit. You can also add new counters in this way, or edit or view them. The details look like:

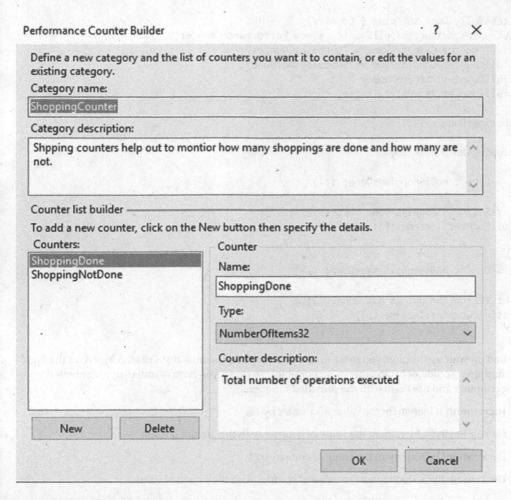

Figure 15-12. *Performance Builder*

The same detail we created is in our code, i.e., two performance counters with provided names and descriptions, etc.

Working with Performance Counter

After creating Performance Counter, these should be used to monitor the performance of an application.

Listing 15-13 shows how you can use them in your application.

Code Snippet

Listing 15-13. Working with Performance Counter

```
// successfully Done shpping (Counter)
PerformanceCounter successfullCounter = new PerformanceCounter();
successfullCounter.CategoryName = "ShoppingCounter";
successfullCounter.CounterName = "ShoppingDone";
successfullCounter.MachineName = ".";
successfullCounter.ReadOnly = false;
```

417

```
// Not successfully Done shopping ( Counter)
PerformanceCounter NotsuccessfullCounter = new PerformanceCounter();
NotsuccessfullCounter.CategoryName = "ShoppingCounter";
NotsuccessfullCounter.CounterName = "ShoppingsNotDone";
NotsuccessfullCounter.MachineName = ".";
NotsuccessfullCounter.ReadOnly = false;

int noOfShoppingsDone = 15;

int noOfShoppingsNotDone = 20;

for (int i = 0; i < noOfShoppingsDone; i++)
{
  Console.WriteLine("Shopping Done Successfully..");
  successfullCounter.Increment();
}

for (int i = 0; i < noOfShoppingsNotDone; i++)
{
  Console.WriteLine("Shoppings Not Done..");
  NotsuccessfullCounter.Increment();
}
```

Somewhere in your application, you make your counter successful and unsuccessful based on the logic (i.e., where shopping would not be possible or be possible). To do so, you have to initialize your created performance counters and use them with the provided functions:

1. **Increment():** Increment the value of counter by 1.

2. **IncrementBy():** Increment the value of counter with the provided value.

3. **Decrement():** Decrement the value of counter by 1.

4. **DecrementBy():** Decrement the value of counter with the provided value.

You can view your change or monitor these performance counters by going to Performance Monitor. Open the application. Select Performance Monitor from the left menu side. Click the green color button of plus (at top). A window of "Add Counters" will pop up in front of you. Search down your Counter Category ➤, click on it, and hit the Add button. This will add the selected counter in the "Added Counter" panel of the same window (you can add as many counters as you want to view). Click on the "OK" button:

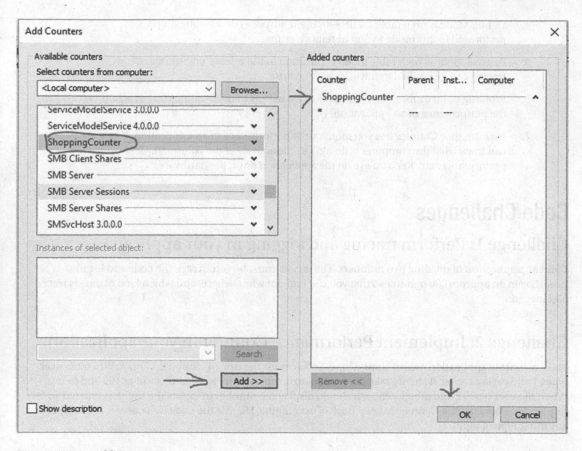

Figure 15-13. *Add Counters*

After clicking on the OK button, the selected counters' performance is viewed in Performance Counter. In such a way, you can monitor your application's health.

■ **Tip** You can further study the Performance Counter from the following link: `https://msdn.microsoft.com/en-us/library/w8f5kw2e(v=vs.110).aspx`

Summary

1. Debugging is the process of finding and removing bugs/errors from your application.

2. Tracing is the process of tracing the errors or issues occurring in your application.

3. Logging is the process to logging traced or debugged errors or issues. Logging is the reporting of errors.

4. Debug Mode is preferable for development purposes and Debugging is performed in this mode to find or remove errors.

5. Release Mode is preferable for an application in the release environment and tracing can be applied to trace/identify an error.

6. Profiling or instrumenting of an application means to insert some code to watch the performance of an application.

7. Performance Counter lets you monitor the performance of an application. You can track what the computer is doing, i.e., the activity of the computer, CPU performance, etc. Keep an eye on the application or on the hardware.

Code Challenges

Challenge 1: Perform tracing and logging in your application.

Build an application of dividing two numbers. The divisor must be zero. Trace the code and log into EventLog in an appropriate manner so that you can find out what, where, and which kind of data is traced and logged.

Challenge 2: Implement Performance Counter in your application.

Make a console application, which should have 2 choices for the user: 1- Input, 2-Output. When the user types 1 and presses enter, it should take the input (single input of any type) and count as 100 and so on. When the user types 2 and presses enter, it should display the number of inputs the user has entered so far. Implement Performance Counter to keep track of user inputs. Handle the code if the user mistakenly enters any other type of input.

■ **Hint** Take the hint from the code written in the Performance Counter topic.

Practice Exam Questions

Question 1

Which class should you preferably use for tracing in Release Mode?

A) Debug

B) Trace

C) TraceSource

D) All of the above

Question 2

To build a project you need a PDB file of:

A) Previous build version

B) Any build version

C) No need of PDB file

D) Same build version

Question 3

Which method is the easiest way of finding the problem if you have no idea what it is?

A) Using Profiler

B) Profiling by Hand

C) Using Performance Counter

D) Debugging

Answers

1. C
2. D
3. A

CHAPTER 16

■ ■ ■

Practice Exam Questions

Microsoft conduct Exam 70-483: Programming in C# from 4 objectives.

1. Manage Program Flow
2. Create and Use Types
3. Debug Application and Implement Security
4. Implement Data Access

In the previous chapters, we covered all the topics included in the objectives. In this chapter, we'll revise these objectives in terms of simple multiple-choice questions. Each objective contains 25 unique questions for your practice and revision.

Objective 1: Manage Program Flow

Question 1

A method name LongRunningMethod(CancellationTokenSource cts), takes a cancellation token source and performs a long-running task. If the calling code requests cancellation, the method must Cancel the long-running task and set the task status to TaskStatus.Canceled.

Which of the following methods should you use?

A) throw new AggregateException();

B) ct.ThrowIfCancellationRequested() ;

C) cts.Cancel();

D) if (ct.IsCancellationRequested) return;

© Ali Asad and Hamza Ali 2017

A. Asad and H. Ali, *The C# Programmer's Study Guide (MCSD)*, DOI 10.1007/978-1-4842-2860-9_16

Question 2

An exception is handled on a method which mathematically calculates numbers. The method contains the following catch blocks:

```
01.
02. catch(ArithmeticException e) { Console.WriteLine("Arithmetic Error"); }
03.

04. catch (ArgumentException e) { Console.WriteLine("Invalid Error"); }
05.
06. catch (Exception e) { Console.WriteLine("General Error"); }
07.
```

You need to add the following code to the method:

```
catch (DivideByZeroException e) { Console.WriteLine("Divide by Zero"); }
```

At which line should you insert the code?

A) 01

B) 03

C) 05

D) 07

Question 3

To create a custom exception, which class is required to be inherited?

A) SystemException

B) System.Exception

C) System.Attribute

D) Enumerable

Question 4

How do you throw an exception so the stack trace preserves the information?

A) throw;

B) throw new Exception();

C) throw ex;

D) return new Exception();

Question 5

You're creating an application that contains the following code:

```
class Test
{
    public event Action Launched;
}
class Program
{
    static void Main(string[] args)
    {
        Test t = new Test();

    }

}
```

How would you subscribe a Launched event in the Main method to the "t" instance?

A) t.Launched += ()=>{..};

B) t.Launched = ()=>{..};

C) t.Launched -= ()=>{..};

D) t.Launched = t.Launched + ()=>{...};

Question 6

You need to reference a method which returns a Boolean value and accepts two int parameters. Which of the following delegates would you use?

A) Func<int, int, bool> func;

B) Action<int, int, bool> act;

C) Func<bool, int, int> func;

D) Action<bool, int, int> act;

Question 7

Which of the following keywords is useful for ignoring the remaining code execution and quickly jumping to the next iteration of the loop?

A) break;

B) yield;

C) jump;

D) continue;

Question 8

Which of the following loops is faster?

A) for

B) do

C) Parallel.for

D) foreach

Question 9

await keyword can only be written with a method whose method signature has:

A) static keyword

B) async keyword

C) lock keyword

D) sealed keyword

Question 10

Which keyword is used to prevent a class from inheriting?

A) sealed

B) lock

C) const

D) static

Question 11

When handling an exception, which block is useful to release resources?

A) try

B) catch

C) finally

D) lock

Question 12

Which of following methods is accurate for holding the execution of a running task for a specific time?

A) Thread.Sleep()

B) Task.Delay()

C) Task.Wait()

D) Task.WaitAll()

Question 13

Which of the following methods is useful for holding the execution of a main thread until all background tasks are executing?

A) Thread.Sleep()

B) Task.WaitAll()

C) Task.Wait()

D) Thread.Join()

Question 14

How would you chain the execution of a task so that every next task runs when the previous task finishes its execution? Which method you would use?

A) task.ContinueWith()

B) Task.Wait()

C) Task.Run()

D) Thread.Join()

Question 15

In a switch statement, which keyword would you use to write a code when no case value satisfies?

A) else

B) default

C) return

D) yield

Question 16

Foreach loop can only run on:

A) anything

B) collection

C) const values

D) static values

Question 17

Which keyword is useful for returning a single value from a method to the calling code?

A) yield

B) return

C) break

D) continue

Question 18

Which of the following collections is a thread-safe?

- **A)** Dictionary<K,V>
- **B)** Stack<T>
- **C)** ConcurrentDictionary<K,V>
- **D)** Queue

Question 19

When running a long-running asynchronous operation that returns a value, which keyword is used to wait and get the result?

- **A)** await
- **B)** yield
- **C)** return
- **D)** async

Question 20

Which of the following is the right syntax for using an asynchronous lambda expression?

- **A)** Task task = async () => { ... };
- **B)** Task<Task> task = async () => { ... };
- **C)** Func<Task> task = async () => { ... };
- **D)** Action<Task> task = async (t) => { ... };

Question 21

Suppose you're developing an application and you want to make a thread-safe code block for execution. Which of the following code blocks would you use to write code?

```
A)
  object o = new object();
  lock (o)
  {
      ...
  }
B)
  object o = new object();
  lock (typeof(o))
  {
      ...
  }
```

```
C)
  lock (new object ())
  {
      ...
  }
D)
  lock
  {
      ...
  }
```

Question 22

Suppose you're creating a method that threw a new exception but it also threw an inner exception. See the following code:

```
01. private void myMethod(int i)
02. {
03.     try
04.     {
05.         ...
06.     }
07.     catch (ArgumentException ex)
08.     {
09.
10.     }
11. }
```

You must preserve the stack trace of the new exception and also throw the inner exception; which code statement would you use in line 09?

A) throw ex;

B) throw new Exception("Unexpected Error", ex);

C) throw;

D) throw new Exception(ex);

Question 23

You're creating an application that has many threads that run in parallel. You need to increment an integer variable "i". How would you increment it in an atomic operation?

```
A)
   int i = 0;
   Interlocked.Increment(ref i);
B)
   int i = 0;
   Interlocked.Increment(i);
```

```
C)
   int i = 0;
   i++;
D)
   int i = 0;
   Interlocked.Increment(out i);
```

Question 24

Which property or method of task can be used as an alternative of the await keyword?

A) Result

B) Wait()

C) WaitAll()

D) Delay()

Question 25

Suppose you're creating an application that needs a delegate that can hold a reference of a method that can return bool and accept an integer parameter. How would you define that delegate?

A) delegate bool myDelegate(int i, int j);

B) delegate bool (int i, int j);

C) delegate myDelegate(int i, int j);

D) delegate bool myDelegate(int i);

Answers

1. B
2. A
3. B
4. A
5. A
6. A
7. D
8. C
9. B
10. A
11. A
12. B
13. B

14. A
15. B
16. B
17. B
18. C
19. A
20. C
21. A
22. B
23. A
24. A
25. A

Objective 2: Create and Use Types

Question 1

Suppose you're creating an application; in the application you need to create a method that can be called by using a varying number of parameters. What should you use?

A) derived classes

B) interface

C) enumeration

D) method overloading

Question 2

You are developing an application that includes the following code segment:

```
interface ILion
{
    void Run();
}
interface IMan
{
    void Run();
}
```

You need to implement both Run() methods in a derived class named Animal that uses the Run() method of each interface.

Which two code segments should you use?

A)
```
var animal = new Animal();
((ILion, IMan)animal).Run();
```

B)
```
class Animal : ILion, IMan
{
    public void IMan.Run()
    {
        ...
    }

    public void ILion.Run()
    {
        ...
    }
}
```

C)
```
class Animal : ILion, IMan
{
    void IMan.Run()
    {
        ...
    }

    void ILion.Run()
    {
        ...
    }
}
```

D)
```
var animal = new Animal();
((ILion)animal).Run();
((IMan)animal).Run();
```

E)
```
var animal = new Animal();
animal.Run(ILion);
animal.Run(IMan);
```

F)
```
var animal = new Animal();
animal.Run();
```

Question 3

You're creating an application that receives a JSON data in the following format:

```
{
    "Name" : "Ali",
    "Age" : "22",
    "Languages": ["Urdu", "English"]
}
```

The application includes the following code segment:

```
01. public class Person
02. {
03.     public string Name { get; set; }
04.     public int Age { get; set; }
05.     public string[] Languages { get; set; }
06. }
07. public static Person ConvertToPerson(string json)
08. {
09.     var ser = new JavaScriptSerializer();
10.
11. }
```

You need to ensure that the ConvertToName() method returns the JSON input string as a Name object. Which code segment should you insert at line 10?

A) Return ser.ConvertToType<Person>(json);

B) Return ser.DeserializeObject(json);

C) Return ser.Deserialize<Person>(json);

D) Return (Person)ser.Serialize(json);

Question 4

You are developing an application. The application converts a Person object to a string by using a method named WriteObject. The WriteObject() method accepts two parameters: a Person object and an XmlObjectSerializer object.

The application includes the following code:

```
01. public enum Gender
02. {
03.     Male,
04.     Female,
05.     Others
06. }
07. [DataContract]
08. public class Person
09. {
10.     [DataMember]
```

```
11.    public string Name { get; set; }
12.    [DataMember]
13.    public Gender Gender { get; set; }
14. }
15. void Demo()
16. {
17.    var person = new Person { Name = "Ali", Gender = Gender.Male };
18.    Console.WriteLine(WriteObject(person,
19.
20.    ));
21. }
```

You need to serialize the Person object as a JSON object. Which code segment should you insert at line 19?

A) new DataContractSerializer(typeof(Person))

B) new XmlSerializer(typeof(Person))

C) new NetDataContractSenalizer()

D) new DataContractJsonSerializer(typeof(Person))

Question 5

Suppose you are developing an application that uses the following C# code:

```
01. public interface IPerson
02. {
03.    string Name { get; set; }
04. }
05.
06. void Demo(object obj)
07. {
08.
09.    if(person != null)
10.    {
11.        System.Console.WriteLine(person.Name);
12.    }
13. }
```

The Demo() method must not throw any exceptions when converting the obj object to the IPerson interface or when accessing the Data property. You need to meet the requirements. Which code segment should you insert at line 08?

A) var person = (IPerson)obj;

B) dynamic person = obj;

C) var person = obj is IPerson;

D) var person = obj as IPerson;

Question 6

Suppose you are creating an application that manages the information of persons. The application includes a class named Person and a method named Save. The Save() method must be strongly typed. It must allow only types inherited from the Person class that use a constructor that accepts no parameters.

You need to implement the Save() method. Which code segment should you use?

A)
```
public static void Save<T>(T target) where T: new(), Person
{
    ...
}
```

B)
```
public static void Save<T>(T target) where T: Person
{
    ...
}
```

C)
```
public static void Save<T>(T target) where T: Person, new()
{
    ...
}
```

D)
```
public static void Save(Person person)
{
    ...
}
```

Question 7

Suppose you are developing an application that includes classes named Car and Vehicle and an interface named IVehicle. The Car class must meet the following requirements:

It must either inherit from the Vehicle class or implement the IVehicle interface. It must be inheritable by other classes in the application. You need to ensure that the Car class meets the requirements.

Which two code segments can you use to achieve this goal?

A)
```
sealed class Car : Vehicle
{
    ...
}
```

B)
```
abstract class Car: Vehicle
{
    ...
}
```

C)
```
sealed class Car : IVehicle
{
    ...
}
```

D)
```
abstract class Car : IVehicle
{

}
```

Question 8

Suppose you're creating an application that concatenates "1" value with a string for a million times. Which of the following codes would you use that minimize the completion time and concatenates the string for the millionth time?

A)
```
string str = "";
for (int i = 0; i < 1000000; i++)
{
    str = string.Concat(str, "1");
}
return str;
```

B)
```
var str = new StringBuilder();
for (int i = 0; i < 1000000; i++)
{
    str.Append("1");
}
return str.ToString();
```

C)
```
var str = null;
for (int i = 0; i < 1000000; i++)
{
    str = str + "1";
}
return str.ToString();
```

D)
```
var str = null;
for (int i = 0; i < 1000000; i++)
{
    str += "1";
}
return str.ToString();
```

Question 9

You are creating a class named Person. The class has a string property named FirstName.

```
01. class Person
02. {
03.     public string FirstName
04.     {
05.         get;
06.         set;
07.     }
08. }
```

The FirstName property value must be accessed and modified only by code within the Person class or within a class derived from the Person class.

Which two actions should you perform?

A)   Replace line 05 with the protected get;

B)   Replace line 06 with the private set;

C)   Replace line 03 with the public string EmployeeType

D)   Replace line 05 with the private get;

E)   Replace line 03 with the protected string EmployeeType

F)   Replace line 06 with the protected set;

Question 10

How would you convert the following values?

```
01. float ft;
02. object o = ft;
03.
04. Console.WriteLine(i);
```

You need to ensure that the application does not throw exceptions on invalid conversions. Which code segment should you insert at line 03?

A)   int i = (int)(float)o;

B)   int i = (int)o;

C)   int i = o;

D)   int i = (int)(double)o;

Question 11

You need to convert a date value entered in string format and you need to parse it into DateTime and convert it to Coordinated Universal Time (UTC). The code must not cause an exception to be thrown. Which code segment should you use?

A)
```
string strDate = "";
bool ValidDate = DateTime.TryParse(strDate,
    CultureInfo.CurrentCulture,
    DateTimeStyles.AdjustToUniversal | DateTimeStyles.AssumeLocal,
    out ValidatedDate);
```
B)
```
string strDate = "";
bool ValidDate = DateTime.TryParse(strDate,
    CultureInfo.CurrentCulture,
    DateTimeStyles.AssumeLocal,
    out ValidatedDate);
```
C)
```
bool validDate = true;
try
{
    ValidatedDate = DateTime.Parse(strDate);
}
catch
{

    validDate = false;
}
```
D)
```
ValidatedDate = DateTime.ParseExact(strDate, "g",
    CultureInfo.CurrentCulture,
    DateTimeStyles.AdjustToUniversal
    | DateTimeStyles.AdjustToUniversal);
```

Question 12

Suppose you are developing an application that includes an object that performs a long-running process. You need to ensure that the garbage collector does not release the object's resources until the process completes.

Which garbage collector method should you use?

A) WaitForFullGCComplete()

B) WaitForFullGCApproach()

C) KeepAlive()

D) WaitForPendingFinalizers()

Question 13

How would you ensure that the class library assembly is strongly named? What should you do?

A) Use the gacutil.exe command-line tool.

B) Use the xsd.exe command-line tool.

C) Use the aspnet_regiis.exe command-line tool.

D) Use assembly attributes.

Question 14

You are developing an application that includes the following code segment:

```
01. class A { }
02. class B : A { }
03. class C
04. {
05.     void Demo(object obj) { Console.WriteLine("Demo(obj)");}
06.     void Demo(C c) { Console.WriteLine("Demo(C)");}
07.     void Demo(A a) { Console.WriteLine("Demo(A)");}
08.     void Demo(B b) { Console.WriteLine("Demo(B)");}
09.
10.     void Start()
11.     {
12.         object o = new B();
13.         Demo(o);
14.     }
15. }
```

You need to ensure that the Demo(B b) method runs. With which code segment should you replace line 13?

A) Demo((B)o);

B) Demo(new B(o));

C) Demo(o is B);

D) Demo((A)o);

Question 15

How would you make sure the garbage collector does not release the object's resources until the process completes? Which garbage collector method should you use?

A) WaitForFullGCComplete()

B) SuppressFinalize()

C) collect()

D) RemoveMemoryPressure()

Question 16

Which of the following methods of assembly is used to get all types?

- **A)** GetTypes()
- **B)** GetType()
- **C)** ToTypeList()
- **D)** Types()

Question 17

Which of the following keywords is used for a dynamic variable?

- **A)** var
- **B)** dynamic
- **C)** const
- **D)** static

Question 18

What should you use to encapsulate an array object?

- **A)** Indexer
- **B)** Property
- **C)** Event
- **D)** Private array

Question 19

How should you create an extension method of an integer?

A)
```
static class ExtensionClass
{
    public static void ExtensionMethod(this int i)
    {
        //do code

    }
}
```
B)
```
static class ExtensionClass
{
    public static void ExtensionMethod(int i)
    {
        //do code
            }
}
```

C)
```
class ExtensionClass
{
    public static void ExtensionMethod(this int i)
    {
        //do code

    }
}
```
D)
```
static class ExtensionClass
{
    public void ExtensionMethod(this int i)
    {
        //do code

    }
}
```

Question 20

Which keyword is used to check or compare one type to another?

A)   as

B)   is

C)   out

D)   in

Question 21

How would you parse a type to another in a way that it doesn't generate an exception in a wrong conversion?

A)   as

B)   is

C)   out

D)   in

Question 22

Which of the following interfaces is necessary to implement for creating a custom collection in C#?

A)   IUnkown

B)   IEnumerable

C)   IComparable

D)   IDisposable

Question 23

Which of the following interfaces is used to manage an unmanaged resource?

A) IUnkown

B) IEnumerable

C) IComparable

D) IDisposable

Question 24

Which class is necessary to inherit while creating a custom attribute?

A) Exception

B) Attribute

C) Serializable

D) IEnumerable

Question 25

Which statement is used to remove the unnecessary resources automatically?

A) using

B) switch

C) Uncheck

D) Check

Answers

1. D
2. B, D
3. C
4. D
5. D
6. C
7. B, D
8. B
9. B, E
10. A
11. A

12. C
13. D
14. A
15. B
16. A
17. B
18. A
19. A
20. B
21. A
22. B
23. D
24. B
25. A

Objective 3: Debug Application and Implement Security

Question 1

You need to create a unique identity for your application assembly. Which two attributes should you include for this purpose?

A) AssemblyTitleAttribute

B) AssemblyCultureAttribute

C) AssemblyVersionAttribute

D) AssemblyKeyNameAttribute

E) AssemblyFileVersion

Question 2

You are working on an application where you need to encrypt highly sensitive data. Which algorithm should you use?

A) DES

B) Aes

C) TripleDES

D) RC2

Question 3

You are required to develop a method which can be called by a varying number of parameters. The method is called:

A) Method Overriding

B) Method Overloading

C) Abstract Method

D) Virtual Method

Question 4

You are required to create a class "Load" with the following requirements:
Include a member that represents the rate of a Loan instance.
Allow an external code to assign a value to a rate member.
Restrict the range of values that can be assigned to the rate member.
To meet these requirements, how would you implement the rate member?

A) public static property

B) public property

C) public static field

D) protected field

Question 5

You are creating a library (.dll file) for your project. You need to make it a strongly typed assembly. What should you do?

A) use the csc.exe/target:Library option when building the application

B) use the AL.exe command line-tool

C) use the aspnet_regiis.exe command line-tool

D) use the EdmGen.exe command line-tool

Question 6

You are required to create a program with the following requirements:
In Debug Mode, console output must display Entering Release Mode.
In Release Mode, console output must display Entering Debug Mode.
Which code segment should you use?

```
A) if DEBUG.DEFINED
   Console.WriteLine("Entering Release Mode");
   else
   Console.WriteLine("Entering Debug Mode");
```

```
B) if RELEASE.DEFINED
   Console.WriteLine("Entering Debug Mode");
   else
   Console.WriteLine("Entering Release Mode");

C) #if DEBUG
   Console.WriteLine("Entering Release Mode");
   #elif RELEASE
   Console.WriteLine("Entering Debug Mode");

D) #if DEBUG
   Console.WriteLine("Entering Debug Mode");
   #elif RELEASE
   Console.WriteLine("Entering Release Mode");
```

Question 7

You are required to create an event source named mySource and a custom log named myLog on the server. You need to write the "Hello" information event to the custom log.

   Which code segment should you use?

```
A) EventLog Log=new EventLog(){Source="mySource"};
   Log.WriteEntry("Hello",EventLogEntryType.Information);

B) EventLog Log=new EventLog(){Source="myLog"};
   Log.WriteEntry("Hello",EventLogEntryType.Information);

C) EventLog Log=new EventLog(){Source="System"};
   Log.WriteEntry("Hello",EventLogEntryType.Information);

D) EventLog Log=new EventLog(){Source="Application"};
   Log.WriteEntry("Hello",EventLogEntryType.Information);
```

Question 8

You have to class ExceptionLogger and its method LogExecption, which logs the exception. You need to log all exceptions that occur and rethrow the original, including the entire exception stack.

   Which code segment should you use for the above requirements?

```
A) Catch(Exception ex)
   {
      ExceptionLogger.LogException(ex);
      throw;
   }
B) Catch(Exception ex)
   {
      ExceptionLogger.LogException(ex);
      throw ex;
   }
```

```
C) Catch(Exception)
   {
     ExceptionLogger.LogException();
     throw;
   }
D) Catch(Exception )
   {
     ExceptionLogger.LogException(ex);
     throw ex;
   }
```

Question 9

You have the following code snippet:

```
If(! PerformanceCounterCategory.Exists("CounterExample"))
{
Var counters=new CounterCreationDataCollection();
Var counter1=new CounterCreationData
{
CounterName="Counter1",
CounterType=PerformanceCounterType.SampleFraction
};
Var counter2=new CounterCreationData
{
CounterName="Counter2"
};

Counters.Add(counter1);
Counters.Add(counter2);

PerformanceCounterCategory.Create("CounterExample","",PerformanceCounterCategoryType.
MultiInstance,counters);
}
```

You need to ensure that counter1 is available for performance monitor. Which code segment should you use?

A) CounterType=PerformanceCounterType.RawBase

B) CounterType=PerformanceCounterType.AverageBase

C) CounterType=PerformanceCounterType.SampleBase

D) CounterType=PerformanceCounterType.CounterMultiBase

Question 10

You are required to install an assembly in GAC. Which action should you take?

A) Use the Assembly Registration tool (regasm.exe)

B) Use the strong name tool (sn.exe)

C) User Microsoft register server (regsvr32.exe)

D) Use the Global Assembly Cache tool (gacutil.exe)

E) Use Windows installer 2.0

Question 11

You need to validate a string which has numbers in **333-456** format. Which pattern should you choose?

A) @"\d\d-\d\d"

B) @"\n{3}-\n{3}"

C) @"[0-9]+-[0-9]"

D) @"\d{3}-\d{3}"

Question 12

How would you throw an exception to preserve stack-trace information?

A) throw;

B) throw new Exception();

C) throw e;

D) return new Exception();

Question 13

The application needs to encrypt highly sensitive data. Which algorithm should you use?

A) DES

B) Aes

C) TripleDES

D) RC2

Question 14

You are developing an application which transmits a large amount of data. You need to ensure the data integrity. Which algorithm should you use?

- A)   RSA
- B)   HMACSHA256
- C)   Aes
- D)   RNGCryptoServiceProvider

Question 15

Salt Hashing is done by:

- A)   Merging data with a random value and performing Cryptography
- B)   Merging data with a random value and performing Cryptanalysis
- C)   Merging data with a random value and performing Encryption
- D)   Merging data with a random value and performing Hashing

Question 16

Which of the following commands is required to create a strong name key?

- A)   sn -k {assembly_name}.snk
- B)   sn k {assembly_name}.snk
- C)   gacutil -i {assembly_name}.snk
- D)   gacutil i {assembly_name}.snk

Question 17

Which of the following methods is used for getting the information of a current assembly?

- A)   Assembly. GetExecutingAssembly();
- B)   Assembly.GetExecutedAssembly();
- C)   Assembly.GetCurrentAssembly();
- D)   Assembly.ExecutingAssembly();

Question 18

Which bindingflags are useful for getting the private data instance?

- A)   BindingFlags.NonPublic | BindingFlags.Instance
- B)   BindingFlags.Private | BindingFlags.Instance
- C)   BindingFlags.NonPrivate | BindingFlags.NonStatic
- D)   BindingFlags.Private | BindingFlags.NonStatic

Question 19

Which class should preferably be used for tracing in Release Mode?

A) Debug

B) Trace

C) TraceSource

D) All of the above

Question 20

To build a project you need a PDB file of:

A) Previous build version

B) Any build version

C) Current Solution File

D) Same build version

Question 21

Which method is easiest to find the problem if you have no idea what it is?

A) Using Profiler

B) Profiling by Hand

C) Using Performance Counter

D) Debugging

Question 22

You need to validate an XML file. What would you use?

A) XSD

B) RegEx

C) StringBuilder

D) JavaScriptSerializer

Question 23

You need to send your data to a receiver and want no one to tamper with your data. What would you use?

A) X509Certificate2.SignHash

B) RSACryptoServiceProvider.Enrypt

C) UnicodeEncoding.GetBytes

D) Marshal.ZeroFreeBSTR

Question 24

You are developing an assembly that will be used by server applications. You want to make the update process of this assembly as smooth as possible. What steps would you take?

A) Create WinMD Assembly

B) Deploy Assembly to GAC

C) Sign the assembly with the storing name

D) Delay sign the assembly

Question 25

You want to configure your application to output more trace data. What would you use for the configuration setting?

A) Listener

B) Filter

C) Switch

D) Trace

Answers

1. B, C
2. B
3. B
4. B
5. B
6. C
7. A
8. A
9. C
10. D, E
11. D
12. A
13. B
14. B
15. D
16. A
17. A

18.	A
19.	C
20.	D
21.	A
22.	A
23.	A, C
24.	B
25.	C

Objective 4: Implement Data Access

Question 1

Suppose you are developing an application that includes the following code:

```
List<int> list = new List<int>
{
    80,
    75,
    60,
    55,
    75
};
```

You have to retrieve all the numbers that are greater than 60 from a list. Which code should you use?

A)
```
        var result = from i in list
                     where i > 60
                     select i;
```

B)
```
        var result = list.Take(60);
```

C)
```
        var result = list.First(i => i > 80);
```

D)
```
        var result = list.Any(i => i > 80);
```

Question 2

Suppose you're developing an application that needs to read the data from a file and then release the file resources. Which code snippet should you use?

A)
```
string data;
using (StreamReader readfile = new StreamReader("data.txt"))
{
    while ((data = readfile.ReadLine()) != null)
    {
        Console.WriteLine(data);
    }
}
```

B)
```
string data;
StreamReader readfile = null;
using ( readfile = new StreamReader("data.txt"))
{
    while ((data = readfile.ReadLine()) != null)
    {
        Console.WriteLine(data);
    }
}
```

C)
```
string data;
StreamReader readfile = new StreamReader("data.txt");
while ((data = readfile.ReadLine()) != null)
{
    Console.WriteLine(data);
}
```

D)
```
string data;
StreamReader readfile = null;
try
{
    readfile = new StreamReader("data.txt");
    while ((data = readfile.ReadLine()) != null)
    {
        Console.WriteLine(data);
    }
    readfile.Close();
    readfile.Dispose();
}
finally
{

}
```

Question 3

Suppose you have a List<Person> people = new List<Person>(); You need to create an extension method that will return the correct number of Person objects from the people list that can be displayed on each page and each page has a uniform page size. Which code snippet should you use?

A)
```
Public static IEnumerable<int> Page(IEnumerable<int> source, int page, int pagesize)
{
    return source.Take((pagesize - 1) * page).Skip(pagesize);
}
```
B)
```
Public static IEnumerable<T> Page(this IEnumerable<T> source, int page, int pagesize)
{
    return source.Skip((page - 1) * pagesize).Take(pagesize);
}
```
C)
```
static IEnumerable<int> Page(IEnumerable<int> source, int page, int pagesize)
{
    return source.Skip((pagesize - 1) * page).Take(pagesize);
}
```
D)
```
Public static IEnumerable<T> Page(this IEnumerable<T> source, int page, int pagesize)
{
    return source.Take((page - 1) * pagesize).Skip(pagesize);
}
```

Question 4

Suppose you're creating an application that includes the following code, which retrieves JSON data. You need to ensure that the code validates the JSON.

```
01. bool ValidateJSON(string json, Dictionary<string,object> result)
02. {
03.
04.   try
05.   {
06.     result = serializer.Deserializer<Dictionary<string, object>>(json);
07.     return true;
08.   }
09.   catch
10.   {
11.     return false;
12.   }
13. }
```

Which code should you insert at line 03?

A)   var serializer = new DataContractSerializer();

B)   DataContractSerializer serializer = new DataContractSerializer();

C)   var serializer = new XmlSerializer();

D)   var serializer = new JavaScriptSerializer();

Question 5

Suppose you have a collection of integer values. You define an integer variable named IntegerToRemove and assign a value to it. You declare an array named filteredIntegers. You must to do the following things.

Remove duplicate integers from the integer array. Sort the array in order from the highest value to the lowest value. Remove the integer value stored in the integerToRemove variable from the integers array.

Which LINQ query would you need to create to meet the requirements?

A)
```
int[] filteredIntegers = integers.Where(value => value !=
integerToRemove).OrderBy(x => x).ToArray();
```
B)
```
int[] filteredIntegers = integers.Where(value => value !=
integerToRemove).OrderByDescending(x => x).ToArray();
```
C)
```
int[] filteredIntegers = integers.Distinct().Where(value => value !=
integerToRemove).OrderByDescending(x => x).ToArray();
```
D)
```
int[] filteredIntegers = integers.Distinct()
.OrderByDescending(x => x).ToArray();
```

Question 6

An application has the following code:

```
01. class Person
02. {
03.     public string Name { get; set; }
04.     public int Age { get; set; }
05. }
06. static IEnumerable<Person> GetPersons(string sqlConnectionString)
07. {
08.     var people = new List<Person>();
09.     SqlConnection sqlConnection = new SqlConnection(sqlConnectionString);
10.      using (sqlConnection)
```

```
11.        {
12.            SqlCommand sqlCommand = new SqlCommand("Select Name, Age From
13.            Persons", sqlConnection);
14.
15.            using (SqlDataReader sqlDataReader = sqlCommand.ExecuteReader())
16.            {
17.
18.                {
19.                    Person person = new Person();
20.                    person.Name = (string)sqlDataReader["Name"];
21.                    person.Age = (int)sqlDataReader["Age"];
22.
23.                    people.Add(person);
24.                }
25.            }
26.        }
27.        return people;
28. }
```

The GetPersons() method must meet the following requirements:

1. Connect to a Microsoft SQL Server database.

2. Create Animal objects and populate them with data from the database.

Which two actions should you perform?

A) Insert the following code segment at line 17:

    ```
    while(sqlDataReader.NextResult())
    ```

B) Insert the following code segment at line 14:

    ```
    sqlConnection.Open();
    ```

C) Insert the following code segment at line 14:

    ```
    sqlConnection.BeginTransaction();
    ```

D) Insert the following code segment at line 17:

    ```
    while(sqlDataReader.Read())
    ```

E) Insert the following code segment at line 17:

    ```
    while(sqlDataReader.GetValues())
    ```

Question 7

You're using ADO.NET Entity Framework to retrieve data from a database in MS SQL Server. Suppose you have the following code snippet:

```
01.   public DataTime? OrderDate;
02.    IQueryable<Order> GetOrderByYear(int year)
03.    {
04.       using (var context = new NortwindEntities())
05.       {
06.           var orders = from order in context.Orders;
07.
08.                         select order;
09.           return orders.ToList().AsQueryable();
10.       }
11.    }
```

You need to ensure the following requirements:

1. Return only orders that have an OrderDate value other than null.

2. Return only orders that were placed in the year specified in the OrderDate property or in a later year.

Which code segment should you insert at line 07?

A) Where order.OrderDate.Value != null && order.OrderDate.Value.Year > = year

B) Where order.OrderDate.Value = = null && order.OrderDate.Value.Year = = year

C) Where order.OrderDate.HasValue && order.OrderDate.Value.Year = = year

D) Where order.OrderDate.Value.Year = = year

Question 8

Suppose you're writing a method named ReadFile that reads data from a file. You must ensure that the ReadFile method meets the following requirements:

1. It must not make changes to the data file.

2. It must allow other processes to access the data file. It must not throw an exception if the application attempts to open a data file that does not exist.

Which code segment should you use?

A) var fs = File.Open(Filename, FileMode.OpenOrCreate, FileAccess.Read, FileShare.ReadWrite);

B) var fs = File.Open(Filename, FileMode.Open, FileAccess.Read, FileShare.ReadWrite);

C) var fs = File.Open(Filename, FileMode.OpenOrCreate, FileAccess.Read, FileShare.Write);

D) var fs = File.ReadAllLines(Filename);

E) var fs = File.ReadAllBytes(Filename);

Question 9

You're creating an application that converts data into multiple output formats; it includes the following code snippets.

```
01.    class TabDelimitedFormatter : IFormatter<string>
02.    {
03.        readonly Func<int, char> suffix =
04.            col => col % 2 == 0 ? '\n' : '\t';
05.        public string Output(IEnumerator<string> iterator, int size)
06.        {
07.
08.        }
09.    }
10.    interface IFormatter<T>
11.    {
12.        string Output(IEnumerator<T> iterator, int size);
13.    }
```

You need to minimize the completion time of the GetOutput() method. Which code segment should you insert at line 07?

A)
```
            string output = null;
            for(int i = 1; iterator.MoveNext(); i++)
            {
                output = string.Concat(output, iterator.Current, suffix(i));
            }
```

B)
```
            var output = new StringBuilder();
            for(int i = 1; iterator.MoveNext(); i++)
            {
                output.Append(iterator.Current);
                output.Append(suffix(i));
            }
```

C)
```
            string output = null;
            for(int i = 1; iterator.MoveNext(); i++)
            {
                output = output + iterator.Current + suffix(i);
            }
```

D)
```
            string output = null;
            for(int i = 1; iterator.MoveNext(); i++)
            {
                output += iterator.Current + suffix(i);
            }
```

Question 10

You are developing a class named Person. See the following code snippet:

```
01.    class People
02.    {
03.        Dictionary<string, int> people = new Dictionary<string, int>();
04.        public void Add(string name, int age)
05.        {
06.            people.Add(name, age);
07.        }
08.
09.    }
```

It has the following unit test:

```
        public void UnitTest1()
        {
            People people = new People();
            people.Add("Ali", 22);
            people.Add("Sundus", 21);
            int expectedAge = 21;
            int actualAge = people["Sundus"];
            Assert.AreEqual(expectedAge, actualAge);
        }
```

You need to ensure the unit test will pass. What code snippet you should insert at line 08?

A)
```
        public Dictionary<string, int> People
        {
            get { return people; }
        }
```
B)
```
        public int this[string name]
        {
            get
            {
                return people[name];
            }
        }
```
C)
```
    public Dictionary<string, int> People = new Dictionary<string, int>();
```
D)
```
        public int salary(string name)
        {
            return people[name];
        }
```

Question 11

You are creating an application that uses a class named Person. The class is decorated with the DataContractAttribute attribute. The application includes the following code snippet:

```
01.    MemoryStream WritePerson(Person person)
02.    {
03.        var ms = new MemoryStream();
04.        var binary = XmlDictionaryWriter.CreateBinary(ms);
05.        var ser = new DataContractSerializer(typeof(Person));
06.        ser.WriteObject(binary, person);
07.
08.        return ms;
09.    }
```

You need to ensure that the entire Person object is serialized to the memory stream object. Which code segment should you insert at line 07?

A)   binary.WriteEndDocument();

B)   binary.WriteEndDocumentAsync();

C)   binary.WriteEndElementAsync();

D)   binary.Flush();

Question 12

You need to choose a collection type which internally stores a key and a value for each collection item, provides objects to iterators in ascending order based on the key, and ensures that items are accessible by a zero-based index or by key. Which collection type should you use?

A)   SortedList

B)   Queue

C)   Array

D)   HashTable

Question 13

You need to store the values in a collection. The values must be stored in the order that they were added to the collection. The values must be accessed in a first-in, first-out order.
   Which type of collection should you use?

A)   SortedList

B)   Queue

C)   ArrayList

D)   Hashtable

Question 14

You are creating an application that will parse a large amount of text. You need to parse the text into separate lines and minimize memory use while processing data. Which object type should you use?

A)   DataContractSerializer

B)   StringBuilder

C)   StringReader

D)   JsonSerializer

Question 15

Which of the following two interfaces should you use to iterate over a collection and release the unmanaged resources.

A)   IEquatable

B)   IEnumerable

C)   IDisposable

D)   IComparable

Question 16

You have a List object that is generated by executing the following code:

```
List<string> subjects = new List<string>()
{
    "English","Computer","Maths","Physics"
};
```

You have a method that contains the following code:

```
01.        bool GetSameSubjs(List<string> subj, string searchSubj)
02.        {
03.            var findSubj = subj.Exists((delegate (string subjName)
04.            {
05.                return subjName.Equals(searchSubj);
06.            }
07.            ));
08.            return findSubj;
09.        }
```

You need to alter the method to use a lambda statement. How should you rewrite lines 03 through 06 of the method?

A)   var findSubj = subj.First(x => x == searchSubj);

B)   var findSubj = subj.Where(x => x == searchSubj);

C)   var findSubj = subj.Exists(x => x.Equals(searchSubj));

D)   var findSubj = subj.Where(x => x.Equals(searchSubj));

Question 17

You're creating an application that counts the number of times a specific word appears in a text file. See the following code snippet:

```
01.    class Demo
02.    {
03.        ConcurrentDictionary<string, int> words =
04.                    new ConcurrentDictionary<string, int>();
05.        public Action<DirectoryInfo> ProcessDir()
06.        {
07.            Action<DirectoryInfo> act = (dirInfo =>
08.            {
09.                var files = dirInfo.GetFiles("*.cs").AsParallel<FileInfo>();
10.                files.ForAll<FileInfo>(
11.                    fileinfo =>
12.                    {
13.                        var content = File.ReadAllText(fileinfo.FullName);
14.                        var sb = new StringBuilder();
15.                        foreach (var item in content)
16.                        {
17.                            sb.Append(char.IsLetter(item) ?
18.                                item.ToString().ToLowerInvariant() : " ");
19.                        }
20.                        var wordlist= sb.ToString().Split(new[] { ' ' },
21.                        StringSplitOptions.RemoveEmptyEntries);
22.                        foreach (var word in wordlist)
23.                        {
24.
25.                        }
26.                    });
27.                var dir = dirInfo.GetDirectories()
28.                        .AsParallel<DirectoryInfo>();
29.                dir.ForAll<DirectoryInfo>(ProcessDir());
30.            });
31.            return act;
32.        }
33.    }
```

You need to populate a words object with the list of words and the number of occurrences of each word, and also ensure that the updates to the ConcurrentDictionary object can happen in parallel. Which code segment should you insert at line 24?

```
A) words.AddOrUpdate(word, 1, (s, n) => n + 1);
B)
   int value;
   if(words.TryGetValue(word, out value))
   {
       words[word] = value++;
   }
   else
   {
       words[word] = 1;
   }
```

C)
```
    var value = words.GetOrAdd(word, 0);
    words[word] = value++;
```
D)

```
    var value = words.GetOrAdd(word, 0);
    words.TryUpdate(word, value + 1, value);
```

Question 18

Suppose you have the following code snippet:

```
01.    class Person
02.    {
03.        public int ID { get; set; }
04.        public string Name { get; set; }
05.        public int Age { get; set; }
06.    }
07.    Dictionary<int, Person> people = new Dictionary<int, Person>
08.    {
09.      {21, new Person {ID = 1, Name="Ali", Age = 22 } },
10.      {22, new Person {ID = 2, Name="Sundus", Age = 21 } },
11.      {23, new Person {ID = 3, Name="Asad", Age = 22 } },
12.      {24, new Person {ID = 5, Name="Naveed", Age = 21 } },
13.    };
14.
15.    people.Add(24, new Person { ID = 6, Name = "Malik", Age = 10 });
```

The application fails at line 15 with the following error message: "An item with the same key has already been added." You need to resolve the error.

Which code segment should you insert at line 14?

A)   if(!people.ContainsKey(24))

B)   foreach (Person person in people.Values.Where(t=>t.ID !=24))

C)   foreach (KeyValuePair<int, Person> key in people.Where(t=>t.Key != 24))

D)   foreach (int key in people.Keys.Where(k=>k!=24))

Question 19

Suppose you have the following code segment:

```
01.            ArrayList arrays = new ArrayList();
02.            int i = 10;
03.            int j;
04.            arrays.Add(i);
05.            j = arrays[0];
```

You need to resolve the error that occurs at line 05 ("Cannot implicitly convert type object to int"). You need to ensure that the error gets removed. Which code should you replace with in line 05?

A) j = arrays[0] is int;

B) j = ((List<int>)arrays) [0];

C) j = arrays[0].Equals(typeof(int));

D) j = (int) arrays[0];

Question 20

Suppose you're writing a method that retrieves the data from an MS Access 2013 database. The method must meet the following requirements:

Be read-only.

Be able to use the data before the entire data set is retrieved.

Minimize the amount of system overhead and the amount of memory usage.

Which type of object should you use in the method?

A) SqlDataAdapter

B) DataContext

C) DbDataAdapter

D) OleDbDataReader

Question 21

Which of the following extension methods is used to join two queries?

A) join()

B) group()

C) skip()

D) aggregate()

Question 22

Which of the following keywords is used to filter the query?

A) select

B) where

C) from

D) join

Question 23

Which of the following collection types is used to retrieve data in a Last In First Out (LIFO) way.

A) Queue

B) HashTable

C) Stack

D) Dictionary

Question 24

Which method is used to return a specific number of objects from a query result?

A) Take()

B) Skip()

C) Join()

D) Select()

Question 25

In entity framework, which class is responsible for maintaining the bridge between a database engine and C# code?

A) DbContext

B) Attribute

C) DbContextTransaction

D) DbSet

Answers

1. A
2. A
3. B
4. D
5. C
6. B, C
7. A
8. A
9. B
10. B
11. A

12. A
13. B
14. B
15. B, C
16. C
17. A
18. A
19. D
20. D
21. A
22. B
23. C
24. A
25. A

Index

Get the eBook for only $5!

Why limit yourself?

With most of our titles available in both PDF and ePUB format, you can access your content wherever and however you wish—on your PC, phone, tablet, or reader.

Since you've purchased this print book, we are happy to offer you the eBook for just $5.

To learn more, go to http://www.apress.com/companion or contact support@apress.com.

Apress®

Printed in the United States
By Bookmasters